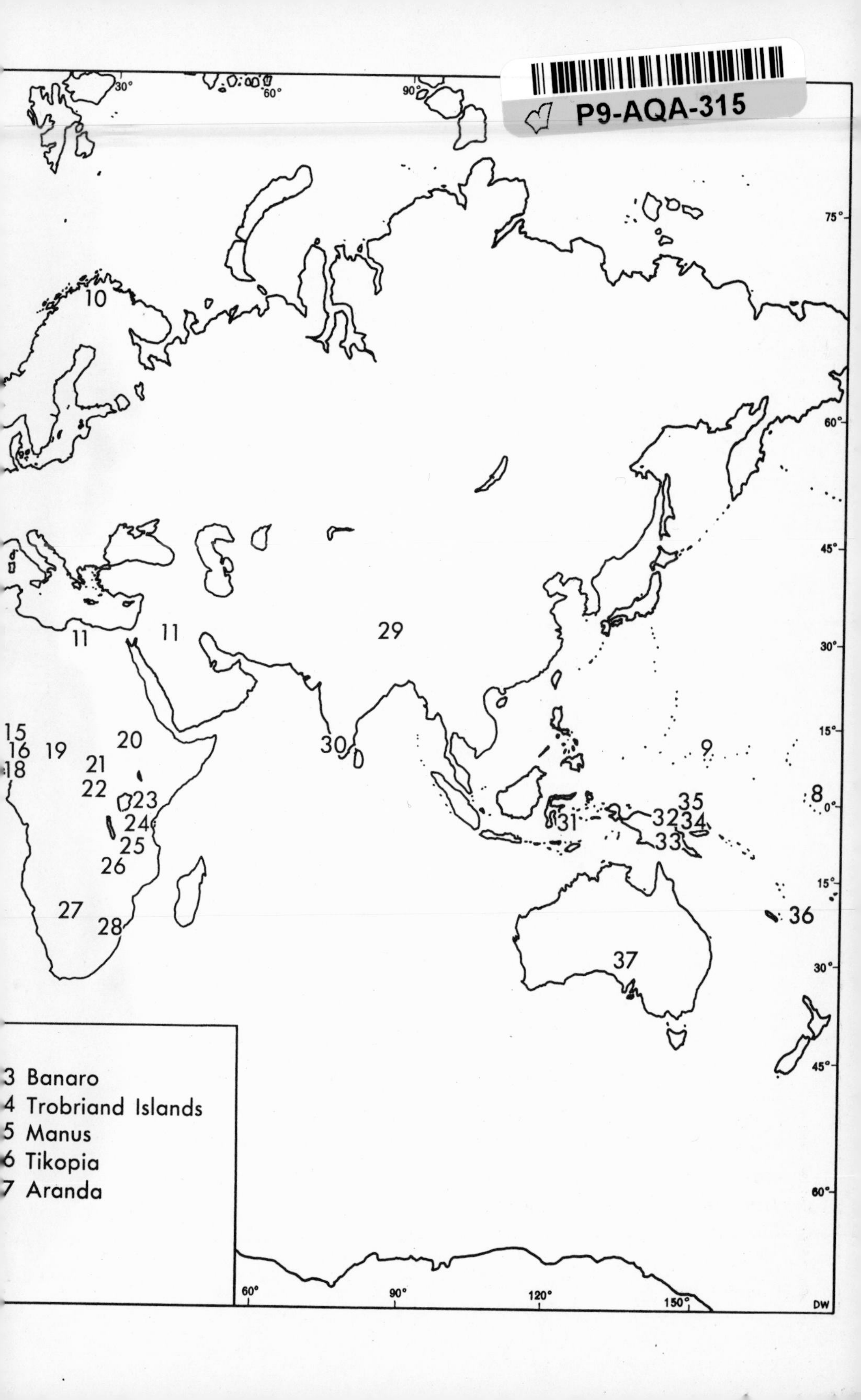

P9-AQA-315
30°
60°
90°
75°
60°
45°
30°
15°
0°
15°
30°
45°
60°
10
11
11
29
15
16
18
19
20
21
22
23
24
25
26
27
28
30
9
8
35
31
32
33
34
36
37
3 Banaro
4 Trobriand Islands
5 Manus
6 Tikopia
7 Aranda
60°
90°
120°
150°
DW

SOCIAL ANTHROPOLOGY

SOCIAL ANTHROPOLOGY

PAUL BOHANNAN
NORTHWESTERN UNIVERSITY

HOLT, RINEHART AND WINSTON
NEW YORK • CHICAGO • SAN FRANCISCO
TORONTO • LONDON

To My Mother and Father

Printed in the United States of America
Library of Congress Catalogue Card Number: 63-13322

ISBN 0-03-012190-6

56789 038 19181716151413

Preface

ANTHROPOLOGY HAS SUBDIVISIONS, but, except historically, it has no beginning. In writing an introductory book or teaching a beginning course in the subject, everything must come first. Since that is impossible it seems appropriate to explain, in a preface, whatever compromise an author has found necessary.

The major task in teaching or in learning anthropology is to get the texture of our own culture and our own lives into conscious perspective so that we are not misled by them when we look at other cultures and other lives; so that, in short, we can see other cultures without warping them and without losing our commitment to our own.

To enable him to work with the facts and interpretation of social, cultural, and psychic life made by all peoples, including his own, the anthropologist must be aware of scientific theories and categories. This book therefore begins, in Part 1, with a discussion of culture, personality, and society—the three major concepts under which the achievements of the science of anthropology can be summed up. It proceeds immediately to considerations of speech and art: the ways in which ordinary men of every culture see and criticize the world. In so doing, the book intends to instill immediately the stereoscopic vision that is the hallmark of all successful anthropology and a necessity of the modern world.

There are certain aspects of the human condition on which all peoples must have views and on which, therefore, anthropologists must have views. Since man is a mammal and is mortal, the biological processes and the biological network of human beings must be expressed in cultural concepts, norms, views, and acts. Because kinship, household, families, divorce are all subject to immense diversity within regularity, they thereby lend themselves to cross-cultural comparison and science. These are the concerns of Part 2.

Similarly, men in all societies make agreements that create ties beyond the biological network. Many societies, but not all, also build social and cultural structures on premises of inequality and hierarchy. Both must be and can be compared and explained. Part 3 is therefore entitled "The Network of Agreements."

All men in all societies must provide for their daily subsistence, and must do it in terms of regularity and predictability. In that sense, all societies have economies, and all cultures provide means for getting a living. In most, there is widespread exchange and allocation of goods, services, and social prerogative. Such allocation also lies at the base of the power structure of the society, but is by no means the only (or perhaps even the dominant) component: all societies must control power in social relationships, must settle disputes, must organize for war (even if they do not carry it out) in order to guard the integrity of their most cherished institutions. Part 4, in short, deals with economy and polity on a broad comparative base.

There seems also to be a limit to the uncertainty that human beings can tolerate over extended periods of time, and there are to be found in all societies ways and means of reducing uncertainty. Science, religion, magic, even witchcraft, are discussed in Part 5. Just as language is a projection of culture and society in one symbolic form, science and religion are projections of the entire physical, social, psychic, and mystical universe, as they are comprehended, into another symbolic form. Without religion of some sort (even if it be agnosticism or atheism) and without science of some sort (no matter what its canons of proof) human culture would be chaotic.

Finally, this book sets forth in Part 6 a theory of social and cultural change which attempts to separate the repetitive processes of social life, the chained events of history, and the evolution of man, the animal with culture, and to show their interrelationships. For too long "functionalism" and "evolution" have been opposed schools of thought when, in fact, each is lost without the other.

Like all books which purport to "introduce" a subject, this one exposes the creed of its author: anthropology is among the best devices yet discovered for turning human animals into self-aware animals.

The more fully one becomes aware of the truth in the truism that everyone is dependent ultimately upon his contemporaries, his neighbors, and his culture, the greater a problem acknowledgment becomes. There are two courses: one can thank everybody from Cro-Magnon to one's infant son; or one can include a truncated list of figures who have proved professionally formative. I have chosen the latter way. I was taught anthropology first by E. H. Spicer and Emil Haury; then by E. E. Evans-Pritchard, Meyer Fortes, and the late Franz Steiner. I have been kept up to snuff by my colleagues and my graduate students, both in Britain and America. I have suffered, more or less gladly, the cogent criticisms of Laura Bohannan, Godfrey Lienhardt, John Beattie, Marion J. Levy, Jr., George Dalton, Francis L. K. Hsu, to name only the most demanding. Rather than merely thank them, I propose to continue to reciprocate in kind.

PAUL BOHANNAN

Evanston, Illinois

Contents

SOCIAL ANTHROPOLOGY

"The noblest study of mankind is man—
says man."

—JAMES THURBER

The nature of anthropology and the nature of man

part 1

1

On the nature and significance of anthropological science

ANTHROPOLOGISTS come in several varieties. There are field anthropologists and armchair anthropologists. There are measuring anthropologists, digging anthropologists, testing anthropologists, and living-in anthropologists. Yet for all their variety, they are basically one.

The word "anthropology" has been current in the English language for some centuries. Derived from the Greek, it means "the study of man." Until about the middle of the nineteenth century the word was used for all humanists and for the philosophical forerunners of modern social scientists. Since that time, anthropology has meant something more specialized; in modern usage, anthropology refers to a recognized social science, and older usages of the word have almost disappeared.

THE DEFINITIONS OF MAN

As we have said, anthropologists come in many varieties; yet all say they are studying man. The way in which they vary is closely associated with the way each defines "man." Each science that deals with human beings has its own definitions (often covert) of man. Economists, for example, define man as a choice-making animal; they study the choices men make for allowing scarce means to achieve the ends they consider of greatest importance. Philosophers regard man as a rationalizing animal —or at least a potentially rational one—and study man's systems of rationality. Such modes of definition are reminiscent of the blind men and the elephant.

There are four major components in an anthropologist's definition of man. He shares each component with at least one other discipline. Furthermore, some of the characteristics in any one component are common to man and other members of the animal kingdom.

Man is, first of all, a mammal, which is to say that he reproduces sexually, the female bearing live young and nurturing them at her mammary glands. Being a mammal, with all that that entails, is a major determinant of the limitations forced upon the human being.

Man is, he has assured himself, not "a mere animal"—he is a "sapient" animal. He has, in his classification of species, called himself Homo sapiens—"man the knowing" or "man the perceiving." A great deal has been written about the characteristics that raise human perception above a subhuman level. It has been said—and proved of doubtful analytical value—that only men have "culture." It has been said that men communicate by symbols whereas other animals have only signs. The crux of most of the arguments, however, would seem to lie in the fact that man communicates his perceptions more efficiently than do other species of mammals.

If a man is to communicate, there must be another creature with whom he communicates. Man is, in other words, a social being. All animals are, of course, to a greater or lesser degree social—all in fact can be seen as a single community of the living. But social man is man in touch with his own kind. Alone, without communication with other human beings, he is not wholly human. Solitude and solitariness must not here be confused; men of many cultures and animals of many habits seek solitude. But none

TABLE 1 BRANCHES OF ANTHROPOLOGY

DEFINITION	BRANCH OF ANTHROPOLOGY	SPECIALTIES	RELATED SUBJECTS
Man is a mammal	Physical Anthropology	Osteology Human Morphology Anthropometry Biometrics Human Serology	Anatomy Biology Palaeontology
Man is a sentient being	Psychological Anthropology	Culture and Personality	Psychology Social Psychology Psychiatry
Man is a social being	Social Anthropology	Comparative Sociology	Sociology
Man is a being who lives by culture	Cultural Anthropology	Prehistory Archeology Linguistics Culturology	All the humanities, arts and sciences

is solitary. "Wolf children," raised by animals, cannot speak, think, or even walk like human beings.

Finally, man communicates through and lives by culture. In his perception of the world, and in his communication of it to others of his kind, man must use sounds and images and material things that are meaningful to him and to the persons with whom he communicates. These meanings, made overt in language, metaphors, things, and behavior, are summed up in the idea of "culture."

For an anthropologist, then, a man is (1) a mammal (2) with highly developed capacities for perceiving and communicating his perception (3) in a symbolic medium or idiom that is called culture, (4) to other human beings with whom he is in social contact.

To oversimplify, physical anthropology concentrates on the first point in the definition; psychological anthropology concentrates on point two; cultural anthropology (including archeology) concentrates on point three; social anthropology concentrates on point four. But—no anthropologist can afford to overlook any of the characteristics covered by the definition.

THE "PROGRESS" OF ANTHROPOLOGY

The subject of anthropology is rooted firmly in the realization of human animality. The discipline grew with man's capacity for self-revelation. The most serious obstacle to greater achievement in anthropology is still—and will doubtless remain—the difficulty inherent in self-knowledge.

Archeology developed relatively early because man's *amour-propre* allows him to consider the material remains of past civilizations with complacency. The rest of cultural anthropology, following archeology, began by studying the material culture of living peoples, much as if it were the remains of bygone peoples. But the subject matter could not reasonably be limited to material "remains"; it also could include the words, the attitudes, the stories. At first all this "nonmaterial" culture was studied in almost precise analogy to material culture: it was broken down into "culture traits" that grouped themselves into greater units variously called patterns or clusters, or any of several other such terms. With the increase in firsthand field experience by anthropologists, and with the impact of the other social sciences, the concept of culture has grown and developed, always bringing with it new horizons of self-awareness for human beings.

Psychological anthropology developed from the impact of the various schools of psychology on the revelations of cultural anthropology. Psychology, particularly depth psychology, was a basic technique of self-revelation; anthropologists were vitally aware that they had much to learn and much to contribute.

Social anthropology developed from the impact of cultural anthropology and early sociology, first American and French, and later German sociology. This is not to say that social anthropology *is* sociology any more than psychological anthropology is psychology or economic anthropology is economics or legal anthropology is jurisprudence.

The essence of anthropology is simultaneous self-examination and examination of other, unlike peoples. Self-examination is always difficult. Social or cultural self-examination is doubly difficult because social relationships, personalities, and ideas are abstract, unlike pots or stone axes. Modern anthropology has, indeed, grown out of a continuous struggle against the tyranny of learned perception. The theme of this book, like the theme of the discipline, is the story of the mastering of human animality by processes and techniques of self-recognition.

Anthropology has long been considered a unified science—a unity of all the subdisciplines based on the various implications of the anthropological definition of man. As the subject has become more complex, it has become necessary for every anthropologist to specialize. Fears have sometimes been expressed that the unity, which was the hallmark of anthropology in its early days, would be lost. Such fears are, however, ungrounded. As long as anthropology studies man, it must study all of him, as that totality can be perceived. As each branch of the subject becomes more complex for its specialists, it must necessarily develop at the same time a set of comprehensive, somewhat abstract but simplifying ideas for use by those who specialize in other branches of the subject.

Social scientists, including anthropologists, do, however, work under a particular difficulty not faced by other scientists, and their significance and their progress must be evaluated in terms of that difficulty. Physical scientists proceed with the assurance that their accomplishments have stacked up since the beginning. There was a sensible, if unenlightened, period before the laws of mechanics were understood or before the atom was "discovered." One can understand the horse and buggy and recognize the automobile as an improvement on it.

However, when one deals with the more abstract items of interest to social science it becomes more difficult to remember or to understand the times and the days before current ideas were part of current knowledge. The idea of money, let alone the material coins themselves, is a case in point. Money is one of the shatteringly simplifying ideas of all time because it is no less than a device by means of which many items and many acts can be valued, added up, and expressed in terms of a single standard. With money, butter and guns—to use the old saw of the economists—are added up and a choice made. To make people understand what life is like in the absence of this simplifying idea is still a major difficulty in teaching anthropology. Coins may have been absent, they recognize; but something "must" have done their job. Anthropologists know better, but find conviction hard to achieve when it means recomplicating the perceptions of their audience.

Another example is the contracts on which our daily lives depend. We get our food by informal contracts that we make with the grocer, paid for by our earnings from more or less formal contracts we make with employers. The grocer gets the food on the basis of a contract he makes with the distributor, who gets it from a producer through unnumbered contractual links. The whole society is fused in a network of contracts. We seldom stop to think that without a vast and dependable legal system, police system, and court system, this series of contracts could not be made to work even as well as it does. We would, in such a world, be forced to fall back on other sorts of sanctions for human relationships.

Modern life is full of simplifying ideas such as "money" and "contract." It could not be carried on without them. The difficulty comes—bringing error in its wake—when we project these ideas backward in an effort to understand the data of history, or outward to understand the data of anthropology.

As anthropologists and other social scientists gain new insights, these very insights (if they are good, and sometimes even if they are not) are quickly diffused into the common culture where they occupy a very different position than do the ideas and discoveries of physical scientists. The latter make discoveries and inventions that obviously improve methods of traveling from point *A* to point *B*. Learning to recognize and use the new way does not, of itself, blot out comprehension of the old way. However, social science deals not merely with the substance of our behavior, but with the very mode of it. It examines not merely our overt ideas but the unconscious categories of our thought. Therefore its discoveries create a new milieu in which the old or the exotic has to be especially studied in order to be comprehensible.

Thus, because anthropologists deal in ways of looking at the universe, their truths and their discoveries become "trite" the moment they are half understood by laymen. These laymen fail to comprehend the part social science plays in the life that goes on around us, or the fundamental differences it has made in the way we live.

The history of physical science becomes a history of technology and of cosmology, which are subjects that can (at least, in historical perspective) be looked at dispassionately. But the history of social science is the history of beliefs about the family, about crime, about emotion—in short, a history of morals. Once it is fully understood, it becomes trite; once outmoded, it seems almost silly. The cross that anthropology must bear is the illusion of the absence of an impressive past. Its rewards are concomitant with that very illusion—they are the basic but usually anonymous contributions that anthropology makes to the mode in which moderns, of whatever era, comprehend the modern world.

If anthropology is right or it "fits," its ideas are soon diffused into the common culture. Children learn them from their parents, and elementary-school students from their teachers. Anthropology first influences the culture in which people are reared to adulthood, then has to hurry to keep ahead not merely of those adults, but of the very children who learn from them. As anthropologists and other social scientists achieve the self-revelation which is their aim, they must simultaneously pursue in some detail the history of their subject in order to realize their achievements. Such is the fertile paradox of anthropology.

THE ANTHROPOLOGIST'S TASK

Anthropologists go to exotic peoples who practice what are to them strange customs and cultures—even when such exotic peoples are to be found in the next block. In order to understand these cultures, they must learn to understand their own. The process provides the anthropologist with a sort of stereoscopic vision—he sees a situation through two lenses at once, and it stands out in a perspective that is sharper and more poignant than it was before he learned to evaluate two or more cultures, each in terms of the other.

The first task a social anthropologist faces is carrying out his field research among such peoples. The second is communicating his findings to his colleagues within a conceptual framework that makes it possible for them to understand the facts from the standpoint of the subject people and, at the same time, to be able to forge better theoretical understanding of society and culture.

It is difficult for anthropologists to realize that there was a time in the history of their own discipline before they had discovered field research. They took their "facts" from the writings of explorers, colonial officials, and missionaries; they interpreted such facts largely without benefit of the interpretation placed on them by the peoples to whom they applied. Then, at the turn of the twentieth century, the Americans and the British "discovered" fieldwork independently and at about the same time. The spiritual heirs of Boas in America and of Haddon and Rivers in Britain, having discovered "the field," never looked back.

ETHNOGRAPHY

Field work for the social anthropologist means becoming an ethnographer. Ethnography is the study in depth of a single people, or small number of closely related peoples. The more comprehensive the ground the ethnographer covers, and the more profoundly he covers it, the better the ethnography that results from his field research. A first-rate ethnography usually takes between a year and two years of field research. During this time the ethnographer learns the language of the people he studies—it probably becomes his second-best language—and discusses his discoveries and insights with the people from whom he is learning. The ethnographic field trip can be a most revealing and valuable personal experience because it puts the ethnographer in a controlled position for seeing two cultures at once—his own (including his anthropological training) and that of the people he is studying. It is just here that he develops stereoscopic social vision.

The ethnographer, once he returns from the field and is again firmly ensconced in his study, must do two things at once: he must complete his ethnography by writing it up, and he must set himself and his data into an expanding tradition of theory. In his latter role he is called an ethnologist,[1] and ethnology is the comparative study of peoples from the ethnographies that have been produced about them. That the two processes are inseparable has led to some of the greatest misunderstandings and arguments in the entire profession.

TRANSLATION

The completion of the ethnography has as its major problem the accurate translation of data from one cultural milieu into another without serious warping of facts and interpretation.

The anthropologist who goes to the field and who over a period of two years or so learns another social system and another culture does so in a strange, usually exotic, non-Indo-European language. As he becomes more and more conversant with this language, he finds that, in the rush to keep his notebooks current and accurate, he writes more and more notes in the language of the people he is studying. Some anthropologists say that eventually they take all their notes in the native language, and even contend that any anthropologist who does otherwise cannot have sufficient command of the language of his people to know what they are talking about.

The anthropologist's problem of translation is on a scale unknown to all save a few literary translators; yet, an example of translation from Japanese provides an instructive parallel. Arthur Waley, when translating Lady Murasaki's *Tale of Genji,* was faced with the problem not merely of getting the story forward, but of making an exotic society and an exotic system of ideas and values understandable in English. His difficulty reached its

[1] In the British scientific dialect, the ethnologist is a person who uses the factual data gathered by the ethnographer in a way reminiscent of the way in which an historian uses the information of the archeologist. In the British terminology, therefore, a "social anthropologist" is one who compares several ethnographies, including that of his own society. The word "ethnology" means, in France, what English speakers term "cultural anthropology."

peak when he had to translate Japanese poems the characters of the novel sent as notes to one another, the purpose of which was to convey two or more meanings simultaneously. In the original Japanese, only the poem itself—seventeen bare syllables—appears. The rest is up to the reader. It is impossible to translate these poems and retain all the shades of meaning. Waley has used a device for explaining them that is very similar to the sort an anthropologist might use: he tells us that the poem "said" such and such, but "meant" something else as well.

The anthropologist's translation difficulty can also be seen, by himself, when he is attempting to explain the system of his own society to the people he studies: informants are as curious as anthropologists. I was once asked by a Nigerian elder, "What are the divisions of your country?" I replied, "We divide the country into forty-eight divisions, which we call states [true at that time]. Each one has a headman who is elected every few years by the people of that state." He looked dubious. "Forty-eight?" he asked; "that is a lot of children for one man to have—you must have skipped some generations when you learned the genealogy." His remark was not a *non-sequitur*. In his own tribe the divisions were said to have been formed by the sons and the subdivisions by the grandsons of the founder and genitor of the whole nation. He was guilty of having translated foreign ideas into his own categories of thought: of giving the ideas of his own culture a more general validity than they actually have.

There is no more complete way to misunderstand a foreign civilization than to see it in terms of one's own civilization. It was a common fault of colonial governments that they looked for "the indigenous authorities"—instead of realizing that authority is a Western concept and that it may even be peculiar to the West. With half a dozen notable exceptions, it has been only within the last generation or two that missionaries have stopped calling all the indigenous spirits whose names and rites they encounter "devils."

The notions of "authorities" and "devils," which were imported from our society and our own culture and language, were curtains that effectively concealed the true meanings of the words and notions employed and expressed in the vernaculars, and hence concealed what is all too often and all too uncomprehendingly called "the mind of primitive man." Today we are wise about such crude notions as authorities and devils. But there are many other such misinterpretations whose existence we are only now coming to recognize.

All the people in the world, in all societies, place an interpretation on the behavior in which they engage and the culture in terms of which they interact with one another. In the process of their interpretation, the culture and social action become organized into sensible chunks or schemes that form sensible connected wholes of one sort or another. This folk organization of actions, beliefs, tools, and ideas is to be found, a living reality, *both* in the language *and* in the institutions of the society.

It is precisely in this system of categories, as it is preserved in the language and in recurrent social behavior, that the ethnographer must report. The categories in which any people systematize their own actions and thoughts are as much facts as any of the component actions or words that one can see or hear.

The ethnographer is, in short, a translator of strange ideas, customs, and things into familiar language. The danger is that he will rob them of their genius by turning them into pale carbon copies of his own culture or of his own discipline. It is through ethnology and its examination of many cultures, and through willingness to examine his own culture and his own scientific concepts, that the anthropologist can avoid the pitfalls of ethnographic translation.

Ethnologists must thus learn not merely many ethnographies, but also to examine the principles and ideas of Western society through eyes conditioned by such exotic cultures. It is just such an experience that allows an anthropologist a certain degree of that disengaged quality usually called "objectivity."

All ethnographic reporting is, to some extent at least, a comparison, overt or covert, of strange customs with familiar ones. It thereby provides a way for examining with awareness what all too often is considered to be "natural" when in fact it is merely habitual: it allows us to distinguish *a* human condition from *the* human condition.

The anthropologist, in passing, may show the members of his own society that their ways of doing things are insular, and that their categories of thought are not general—nor, perhaps, even the best. He demonstrates to his own people that they can learn a great deal about their own ways by learning the ways of others. The anthropologist's job is, in part, to make members of his own culture ask—about their own institutions and ideas—questions that have never been asked before.

THE CREATION OF ANTHROPOLOGICAL THEORY

Social anthropologists are more than ethnographers; they are, in fact, even more than ethnologists, although they must first be both. Besides translating his field data and comparing it with other such data, the social anthropologist must proceed along general lines of scientific method for arriving at and presenting his conclusions. Besides understanding the folk conceptions of exotic peoples and those of his own society, the social anthropologist must create analytical theory for the fuller comprehension of both folk theories and the perceived social facts on which they are based.

Whereas a scientific theory in the physical or life sciences has to cope only with the "facts" and their theoretical organization, the behavioral sciences and particularly anthropology must deal with "facts," with folk organization of "facts," and only then with theoretical organizations of both. The rightness or wrongness of a people's own folk organization of "facts" is for the anthropologist in itself a key fact.

Here, then, is the basic problem. The anthropologist always learns some sort of folk organization of his data from his informants. But this folk organization is not in itself adequate for his purposes, so he must create an additional organization—an analytical organization—in order to compare the facts and the folk theories.

Now, both the folk and the analytical viewpoints may be perfectly sound, but they must not be confused with each other. The folk organization has as its purpose action in daily life. Overt or covert, it is adequate to the extent that it is successful from the point of view of the actors. The analytical organization, on the other hand, has analysis and theorizing as its purpose. It should be entirely overt, and it is as adequate as the theory and understanding to which it leads.

The direst trap for the anthropologist is to confuse folk organization with analytical organization. The most heinous fault that a work of social anthropology can have is assignment of ideas from an analytical system to people who act merely in terms of a folk system.

To take an example: a book on the law of an African tribe, say, based on sensitive and thorough field research, can be irrevocably spoiled if the author assumes a theoretical framework such as that established by Roman law, canon law, or common law and assigns these categories to the ideas and acts of Africans without first discovering and explaining the framework of "folk theory," so to speak, on which the Africans themselves organize the facts. To take another example: in the past, anthropologists have noted quite correctly that a certain ritual increases community solidarity (whatever definition they may have given for that), and then spoiled it all by saying that the participants performed the ritual for the purpose of achieving solidarity, which they almost surely did not.

KEY TERMS

It is a matter of empirically verifiable fact that every culture has certain key words in its language. Almost without exception it is not possible for a person who uses that culture to say what they are. Those key words may be relatively few, as among some African groups or some American Indian tribes. They may be, on the other hand, so numerous that their very complexity makes it seem as if there were no key words at all, or that this method of proceeding is not applicable in such an instance.

If an anthropologist learns the language of the people he studies—

learns it really well—he should be able, in the process of translation, to pick out these key terms: they are no more than the terms that allow him to get his ethnography sensibly into as few folk categories as possible. I shall take examples from my own fieldwork among the Tiv of central Nigeria. One such key word for Tiv ethnography is *tiev,* which means farm or garden. To describe the farms, the emotional attitudes to them, is to set *tiev* into its native context. Another such word is *jir,* which means court, court case, moot. Tiv spend a great deal of time settling disputes in *jir,* and all of their ideas of justice and ethics among human beings eventually impinge on this activity. Another such term is *tsav,* a substance that grows on the hearts of "witches" and that forms the keystone of Tiv magical and religious ideas. Another is *kasoa,* which refers to what we would call a "market," but is much broader in concept than our term. There are some half dozen other such key words. If I write about these words, explaining them and their context fully, I can organize most of my field notes, and can communicate the major part of what I know about these people. The translation has been achieved. The anthropologist has explained alien concepts in English without assimilating them to Western concepts, which would destroy them.

THEORY FORMATION

The task of translation and comparison can be achieved in only one way: erection of an "analytical system"—a "theory," if anyone prefers the term—by means of which the Anglo-American or Western notions can be compared with the exotic ones, and the latter with one another, in such a way that none of them loses its individualizing traits—its "genius," to use the eighteenth-century word.

In its processes of gathering data, anthropology resembles history. Anthropologists are interested in description of events, and in the generalizations and explanations made by the actors in those events. An anthropologist can acknowledge no finer master than Marc Bloch, the great French historian, in dealing with this aspect of his problem. Bloch's *Apologie pour l'histoire* (1952) sets the ethnographer's problem as ably as it sets the historian's problem.

However, when it comes to theory formation, anthropology resembles science. The rudiments of anthropological theorizing can be set forth in a diagram (Figure 1).

The ethnographic, or "historical," aspects of our study allows us to arrive at box N via box M. Box N, then, is to be understood on the same level as box B, the folk explanations current in our own society and, on a different level but performing a comparable function so far as the anthropologist is concerned, the theories of the social sciences of our own

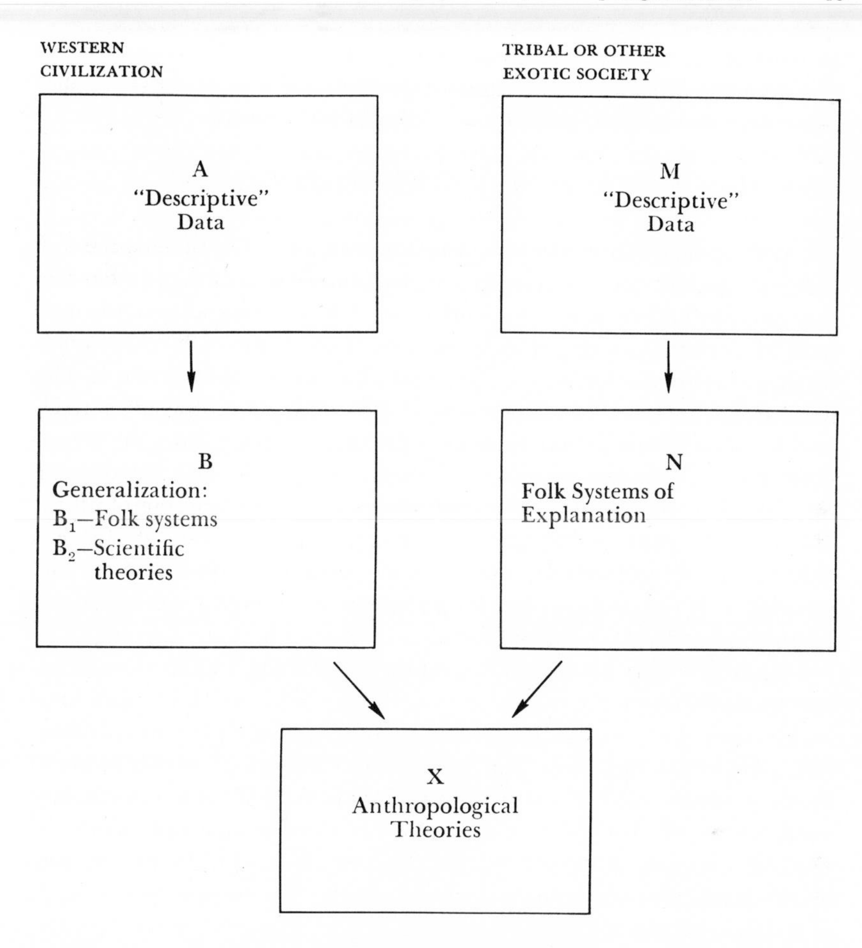

FIGURE 1 Anthropological Theorizing

society. Insofar as any idea in either box B or box N explains adequately everything in boxes A, B, M, and N, it is adequate anthropological theory and can be put into box X. If it does not, then anthropological theory must be a new and original statement of sensible relationships among these four boxes. The most common anthropological errors are (1) explaining box M in terms of box B, omitting box N altogether—that is confusion of B_2 and X; (2) explaining box N by box B without first determining that the contents of box N can in fact be derived from box M.

Anthropological theory can, eventually, make predictions on the basis of manipulating the theory in box X. What it can never do is make these predictions in terms of specific events *unless* it discovers a way to feed back the material of boxes M and N, which was removed in the process of arriving at the propositions in box X. Even then, accurate prognostication is extremely difficult for the simple reason that the same processes may take place in many superficially different cultural forms.

THE SIGNIFICANCE OF ANTHROPOLOGY

Anthropology, then, has two sorts of significance. On the one hand, it collects, classifies, and analyzes knowledge about human beings, how they live, and what they make. On the other hand, it questions some of the most basic ideas of the contemporary world, brings comparative insights to bear on them, and makes us more aware of what we are by confronting us with what we are not. As Clyde Kluckhohn (1949) once put it, it would scarcely be a fish that discovered the existence of water. In other words, de Toqueville's insights into America could never have been made by a home-grown observer. It is the purpose of anthropology, as it is the purpose of all the rest of the humanities and social sciences, to make us aware of ourselves and our society, and thus transform our self-awareness into knowledge and security. It is the method of social anthropology to reveal folk systems of understanding by the creation of analytical systems of understanding.

Anthropology is, like history or science, an "attitude." That attitude consists in developing a stereoscopic view of human activities and human ideas by means of concepts that have been discovered in the processes of translating key organizing ideas from one cultural idiom into the language of another culture, usually our own, thus making these ideas in some degree available to all. Any given anthropological theories, like the theories of physical scientists, or indeed like the interpretations of historians, may go by the board. But the anthropological attitude, like the scientific attitude of which it is a mode, is here to stay.

2

Culture, personality, and society

A SIGNAL ACHIEVEMENT of anthropology in the first three decades of the twentieth century was the ability to distinguish culture from race and from language. The subject had inherited from the common pool of Western culture an unthinkingly repeated mixture of biological, linguistic, and behavioral characteristics. Like other correct discoveries of social science this distinction, although it is encountering strong vested interests, is now in process of reducing itself to "common sense" in the greater culture.

An analogous confusion still exists, however: an unthinkingly repeated association of culture, personality, and society. Personality is still used even by eminent scientists to give a false genetic basis to cultural factors (Muller, 1962): many social scientists still compound confusion by saying that since culture and society cannot be "objectively" separated into two categories they are the same thing.

DISTINGUISHING CULTURE, PERSONALITY, AND SOCIETY

The problem of distinguishing race, language, and culture is of precisely the same sort as the problem of distinguishing culture, personality, and society. Both problems can be solved only by a clear differentiation of the criteria used for classification. Race is a summary of biophysical phenomena, culture is a summary of behavioral phenomena, and language is a summary of a specific type of behavioral phenomena (in some contexts part of culture, although interestingly independent of the rest of culture). Since the three concepts deal with different characteristics or activities of people —and since all people have manifold characteristics—race, language, and culture may vary independently of one another, and the different modes of association of the three can be scientifically explored.

Personality, culture, and society have been difficult to distinguish for a similar reason: each deals with a different aspect of the same thing. In this case, however, the "thing" is not the human individual but rather a more difficult entity: social behavior. Social behavior demands at least two human beings, and so stands at the basis of society. Further, it demands common knowledge and expectations of those two or more people, and so a common culture is essential. Social behavior also demands people who can interact with some degree of dependability—and social behavior seen from the standpoint of such individuals is one aspect of personality.

People have to be "socialized" and "enculturated," to use two jargon terms for "taught the manners and technology of their elders." In bringing about this situation, the child participates in social relationships and learns techniques and ideas. There is, in the individual, a residue from this activity that (taken in some unknown mixture with his genetic inclinations and capabilities) creates the "personality."

At the same time that the individual absorbs his culture and learns to use it for communication and expression, he is participating in the social relationships that (rather than the individual himself) become the weft of the society. The techniques and ideas themselves become the medium or idiom in which both personality and social relationships are expressed. They are the culture.

THE INTERRELATION OF THE CONCEPTS

The point is that culture, society, and personality are not empirically separable each from the other. In order to have social relationships, we must have culture as the means with which to express them, and we must have personalities that handle the culture and play the roles in the social relationships. No matter with which we begin, the other two are necessary dimensions. Only analytically can a separation be made.

An analogy to electricity is helpful. As a glance into a dictionary will show, electricity is very difficult to define— so indeed is the flow of social and cultural reality. In order to define electricity, to measure it, and hence to control it, some scales must be established. It was necessary to create concepts like volt, ohm, ampere, and the like. The interesting point is, however, that "volt" has, by itself, no meaning at all. Before a volt has meaning, the corresponding notions of ohm and ampere must be brought forward. A *volt* of electricity measures force. An *ohm* measures resistance. An *ampere* measures current. A volt, then, is the electromotive force necessary to create one ampere of current when steadily applied to a conductor with a resistance of one ohm. We add the term *watt* when we change our viewpoint to the amount of work that unit of electricity does. When we add a further factor—one second of time—we get the notion of *coulombs* or *joules.*

The point is clear enough. We have an electrical phenomenon. If we look at it from the standpoint of measurement (of electric current), we see amperes. If we look at it from the standpoint of resistance, we see ohms;

and if we look at it from the standpoint of force, we see volts. Yet, so far as the "reality" of the situation goes—whatever one may make "reality" mean—there is a single situation. The plurality is in the analysis.

The social situation can be seen in analogy to the electrical situation. Social reality—social events—exists. Social reality flows on in time (itself a cultural idea); it is difficult to define. When we begin to look at the situation with a view to explaining it, we must create artificial units and viewpoints.

Out of this social flux, we must separate an analytical unit called a "social relationship." A social relationship is played out between two persons, in a sense, but certainly not between two total persons. It is, therefore, well to factor the person by his relationships, and to call each factor a "role." We can then say that a relationship exists between two roles, and that each social person is composed of many roles centering in a single individual.

A social relationship takes place in a medium of "culture," and is one of many social relationships. The totality of the medium is the culture, and another viewpoint is thus added. We can, to pursue our analogy (it will give way presently), note that social relationships are the "current" of social reality, culture is its "force," and personality is the "resistance."

Just as in the case of electricity, it is possible to add still new viewpoints. Here it is enough to note that culture,social relationships, and personality must be interdefined. They are different ways of looking at the same thing.

HABITUATION AND EDUCATION

Into every culture and every civilization, year after year, hordes of uncultured "barbarians" descend in the form of newborn babies. In every society, a major—indeed, an overwhelming—amount of social energy must be spent in making cultured creatures out of this human plasm. Babies, whatever their potential may be, have few inborn abilities. They can grasp (a newly born baby can support its own weight by its grasp), but probably have to learn to utilize the capacity. They have to be taught to suck—for some, learning takes a minute or two, for others as much as a day or two. Some children are brighter than others, and the difference begins to show very early in life.

It is one of the characteristics of human beings that their children remain helpless for a very long period. Horses can walk and run a few hours after birth. Apes mature in about a third of the time that it takes human beings to mature. Even elephants, whose period of gestation is almost twice that of human beings, and whose life span is only a little shorter, are self-sufficient within about three years. Under minimal conditions, the human being requires ten or twelve years to become self-sufficient; under most conditions of culture, some fifteen years or so; and under our own system, with its complex material culture and vast need for training and education, somewhat longer than that.

Human beings, whether they are a few days old, a few years old, or a few decades old, have many needs because of the sheer fact that they are animals. Some of these needs, if left unfulfilled, will lead to the death of the animal. They must be fed, they must have a certain environmental temperature, and they need at least a certain minimal contact with others. If human babies are left without human contact, they die—even if their other needs are well attended (Spitz, 1949).

Babies, being helpless, have their needs fulfilled for them. In the course of the fulfillment of these needs, the way in which the need is fulfilled comes to be almost as important as the fact of fulfillment. By the time a child is nearly adult enough to fulfill some of his own requirements for food and sleep, his habits are well established. These habits may be changed several times during the course of maturation, but even the need to change and the capacity to change are developed into habits. If it were not possible to change habits, any sort of "progress" or social change would be quite impossible.

The habits that are acquired by youngsters are part of the culture in accordance with which they are brought up. In one sense, the habits *are* the culture: if all the habits of all the people were changed, the culture would have changed.

There are, however, two ways in which culture can be "internalized." One is by habituation and the other by purposeful education. Western children are taught, rather systematically, to use a fork (a most clumsy instrument until you have mastered it); but they are not taught food preferences in the same purposeful way (although they may be taught, very purposefully indeed, what not to eat).

In habituation, human beings learn those aspects of culture that are not regarded in the culture as specifically learnable techniques. In education they are taught—specifically taught—the techniques. Education is usually defined as the directed learning process, either formally or informally carried out. The purpose here is not to make a pedantic distinction between these two aspects of education—many situations of human learning cannot be specifically set out as one or the other, but partake of both. It is merely to point out that human beings learn a great deal more than is specifically taught them: people pick up habits, without questioning them, because "that's the way it is done." Yet nobody picks up reading as a habit the way he picks up a taste for wheat bread and meat instead of millet porridge and fish.

Both of these processes—habituation and education—make it possible to live in the society in which we are born or in which we find ourselves. Neither stops, however, when the learner becomes a full-fledged member of adult society. Rather, he continues throughout his entire life to learn his culture—new culture or new fields of traditional culture. Education and habituation continue to the grave. There is no culture that it is possible completely to master, even though it is possible in some—but not in our own—to be "old and full of years," satiated with sufficient of one's culture that death is not an objectionable alternative to finishing the job.

Thus, as man's primary needs are cared for—those whose neglect would cause his death—he is habituated and educated. The habituation and education themselves set up a secondary set of needs for the primary needs to be cared for in certain ways. They may become as grave a need as the substantive needs.

HABITUATING AND EDUCATING AGENTS

Education may be carried on by any number of agencies. The family is probably the most important educating agency in every society. In some societies, a part of the job is taken over by professionals when the child is about six years old. Even in societies that lack any sort of formal schooling, the family may be assisted by other elements of the society when the child reaches about this age. Sometimes children are sent to their grandparents, because grandparents are thought in that culture, for one reason or another, to be the best formal instructors during certain periods of a child's life. In other societies, a child goes to his father's sister because it is thought that the parents themselves may be so fond of the child as to be too indulgent to insist on adequate training for coping with life and society. The father's sister, the evaluation in such a society runs, is a close kinswoman and hence will be kind and proffer some affection, but she is far enough removed that she will insist on the child's continuing education to the point of being strict if it is necessary. Some societies have formalized age associations that organize children to teach younger children.

Finally, the community as a whole may act as an habituating and educating agency simply by withholding its approval from people who do not behave "properly," or by rewarding behavior that is esteemed. The community may be to its members what Pavlov was to his dogs: in the end the individual learns to do what the community expects and even to like it, just as one of Pavlov's dogs told a peer who belonged to a different master: "I've got my guy trained to ring a bell every time he's about to feed me."

There are, of course, some failures. These are the people that the society brands neurotic, sick, criminal, or all three. Yet even these "failures" are habituated and to some degree educated: they rebel in terms of their own culture. They speak the language, wear the clothes, eat the food of the society they are rebelling against. They sing songs written with the same scales and notes, and they recognize the same norms, even by valuing perversions of them.

CULTURE AS THE IDIOM OF PERSONALITY

Kluckhohn and Murray once wrote that "every man is in certain respects like all other men, like some other men, and like no other man" (1949, p. 35). Thus, some determinants of personality are universal: every person is born, learns to use his body for movement, explores his environment, and learns to protect himself. Every person experiences hunger and sexual tensions. Furthermore, all men must adjust to the condition of being social animals, which means learning to live in groups; they must do so in terms of some culture or other and hence have to learn to gratify, at least minimally, the expectations of others. All persons experience illness.

Other similarities are more limited. All of us are in some ways like some men who are part of our social and cultural environment, and different from those in other environments—men living in different societies, by means of different cultures. These more limited similarities arise from learned responses that we make to situations to which there may be many possible responses. Groups whose members share numerous experiences of habituation and education share the characteristics resulting from that particular experience.

Finally, there are unique qualities in every personality. Unique qualities are, of course, dependent on physical nature or social conditioning. However, some aspects of that physical and social nature allow of eccentricity whereas others do not.

All these ideas can be put into another set of terms; indeed, the two sets of terms are more enlightening than either single one. This second set of terms is somewhat more metaphorical; nonetheless, it brings out an important distinction in the first set. Children, when they are born, are without culture, and hence are without personality, and almost without social relationships. The very fact of birth may be described as the termination of a biophysical relationship and, in the usual course of events, its replacement with a social relationship. Social relationships, then, expand with maturation; new culture is demanded in which to respond to other people so that the relationships are possible. The acquisition of that culture is *ipso facto* the growth of the personality. As the personality develops, the characteristic way of responding to given stimuli (some of the responses being universal, some culturally normal, and some eccentric) becomes more highly developed and, at the same time, more set.

Culture, as it is acquired with the growth of personality, becomes the *medium* of that personality. You cannot swim without water, and water is the medium of swimming; you cannot paint a picture without paint, and the paint becomes the medium for expressing the message of the picture. The difference between culture and personality is the same as the difference between the medium and the content of a picture. They are, at one level, the same thing. At another level, they are distinct because they have been viewed with completely different purposes and techniques.

BASIC PERSONALITY AND MODAL PERSONALITY

The experiences shared by all men, and hence the aspects of the personality shared by all men, are best brought out by comparison of the behavior of men to the behavior of other animals. As universals, they are of minimal interest to anthropologists (although some anthropologists would disagree with this statement because they are primarily interested in the fact that in some regards men are the same the whole world over). At the other end of the scale, the eccentric elements are also of little interest to anthropologists, for anthropologists deal in cultural generalizations that can be made about groups of people.

The primary field of the anthropologist's interest in personality concerns that part of the personality men share with other men of their own culture, but which they do not share with all other men. The premise is that certain ways of habituation and education, as well as certain substantive aspects of habits and learning, are associated with certain features of personality.

The sort of groups in which children are taught their culture leaves an indelible mark upon them. The basic values of the subject matter leave an equally permanent mark. The framework of a house can be seen in the finished building, if you know how to look for it. In the same way, the techniques and ideas that children learn have a lasting effect on the sort of adults they become.

Each set of cultural norms and social institutions produces in men and women a characteristic type (or types) of personality structure. The part of their personalities that is shared by a large proportion of the people of a single society is usually called the "basic personality."

Basic personality is "a structure of articulated personality characteristics and processes attributable, nonstatistically, to almost all members of some culturally bounded population" (Wallace, 1961, p. 106). The emphasis in the basic personality has been placed on the fact that it is regular, and that it is "a structure," which means that its "characteristics and processes" are always correlated with one another in the same way. Some anthropologists have called such a structure a pattern.

The term "modal personality" is also used for this same general phenomenon, but is arrived at in a different way. It is usually handled statistically, with the various characteristics of the structure elicited by personality tests such as the Rorschach or the Thematic Apperception Test. The greatest dimension to be added by such tests is that they can give a hint of the large variety of types that can actually exist within a single cultural group (Wallace, 1961, pp. 109-110).

It is this variation within the group that is not always adequately explained by reference to basic or modal personality. In their effort to see the exotic group as different from ourselves, anthropologists have sometimes underemphasized the fact that there is likely to be as great a difference in the personalities of members of an exotic society as there is among members of Western society. There are likely to be many personality types in any social group, even though the pattern of strains and conflicts within each may be significantly different from one culture to the next.

What is true, however, is that a culture may select certain types of personality for special reward. Even if culture cannot fundamentally change anybody (a moot point), it can be so oriented that one personality type is rewarded more significantly than some others. Therefore, those individuals who are most malleable, and those parts of each individual's makeup that are most pliable, are attracted toward and ultimately become representative of the dominant, best-rewarded personality type.

In a social group that rewards men of action over men of thought, those persons who are not strongly one or the other have a choice: they can play either role with a modicum of success, so they choose the one in which they see most rewards. The inclination of that social group to regard men of action as worthwhile is thereby reinforced. However, there *may* be some men who could only with real damage to themselves be men of action, so as far as they are concerned they take the greater rewards, which the culture brands as lesser.

It is possible, then, to characterize social or cultural groups by the sorts of personalities they hold in greatest esteem. There are more of such personalities, and hence concomitantly more are developed. We can, in this way, pick out the favored and dominant personality types within our own society or any other. They may change from one generation to another; in fact, they have changed markedly in the United States within the last generation (Riesman, 1950).

In summary, personality develops as cultural capacity grows. Personality can be expressed only in terms of culture. For these two reasons, and probably many others as well, it is easy to confuse culture and personality.

Culture can be viewed—among other views—as the qualitative or idiomatic aspect of personality. Modal or basic personality is the personality expressed more or less in common, and maximally rewarded, among a group of people who communicate and interact with one another. As the human individual matures and learns to communicate with his elders and his peers, he learns certain modes and manners of expressing himself and of fulfilling his requirements, and he also learns to expect consistent behavior from these others. The human personality would seem to be pliable enough that it can be taught to express itself in almost any cultural idiom, however difficult it may be to change certain basic particulars in the idiom after adulthood.

The basic problem, however, is a simple one: personality must not be confused with culture any more than either should be confused with "race."

CULTURE AS THE IDIOM OF SOCIETY

Just as culture is inseparable from the personality but must be analytically distinguished from it, so culture is inseparable from social relationships, but must be distinguished from them. In order for either culture or personality to exist, there must be two or more individuals, with their personalities, who affect one another. Culture is the idiom of society just as it is the idiom of personality.

From the time of Defoe, and long before, it has been stylish among novelists and certain types of philosophers to imagine what human beings would be like if they did not engage in any social relationships at all. Just what is a "neat" human being, with nothing in the way of other human beings to influence and dilute him? The classic exposition of the problem is, of course, the fictional case of Robinson Crusoe.

The pertinent question about Robinson Crusoe is, however, seldom asked: How old was he when he was washed ashore on his desert island? The answer is given—he was a full-grown, married man, between youth and early middle age.

His whole personality, and his capacity to grasp and cope with the problems of life—even life that had to be lived out alone—had been formed before he was cast up on his desert island. He knew about boats—all he had to do was build one, and he had a pretty good knowledge of how to go about it. He knew techniques for getting food and building shelters. And he knew what he was missing: only the most stern discipline made life livable.

The romance of Robinson Crusoe derives from the fact that a man, forced by circumstances to do for himself everything that society normally provides, still longs for company. The situation is made more poignant, and the point driven home, when he finds a footprint in the sand and experiences again the combination of anticipation and dread that accompanies social relationships.

Another attempt at the theme was made more recently in William Golding's *Lord of the Flies,* a novel in which about thirty young boys are trapped on an island and, with only the knowledge of twelve-year-olds, must try to work out a human society and culture. Their problems are enlightening and Golding's findings offer a devastating satire on our own present culture. However, a social scientist cannot allow Golding's ultimate theme to go unstressed: in order to avoid the story's ending in the total collapse of human society, tradition—in the form of adults and a higher authority—had to be reintroduced. Society is the very *deus ex machina* that allows human life to continue.

THE PROCESS OF SOCIAL RELATIONSHIPS

The habituation and education of an individual is necessarily carried out by other individuals—or, occasionally, by himself in his relationships with other individuals. As such a person takes on habits and learns to do things, he takes on at the same time—and usually without realizing it fully—a whole set of social obligations.

Children behave as they do because their parents, and later others, make certain demands on them. They continue to behave as they do, either because they continue to behave in accordance with those demands—first of their parents, then of others—or because they positively do not comply with the demands.

A child's first social relationship is with his mother. Within a few weeks or months, the child's world enlarges to include, normally, father and siblings. At about three, say, it enlarges to include something of a peer group outside the family. The process of enlargement goes on until middle age at any rate, and probably until death—although after a point the changes may be no more than substitution of personnel.

Each one of these people affects the individual's behavior, and vice versa. That is about as clear a definition of a social relationship as can be given: if two people are in association, each affecting the behavior of the other, a social relationship exists. It should be specifically noted that a relationship exists only if *both* parties to it are affected. No social relationship is created, for example, if you read a book of Rousseau. Rousseau affects the reader, but Rousseau is not affected—he is dead. Rousseau is thus part of what can be called the cultural tradition. Modern individuals have developed ways, via writing and other forms of nonpersonal communication, to absorb tradition in situations that are fundamentally nonsocial: such is, in fact, one of the marks of civilization. Yet, reading and writing may provide—and in a literate civilization do so daily—a form, such as the business letter, for carrying on social relationships.

Neither is listening to the radio or watching television a social relationship. The ad-man does not react to a shouted, "Shut up, you blithering hireling!" One of the fundamental characteristics of Western culture is that we have developed nonsocial tools for educating our population, and so have created fundamental changes in social life.

BEHAVIORAL EXPECTATIONS

As children grow up, they learn to expect certain kinds of behavior from the people around them. The word "expect" is important, because the child very quickly acquires expectations of what first his mother, later his siblings and his father, and still later his peers, will do. The expectations are also held in the minds of the other persons engaging in the relationships. The mother, who is expected by the child to do such and such, also has a picture of these activities that she expects to carry out. And more importantly, she expects and demands certain types of activity on the part of the child. The performance of acts in accordance with the mother's expectation leads to approval, food, warmth, shelter, love, and all the other requirements and good things. An act not in accordance with the expectations may very quickly lead to the opposite.

Therefore, a child picks up, just as he picks up language, a knowledge of expected rewards, gained rewards, and a complementary set of expectations to those of his mother and other persons in his life. It is possible to say—and has indeed, been said (Parsons, 1951)—that the unit of social life is the expectation.

Expectations must be held in human minds (whatever we may give for a definition of mind), either consciously or unconsciously. The expectations form what can be called an "image" of sensible behavior (Boulding, 1956). The images of two interacting people must be in some degree complementary: if person *A* does one thing, person *B* must be able to put such a construction on it that he can perform the next "reasonable" act in sequence. If a child has one image of a situation and his mother another, only misunderstanding results.

It is, of course, not necessary for both parties to a relationship to hold images that mesh in total congruity. It is probably true that no two people see even the simplest social situation in precisely the same terms. It is necessary, however, that their images be sufficiently similar to allow each to achieve an optimum proportion of his intentions. Complementary images are at the very root of every social relationship.

SOCIETY AND INDIVIDUALS

Social scientists, from their earliest days, have been pestered with a common-sense idea, rife in the Western tradition for millenia: the idea that the "individual" is the unit of society. To question the scientific usefulness of the idea is even today often confused with the moral problem of questioning the "value of the human individual." As a moral position, the Western one seems both inviolate and culturally useful: every individual is valuable for himself and is worth developing to his maximum capacities.

When the moral position about the nature of the individual was "scientized," so to speak, by a seventeenth-century philosopher named Thomas Hobbes, the result was more equivocal. The first edition of his *Leviathan* contains a frontispiece of absolutely Düreresque mood that has what seems to be hundreds of small individuals crawling all up and down the page, through the letters and into the publisher's credits. There is, moreover, a neat frame around the drawing. Here are all these people making up the Leviathan, which was Hobbes's metaphor for society, and they are hemmed in by the boundaries of the printer's matrix.

Here we have, presented in grotesque and impressive form, a problem we are still cursed with: the notion that society is a collection of individuals. At one level, that idea need not and probably cannot be negated. But at a level that allows of scientific analysis, it is impossible to do anything with such an idea. It leads quite naturally to the organic metaphor of society: the individual people in one industry are the liver, those in another the kidneys, and those of the church (or the king) are the endocrine gland. Each person does his bit in creating the totality that is a functioning society.

The organic metaphor is valuable until it is carried too far. As long as the individual remains the "unit of society," the metaphor is unavoidable; social science either bogs down or the metaphor must change. It can change in two ways. The whole question of the unit of society could be begged completely and "society" understood on the basis of dictionary definition or seen as some sort of *Gestalt*. The other way—and the one that has been chosen—is that the unit of society can be considered to be some unit other than the human individual.

ROLES

The first great idea for superseding the individual as the conceptual unit of society was the idea of "role." This new analogy, taken frankly from the theater, was put forward by social science in the early twentieth century. One can go back to Shakespeare's "All the world's a stage, and all the men and women merely players," or beyond to find a metaphor of "role" of "action." John Gielgud plays the "role" of Hamlet; John Kennedy plays the "role" of President; and John Doe plays the "role" of father. The advantage of this analogy is that the expectations for behavior are lumped together into "roles" on the one hand and separated from any particular individual on the other.

On the basis of this analogy, sociologists and anthropologists have set up their notion that there is a "role" of mother, say, and a role of son. This procedure has the advantage that it does not confuse the role of mother with "the real me" of the woman who plays that role. Carrying the analogy a step further, she becomes the "actor." There are certain things that mothers must do. When a woman does them, she is acting the role of mother.

The child, as he learns the expectations and techniques, learns to play the role of son or daughter. These roles allow the scientist to get rid of the individual in analyses of social structure and of culture patterns, but to keep him, as "actor," for other purposes.

Using the theatrical metaphor, it becomes possible to say that the mother-son relationship is composed of an image of complementary expectations about the nature of the role mother, the nature of the role son, and the way the two roles should fit together. It is also quite obvious that any person, during his life, is going to play many roles, vis-à-vis many people.

It must also be pointed out that every woman who is a mother plays the role of mother in a somewhat idiosyncratic way. Every actor has something that can only be called "style." This word has been in anthropology at least since 1919, and in theatrical criticism much longer. Jessica Tandy plays Blanche Dubois in a different style than does Vivian Leigh. But it is Blanche Dubois nonetheless—the words are the same; the point of the play may be made and indeed remade by each actress, but ultimately it is only a new dimension to the same role. Each is limited by the role; each is given freedom to develop style—and indeed her own personality—in the role.

All fathers are alike—in spite of their manifold differences. Or, better, all fathers have something in common. But all American fathers have a little more in common with one another than they have with African fathers. All priests are alike, but Jesuits and witch doctors have little in common beyond the bare fact that both deal by metamortal means with mortal well-being. Role allows us to compare all sorts of similarities. And it is to be remembered: a "role" is a set of expectations, not just some individual climbing up the second letter of Leviathan.

A role is something that the actor must perform with minimal efficiency. Otherwise he must relinquish the role or improve his style. It is possible, in some situations, to walk out on some roles. It is indeed possible to cease being a "father" in one sense. The fact that a man begot a child remains true but may be considered the least important part of paternity. If a man deserts his child, he has rejected the role of father. The degree to which various societies allow persons to reject different roles may prove to be one of the most diagnostic characteristics of those societies. However, so long as a man does not reject a role, and is not pushed out of it by others, he must *do* something.

Many people play roles badly—there is bad human behavior as well as bad theater. Indeed, modern Westerners have had to invent new roles—social workers—because some people perform their roles in the family so badly. Everyone, to live social life (which means to live at all), must play roles.

The criteria for what is good and what is bad in the way roles are played can be stated quite simply. The consensus of the members of any social group concerned provides the critical standard by which the capacity in role playing must be judged. If all the members of a social group agree that one person plays his role well, then he is "good." If the members of the society agree that motherhood involves doing *A*, *B*, *C*, and *D*, and this particular woman does them with a fair degree of alacrity and efficiency, she is a good mother. If you were to transport her to Japan, or to the Eskimos, or to Polynesia, and she did the same thing, people there might very well object that she was an impossible mother. But, if people approve of the way in which a role is played out, and of the results in social terms, the actor is successful.

INDIVIDUAL PERSONALITY AND SOCIAL PERSONALITY

It is now possible, and probably necessary, to distinguish between the individual personality and the social personality. The individual personality is "the real me" and is examined by one set of tools—depth psychology, intelligence and personality tests, and the like. Here is a device for studying "style" in social relationships, if you will, and of the determinants of style within the individual. The social personality, on the other hand, is the capacity and the quality in playing roles themselves.

Social personalities, and ultimately all of social life, are colored by actors with their individual personalities. The Presidency is perhaps the most dramatic example. The Presidency exceeds and supercedes any of its occupants. Indeed, as the remarks of ex-Presidents too often show, the Presidency sometimes forces greatness upon a man. Yet the Presidency is never the same when any given individual, with his style, has finished with it as it was before he assumed the role. There is a residue in the role from each particular incumbent. When roles are repeated innumerable times throughout society, such as the roles of mother or of son, the change is slow and results from forces that are less personal. A good mother changes the role of mother less than a good President changes the role of President. The reason is that opinion about what makes a good mother is held in many more heads and is of a more precise nature than is the knowledge or opinion of what makes a good President.

Roles, activated by the actors who play them, are the "poles" of social relationships. A parent is unthinkable without a child; an employer cannot exist without an employee. Roles come in pairs, and the nexus between them is the congruity of the image and the complementarity of expectations.

SYNDROMES

There is another sort of nexus of roles, however. Some roles go together because the members of the society expect them always to be played by the same person. Thus "mother" goes with "wife" in the normal course of events in our society and in most others. To separate the two roles is, in one sense, to be pedantic—but there are two words for the roles, probably in all languages. The husband, in the same way, is also father. Indeed, as we shall see, the nuclear family can be looked upon as a concatenation of eight relationships and eight roles.

When a single individual plays two or more roles, a "syndrome" of roles can be said to exist. The term "syndrome" is a medical term for a collection of symptoms that are found empirically to accompany one another. There are two sorts of syndromes. One sort is a dimension of social personality in that two roles are specifically linked into a primary social group. Husband and father is a case in point; employee and junior executive is another. Such syndromes can be called primary. There are also secondary syndromes that link two primary social groups. Husband/executive is such a secondary syndrome. The difference between a primary and a secondary syndrome is that the roles of a primary syndrome form relationships with other roles that are themselves linked by relationships to one another. In a secondary syndrome, the roles that form the relationships to other roles in the syndrome are not themselves formed into other relationships with one another. Thus, huband/father is a primary syndrome because the wife and son form themselves into a mother-son relationship. Husband/executive is a secondary syndrome because wife and company officer need have no social relationship.

A primary social group is a concatenation of roles, relationships, and primary syndromes. Primary social groups are then linked to one another by secondary syndromes.

The family, as we know it, is perhaps the most widespread example of a primary social structure. Here is a recognized, repeated structuring of a set of social relationships that are themselves recognized and are broken into roles with names and a content of expectations. The roles are grouped not only into relationships, but also into syndromes.

Another important primary social group in our own society is the production group—a firm that produces tires can provide an example. The firm, like the family, is a collection of roles, syndromes, relationships, and expectations. All of the people in the firm have a fairly clear idea (although it may be very vague about those furthest removed from them within the group) of what the others do. There is a total mutual dependence among the roles.

Such primary structures are linked by secondary syndromes. One of the aspects of the syndrome husband/father, in most American families, is that of the "breadwinner." As "breadwinner," the same man goes into the tire factory, to become, say, a salesman. There he is linked by relationships, based on contract, to other members of the firm. The family life of the man who plays the two sets of roles in the two syndromes may affect the "style" with which he plays the role of tire salesman. It does not, however, affect the substance of the role or the relationships in which the role stands to other roles in the structure of the factory. In fact, the "style" in which a man is a father has little to do with the "style" in which he is a tire salesman —for his customers to see him playing with his son might be embarrassing, and almost surely he would just as soon his wife did not know the shenanigans involved in selling tires. There is a feedback from one to the other, of course. Frustration in one can lead to inadequacy in the other. The "style" *is* the individual personality. All a man's roles are thus related by his style, but some are also related structurally into primary groups whereas others are merely related in a manner reminiscent of a network holding various primary social groups together.

The distinction between primary and secondary syndromes can be seen in another way as creating the difference between primary groups and networks. Primary groups are tightly knit, and each role is compounded into syndromes that tie each individual to many other members of the group.

Secondary syndromes knit the primary groups together into a social network, and ultimately all social groups, all actors, have a sort of association at second, third, fourth and *n*th hand.

CULTURE AS THE IDIOM OF SOCIAL STRUCTURE

Social structures are therefore made up of roles, relationships, and syndromes in two sorts of nexus: primary social groups, within which the roles form primary syndromes, and social networks in which the nexus is by roles held together in secondary syndromes.

Every role is a part of a relationship. Every role is also linked to other roles in syndromes. Roles consist in the expectations held in the minds of the people who play the roles as well as most of the rest of the people of the society: the content of a role may often be given fairly accurately by a person not directly associated with anyone playing it.

In just such facts is to be found the fertile paradox of sociology: a relationship cannot have a view of itself; a role is an image in the minds of actors or potential actors. Thus, social relationships are possible only when there is good agreement on what the content of a role should be and the way that one role should fit into another, what the individual gets out of the role and the relationship, and what sort of emphasis he should put on it.

One further point remains to be underlined. For roles to be played, relationships to exist, syndromes to persist, there must be not just the idea of what they should be, but also a means to play them out. The means—the quality of the roles, relationships, and syndromes—is culture.

Similar family structures may allow vastly different cultural qualities. Such, indeed, is the case among the families of the Americans and of the

Pygmies of the Congo forests. On the other hand, the culture may be much the same, but the structure different as is the case if one compares the Bushong of the Congo, who are monogamous, with their polygynous neighbors.

Just as culture is the overt quality, the very essence, of personality, so it is also the overt quality of social relationships.

Obviously, in looking at human beings with personalities, acting out the roles of social relationships in a medium of culture, it is necessary for the social scientist to take up a viewpoint. He must adjust his vision in order to see at all. A social anthropologist focuses primarily on the social relationships, he considers personality in terms of "style," and notes that some styles are preferred to others. He knows that his view of personality does not exhaust the concept—it merely makes it consistent with his mode of explanation. To him, culture is the all-important quality in which social relationships are made empirically manifest. But another social scientist, from the same empirical, factual situation, can abstract the culture: that is, he can focus on the words, ideas, equipment, and overtly approved or disapproved attitudes. Such a scientist is a cultural anthropologist. For him the social organization is examined as if it were another cultural tool for achieving the culture's ends, and personalty is the living plasm in which the culture is made manifest: the "locus" of culture, as it has been called. Still another social scientist—the psychological anthropologist—can focus on the personality and the values and modes of perception held by individuals within the culture. For such a scientist, social relationships become knots of value orientations, and the culture is the means of expressing overtly the innermost forces that have shaped the psyche.

All these men take up a view and may even fight for their views, but the more they differ the more they counterilluminate one another's insights. Anthropology ultimately is a single subject precisely because man, living socially by means of culture, provides a unitary set of phenomena.

3

Art, language, and science

IN DESCRIBING the interrelationships of culture, personality, and social structure, it was noted that there must be common understandings and expectations among the people who are themselves engaged in playing out social relationships, and among the other people who live with them. Social "reality" is what somebody—usually several somebodies—may make of it. It lies in the image that the actors have of it, and teach one another about it. Things can be no more than they seem to someone.

It is obvious that people in different cultures have different images of situations, of society, and of the world: indeed, that very quality creates the "differentness" of cultures. One cultural image is as valid for purposes of social behavior as is another. What is usually called "cultural relativism" is the realization that it is impossible fully to evaluate one image of "reality" unimpaired by the reflection of another image.

It remains a philosophical question, probably unanswerable by science, and certainly irrelevant to it, whether or not there is any reality beyond human perception. But it is certainly true that no situation can be perceived without a perceiving individual; it cannot be communicated without two perceiving individuals. Reality must thus be perceived before it can enter into the social world. Social scientists can afford to beg the question of the nature of reality because it is perception alone with which they deal.

There are two aspects of most perception. There are some aspects of which people are aware, and others of which they are not aware: the overt and covert aspects of culture. Every individual behaves in terms of the overt and covert aspects of his image of himself, of his society, and of the situation at hand. It is the task of anthropologists to determine what the images are and to compare them one with another.

The common image that a people has of any situation is necessarily sketched in by, but not necessarily limited by, the horizons of language. Language, although it is an element in overt images, is overwhelmingly associated with the covert aspects. Concepts held in common by a number of people are, however, more easily examined in the form of art than in the form of mere language. From one point of view, art *is* a folk mode of analyzing cultural images for better communication and more subtle appreciation. Language and art, in short, are methods of communication and cultural statement—of capturing the image and transmitting it.

PERCEPTION AND COMMUNICATION

Unless I can communicate to you, either by speech, writing, gesture, or signs, what it is that I know, there is no way for you to know that I know it. If what one organism perceives is willed by another (that is, if we were meant by another person to perceive a fact in a particular way), we can call the result "communication."

Becoming *Homo "sapiens"*—learning to communicate one's perception—is part of the growing-up process. It is so much a part of everyone's experience that it is difficult to separate the process of knowing, the way human beings become sapient, from the sheer process of physical maturation. By the time that a baby is old enough to know anything, he already knows something.

Fortunately for social science, however, there are some exceptions. One of the most notable of the exceptions is that strange and wonderful woman, Helen Keller. Because she was deaf and blind, her experiences in learning to perceive and to communicate were enough out of the ordinary that her teacher could write them down in detail. This teacher was an uneducated but exceptional young woman named Anne Sullivan, whose letters provide one of the most illuminating records of human achievement and learning that we have. The Sullivan record puts the experiences in plain terms:

> We went to the pump, where I had Helen hold her cup under the opening while I pumped. As the cold water poured forth and filled the cup, I spelled out "water" by tapping on her free hand. The word, which followed so immediately upon the sensation of the cold water running over her hand, seemed to puzzle her. Then she let the cup fall and stood as if she were rooted there. A completely new expression lighted her features. She spelled out the word "water" again and again. She knelt down and touched the earth and wanted to know its name, and she did the same for the pump and the nearby trellis. Then she turned around and inquired about my name. I spelled out "teacher" on her hand. At this moment, Helen's little sister's nurse brought her to the pump. Helen spelled "baby" and got the meaning of her nurse. All the way back she was terribly excited and inquired after the name of everything she touched, so that in only a little over an hour, she had learned thirty words [1904, p. 316].

This passage, which is often quoted and even made the basis for a signally successful drama, has been analyzed by Ernst Cassirer (1944), the

German-turned-American philosopher. His investigation is almost as exciting as the original passage. The teacher did not recognize, as Cassirer the philosopher did, that Helen Keller, at that moment, at the age of about five, had made a discovery most of us make long before anyone can be aware of it: the basic mode of communicating—the symbolic value of words. The taps that spelled out "w-a-t-e-r" on her hand *were* water. She learned thirty words within an hour, her first day of learning in this way. Her handicap had made her slow; so slow that the teacher could record the rush of learning when it finally came.

But all of us recognize the type of learning, the way of knowing. Helen Keller became "sapient" in the moment that she made a simple connection with "water" and a cold, moist sensation. She became fully human when she herself performed an act meant to communicate that sensation of the teacher. She had begun the process of symbolizing the world of things and of sensation that creates the image behind communication, social life, and all culture. Symbolizing, of the sort that we have watched Helen Keller learn, is the basic capacity of mankind that makes all culture and progress possible.

LANGUAGE

Language, by means of speech and highly abstract symbols, allows human beings to communicate abstract details to one another. Words and grammar enable us to call up in someone else the sort of sensations that are (so far as we can tell) analogous to our own, so that some sort of common goal or activity is possible.

All human beings speak, unless they are abnormal. Their speech represents or symbolizes the set of common understandings that is culture. Speech is a reflection of culture, because it is the means by which we symbolize all culture for purposes of communication. There are also other, more specialized, ways of symbolizing culture for communication. Gestures may be systematized and widely known—and may, in fact, communicate much even if they are not systematized. Music is a more general and less precise type of symbolization for communication than is art. Nevertheless, music can communicate emotion of a sort, a sense of order that challenges even mathematics, and if it is really good music, much more. However, language is both the most common and the most extensive symbol system.

But language is a two-edged sword: at the same time that it allows people to cut through the morass of sensation and communicate not merely gross impression but the intricacies of idea and interpretation, it also creates disjointed pieces and characteristic unions of them that imprison the mind within a single mode of perception. Language (or art) is the mold into which perception must be fitted if it is to be communicated. Any single language imprints its own "genius" on the message. We have already seen that the task of the anthropologist is to explore and illuminate the linguistic and cultural vise that holds firmly the minds of the people of his own society and of others.

Probably the most popular, because it is the most vivid, example for describing the cultural categories that the necessity to communicate creates in human perception is to compare the ways in which different peoples cut up colors into communicable units. The spectrum is a continuum of light waves, with frequencies that (when measured in length) increase at a continuous rate. That part of the continuum of waves that can be perceived by the human eye is called the spectrum. The longer waves we see as violet, the shorter as red; all the other colors of the spectrum fall between them. The perception of light, broken into colors, seems to be the same for all human beings except the color blind, and even they have the same range. But the ways different cultures organize these sensations for communication show some strange differences.

The Japanese, for example, have one word, *aoi,* which covers both blue and green ranges of the spectrum: actually, it means a sort of "nature color." The fact that the Japanese do not make a linguistic distinction does not mean that they cannot tell blue from green, because they obviously can, and can describe the differences in metaphors if they so desire. It means, rather, that the Japanese language, and hence Japanese culture as a whole, sees no need to make this distinction for purposes of ordinary living.

The noted Danish linguist, Louis Hjelmslev (1953), has compared the color words of English and Welsh; in Figure 2 I have added the color words from the Tiv language. The Welsh word *glas* covers everything English

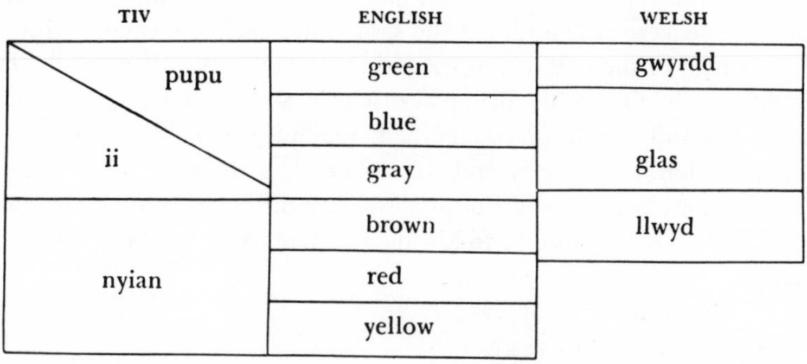

<table>
<tr><th>TIV</th><th>ENGLISH</th><th>WELSH</th></tr>
<tr><td rowspan="3">pupu
ii</td><td>green</td><td>gwyrdd</td></tr>
<tr><td>blue</td><td rowspan="2">glas</td></tr>
<tr><td>gray</td></tr>
<tr><td rowspan="3">nyian</td><td>brown</td><td>llwyd</td></tr>
<tr><td>red</td><td rowspan="2"></td></tr>
<tr><td>yellow</td></tr>
</table>

FIGURE 2 Color Words

would call blue, some the colors English would call green, and some it would call gray. *Llwyd* takes up the rest of the gray and runs over into brown. In Tiv, on the other hand, all green, some blues, and some grays are *ii*. But very light blues and light grays are *pupu. Nyian,* which covers brown, also covers all warm colors through red to yellow. The distinction between *ii* and *pupu* actually is not in terms of color, but in terms of what we would call shade—darkness and lightness. Very light blue, gray, or white are all *pupu. Ii* means dark and covers all dark colors and black—unless there is a warm color present: brown, red, and yellow are all *nyian.* Tiv can distinguish colors and do color-blind tests, but their culture does not require—or allow—that they make some of the color distinctions that Westerners make. Westerners are among the most color-conscious of peoples.

Although colors provide the most obvious example, they are not unique in being culturally and not "naturally" determined segments of reality. Indeed, all human perception is of this sort.

As a second example, take the English, German, Danish, and Tiv words for wood and trees (Figure 3). German and English both have three words.

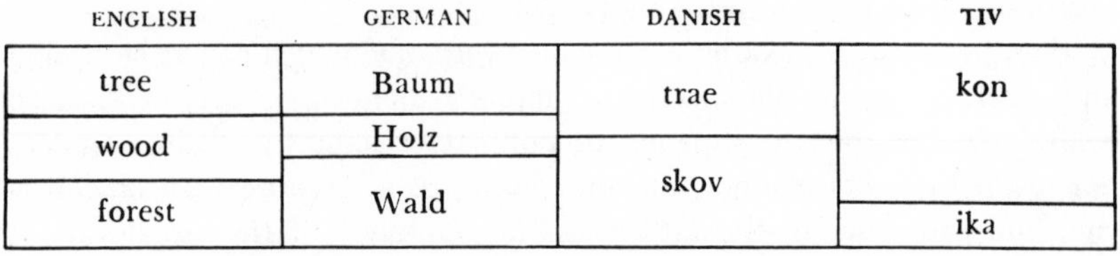

ENGLISH	GERMAN	DANISH	TIV
tree	Baum	trae	kon
wood	Holz	skov	
forest	Wald		ika

FIGURE 3 Tree Words

Tree and *Baum* cut the continuum in about the same place. But the English word "wood" has a wider field of meaning than the German word *Holz;* that is, a wood is, in English (Americans use the plural), a forest that is not very dense. This kind of "wood" and "forest" itself are both *Wald* in German. Speakers of Danish cut the same total field of meaning with two words instead of three. Tiv also use only two words, but they cut the field very differently. Obviously, distinction within a perceived field is a matter that is culturally conditioned, learned, and passed on. For purposes of communication, one way is probably as good as the next in a common-sense situation; but the points of precision are different from one language to the next. The "culture", following the language, shows a significant variation.

DIFFERENCES IN STRUCTURE

When one comes to the structure of ideas as reflected in sentences, the matter becomes even more complex:

jeg ved det ikke Danish
I do not know English

Je ne sais pas	French
en tieda	Finnish
naluvara	Eskimo

The meanings of these short sentences are all more or less the same—at least, they are translations of one another. But the ways in which the idea is cut up for communication varies widely (Hjelmslev, 1953). In Danish the first word, *jeg,* means "I," then *ved* (know, present indicative), then an object *det* (it), and finally a negative, *ikke.* Very straightforward and sensible, but different from English where the first word is "I," then a verbal concept of the sort that would be called a modal auxiliary in German—and which is not represented in the Danish sentence at all—then the negation, and only when the word "know" which tells us what it is all about—and there is no case in the verb, and no object in the sentence. In French, there is first "I," then a kind of negation that is, however, completely different from that of English or Danish because it does not function as a negative in all combinations, then "know" (first person, present indicative), and finally a very peculiar particle (*pas*) that some people claim is a negative but that can also mean "step" and that acts grammatically as an adverb; as in Engish, there is no object. In Finnish, there is first a verb signifying "not I" (*et* means thou not; *ei,* he not; *emme,* we not; and so on), followed by the concept "know" in a form that has imperative meanings in other combinations; there is no object. Finally, in Eskimo the whole thing is a verb—"not-knowing-am-I-it"—derived from *malo,* ignorance, with the suffix of the first person subject and the third person object.

The point is that people use different types of linguistic units for breaking up experience into communicable bits, as well as vastly different principles for putting the bits back together again. Obviously, most people do not think about such matters when they are talking. The regularities are epiphenomenal to the activities of communication. Nevertheless, they are always there, for if they were not, communication would not be possible.

It is the process of breaking up perception into linguistic chunks for communication that creates the image. The image, seen in another light, is itself the vise in which every mind is ruthlessly held. All sensations, all input of ideas or impression, must either be fitted into the categories of communcation that are already in the mind, or they must remain uncommunicated (and hence not fully realized). The only alternative is that they break the mold of linguistic and ideational categories and establish a new outlook.

All too seldom are people aware that their images are limited by language and culture. They are easily aware of constant broadening created by learning but not so easily aware of the equally constant narrowing created concomitantly. The enlargement of knowledge is education; the concomitant narrowing and hardening of the mode of perception and communication is a form of what we have already called habituation.

Education itself can be divided into two elements. There is on the one hand the process of training in which culture, ideas, and technique are poured into the student, utilizing the pigeonholes of communication to which he has already become habituated. He looked at his new knowledge and techniques through the old glasses, in terms of the old pigeonholes. But on the other hand there is another process that lies at the heart of a liberal education: creating awareness in a person of the fact that his image is limited by the pigeonholes of his culture and that he must seek actively for a means of increasing its scope and quality.

GRAMMAR

The regularities that any language demands if it is to be a suitable vehicle for communication were first (so far as we know) discovered several thousand years ago, in India, by a scholar of genius named Pāṇini. He made the first grammar—of Sanskrit. His idea of lifting out the regularities of usage of a language from the various acts of speech and writing was a new and daring process. Pāṇini's achievement was that he created a system of analytical thought which allowed him to understand the phenomena of speech in a new way. The regularities were inherent in Sanskrit—the recurrences he picked out can be likened to recurrent chemical reactions. But they had never been picked out before. Grammar has changed Sanskrit very little more than the science of chemistry has changed oxidation. But grammar and chemistry provided a new and better way of understanding the phenomena each comprehends.

Let us hasten to add that the analogy between grammar and chemistry is of limited use. People speak, and the matrices of their thought allow for change at a very much more rapid rate than phenomena comprehended by the so-called rules of chemistry. However, the idea of selecting regularities in occurrences or events, and explaining them with a "theory," is a sound one.

The Greeks obviously seem to have known Pāṇini's grammar, but they misunderstood it. Instead of looking at his *method* of reducing regularities to a statement of rules, they took the rules he had worked out for Sanskrit and tried to make them work in Greek. Greek is the first language, thus, to have a bad grammar, given to it by people who took their model from another language. The mistake has been often repeated: for centuries English was forced into the categories of Latin grammar (which, by and large, do not fit) because grammarians had accepted the *result* of the works of Latin grammarians—the forms—rather than the *principles* of grammar making—the activity.

There are, then, three different levels of analysis to be considered. First are the regularities in the vocal events that occur when a language is spoken (or in manual events when it is written). There are, in the second place, the "rules" of Sanskrit grammar, which can be elicited from the original regularities and stated more or less as "scientific" laws. Third and most elusive, there is the idea of the activity involved in seeking and discovering rules in regularities, and of organizing them into consistent bodies of thought. The first is event, the second is science, and the third is scientific method—the epistemology of science. Science must always be based on regularities occurring in the data that are to be explained. Scientific epistemology—"the philosophy of science"—must always be based on the regularities in the activity of scientists. The first set of regularities is one in communication, the second one in science, the third one in philosophy.

The analogy from language to the rest of culture should be obvious: there are regularities of behavior that can be observed. With observation, the "rules" (in the sense of the statistical mean, not the morally required minimum) of behavior can be established by scientists by and for people who live by means of that culture; moreover, the people who live the culture have already established their own rules. This second, or scientific process leads to "ethnographic theory," if the purpose be to explain and translate a single culture, or to "ethnological theory" if the purpose be to compare many cultures. Finally, there is the science of anthropology, which is a set of rules for examining behavior and creating ethnological theory. Anthropology is thus, at its most abstract level, interested in determining how it is that people know what they know, whether it be on the psychic, the scientific, or the epistemological levels.

LINGUISTICS

It has been said (Whorf, 1956, p. 232) that the beginning of scientific linguistics can be dated from the rediscovery of Pānini 's grammar in the eighteenth century. For millenia after the original creation of grammar, no new regularities in languages and speech were either discovered or sought. It is practically within our own time that the next great surge of progress in the study of language has come. The result is that linguistics is the most scientifically advanced branch of cultural anthropology: indeed, linguistics provides the model on which cultural analysis is proceeding. Cultural anthropology, which treats of culture in relation to people and society much as linguistics treats of the phenomena of language in relation to the intricacies of meaning, has found—at least for the moment—a mode of progress.

The "secret" of the success of linguistics is an open one: there are many different sorts of regularities that can be discovered in the same body of phenomena. Linguistics has discovered that the number of sounds used by any language is limited; phonetics and phonemics have resulted. The characteristic ways that sounds are combined to communicate chunks of meaning have given rise to the concept of the morphemic system; tones, if they are important, can be understood in terms of a tonic system. There are many other possible systems.

Any sound that a language uses is called a *phoneme.* Phonemes can be easily discovered: if changing the sound changes the meaning, there are two phonemes; if it does not, there is only one. Thus, in English *r* and *l* are separate phonemes because there is a difference in meaning between rim and lim(b). In many West African languages, these two sounds are not separate phonemes. Conversely, in many African languages an exploded "b" of the sort found in English and the imploded "ɓ" that an English speaker would not even notice are separate phonemes. There would be, that is, a change of meaning between boy and ɓoy. Phonemics is not composed solely of the observation of individual sounds, but also of the characteristic ways in which languages put these sounds together. For example, no word in English begins with "s-r," although the combination is a common one in Italian.

Linguistics has reduced speech, the most important means by which we communicate, to order and made it amenable to scientific description and discussion. We know a great deal about how phonemic systems change, and can predict with almost uncanny accuracy what will happen to a "k" sound if it begins to come into conflict with a broad "a." Predictions can be made in the rest of the system.

However, note that the basic *communication* has not been touched. Linguistics, at this level, is dealing with the regularities in the *instrument* of communcation, not with the ideas it contains. It has been dealing with a part of what communications engineers would call the matrix or the code, not with what they would call the message.

A matrix is as good as its ability to carry a message. What linguists study are the differences among and the systems within which people speak with one another and communicate their ideas. By their own choice, linguists have limited themselves to language. But cultural anthropologists do something of the same thing. They study the matrices within which people live with one another and communicate their lives. Whatever reality may be, the data that the anthropologist must work with is communication through act, word, or some other form. Presumably, by studying the differences in the matrix from one culture to another, we can ultimately learn something about human perception and various images to which it gives rise.

Linguistics is an extremely important and practical branch of anthropology. Besides the fact that it deals scientifically with one of the universal aspects of culture, it is of immense value on two other grounds. First, as the most scientifically advanced of the cultural sciences, it provides a necessary model. People can dissociate themselves from their languages with a fair degree of ease; self-consciousness and *amour-propre* soon disappear from a consideration of it. Therefore, the scientization of linguistics has proceeded rapidly, and the analogy to the activities of linguists can provide many scientific guideposts for men who are investigating other aspects of culture. Second, and even more practical, a firm knowledge of linguistics dramatically reduces the time required to learn new languages, and is hence an indispensable tool for the fieldworker.

SEMANTICS AND THE WHORFIAN HYPOTHESIS

Benjamin Lee Whorf was a linguist so startlingly original that he is still persistently misunderstood by many members of his profession. He is misunderstood for precisely the same reasons that James Joyce or Picasso, say, were not accepted for many years by some critics or much of public. In order to communicate new and deeply original perceptions, they all had to go beyond traditional modes of communication. Sometimes communication of new insights is clumsy. That is the worst charge that can be leveled against Whorf: he tried to express, in terms of the old categories of semantics, some new ideas that had to burst them.

What has come to be known as the "Whorfian hypothesis"—Whorf, had he lived, might well have joined the ranks of Marx and Freud by stating, "I am no Whorfian"—is merely this: people break up not just their language, but by means of their language their whole culture into bits for purposes of communication. As they learn the "code" or matrix in the process of maturation, there is an automatic knowledge and response in perception. The code units are words, and most of the knowledge and perception—certainly all that is communicated—is seen in terms of these words. The words become categories of reality. The mode of putting them together becomes the "natural organization" of reality, and the point of education and thought is to discover that the "naturalness" is itself open to questioning and to change.

Besides the words, there are larger categories that form the grammatical elements: the "parts of speech." They are the manner in which we put these word categories together when we communicate. Whorf pointed out (what we had, on a more primitive level, already known) that all Indo-European languages break things into two big, inclusive grammatical categories. There are things and there are qualities. The qualities we call verbs, adjectives, and adverbs. The things we call nouns and pronouns. The other grammatical bits such as postpositions, prepositions, and conjunctions are hooks for tying the main units together in the right juxtapositions. Every sentence we utter has a subject and a predicate. But we can, as a result of Whorf, see that fact in a new light. Every idea that we have and express in English *must* be broken down into things and qualities. The universe, indeed, must be classified into two boxes: things and qualities.

It is not possible to divide words themselves into two groups, some for things and other for qualities. The word "man," for example, represents a thing. But if you say "he is a man," the word "man" is a quality. If you say, "the ship is manned," the word "man" becomes a quality of the ship. You can take the word "run," which is a quality of some animal, and turn it into a noun or thing quite easily.

This particular system is not quite universal. The Salish languages apparently do not so break the world into two great segments for communication. These languages seem to be made entirely of concepts that represent entities interrelated or juxtaposed. "I go down the path" comes out "I foot path." The qualities may be inherent in the nouns, but the world is not broken up in the same way as for the Indo-European languages. The point is that the matrix affects thought and very often changes the intricacies of thought, but one can say anything in any language. It may not come out the same, but the meaning can be got across. However, the people who speak the language habitually may not understand what a foreign speaker says in the language, even though he says it correctly, if they do not have the ideas themselves in at least some attenuated form.

Thus, a language is not merely part of the culture, but it is also a reflection of the total culture. It is a reflection, more importantly perhaps, of the *organization* of that total culture. To be perceived it must be broken up into bits. To be used, the bits must be organized, and it is the organization that is important.

THE TRAP OF LANGUAGE

One of the best ways to see that any language provides a trap at the same time it provides a means of expression is to examine some of the problems that have come to light in the course of translations. The Bible is the most widely translated book with which we are intimately acquainted. It has been set into the languages of "civilized" and "primitive" peoples, and into all the linguistic families of the world. Eugene Nida has written a book called *God's Word in Man's Language* (1952), which rehearses in some detail problems that have arisen in translating the Bible into some of these languages.

One of the most common problems is that language may mirror social ranking and social organization, and the social system of the Bible may not correspond in any detail. One vivid example can be taken from the Japanese. In that language, a writer cannot use direct quotation without at the same time indicating the relative social rank of the two persons involved. Japanese verb endings—and the verbs must have endings—always indicate whether the speaker is socially superior, inferior, or equal to the addressee. There are, moreover, several grades of superior and inferior. When Christ turned to the man he had cured and said, "Pick up thy bed and walk," what verb endings would he have used had he been speaking Japanese? Were Christ and the patient equals? Was one the social superior or inferior of the other? These are theological problems created by the processes of translation.

In the original Greek—and indeed in English—there is nothing in the grammar to indicate relative social position; at most there would be something in the vocabulary or the tone of voice. In Japanese, the matter of rank is always present in the grammar. The social structure must thus be known or assumed even to *speak* Japanese. The same is true of some American Indian languages and some of the African languages. What we do with manner and choice of words, they do with grammar. Introduction of social organization into the forms of a language creates a difficult translation problem, and elucidates the nature of the language trap.

Our languages may also stamp our notions of credibility and proof. "Truth" is for Westerners a complex but single idea. Most West African languages have two words for "truth." There is one kind meaning "social correctness" and another meaning "what actually happened." If I know perfectly well that my brother's wife committed adultery and my brother asks me about it, I can tell the socially correct "truth" and save everyone a lot of trouble, or I can tell the precise "truth" and create trouble. The truth of right action, in the Tiv language, is called *mimi*. The truth of verifiable occurrence is called *vough*. The antonym of both these words is *yie*, which must be translated "lie." *Mimi* may coincide with *vough*—but it may not. Among close personal acquaintances and kinsmen, it is moral to use *mimi;* among others, it is wise to use *vough*. In court cases, when an oath is taken by a witness before he gives evidence, he swears to speak *vough*. But the defendant and the plaintiff are, in most parts of Africa, refused the right to swear, because each is expected to tell his version of *mimi*.

One of Whorf's favorite examples of the tyranny of language is the concept of time. We assume time, velocity, matter. Time is something in our concepts, which the physicists call *t*. It has a beginning—at least until Einstein, we thought it would have an end. It runs forward in one direction, at a uniform rate. It "exists." The idea of its existence has become more pronounced in the last 200 years. Since time has entered the market, it has become money. Time is divided into hours; hours cost money. And time is running out.

The Hopi people of our own Southwest, whose language was analyzed by Whorf, do not have this kind of an idea of time. To put it into a metaphor, time is to them a sort of cylinder that turns over slowly. There is night on one side and day on the other; first night comes round and then, as the cylinder turns, day. Both recur. The recurrences can be counted. However, it is not possible to compute duration. Time, *t*, in our own idea, has duration—"five days." The Hopi language puts it, "day came five times." There is a difference, even though the message is much the same. "I left the fifth time day came around" means the same thing as "I stayed five days."

The same conceptualization occurs among some African peoples with reference to generation—there are constantly two generations. You name your children for your parents, and they are in some sense reincarnations of the parents. The same principle may be applied to three or more generations as to two.

Time is a necessary dimension of English grammar—present, past, and future tense. Every speaker who would assert existence must indicate either that something is happening now or that it happened in the past. Hopi does not demand such a built-in statement about time. Neither does Japanese. The distinction between past and present is not built into some languages, yet the distinction can be made with adverbs or some other such way, if it is desired. In English the distinction is one that must be made in the sheer process of description or narrative: speakers of English are stuck with tense, and hence with a limited concept of time, just as speakers of Japanese are stuck with a mode of social organization.

English, furthermore, cannot put a statement into the future without implicit prognostication. But the Hopi language can. Hopi divide the world into what Whorf calls the manifest and the nonmanifest. The manifest "tense" has absolutely nothing to say about the present, last week, or a decade since. It "is." Everything that one wishes, knows, but does not see, such as religious ideas, are categorized together with the future in the nonmanifest. In this case one can immediately see how wrong it would be to say that all religion is in "the future tense" in Hopi: that would be seeing it in our terms. Rather, certain religious phenomena are unmanifested and and therefore are so indicated grammatically.

There is, also, another Hopi "tense" for things that are constant and immutable in the world. Therefore, we have manifest-mutable, manifest-immutable, and nonmanifest. It is as good a way of dividing the world up as is the Indo-European.

A similar set of statements can be made about space. Our own ideas of dimension and space are probably unique in the world. In 1732 a device called the sextant was invented. It changed the culture of the world far more than it is given credit for, in only a little over two centuries. With this instrument and some other surveying equipment and the idea that positions on the earth are fixed relatively to the stars, we have been able to put on paper, or on globes, a grid. We can then pick out a point on the grid that is referable to the stars. Then, with other devices we measure out other points on the grid. And the result is something called a map. Scientifically, modern maps are "correct." But they and the instruments that produce them have led to a very pronounced and definite way of viewing space. People who do not have the same gadgetry do not see space in this mechanistic way—most of them see it in terms of social relations, kinsmen, time, and effort. In the Tiv language the word *cha,* which is usually translated "far", has three referents: it is far if when you go someplace it takes you a long time to get there; it is far if the distance is great; and it is far if you go into an area where you are a stranger.

THE VALUE OF WHORFIAN CONCEPTS

Whorf's ideas are so simple and so vital that it would seem that some of his critics wilfully refuse to understand them. Simplicity often makes for difficulty in understanding, especially if what is simplified includes ideas that people would just as soon continue to be muddled about.

Whorf was searching for a language different enough from English to enable him to pin down his ideas. He found the language in Hopi. There have been two kinds of criticism of Whorf. One of these is the *pars-pro-toto* type of criticism—the critic proves that two or three of Whorf's points in Hopi were wrong, so he throws out the hypothesis. This is the baby-with-the-bath fallacy. The other type of criticism is the sidetrack type of criticism—to criticize Whorf for something he did not do: he did *not* try to establish a "relationship between language and culture" or between language and the rest of culture. He has been extensively criticized (Hockett, 1954) as if he had.

It may sound a little shocking to say that it is a matter of complete indifference whether Whorf's analyses of the nature of Hopi turn out to be right or wrong. But reconsider: he has allowed us to see something in English that we could not have seen had it not been for his ideas and his perceptions in Hopi. It would be "nicer" if Whorf's analyses of Hopi were correct. But in the long run, it is beside the point whether they are right or not. Whorf based his ideas on something that is very right in English—he illustrated it by constrast from Hopi. His vision into Hopi—correct or erroneous, it does not matter—allowed him to see some of the pigeonholes and integrating devices in English.

Whorf was stating something very simple, almost axiomatic: I cannot know the nature of reality, for I have no way of perceiving it save through my senses and the instrumental extensions of them that I create. Therefore, I must work with perceived reality, and the more I know about the nature of the perceiver, the more nearly I will ultimately know the reality. The proper subject for study—indeed the only possible subject for study—is, therefore, perception.

ART

Every perception that forms the basis of a communication is a part of culture. The most common code, or matrix, of the message is language.

Perceptions may, moreover, be communicated in media other than language. The plastic and graphic arts constitute such a medium. Music constitutes another. It is the task (among other tasks) of art historians and of those anthropologists who are specialists in such matters to examine the stylistics of art in a way reminiscent of the way in which Pāṇini investigated grammar. It is the task of the comparative musicologist to discover the regularities in musical communication and to organize into a scientific framework the repeated elements of a musical style, and to isolate its principles.

Man must cut the field of perception into bits or elements for artistic communication just as surely as he must for linguistic communication. The way in which the limited selection of pieces is organized constitutes an art style. One anthropologist, also a competent art historian, has drawn up a list of approximately 400 basic motifs. The problem, then, becomes to find a mode of classifying the ways in which these motifs are put together into systems so that the superficial aspects of a sculpture or a painting can be catalogued. Once the anthropologist has been able to do this, if indeed he is able to do it, he will be in a position (at least, he hopes to be in a position) to make a study of comparative design in various cultures and various centuries.

An important fact must be noted: in order to make such a study of comparative design, it is vital that the design be divorced from the "message" in precisely the same way that grammar or phonemics can be divorced from the message in language. Even in making such a statement, a writer must immediately placate the art appreciators: you spoil it, they say. But such critics misunderstand our purpose. To diagram all the sentences in *War and Peace* might be a foolish—although it might just be an enlightening—process. But it would have no effect whatever on *War and Peace*. Just so, to create a "grammar" of art will not destroy art or "mechanize" it or besmirch it.

Stylistics in art is not about the subject matter or "message" of art any more than rhetorical exercise of dividing feet of poetry into iambs or dactyls and counting lines by quadrameter or pentameter or alexandrines is about the "message" of poetry. A phonetic study of the language of *Hiawatha* neither improves nor cheapens the verses.

Art as a symbol system is, however, much more vague than is language. Therein lies the difficulty. "Style" in art is more diffuse than is grammar—there would seem to be more "parts of painting" than there are parts of speech. Yet, the concept of "style" is of the same order. As the art critic Meyer Schapiro has expressed it, "style is the constant form—and, sometimes, the constant elements, qualities, and expression—in the art of an individual or a group" (1953, p. 287). Style is the code or matrix in which a message is communicated. And style is subject to examination divorced from the message:

> Style is above all, a system of forms with a quality and a meaningful expression through which the personality of the artist and the broad outlook of a group are visible. It is also a vehicle of expression within the group, communicating and fixing certain values of religious, social and moral life through the emotional suggestiveness of forms. It is, besides, a common ground against which innovations and the individuality of particular works may be measured [Schapiro, 1953, p.287].

Just as a language selects certain phonemes and disregards other sounds, so an art style selects certain motifs and disregards others. The alphabet of style, however, is much broader than is that of phonemes. Just as the American language is changing, so American art styles are changing—and much more rapidly, and in many more directions. Yet, when painters invent a new style, they do not throw out everything of the old, even when they like to think that they do. Even across the abrupt breaks in style there are transitions that the art historian can discern. When musicians turn to twelve-tone scales, they think they have set the world on its ear. It is fifty years later that musicologists come to realize that the rules of twelve-tone writing and the principles of polyphony have much in common. Just so, when Braques and Picasso broke with the tradition of nineteenth-century painting, they retained more than even they knew.

Stylistics as a branch of the study of art is practicable, and it is being developed by museologists and art critics such as Schapiro. Just as a sudden inundation of primitive art brought Picasso and Braques to their feet and gave them courage and inspiration to break with some aspects of Western tradition, the sudden importance in the nineteenth century of Oriental and exotic art made it possible for critics and scholars to see new ways of artistic communcation, and then to widen their ideas of style to include them all. With increased variety, stylistics becomes more practicable.

Music is an even less precise matrix for communication, as befits a medium whose primary quality is being able to communicate unstated emotion. And yet, the "grammar" of music has probably been made more precise than has any other symbol system. A composer must know more of the analytical lore of his medium than a painter. A writer, although he must know how to use his language grammatically, need know no linguistics, or even grammar, at all. Music in non-Western traditions has been seriously neglected by all but a handful of anthropologists, in spite of the fact that it has been proved one of the most diagnostic traits of any culture.

Just as any language is a rigid way of perceiving and communicating the world, so an art style or a musical style imprints its categories and organizational genius on decoration and on sound. As modern artists know, it is only with great efforts of will and vision that the vise of style can be broken —and even when it is, the new style quickly becomes as rigid as the old.

ART FORMS

Art is of very great interest to anthropologists of every persuasion because it is one of the primary means through which a people can examine its own images. The purpose of art is to make the image overt and realizable.

Artistic images are more than a message embedded in an idiom, however. They also have recognizable forms. The form is to art something of the same thing as a program is to a computer. The analogy to computers is useful: data must be put into a computer, but it must be so within the limitations of the code or matrix. The program, then, is a manipulated statement of the range of permitted questions and expectations. Without any one of these three requirements—message, matrix, program—a computer is unable to work. So is an artist.

Form, in giving a medium to encoded messages, also creates strict limitations: it is the ultimate paradox in art, as in life, that freedom in one area requires the pinning down of other areas to known dimensions and qualities.

One of the most characteristic attributes of any recognizable artistic form is that it provides a mechanism for reducing ideas or problems from the disparities of life to the reasoned regularities of games. A court trial takes a problem in social life and reduces it to an encompassed "game," with a known and enforceable set of rules. A decision is arrived at, and the people are then dismissed back into the total range of their social lives— the "game" is over. A painting is of the same sort: the painter takes his vision of the world—his image—and he *reduces* it to canvas. In this small-scale arena, with specific rules (even if he made them himself), the problem can be solved. A statement can be made. And then it is returned to the larger arena of life. The artist has become a commentator on his own society.

Perhaps the most obvious example of the reductive quality in art is to be found in drama; drama is (at least, superficially) also relatively easy to appreciate cross culturally. Primarily, drama is a way of reducing events of the world as we know it to a less inclusive framework so that we can examine that "world" and communicate about its nature. Just as language must reduce reality, so drama is a form for taking a chunk of reality, changing the framework within which we see it, and investigating it. Every drama—every Broadway play, every piece of Racine or Shakespeare—is "about" something, whether its author intended it to be or not. Drama is one of the most powerful of propaganda weapons, for it cannot do *other* than make moral statements and intellectual examinations of the human condition. Small wonder that it has often been the concern of princes and priests, as well as of artists.

Drama of one sort or another seems to be almost universal. In West Africa, religious dramatic presentations with masks, costumes, and known *dramatis personae* accompany many religious rites and court cases. In parts of what is now the Republic of Ivory Coast, criminals must go before tribunals made up of masked figures. The persons who wear the masks lose their individuality: the wearers *become* the demons, lending their vitality to abstract principles of thought and idea expressed in the mask. It is symbolically like the classical Western image of justice, blindfolded, with scales in one hand and a sword in the other. The difference is what we do not make our representations of justice carnate, whereas the West African masks are made carnate. The principle of justice is in the expressionless or demonic mask, to which a "judge" merely lends his vitality. The masks are the purest art—the form is political drama.

Drama may be brought into the service of religion just as it is brought into the service of politics. And, more important to us, it may be brought into the service of recreation. But such is an illusion—for always a drama by its nature presents us with social problems decked out in a form that makes it possible for us to consider them in small scale. To take only two well-known commercial dramas of our own time: Thornton Wilder's *Our Town,* which is an enjoyable play, is also and unobtrusively an essay on the various kinds of love. The playwright has, with the aid of a simple story and a few characters and situations, reduced the whole field of love to a dimension in which it is possible to comment on it and make us realize anew some of the problems involved. Arthur Miller's *The Crucible* is about tyranny. It has reduced the whole subject of tyranny, which the playwright obviously considers to be the most important moral and ethical problem of our time, to a dimension in which he can renew and examine his image of it and create in his audience a capacity for re-examining their images of it. Even TV Westerns have a strict moral system.

Similarly, in many tribes of West Africa, young men must undergo a long and painful initiation that usually demands months or even years of segregation and schooling, cut off from the rest of society. It usually involves the operation of circumcision; certainly, it involves ordeals of other sorts. In these situations, the instruction, the ordeal, the operation are all performed by masked men. The reasoning is obvious: such men are no longer themselves; they are forces of nature or principles of society such as rain, growth, justice, adulthood, law and order, and the like. The high point of the ceremonies accompanying these schools, after the education or training is complete so that the boys are capable of taking their places in society, after they have undergone their operations and humiliation, is when the wearers of the mask in a tense and frightful moment *remove* the masks, and place them, or some like them, on the boys themselves.

Here we have the purest drama—the turning of the small, enclosed, limited world of the play into the full world of reality. What has been symbolized, of the world, of society, of God, is turned in on oneself—one learns to play the parts. Drama is, par excellence, the field in which a limited set of symbols, with definite rules for their manipulation, is made to instruct and eventually to stand for something else: something larger.

The art of any society takes many forms: drama and poetry, the novel and the epic—these are art forms that express ideas in a medium of words. Sculpture and painting express ideas in a medium of wood or colors. Music expresses ideas in a medium of sound. They have in common the fact that they allow the cultural images to be made overt and, in some instances, to be changed.

Art is, however, more than *mere* communication and comment. Good art necessarily contains an element of mystery. The element of mystery may be, in fact, the most valued aspect of art; many other aspects or forms of culture may also be in part a culturally appreciated mystery. Ultimately, religion is a mystery, and it is the very quality of mystery for which it may be valued. There is a fundamental mystery in love and in life that cannot be penetrated by biology, no matter how much biology we come to know. The mystery in art is the ineffable quality that distinguishes Mozart from Telemann, Braques from Grandma Moses. Mystery, as a culturally valued phenomenon, can even be reduced to order scientifically without in any wise touching the mystery or its power. Mystery in art, as in theology, may be its most prized characteristic; but the characteristics that concern the anthropologist are also present—art cannot escape being communication.

ART AND SCIENCE

The point of this chapter was to analyze the truism that in acquiring culture a person must learn at least one language. In communicating he must use cultural mediums and forms. In criticizing his culture and remaking it, he must use the forms of art and, as we shall see below, of science. Man cannot even perceive his surroundings in a human fashion without language and without a style. Therefore, he sees the world in terms imposed by the languages and the styles he knows.

Language and art, in short, pervade perception and provide some of the major determinants of the images with which people face one another and all the problems of life.

Every individual, in order to live, must have an image of his world, and that image must be more or less congruent with the images of the other people around him. There are two sorts of images, which correspond to the distinction already made: there is the "folk image," or image people learn and create for purposes of living out their lives. There is the "scientific image," or image social scientists create for purposes of analyzing and comparing social and cultural activity.

Language and art provide the key to the folk or organizational image. That key is especially important because so many aspects of the image are covert. We are not aware that we in fact assume most of the assumptions that are necessarily a part of any folk image. Until a fair degree of sophistication is reached, people do not know that they speak grammatically, but rather they know only that there are right and wrong ways to say something. Most people do not know anything about art, but do know what they like.

In spite of the fact that science is old, the scientific image is a recent phenomenon. Science has become a powerful way of looking at the world of reality, an overwhelming means of examining and fashioning our images of the cosmos, the world, and of society itself. The canons of science, as those of art, change from one age to the next; only within the last few centuries has "scientific method" developed to the point that science can be set off from art. Science is a point of view. Like drama or the sonnet, or like sculpture, it is a "form" that may deal with any or with all of the messages in the world. Its unique characteristic is in the peculiar rationality of the interrelationships of the elements in its code or matrix.

Whereas art is judged by standards of truth and beauty, science is judged by standards of verifiability and elegance. The social sciences do more however, than merely study the behavior of man: they study no less than the folk images of men. In so doing, they create their own images—they deal in images of images as well as in the meaning of meaning.

Insofar as the images of social science have any use or relevance, they have one important difference from the folk images. The folk image is both a product and a cause of social behavior. An analytical image, although it often influences folk images, is a mode of examining behavior. The only behavior it produces or causes is the behavior of the scientist, within the brotherhood of scientists. The end of the folk image is living. The end of social science is a particular type of knowledge.

The biological network

part 2

4

Kinship networks and kinship terminology

MAN IS A MAMMAL. As we have seen, such a statement implies that man is mortal, that he reproduces sexually, and that since his young are born immature they demand nurture and training to enable them to take their places in the network of human life. Mortality assumes social relationships the aim of which is replacement of the population. Reproduction demands —indeed, it *is*—social relationships. Education involves some of the most intense of social relationships.

The cultural dimensions of these biological and social facts are simple: every culture provides a set of concepts or images for viewing the situations of reproduction, care for the young, and the passage from generation to generation. Anthropology has summed all this up as "kinship."

KINSHIP

The word "kinship" has been used to mean several things—indeed, the situation is so complex that it is necessary to simplify it in order to study it. "Kinship relationships" have several referents, which must be kept sharply separated analytically. There are biological referents, behavioral referents, and linguistic referents (among others). It is of utmost importance that these three be kept separate, and that it be remembered that kinship is a maze of complex phenomena which any description must oversimplify, given the present state of our knowledge.

People who are genetically and biologically related to one another are "kinsmen." People have sires and dams and mates (to avoid momentarily the terms we use to describe the specifically human attributes of such roles). Kinship relationships, so viewed, form biological networks. Every living individual is at a node in a biological network. He is a recipient of genes and probably a donor of genes. The biological network stretches far beyond the awareness of any human individual and presumably includes all human beings.

There are two types of biological relationships that can exist between mammals. One of these two types is a relationship of descent. The other is a sexual relationship. In the biological sense, all kinship relationships comprise one link or a series of links either of descent or of sexual union. Adoption and other forms of "quasi-kinship" are made to serve as socially approved substitutes for the biological relationship, thereby merely underscoring its primacy.

The study of kinship is not, however, the study of mere biology. If it were, kinship would be the same in all societies. In fact, kinship provides one of the areas of widest differences in all culture.

People who are kinsmen are always aware, in one way or another, of at least some of their biological relations. They in all probability have extremely complex views about what the biology of the situation implies socially and culturally. There are thus two particular ramifications of such views. First, all people classify kinsmen into various categories and give these categories names, called "kinship terms." Secondly, each named category will be found to have certain modes of behavior expected from the people who are fitted into it. In other words, a kinship term is a linguistic tag for a role; the role has biological criteria or admitted substitutes for admission to it, and it also has cultural criteria for performance. Kinship terms are role terms.

Two warnings must be made immediately: there are many criteria that can be used for assigning kinsmen, biological or putative, to roles—and no culture has been found that uses all the criteria that have been discovered. There are, moreover, many different behavioral requirements that can be assigned even to roles that are delineated by identical criteria.

In short, kinship is a complicated subject. But the tools exist for simplifying it. It can be, initially and briefly, defined as a study of the cultural interpretations of social relationships, social categories, and social groups that are formed among people who stand in biological or quasibiological relationships or chains of relationships to one another.

Generations of anthropologists have begun the study of kinship by citing a simple diagram (Figure 4). The diagram can be read: "A man [♂] marries [=] a woman [♀] and they produce [|] children[♂┐♀]." This information, sometimes called the facts of life, is certainly the basic

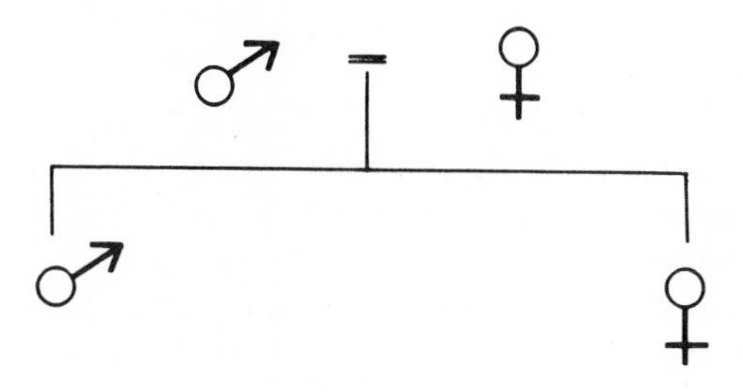

FIGURE 4 The Family

fact of the science of life and, since man is a self-aware animal, it is one of the basic facts of the sciences of behavior.

It should be pointed out, however, that the words we have used are already loaded: "marry" is an extremely complex word, meaning much more than merely "to mate with." "Children" are more than mere offspring. The moment we go further to speak of husband and wife instead of mates, of father and mother instead of sire and dam, we have slipped irrevocably beyond biology. Escape from the problem is not to be found in avoiding the fields beyond biology, but rather in entering them with full awareness. Human reproduction takes place in a melee of attitudes and values—it is impossible even to discuss it without calling up many of them with the very words we use. Since they cannot be avoided, they must be investigated.

There are, as we have seen, two kinds of biological relationship—sexuality and descent. Each can take place in one of two modes: the direct and the shared. Mates have a direct sexual union. Co-spouses (such as the wives of one man in a polygynous situation) share a mate. Parent and child have a direct descent union; siblings or other collaterals share descent. These two distinctions form a neat four-square table. (Table 2).

TABLE 2 TYPES OF KINSHIP RELATIONSHIP

	DIRECT	SHARED
SEXUALITY	Spouses	Co-spouses
DESCENT	Lineal kinsmen	Collaterals

The traditional method of the genealogical chart emphasizes roles and actors—husbands, fathers, sons, and brothers. Sex and generation are attributes of individuals who act out roles. The four-square diagram emphasizes relationships. Sexuality and descent are attributes of relationships. This distinction, kept clearly in mind, will see us through most of the intricacy of kinship studies.

MEN AND WOMEN

Every society recognizes the physical differences between men and women, but may assign vastly different roles to each. Yet, those social roles are always consonant with the facts of biological reproduction. Women need not be "feminine," but nevertheless they are female; they do bear the children. This fact, and the other fact that their bodies are designed for producing children, which puts certain limitations on their time and their glandular systems, must be recognized. Because men (whatever other disabilities they may suffer) do not have to cope with this particular disability—biologically, a man is no different after he becomes a father than he is before and psychically he is no different unless his culture demands it—and because men need not expend so much strength to nurture and bear young, men have the time and energy to range more widely and to carry on a sweeping range of activities. So much is biological and social fact. What a culture does with these facts by way of interpretation and role assignment varies widely.

Social life starts in a dichotomy of the sexes. But the fact of separation means that there must be a relationship between them. That relationship to which the sexual dichotomy is basic is, of course, mating. When mating takes place in a more or less permanent relationship and is publicly recognized, it can be called marriage. Thus, the first relationship symbol on Figure 4, the equals sign, stands for marriage.[1] Marriages create the type of relationship called *affinity*. A person is an affine of his spouse and of all his spouse's kinsmen save her affines.

Just as the roles of male and female are subject to a wide range of cultural interpretation, marriage is subject to even wider ranges of interpretation. What is involved in marriage? What sort of relationship is it? In our own society, the answers are apparent: marriage involves sexual and domestic rights and privileges. It is said ideally to derive from an emotional state, love. It involves a direct contract, sometimes written, between the two people who marry each other, and a whole set of vaguely defined avoidance relationships among the affines created by the marriage. It is the only condition in which a person may beget or bear children who do not have at least some legal or social disability. Marriage implies a set of ideal behavior patterns and norms in which we are all closely enmeshed, whether we are ourselves actually married or not.

"Marriage" is a word that, when it is used within the context of a single culture, accretes to itself a great many covert connotations of detail. Marriage performs many tasks within any society, and the term calls up the values associated with each task.

However, when the same term, "marriage," is used cross culturally—that is, when it is used for comparison of two different cultures—the field of meaning must be vastly reduced. The "marriage" of an Indian princess is not quite the same thing as the marriage of your cousin. The differences lie in the fact that of the many different aspects of life that can be associated with marriage, there is likely to be a difference between the Indian society

---

[1] In instances in which it is necessary to show a mating relationship that is not socially honored as marriage in a particular society, a single line dash is usually used.

and yours. Thus, when we talk about marriage cross culturally, we necessarily establish minimal requirements, and then describe which other values and practices are associated with marriage in any given culture. This problem arises in all anthropological terminology: terms used cross culturally bear different and fewer connotations than the same terms used within a single culture. It is especially noticeable in dealing with kinship; fortunately, however, kinship is also the field in which we are most ready to grasp and admit the notion of dual fields of connotation.

The very variation in the content of marriage—of the equals sign—from one culture to another allows anthropologists some of their most important and significant theorizing.

PARENTS AND CHILDREN

When a child is born to a mated pair, it is related to both of them by the type of relationship called descent, indicated in Figure 4 by a vertical line. One's lineal kinsman is one to whom one is related only through such lineal links. Every link in the relationship must be readable as an Old Testament "begat" or, in the case of a female parent, "bore."

When a second child is born to the mated pair, not only are new relationships of descent created. There is, moreover, the relationship of collaterality or of shared descent, indicated on the figure by a horizontal line. Two children of the same parents share descent and are hence collaterals, but they are not lineal kinsmen. My mother's brother and I share descent from the persons who are his parents and my grandparents, but since he did not beget me nor I him we are collateral rather than lineal kin.

In popular language, relationships of descent and collaterality are conjoined and called "relationship by blood" or "consanguinity." This word is useful as a general term for joining descent and collaterality, and is common in Western folk evaluations and kinship nomenclature. It contains, however, an error when used cross culturally. The word, in Indo-European languages, petrifies within itself an idiom that makes blood synonymous with biological relationship. Obviously, such is not the case. The genes, linked into choromosomes, are the mechanism of biological relationship. Although blood is heritable by Mendelian principles, it is not the "true" link any more than is hair, skin, or bones. When we carry blood imagery into cultures where it is absent, our description may be warped unless we recognize the metaphor in our own culture. With such a warning, however, "consanguines" is a sufficiently good term to oppose to "affines."

The cultural content of the relationships of descent varies as widely as does that of marriage. The biological fact is that people who are related to one another lineally are necessarily members of different generations. A man is in an adjacent generation to his parents and his children; he is in an alternate generation to his grandparents and grandchildren.

The fact that in all societies one generation must, in some way or another, socialize and enculturate the next younger generation leads to some of the most important problems in social life. The problems indeed form a never-ending chain: not only must parents tame their children, but they must at the same time spend the rest of their lives getting over the process as it was carried out on them by their own parents.

When we investigate descent, it is necessary to go into the ideas about procreation held by the people we study. Different peoples postulate that different physical and personal qualities derive from descent. Some say blood derives from the mother, bone from the father; others that the body derives from the mother, the spirit or personality from the father.

In fact, most cultures also link many nonbiological phenomena to descent, and may even claim that they are "inherited" by the same mechanism as one inherits eye color. In almost all societies, some legal rights are linked with actual or putative descent. Thus, in the matter of descent, kinship overlaps the law—and the earliest treatises on kinship, such as those of Blackstone, were legal treatises on interpretations of biological fact. Inheritance to office or valued social roles is easily distinguishable from descent, but the two are linked in all but a few cultures.

It is of importance that some societies link the most important cultural rights with descent from and through males, whereas others link similar rights with descent through and from females. A descent link from a man to a child is called an *agnatic* link. A descent link from a woman to a child is called a *uterine* link.[2] Many—probably most—societies evaluate agnatic links in a different way than they evaluate uterine links: different qualities and different social requisites and privileges are made to attend them.

COLLATERALS

Finally, Figure 4 contains a horizontal line, which links siblings. The problems of brotherhood are well known, but are subject to even greater cultural variation than are marriage or descent. Whereas marriage performs the basic functions of controlling and channeling the sexual activity of members of society, and whereas lineal kinship is concerned with the functions of bearing and enculturating the young, there is no function that is so "biologically" linked with the relationship between siblings. Therefore, the uses to which the relationship can be put varies widely from one society to the next.

[2] Many anthropologists call these patrilineal and matrilineal links. I hesitate to do so because in some contexts the emphasis on lineality obscures the point.

In summary, no matter what the cultural content of the relationships, if the chain of relationships linking two persons contains an equals sign, they are affines. If it contains no equal signs and at least one horizontal line, they are collaterals. If it contains no equals signs and no horizontal lines, they are descendants and ascendants—lineal kinsmen.

KINSHIP RELATIONSHIPS

Having considered both the symbols in Figure 4 and the boxes in the four-square (Table 2), we have found two sex roles (male and female), two generations (senior and junior), two types of direct biological relationship (sexuality and descent), and two types of shared biological relationship (affinity and collaterality). We can now change our focal length and approach the chart and the square from nearer at hand: as a series of more precise relationships and roles.

The female role, seen from the viewpoint of affinity, is that of wife or co-wife. Seen from the aspect of descent, it is either mother or daughter; seen from the aspect of collaterality, it is sister. Conversely, the male role is husband or co-husband if viewed affinally, brother if view collaterally, and father or son if viewed lineally.

These are the ten basic kinship roles: wife, co-wife, mother, daughter; husband, co-husband, father, son; brother, sister. All other roles can be described by breaking them down into a chain of primary roles—mother's brother, father's father, and so on.[3]

The relationships linking the ten roles can be readily seen in a reinterpretation of the four-square (Table 3). These relationships are (1) the

TABLE 3 KINSHIP RELATIONSHIPS

	DIRECT	SHARED
SEXUALITY	Hu–Wi	CoWi-CoWi CoHu-CoHu
DESCENT	Fa–So Mo–So Fa–Da Mo–Da	Br–Br Si–Si Br–Si

direct affinal relationship of husband-wife, (2) the indirect affinal relationships of co-wife to co-wife and of co-husband to co-husband, (3) the four

[3] Kroeber, in his 1909 article which first established the criteria for delimiting the roles recognized by kinship terms, covered most of these points of distinctions of sex, generation, and affinity *vs.* consanguinity. Here we are working with relationships rather than roles, and the relevant distinctions in the relationships are male-female; affine-consanguine; descendant-collateral; direct-shared.

direct relationships of descent between parents and children, and (4) the three relationships of shared descent among siblings.

When we come to consider the cultural image of these biological facts, we run immediately into kinship terminology. Every language may categorize the kinsmen differently, so that in one culture the kinsmen (computed biologically) fall into different categories than those same kinsmen fall into in a different culture. Kinship terms are not mere categories of biological kinsmen, they are also referents for certain types of behavior. The system of kinship terms is, thus, a type of classification system for assigning people of given biological connections into social roles.

There are many sorts of folk images of the roles various kinsmen must play. Indeed, when we enter the realm of kinship terminologies, we are leaving the scientific image of biological reality far behind, and entering the realm of cultural perception. The earliest scientific attempts to deal with kinship—stemming from the middle of the nineteenth century—were attempts at classification of the cultural matrices or codes in which the "message" of biological kinship is clothed. Many modern studies of kinship —now called "componential analysis"—do the same thing.

A kinship system can be broken down, then, into three subsystems. There is first the subsystem of terminology, which has received the greatest amount of attention. There is, second, the subsystem of ideal behavior associated with roles marked out by the terms. There is, third, a subsystem of social groups, eligibility for membership in which is based on criteria of kinship, either terminological or behavioral. This chapter deals with the first two subsystems; the third is the subject of the subsequent chapters.

KINSHIP TERMS

Like almost everything else, kinsmen standing to one another in various categories of relationship must be given names. These words, which make perfectly simple sense in any single language and culture, are sometimes amazingly difficult to translate. In fact, kinship terms are probably among the most difficult of all words to translate from one language to another. As we shall see, inept translation of terms held up general understanding of kinship phenomena for almost a century.

The fact that there are scores of ways of grouping kinsmen and many different principles of categorization has been known for a very long time, but it was not until the middle of the nineteenth century that orderly investigation was begun.

The scientific study of kinship began with Lewis H. Morgan (1871). Although several attempts have been made to discredit Morgan as the founder of kinship studies, such attempts have amounted to little more than have attempts to discredit Darwin merely because he used ideas that were current in his day and could be traced to his less illustrious predecessors. Professor Radcliffe-Brown (1950, p. 8) has traced concern with and interest in the kinship terminology of the Iroquois Indians back to Lafitau in the eighteenth century, and has been widely quoted either with or without reference. But he cannot deprive Morgan of the position that he holds: the first man ever to deal exhaustively and sensibly with the vagaries of the world's systems of kinship terminologies. Morgan, of course, dealt with ideas current in his time, but he left on them the impression of a vivid and original mind.

Morgan became interested in kinship terms while he was working among the Iroquois and Ojibwa Indians and investigating their culture. His book on the Iroquois sets forth systematically, but very briefly, some of the ways in which the kinship terminology used in this Indian language differs from that used in American English. When he discovered similar usage among the Ojibwa he began to collect terminologies from hundreds of languages by sending out questionnaires to administrative officers and missionaries in faraway places and to travelers who did not follow beaten trails. He requested that they fill out his questionnaires, which were set up in descriptive terms such as "mother's brother" and "father's brother" instead of in English terms such as "uncle." The result of his researches, *Systems of Consanguinity and Affinity in the Human Family,* published in 1871 by the Smithsonian Institution of Washington, is surely one of the monumental books of modern times. As in the case of so many monuments, its very size and comprehensiveness led to its neglect.

Morgan's starting point was the terminology. He then made a methodological error: assumptions about the correlation of kinship terminology with behavior and groups were made axiomatic. His initial step was empirically grounded to such an extent that it seems almost impossible to believe, today, that an empirical referent could have been so deftly avoided in his succeeding steps. With admirable objectivity, Morgan classified his terminologies into types. Then, with almost pure lack of objectivity, he associated these terminologies *not* with ideal or actual behavior in social roles, but with social groups—either those that existed or others that he assumed must once have existed.

Morgan's contribution to kinship studies is incalculable. It must not be forgotten in evaluating his work that he was working in the days when Tylor was just adapting the word "culture" to the anthropological ends that have since become commonplaces, when sociology was still struggling to free itself from philosophy, and when psychology was still in the initial throes of the pleasure-pain dichotomy and had not even discovered rats and mazes, let alone the unconscious. It must also be remembered that reading Morgan's theory (not his empirical fieldwork, which even with its errors stands up) led Marx and Engels into some questionable statements that have since become enshrined as Communist dogma.

Morgan, in organizing his vast quantities of data, said that some kinship terms—and by extension, some terminological systems—are descriptive, whereas others are classificatory. In its purest form, a descriptive system uses only primary terms such as father, mother, son, daughter, husband, wife, and perhaps brother and sister. All other kin are described by combinations or juxtapositions of the primary terms. The classificatory system, on the other hand, is that in which several different types of kinsmen (by descriptive criteria) are lumped into single terminological categories.The English term "uncle" is such a one, because it categorizes mother's brother, father's brother, mother's sister's husband, and father's sister's husband. However it was not this type of grouping to which Morgan referred. His "classificatory" meant terminological union of some or all of the collateral kin with the lineal kin. Thus, in a "classificatory system," such as the Iroquois, the father and the father's brother were called by the same term.

Morgan then subdivided his "classificatory" type of terminology into two: the Malayan type, in which all collaterals were terminologically merged with the lineal kinsmen of the same generation, and the American Indian type (he called it Turanian-Ganouanian), in which only part of the collaterals were so merged with the lineal.

It was Rivers (1924), the great English psychologist and ethnologist, who corrected Morgan's dichotomy by making a tripartite division. He retained Morgan's classificatory, but broke "descriptive" into two: descriptive to Rivers meant literally the compilation of primary terms (father's brother's son), whereas "denotative" terms referred to classes of kin formed on principles other than merging of lineals and collaterals into single terminological units (cousin).

The first indication that we are dealing with a "classificatory kinship terminology" is that some of ego's collateral relatives are called by the same terms as some of his lineal relatives. We never do this in English, but in some terminologies considerations of common generation and shared descent override or displace lineal considerations in the creation of terms. In such a system, my father and all his siblings are called by the same term. Now note, I did not say that the father's siblings are called "father." This pedantic point—pedantic only in the microcosm—lies behind what is still the major source of misunderstanding in kinship terminologies: faulty translation. The English word "father" recognizes two principles: generation and descent. The Iroquois term *hanih* recognizes two principles: generation and collaterality. Therefore, to translate the term *hanih* to "father" is an incorrect translation.

Morgan's book set the tone for the studies that followed for the next sixty years. Like Morgan, almost all of them began with the terminologies, and like him most of them correlated the terminological subsystem with the behavioral subsystem not at all, and with the subsystem of social groups by theoretical rather than empirical links, thereby creating false sociology.

The next major contribution to the study of kinship terminology was contained in a short article of Kroeber in 1909. The great advance he made was to recognize eight distinctions by which terms for kinship roles could be differentiated from one another. Of them, we have so far considered terms that show (1) differences in generation, (2) differences between lineal and collateral kinship, (3) differences between affines and consanguines, and (4) differences of sex. Kroeber added to them: (5) differences of age, (6) differences in the speaker's sex, (7) differences in the sex of a relative standing between the speaker and the kinsman to whom the term is applied, and (8) the life or death of a connecting relative.

Lowie (1920) and others have pointed out gaps in Kroeber's analysis. Lowie emphasized the presence of reciprocity in some systems in which kinsmen call one another by reciprocal terms—the typical example is between lineal kinsmen of the same sex but of alternate generations: grandfathers call their grandsons by the same term the grandsons call them. Murdock (1949) refers to this characteristic as "polarity."

It was Lowie, in the fourteenth edition of the *Encyclopaedia Britannica,* who modernized Morgan and successfully divorced the terminological subsystem from the others. He was using material and ideas that "everybody knew" at the time, yet his analyses bear strong personal marks, and in his precise statements we get all these tenuous notions firmly brought to page. Lowie retained Morgan's main mode of classification: whether or not the terminological system united or separated lineal and collateral kinsmen. He then set up four gross categories into which he could, with more or less discomfiture, put all terminological systems.

These four modes of classing kinsmen were based on the terms for kinsmen in the immediately ascending generation from "ego," the person who supplies the reference point necessary in any system of terminology. In a "generation" system, ego's father, his father's brother, and his mother's brother are all called by the same term. In Kroeber's terms, only distinctions of sex and generation are considered in the terms for kinsmen of the ascending generation; there is a perfect terminological merging of the collateral with the lineal kin—that is, the collateral-lineal distinction is not recognized in the terms of the system.

If we add an additional Kroeberian distinction—that of distinguishing between lineal and collateral kin—and only that one, we get what Lowie called the "lineal" type of kinship terminology. Here the collaterals (that is, the mother's brother and the father's brother) are separated terminologically from the lineal kinsman (the father) but not from each other. Still another distinction must be added, and we have arrived at what Lowie called "bifurcation" between the collateral kinsmen. This newly added distinction is that of the sex of the relative standing between ego and the kinsman to whom the term is applied. That is, we take (1) the male kinsmen (2) of the ascending generation. We then divide them (3) on the basis of the lineal-collateral distinction and (4) again in the case of the collaterals on the basis of the sex of the relative who stands between them and ego.

So conceived, however, there are two types of bifurcating terminology. One, which might be called "neat bifurcating" but which Lowie called "bifurcate collateral," in which only these four principles are recognized. The result is three terms: one for father, one for father's brother, and one for mother's brother. The other type of bifurcating terminology results when still a fifth distinction is added—one not recognized by Kroeber, but added much later by Radcliffe-Brown—the idea of the unity of the sibling group, sometimes called the principle of the equivalence of siblings. That principal merely states that for some purposes, be they behavioral, terminological, or other, siblings are not distinguished from one another (for other purposes, obviously, they will be). In some contexts, one brother is as good as the next. Now *if* the distinction between the sex of the relatives standing between ego and referent is maintained, and then the distinction between lineal and collateral overriden by the principle of equivalence of siblings, the father's brother is terminologically linked with the father. We have, thus, what Lowie called the "bifurcate-merging" type of terminology; that is, collaterals are distinguished from one another, but one of them is terminologically merged with the lineal on the principle of the equivalence of siblings. The four types are shown in Figure 5.

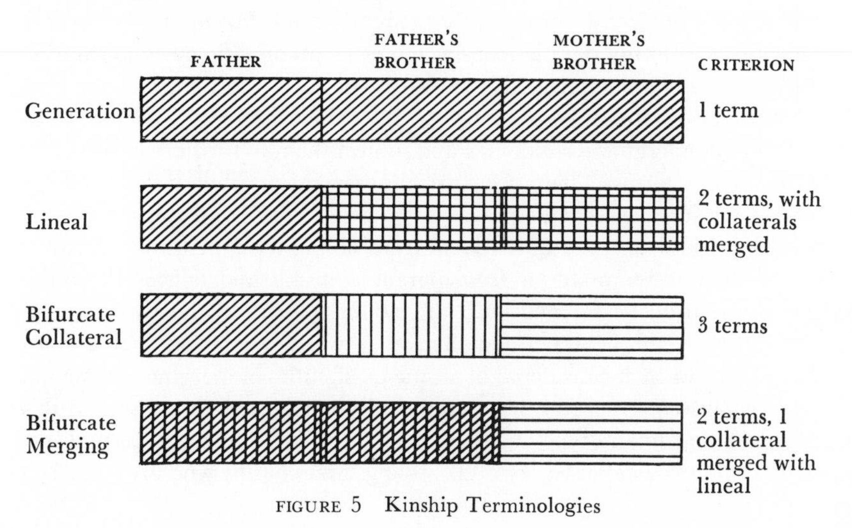

FIGURE 5 Kinship Terminologies

Bifurcate-merging terminology is very common, and based as it is only on the terms for collaterals in the ascending proximate generation, it contains systems that are in other regards greatly at variance. In order to bring further order into the matter, Lowie went to a monograph by Leslie Spier (1925), which is notable for making a significant contribution in the absence of logical rigor. Spier's eight classes are not in any wise mutually exclusive, and his classification would be of only passing interest had it not been that Lowie took up some of his terminology and gave it special meanings. Spier found that in some cases systems could reasonably be grouped by the terms for collateral kinsmen in ego's generation. What he called the "Salish" type of terminology grouped siblings and all cousins under a single term. It therefore corresponds, in ego's generation, with Lowie's "generational" in the ascending generation, and we can say that there are generational systems which are and others which are not of the Salish type.

The other two modes found by Spier have to do with distinctions made in the terms of siblings and cousins similar to those made by Lowie in terms of parents and parents' siblings.

There are four kinsmen (eight if sex of the referent kinsmen be included; many more if age of the kinsman or relative ages of intermediate kinsmen be included) who may be cousins: the father's brother's child, the father's sister's child, the mother's brother's child, and the mother's sister's child. On the basis of wide experience, anthropologists have grouped these four kinsmen into two groups. Parallel cousins are those to whom one is related through two members of the ascendant generation who are of the same sex—that is, one's father and father's brother have children who are parallel cousins, so do one's mother and mother's sister. But when the parents of the cousins are of opposite sex, the cousins are cross cousins: the mother's brother's child or the father's sister's child. Put in another way, I am connected to my parallel cousins either by all agnatic or by all uterine links, whereas I am connected to my cross cousins by a mixture of the two.

What Lowie did, then, was to take all of the examples he could find of his bifurcate-merging terminology and subject them to further classification by the cousin terms. There are, logically, several possibilities: all siblings and all cousins may be called by a single term (Salish); all cousins may be called by a single term, differentiated from sibling terms; cross cousins may be called by different terms from parallel cousins, and one or the other may in addition be merged with the siblings. Further, the two types of cross cousins can be separated, and the two types of parallel cousins separated, and each considered in all the possibilities of merging. Two main types of bifurcate merging were empirically recognized as a result of this exercise: the Omaha type and the Crow type. The Omaha type makes a single terminological category of all siblings and cousins who are joined to ego entirely by agnatic links. Again, there is a different term for all cousins and half siblings who are ego's mother's agnates. The Crow system is the precise opposite: it has one term for all siblings and cousins who are linked solely by uterine links, and again a different term for all half siblings and cousins who are one's father's uterine kin.

KINSHIP TERMS AND SOCIAL ROLES

It was becoming obvious that unless anthropologists wanted the terminology in the analytical system to be even more complex than that in the folk systems under study, they had to stop some place. Actually, the stop came when they began to associate terminology with social roles instead of with institutions or social groups. There have been numerous scattered contributions to the theory of kinship terminology since Lowie's stupendous article in the *Encyclopaedia Britannica*—most of them minor. We have covered enough at this point to allow the student to get through most of the specialist articles on the subject.

The study of kinship terminologies is likely to omit one of the most important discoveries of twentieth-century social anthropology: that kinship terms refer not merely (and often not even primarily) to the facts of biological relationship, but also to the cultural image of them—that is, to the social facts of role expectations. Classification of kinship terminologies may even turn out to be as futile an exercise as was the computation of the cephalic index.

Morgan's basic mistake, as we have seen, was to assume that every kinship term had as its equivalent not a mode of behavior, but rather a recognized institutional entity in an analytical image. Thus, in instances in which a person called his mother and his mother's sister by the same term, the assumption was made that he did not distinguish between them.

Actually, a great deal of trouble could have been saved and problems solved much earlier if the analysts had not done their analyses in translation. In the above case, the word applied both to a mother and her sister was translated as "mother," when in fact it means no such thing. A better translation—no matter for the moment how pedantic—would be "a female uterine relative of the ascending generation." The emotional connotation to the scientist of the English word "mother" is absent, and he is thus in a position to investigate the emotional connotation of the new word. We have been, in the past, tricked into saying that a person calls his mother's sister "mother" instead of saying that a person calls his mother and his mother's sister by the same term—obviously two very different things.

Once we have focused on the term in the native language, we can ask "What is the meaning of the term?" Early investigators, instead of looking for the "meaning" of the term in the folk evaluation, assumed the meaning that was present in the translation term in their own, Western, folk evaluation—the sin that anthropologists label "ethnocentrism."

Let us take two systems of kinship terminology and trace them through a translation, step by step, to illustrate how it should be done. I have purposely chosen simple systems, for the method is as well illustrated with simple systems as with complex ones. The first is that of the Ashanti of Ghana. It is bifurcate merging, Crow type, in Lowie's terminology. The second will be that of the Tiv of central Nigeria, which is a variant of Lowie's lineal type.

Like most systems of kinship terminology, the Ashanti system is simple and logical, but only when it is looked at from the right vantage point. First of all, there are five primary terms for uterine kinsmen. One means "uterine kinsman of my own generation" (*nua*). This can be full brother, full sister, or any uterine cousin, no matter how distant. There is another word meaning "female uterine kinsman of the ascending generation" (*ena*); it includes the mother, mother's sisters, mother's mother's sisters' daughters, and so on. There is another term meaning "male uterine kinsman of the ascending generation" (*wofa*), which includes the mother's brother, the mother's mother's sisters' sons, and so on. There is a word meaning "uterine kinsman of the descending generation" (*ba*). This term can be used *only* by women. Obviously, no male has uterine descendants, and males use another term (*wofase*) to apply to all uterine descendants of anyone they call *nua*. This, then, makes five terms for uterine kinsmen.

There are, next, two further words for the father's uterine kinsmen—one for males (*agya*), which includes the father, and one for females (*sewa*). There is another word (*nana*) that has two primary referents: it is, first, all persons to whom one is related lineally in alternate generations, and, second, all uterine kinsmen in alternate generations. There is a word (*ntoro*) used to describe the relationship of agnation, but it is not applied to agnates beyond saying "We are of the same *ntoro*."

There is one word (*akonta*) that means "affine of my own generation" and is applied to all save the spouse (there are special terms for husband and wife). All other Ashanti kinship terms are modifications of these basic ones. Obviously, it is simple precisely because we have found the correct framework for viewing it: the merging of uterine kin by generations. This is a characteristic of bifurcate-merging systems: uterine or agnatic links are of utmost importance—as they also are for the unilineal descent groups that so often occur in these societies. It is wrong, however, to cite a causal relationship between terms and institutions such as unilineal descent groups, for many societies are marked by strong unilineal descent groups but do not have bifurcate-merging terminologies. The Tiv are such.

The Tiv system is even simpler than the Ashanti. In spite of strong unilineal descent group organization, kinship terminology shows no trace of merging. Tiv have a single term (*ityo*) which means "agnatic kinsman." They have another (*igba*) which means "mother's agnatic kinsman." These terms, seldom used in address, do not recognize age, generation, or sex differences.

The chief terminological distinction Tiv make is between lineal and collateral kinsmen. All male ascendants are called by the same term (*ter*). The word is applied alike to father, father's father, father's father's father, and so on, or to mother's father, mother's mother's father, and so on. The word can be translated "male ancestor." There is another, equivalent, word (*ngo*) for "female ancestor," which includes the mother, both grandmothers, all the great grandmothers, and so on. All collaterals with whom I share a female ancestor in any line may be called "child of my mother" (*wangho*). All collaterals with whom I share a male ancestor may be called "child of my father" (*wanter*). Ego's descendants are all called children; this term may be extended to those collaterals who are descended from kinsmen of ego's own or junior generations, and it can be extended to any woman who is ego's agnate. Tiv have another term, difficult because it is unique so far as I am aware, which means "someone to whom I am related through two routes" (*wangban*): full siblings, double cousins, and other more distant kinsmen to whom I can trace two relationships. These, with the words for husband and wife, and a single word for affine (which literally means "outside") finish it off. Tiv classify kin into very broad categories whose main purpose is first to separate one's juniors from one's contemporaries and seniors, and secondly, to separate those of one's seniors who are lineal kin from those who are collateral kin.

If we had chosen some Australian systems, the translation problem would have been more complex, but it would not have been fundamentally different.

In summary, all societies have terms for the categories into which they classify those kinsmen they recognize. The terminological systems show a wide variation, and there is always, in the folk evaluation, a relationship between the kinship term and the ideal mode of behavior. There may also be regularities between kinship terms and specific institutions, but such relationships are empirical. The presence of the term never allows an anthropologist to infer the institution or vice versa, but only to give *post hoc* explanations of the folk evaluation.

KINSHIP BEHAVIOR

Every experienced fieldworker has been addressed by at least some of the kinship terms in the language of the people he studied. In all cases, these terms are to be understood as signs requesting certain types of behavior, not as a mistaken referent to biological connection. My own experience with the Tiv is that if a Tiv wanted me to give him something, he called me "my father." If he wanted to correct my grammar or put me right on a point of etiquette, he called me "my child." If he wanted to include me with him against somebody he was arguing with, he called me "son of my mother." If he wanted to offer me a drink he used the nonkinship term "my age mate." I have been addressed by every kinship term for a male in the Tiv language.And certainly no Tiv ever thought there was a biological connection between us. The point was the expected behavior.[4]

The most important fact about a kinship system is that it is a set of role tags which make it possible for a person to know what to expect from his kinsmen and what they expect from him. It is only secondarily true that in all societies some or all of these categories include persons who are related by different biophysical links.

These differing systems of linguistic categories indicate that every culture looks at the biological facts of kinship in its characteristic way. The connection between term and behavior is empirical *in every case*. Comparison of terms and behavior must be made afresh in each new culture. Analysis may, in turn, lump the behavior-term units, but it must be remembered when this is done that a folk evaluation can *never* be deduced from an analytical evaluation. It is just here that much of the early analysis went astray.

The correspondence between ideal behavior patterns and terminology was obscured for many years while arguments raged about whether kinship terms had social referents, by which the arguers meant referents in an analytical system. They put such propositions as "A special term for mother's brother signifies the avunculate." What was involved here is a confusion between a folk evaluation specifically utilized by the actors for living in the system (a term for mother's brother) and an analytical evaluation, which is that designed by the social or cultural analyst for purposes of comparison of various systems (the avunculate). It can be stated axiomatically that, within the folk image, there is a relationship between kinship terms and kinship behavior—that in fact the terms are used to call up the behavior. The sort of behavior that ought, in the values of the culture, to be associated with the specific named kinship role can be described by almost any informant, provided the question is stated clearly in his cultural idiom.

There is little to say on a theoretical level about the relationship between kinship terms and the behavior of kinsmen. Here is an extremely

---

[4] A reader has pointed out that in this passage, I do what I have warned against: use translations of terms. I concur—and apologize—and leave the original wording so that the anecdote comes across. The threshold of pedantry is always difficult to gauge.

important point to be described for each society in order that much of the motivation for other action within that society can be made clear. But the relationship between term and behavior is symbolic and historical; therefore, it yields comparatively little theory. Kinship terms in their relationship to behavior must be studied anew for each society. The problem must be understood as an important source of the anthropologist's understanding of the rational element in the folk image of perceiving a culture. It is not, however, an ultimate cause in any sense in the folk system or in the analytical system dealing with social relationships, for all that it may be the point in which the great break can be made in understanding the processes of symbolization.

For an example of excellent description of the behavioral meanings of a set of kinship terms, one can do no better than to examine Hilda Kuper's article on Swazi kinship in *African Systems of Kinship and Marriage* (1950).

Finally, neither terminology nor behavior is to be confused with kinship groups, although both are congruent with them, in the sense that roles and relationships are parts, or units, of social groups. A kinship group is a group made up of roles marked by kinship terms (or of roles that form syndromes with sets of kinship terms), in which the relationship consists of behavior either wholly or in part colored by the moral values associated with kinship relationships, and which recognizes some sort of biological connection or culturally accepted pseudobiological connection among the members.

5

Marriage and the nuclear family

THE PREVIOUS CHAPTER dealt summarily with two aspects of kinship systems: the terminological subsystem and the behavioral subsystem. This chapter begins a consideration of the third aspect: the subsystem of kinship groups. A kinship group is a number of roles bound together in socially recognized kinship relationships and syndromes; it is an entity in the "real" world in the sense that people who play the roles recognize it in their daily lives and perhaps give it a name. The kinship group must be distinguished from the kinship category, which is a group of kinsmen who happen to be called by the same term. It must also be distinguished from a kinship network, which is composed of the biological relationships among human beings.

There are two kinds of kinship groups. One is called a family; it contains affines as well as consanguines. The other can be called the consanguine kinship group; it contains no affines. Both families and consanguine kinship groups can be limited by increasing the number of criteria used for determining eligibility to membership.

There has never been discovered a kinship group that contains within it all of the ten basic kinship relationships. A family based on the group marriage of Morganian tradition would have contained all. This fictive kinship group, postulated by Morgan to have existed in some prehistoric epoch (but never empirically discovered except, as Hooten was fond of pointing out, among the howler monkeys of Panama), was said to have been made up of a group of men who espoused a group of women. All men had equal rights in all women (and vice versa), and all children were acknowledged by all alike, men *and* women. Such a group was, apparently, one of the many figments of the Victorian imagination.

All existing kinship groups that have been studied in empirical detail are formed by the systematic exclusion of some kinsmen. Such exclusion occurs whenever new criteria are added to determine eligibility to membership in any group. The criteria may be of a kinship nature, resulting in refusal to recognize for the purpose of eligibility to the group some of the basic relationships, or else in drawing the line at a given genealogical distance from some ego. The added criteria may also be of a nonkinship nature, and membership depend primarily on kinship but secondarily on such matters as residence in a given area, following of a certain calling, or subscribing to a given religious doctrine. Thus, all families exclude at least one of the relationships of shared sexuality, or (in a monogamous society such as our own) both of them. Consanguine kinship groups exclude all relationships of sexuality, and (except for a handful) recognize many other criteria of exclusion as well.

THE NUCLEAR FAMILY

The family most familiar to Westerners is the "nuclear" family, which excludes both relationships of shared sexuality, but contains all eight of the other basic relationships (see Table 4).

TABLE 4 RELATIONSHIPS IN THE NUCLEAR FAMILY (CRITERIA OF SEX AND GENERATION ONLY)

	DIRECT		SHARED
SEXUALITY	HU-Wi		[hatched]
DESCENT	Fa–So Fa–Da	Mo–So Mo–Da	Br–Br Si–Si Br–Si

There are, besides the eight relationships, also eight roles in the nuclear family: husband, wife, father, mother, brother, sister, son, and daughter.[1]

There are only four syndromes in the nuclear family: husband/father, wife/mother, brother/son, and sister/daughter. If more syndromes are included, the family is no longer a nuclear family. Other terms may be encountered for the group that is here called a nuclear family. Two of the most common are "biological family" and "elementary family." Yet the nuclear family is no more and no less "biological" than is any other, and it is not precisely speaking elementary—the matricentric family, composed of a mother and her children, is both more nearly universal and more "elementary" than is the nuclear family. Indeed, claiming universality for the nuclear family can put analysts in an awkward position (Murdock, 1949; Parsons, 1954).

The matricentric family is considered, in some cultures, to be a unit. It

[1] It is important to remember that we are using two criteria of role differentiation: sex and generation. If one of these criteria is omitted, say sex, then the number of relationships is reduced—to parent-child, co-members of senior generation, and co-members of junior generation. If other criteria, such as those pointed out by Kroeber 1909, are added, the number of possible relationships is increased.

contains a woman and her children, and hence five relationships: mother-son, mother-daughter, and the three sibling relationships. This matricentric family may then be "hooked on" to a male or a group of males to create one of several kinds of family. There are instances, particularly in the Caribbean and in other societies with a past tradition of slave economy, in which the linkage to the male is weak, and in which the husband-wife and father-child relationships are but weakly developed. Indeed, one of the primary problems facing social workers in America today is the tenuousness of the relationships that hook a matricentric family with a man to act as husband/father.

Anthropologists in the past have sometimes accepted the matricentric family as one of the "building blocks" of families. If that assumption is made, it is obvious that if a matricentric family is linked with one man in "monogamous marriage," then the nuclear family results. If two or more matricentric families are linked to one man, the "polygynous family" results. If one matricentric family is linked to two or more men (who are, in all empirically known cases, already linked by other bonds), then the polyandrous family results. This mode of analysis is sensible so long as "family" remains the focal point. As we shall see, matricentric families can also be linked together into units that resemble consanguine groups.

MARRIAGE

The only relationships contained within a family that may not be contained within a consanguine kinship group are those based on sexuality and affinity. It therefore behooves us to begin our examination of the family with marriage.

Marriage is a complex matter. Its complexity is attested to by the fact that it is possible for so many of its qualities to vary, yet for marriage to continue to be recognizable cross culturally in spite of the variations. At least nine qualities of marriage can vary and have hence been used as a basis for classifying marriages (Davis, 1948):

1) Number of mates (monogamy, polygamy)
2) Degree of authority (equalitarian, patriarchal, matriarchal)
3) Residence after marriage (patrilocal, matrilocal, neolocal)
4) Choice of mate:
    a) Who determines choice? (free selection by young people, with courtship; controlled selection by parents)
    b) Bases of choice (kinship, caste, class, region, religion)
5) Exchange at marriage (bridewealth, groomprice, equal exchange)
6) Age at marriage (early or child marriage, late)

7) Strength of the bond (temporary, loose with easy divorce, unbreakable with no divorce)
8) Possibility of remarriage (no marriage after death or divorce, permissive remarriage, mandatory remarriage)
9) Kind of mates (marriage, concubinage)

The question is: How many of these variables make good, or even satisfactory, bases for classification and discussion of marriage? To begin, how many of the variables are actually about marriage and how many concern other matters that may be more or less closely connected with it?

The first point, the number of mates, leads to a classification into monogamous and polygamous unions. A polygamous marriage is a marriage between persons, one of whom is currently already married to somebody else. In modern Western society, all such marriages are illegal. In many societies they are the norm—at least, the goal. Although the behavior required in the husband-wife relationship may be altered by plural marriage of one of the spouses (but, of course, requirements in many cultures may be minimal, so that the alteration is negligible), it is primarily in the legal sense that the marital state of one of the partners to a new marriage can affect it. Other than by legal fiat, a marriage is a marriage, no matter whether its spouses are also concurrently married to other people. Therefore, the word "polygamous" refers not to marriage alone, where its meaning is limited, but more importantly to the family and the household. The polygamous family is an important unit worthy of study; the polygamous household presents many problems, both to its residents and to students of it. Polygamous marriages themselves are of importance only in that they lead to such families and such households.

The second point—on the degree of authority in the marriage—is of interest in studying norms of the husband-wife relationship in any given culture, but basically it refers to qualities of family life, not merely of marriage. Equalitarian, patriarchal, and matriarchal are adjectives that are meaningful when they modify the word "family," but not when they are used to describe "marriage." Is there such a thing as a matriarchal marriage? If there is, it applies to the power structure within the family. It is becoming apparent that one of the problems is that the word "marriage" has been used to mean the creating of a husband-wife relationship, its cultural content, and its place in the family.

The next point, on residence, does not apply to marriage at all. It applies to households. There has been a lot of loose discussion about "patrilocal marriage." What is patrilocal is not the marriage, but the household that may emerge from it. Several items have been confused—marriage is a relationship, a family is a kinship group, a household is a local group.

The next points, 4 and 5, deal with variation in the ways the marriage comes about: the choice of mate and the pseudoeconomic exchange at marriage. Both of these matters are more sensibly examined as classifications of courtship. A successful courtship is concluded by a marriage, but the type of courtship activity is not a very good overall way to classify marriage. Be that as it may, it is the usual one. The basic question here seems to be "How do men get women?"—a problem in courtship rather than marriage.

The question, "How do men get women?" is a male question. In the past it has been males who have been the primary analysts of marriage customs. Men spend so much of their early adulthood getting women that they have even invented a myth—which, like all myths, may be true—that women spend all of their time getting a man. Most discussions in anthropology textbooks classify marriages into those in which the bride is captured, those in which she is the reward of labor, those in which she is bought, those in which she is stolen, those in which she is the object of a contract, and those in which she is merely convinced. Remarriages may include all of these ways, plus others such as those in which the bride is inherited.

How men get women has, of late years, even been put on an economistic basis (Levi-Strauss, 1949, Homans and Schneider, 1955, Needham, 1962). Women, this theory runs, must be "distributed" in a way analogous to the ways in which "goods and services" are distributed among the members of a society. Women, the analogy continues, are a scarce commodity, and therefore there must be rules for their distribution and use.

Now, let it be granted that finding a woman is important in the life of most men, from time to time at least, and that courtship is a well-defined activity in all societies, showing variations which make it subject to classification. But marriage is more than acquiring a woman. Marriage, in fact, *begins* with the act that ends the successful courtship. To study its content, we must know more than how it was brought about.

The most complete classification of marriage by mode of courtship is Hoebel's (1949); he makes an eightfold division:

1) Marriage by purchase
2) Suitor service
3) Exchange marriage
4) Marriage by capture
5) Inheritance of wives
6) Adoptive marriage
7) Fictive marriage
8) Elopement

There are no difficulties in this straightforward classification save in categories 6 and 7. "Adoptive marriage" is a special form based on the criterion, not particularly of how men get women, but how men get sons-in-law. This category includes practices, such as those of traditional Japan, in which a man without sons adopts a man who becomes his daughter's husband and his own heir.

More devious is the matter of "fictive marriage," for by any criterion of how men get women, it is not marriage at all. Indeed, "fictive marriage" always arises because the people of a culture explain nonmarriage phenomena by analogy to marriage. Hoebel's prime example is of "marriages" between members of the same sex, for the sole sake of passing property. Marriage does legitimize children so that property can be passed in accordance with the norms of that society; legitimizing other lines for passage of property may (and sensibly) be made publicly to resemble marriage ceremonies. Analogies in a folk image should not, however, be transferred into an analytical theory. The point to be garnered from fictive marriage is that marriage is deeply enmeshed in any culture, that marriage is difficult to define in detail cross culturally, precisely because so many different aspects of a culture can be seen in analogy to it.

The age of the parties to a marriage (point 6 of the Davis classification) is a vital point, especially for demographers, for it may have important repercussions in the fertility rates. Classification on this basis is perfectly sensible—indeed, so is it on all the points so long as it be realized that each point answers only specific questions. A demographic point of this sort has comparatively little to do with other aspects of marriage, though early or late marriage may have important bearing on other aspects of the culture.

Two points in Davis' list, 7 and 8, are useful to classify marriages by means of the way that they can be superseded. Point 7 is about divorce, not marriage. Point 8 is about remarriage. Here are indeed important aspects of the husband-wife relationship and of the family, into which we later must delve in detail, but they do not lead to a satisfactory notion of what marriage is.

ROLES IN MARRIAGE

It is the last point in the list—number 9—that is to be emphasized here: what Kingsley Davis and others have called "the kind of mates." The division of mating relationships into "marriage and concubinage," which Davis notes, is unfortunate because it imports one of our own Western folk criteria into the analytical image, and hence gives an impression of meaning more than it in fact does. In order to investigate the kind of mates, it is necessary to examine the behavioral content of the roles in marriage. In so doing, much of the material that can be made relevant to the other types of classification can be subsumed. It is useful first to study the roles of husband and wife in jural terms, which is to say that we must analyze and ultimately classify the rights in and duties toward one another that husbands and wives may have in many different societies.

Examination of jural aspects of marriage begins with factoring out several basic types of rights in women that a man himself, or his social group, can acquire on marriage. It is, in fact, possible to make a jural definition of marriage dealing only with the acquisition by a male or his social group of any or all of these rights in a woman, if he is to exercise the rights himself and not assign them to somebody else, as he may on occasion do. It would be equally possible, and probably just as enlightening, if a feminist anthropologist were to study the acquisition by the bride of rights in her groom. However, from the legal point of view—whether we like it or not—it is a man's world in almost all societies. Therefore, we take the man's point of view and ask what rights in his wife he acquires at marriage, remembering that he has corresponding obligations which are the rights his wife acquires.

The rights in women acquired on marriage can be divided into two sorts: the domestic rights and the kinship rights. This distinction depends on another: the distinction between family and household. A family is a kinship group, marked by kinship relationships. A household is a local or spatial group, marked by propinquity. A family need not live together as a household (although such is the norm in most societies). A household need not be made up solely, or even primarily, of family members. The family and the household, even if they contain the same personnel—indeed, especially if they do—must not be confused.

The rights in a wife, which a man acquires at marriage and which form the basis of the household, can be called "domestic rights." Such rights include his right to live with her and to form with her a basic unit defined by the division of labor between the sexes. A man provides meat and a woman cooks; a man provides clothing and a woman provides house furnishings.

The rights and obligations we have called domestic rights are those that are contingent upon the household. The precise and detailed content of those rights varies from one culture to the next. What does not vary is that wherever the family does form a basis for household formation—and that is almost everywhere—there are domestic duties and there is a division of labor between the sexes.

To the basic domestic rights may be added another: economic rights in a woman beyond those implied in the domestic situation. In most societies these two sets of rights can be said to belong to a girl's father or mother, or some other relative who acts as foster parent, until marriage. The right may not be exercised—that is, the girl may not be required to do any work. The society of the Trobriand Islands provides a good example of a place where girls are not expected to do any work before marriage. Many classes in American society exhibit the same phenomenon: there is complete freedom from work for unmarried girls, up to a certain age. These rights to the woman's extradomestic labor may be acquired at marriage, or they may not be. Certainly the rights to a woman's domestic chores and the rights to her extradomestic labor are divisible and one or both may be acquired. In twentieth-century American society, rights to a woman's domestic services are acquired at marriage (in some states her refusal over a long period to carry out domestic obligations constitutes grounds for divorce). Today, however, rights to her extradomestic labor are not so unequivocally the "property" of her husband as they were in the nineteenth century. A married woman can keep her own bank account, pay her own income tax. In Africa, by and large, the domestic rights are transferred—farming, cooking, and so on. However in almost *no* African society are a woman's earnings from extradomestic labor to be touched by her husband. She retains rights to her earnings outside the domestic circle; her husband has no jural lien on them.

The other set of rights a man may acquire in a woman at the time of marriage can be called "kinship rights." The kinship rights are primarily of two sorts: sexual rights and rights to children. The two must not be confused, for there are a few societies that distinguish them; even where they are not distinguished the distinction in the analytical image proves helpful.

In most societies, control of sexual rights in a woman is felt to be held by parents and legitimately exercised by no one until marriage; among many peoples—the Zulu are an example—a man can sue his daughter's seducer and get damages. By most Westerners, the acquisition of sexual rights in a woman is the basis of the folk definition of marriage. In Western societies, in which relatively late marriage is the rule even though age at marriage is getting lower steadily, the parents of the girl fade into the background; it is usually considered that after a girl comes of age she becomes her own mentor in matters of her sexual behavior.

Sexual rights must not, of themselves, be confused with the right of the husband (and, concomitantly, of the wife) to children. Most societies consider it the obligation of a spouse to provide children if the other desires them; and only in a few societies (our own among them) are children not universally desired. This right to children must be, in analysis, kept absolutely distinct from sexual rights. We in the West confuse the two, in part because until recent decades some of the most influential segments of Western society paid lip service to the idea that procreation is the only socially approved point of sexual relations. Most non-Westerners have never made such an assumption and state quite explicitly the difference between sexual rights and rights to children.

The rights to a woman's children can be called rights *in genetricem*—rights in the woman as the bearer of children. If a man acquires these rights at marriage, any children his wife bears during her marriage to him are legally his children, unless he specifically repudiates them. In modern

America, rights *in genetricem* are acquired by men at marriage—in order legally to repudiate his wife's child, a man must present before a court incontrovertible proof that he *could* not have begotten it. Not proof that he did not, but proof that he *could* not, because of physical absence.

Much as extradomestic economic rights may be attached to domestic rights, an additional set of rights may be attached to the rights *in genetricem*. These are the rights to filiate the children to the husband's social group. Filiation of children is not to be confused with their acquisition of of a surname. Our own society is an example of the situation in which a child acquires the surname of the man who has rights *in genetricem* in his mother. His father does not, for that reason, determine irrevocably his membership in any specific social group.

If it is not possible to transfer the right to filiate a woman's children, or if in the preponderant number of cases the right is not in fact transferred, then that society is likely to be described as matrilineal. If it is possible and most marriages are accompanied by the right of the man to filiate his wife's children to his social group, then that society will probably be called patrilineal.

It is now possible to note two facts: we have defined marriage in terms of the rights that can be acquired by a man in his bride at the time of the "wedding" (which in some societies, such as the Nuer of the Sudan, is a series of ceremonies stretching over a period of years). Marriage is the public recognition of the fact that the husband, and perhaps his social group, has been granted household and/or kinship rights in a woman.

SUBROLES IN MARRIAGE

It can be seen that we have factored the role of wife into four different aspects for which we shall use the rather ugly term "subrole." The various subroles may or may not be activated in any specific culture. The subroles are (1) the housewife, which is brought into being when the husband acquires domestic rights in his wife; (2) the sexual consort, which is brought into being when he acquires sexual rights: (3) the "bearer of children," which is brought into being when he acquires rights *in genetricem;* and (4) "child's *mater,*" which is brought into being when he acquires the right to filiate the child to his social group. (See Table 5.) These subroles are quite clear except for the fourth, which will require further explanation later.

So far, the subroles discussed are those of "wife." Obviously, the "ego" in discussing the roles of wife is the husband—the husband is the person that a woman is wife to. If the role of wife can be subdivided, however, the role of mother—the other role in the syndrome wife/mother, which is one of the four basic syndromes in the nuclear family—can also be subdivided.

TABLE 5. SUBROLES IN THE FAMILY

	WIFE/MOTHER SYNDROME		HUSBAND/FATHER SYNDROME	
Rights in the Woman	Mother (ego is child)	Wife (ego is Hu)	Husband (ego is Wi)	Father (ego is child)
HOUSEHOLD				
1. Domestic Rights (extra-domestic economic rights may be added in some cultural situations, leading to the "economic household")	Fosterer ♀	Housewife	Householder	Fosterer ♂
FAMILY				
2. Sexual Rights	—	Consort ♀	Consort ♂	—
3. Rights *in genetricem* (right to filiate children may be added, leading to the "jural family")	Genetrix	Bearer of children	Begetter of children	Genitor
	Mater	Child's mater	Child's pater	Pater

For the role of mother, the reciprocal is the child instead of the husband. The subrole of mother that relates to the household is the fostering female—it is she who takes care of the children, provides for some of their wants and a part of their training.

There is no mother subrole that concords with the consort subrole of the wife. Such a fact is a reflection of the universality of incest prohibitions.

The "bearer of children" subrole of the wife has as its corollary the subrole of mother, the "genetrix." A woman's obligation to bear children to her husband creates, if she is successful, the subrole of genetrix of children.

The subrole of fostering female and that of genetrix need not be played by the same woman. Stepmothers are famous—or infamous—throughout the world. This problem will be studied more closely at a later point.

If the role of "child's *mater*" is acknowledged by the society, then the mother subrole of "*mater*" is acknowledged. As we know, this is an entirely jural or legal matter. If the husband has a right to filiate his wife's child to his social group, then she becomes the mater to his children; and it may well be that *her* social group determines the standing of the child within the social group of her husband. Again, this matter will be investigated in some detail later.

When a man acquires rights in a woman, he concomitantly acquires obligations to her, which may of course be seen as the rights acquired by the woman at the time of marriage. Table 5 indicates that the husband/father syndrome can be factored into behavioral subroles that precisely equate those of wife/mother syndrome; that is, the husband who acquires domestic rights in a woman as his housewife thereby takes on obligations to her, which make him a householder. When he acquires sexual rights and she becomes his consort, he equally becomes her consort. When he acquires rights in her as a bearer of children, he assumes obligations as a begetter of children. And when he acquires the right to filiate the children of the wife, he becomes the *pater* to the children—the legal father from whom the children inherit at least some of their social positions.

The father role can be broken into subroles that are precisely congruent with the husband role in the husband/father syndrome: they consist of the fostering father, the genitor, and the *pater*.

It was, in fact, the subroles within the role of father that were first discerned by anthropologists—all the others in Table 5 have been added since that time. The first and the classical study in subdividing the role of husband is Evans-Pritchard's "Some Aspects of Marriage and the Family among the Nuer" (1945). The most important aspect of Nuer marriage is the way in which the Nuer themselves factor the role of husband. When a Nuer marries, with full bridewealth payments and full ceremonies, he acquires sexual rights, rights *in genetricem*, and rights to filiate the children. After the birth of a child, he acquires domestic rights. The situation is in no way unusual except that if he dies, he—Nuer say his "ghost"—still holds the rights to filiate children and even the rights *in genetricem*. If the woman remarries one of the kinsmen of her dead husband, which is what Nuer prefer her to do, the new "husband" has only domestic rights and sexual rights. The woman still has a duty to bear children to the ghost, and children are still counted jurally as children of the ghost. In order to keep these matters straight, Evans-Pritchard called the living husband (the holder of domestic and sexual rights) the "pro-husband" and noted that the ghost (holder of rights *in genetricem* and rights to filiate children) is still the "husband."

In this new situation, the husband/father syndrome is divided between the pro-husband and the ghost. The pro-husband is fostering father to all the children and genitor to those that are begotten after the death of the ghost; he is also householder, consort, and begetter of children. However, the ghost is the pater to the children and the child's pater to the wife; he may also have been genitor to the older children of the family.

The situation is not limited to remarriages. Nuer consider it very unfortunate for a man to die unmarried or before he has sons who will maintain his name and his position in the genealogy of the lineage. In cases in which a man dies childless, his brothers must "raise up seed to him" by begetting children on his wife. If a man dies unmarried, one of his brothers must "marry a wife to his name"—that is, the dead man is the husband, the living brother is the pro-husband. Children are, for legal purposes of inheritance and succession, children of the dead man, although they were of course begotten and nurtured by the pro-husband.

As Evans-Pritchard puts it, a "ghost-family," which is a translation of the Nuer word, contains a dead husband, a pro-husband, a wife, and the children of the wife. To the casual observer, however, this family appears to be the same as any other family in the society.

The most bizarre illustration of the factoring of the roles in the family is "woman marriage" in Africa—a type of the fictive marriage we examined above, but one that is based on considerations other than property. In a culture such as that of traditional Dahomey, a woman can acquire great wealth through trading; in order to secure her position, she may decide that she needs dependents. In such a situation, she can "marry a wife"—that is to say, she can become householder and child's pater to a girl whom she "marries." She then gives the sexual rights to another—her son or a trusted employee. The trusted employee is the genitor and may be the fostering father of the child, but the wealthy trading woman is the "pater." "Woman marriage" is not an enigma when it is examined in terms of rights and the structure of subroles.

FUNCTIONS OF THE FAMILY

Marriage is, as Malinowski remarked, the "fountainhead of kinship." A new family is brought into being with marriage—at least, a new potential family is brought into being.[2]

A corollary of the fact that a man obtains sexual rights in a woman at the time of marriage is the fact that marriage and the resultant family is, everywhere, one of the main modes by which sexual activity within the society is controlled. Unregulated sexual activity, like any other sort of unregulated activity, produces chaos. Patterns of expectations are, under conditions of no restraint, inadequate for prediction of behavior.

Sex *can* be regulated and given avenues of expression (which is the same thing) by means of many institutions. But the family is almost every-

[2] Talcott Parsons, in his discussion of the family, has phrased the matter forthrightly and succinctly: "A stable attachment of a man to a woman with inclusion of sexual relations taken for granted, almost automatically results in a family" (1952, p. 156).

where the bulwarking institution, and in many areas it is the only one recognized as legitimate. There are enough exceptions to this point to allow us firmly to state the rule or the norm. Many cultures allow certain periods of sexual freedom, either in association with ceremonial occasions dedicated to fertility and abundance or at certain stages in the life cycle. Many other societies admit nonfamilial institutionalization of sex: approved and controlled prostitution is the most obvious example, though some societies have institutionalized extramarital liaisons or homosexuality. The study of the institutionalization of sex is a subject to itself, and we cannot go further into it here save to note that every society has a certain range of permissiveness for its members to overstep the institutions. The range may be very narrow indeed: peoples such as the Gusii of Kenya and many North American Indians are extremely strict. They offer no legitimate sexual activity save that within the marriage relationship, and they are strict in disallowing deviation. Our own society recognizes the same norm, but is not nearly so strict in its demands of concurrence. At the other extreme, many societies offer their members such a wide range of sexual opportunity that the subject ceases to be particularly interesting to the actors.

The fact that a man acquires rights to children when he marries is a corollary to the fact that the family is overwhelmingly the means by which the necessity for replacement of the mortal members of the social group is met. Again, there are ways and means other than the family for human groups to recruit members. Science-fiction writers have thought of many. But in "real life" the number is limited indeed.

The two functions of the family then are regulation of sex and provision of new members of the community.

The functions of the *household* are somewhat different—again, the distinction between family and household must be maintained, even when the two may contain the same people, or be based on the same fundamental relationships. The corollary of the exchange of domestic obligations at the time of marriage means that the functions of maintaining the life of the human individuals can be satisfied. Food getting, provision of shelter and bodily comfort can be—and in technologically simple societies usually are—functions performed by the household. A better way of saying all this is that the function associated with the acquisition of domestic rights is the provision of an institution—the domestic institution—which forms a basis for division of labor required to fulfill the material and spiritual needs of members.

The household also has another vitally important function: almost everywhere it is the unit responsible for bringing up the children and teaching them the culture they must live by. This function, called "the socialization of children" by sociologists and "enculturation" by some anthropologists, is carried out by the household. In only a very few instances is any other institution held primarily responsible until the child reaches the age of six years or so.

This chapter has made several distinctions that must be kept in mind. It has distinguished kinship groups such as families from local groups such as households, and noted that families are responsible almost everywhere for control of sexual activity and recruitment of new members of society whereas households almost everywhere are charged with the basic "domestic economy" and the education and training of the young.

We have also noted that marriage is a complex phenomenon. It is the final stage of successful courtship and the initial stage of family formation. The husband-wife relationship, created at marriage, can be given many different sorts of cultural content, which means that the roles of husband and wife must be factored into several different aspects before cross-cultural comparison becomes meaningful. Some—but by no means all—of the different aspects have been examined here and summarized in Table 5. Marriage is, in short, a very complex institution.[3] In all societies much energy goes into marriage. Necessarily, then, much of the energy of social scientists must be given to it if they are to explain the ways that people live.

---

[3] "But I am not yet ready for an institution" is a quip attributed to that modern earth-mother, Mae West.

6

The household

The distinction between household and family played a prominent part in the foregoing analysis of the family. It therefore behooves us now to investigate the household further. As we have seen, the family need not live together in order to be a family. A family, in other words, cannot be defined as being a local group, for there are societies in which the family is not a local group and in which its members neither live together nor think they should live together. The family is, in short, a kinship group and must be defined on the basis of the kinship relationships (putative or real) among its members. The household, on the other hand, is a group of people who live together and form a functioning domestic unit. They may or may not constitute a family, and if they do, it may or may not be a simple nuclear family.

It is little short of astounding how many books, even modern ones, define the family as "a man, a woman, and their children"—and then add a rider, "who live together." The problems in such a definition should be obvious. There are two criteria, and any definition with two criteria creates room for four classes:

1) Those examples in which both A and B are present
2) Examples in which A is present, B absent
3) Examples in which B is present, A absent
4) Examples in which both A and B are absent

Furthermore, the two criteria of such a definition do not even belong to the same universe of discourse—as we have seen, one is a matter of kinship, the other of propinquity.

The difficulty probably arises from the fact that in the American folk image of kinship relationships there is a word that covers both criteria (a different matter from allowing a confused situation to occur in an analytical image). The American word "home," until it was commercially vulgarized and despoiled, meant "a family living in a household." The American morality declares that families *should* form households and it provides us with a word—home—for the desired result. The concept "home," however, is not part of the armory of analytical social science (except as it may be applied in our own culture).

Put another way: even though persons depend as much on kith as on kin, the two are separate. Indeed, *Webster's Collegiate Dictionary* defines kith as "familiar friends, neighbors, and relatives collectively" whereas kin are "one's relatives, collectively." Thus, the two ideas are not antithetical: they are merely defined by different criteria, and therefore whether they overlap is beside the point—certainly it is no more than empirical fact.

RESIDENCE CLASSIFICATION

However, it is true that a husband and wife usually live with each other and their children usually live with them. Such families must settle somewhere in space. That being the case, the positions in space occupied by families can be classified. This sort of classification—called "residence classification"—is one of the oldest problems, and by now one of the thorniest, in social anthropology.

The earliest method—and until recently it remained unchallenged—of classifying residence was to consider the place at which a newly married couple established a household vis-a-vis their parents. The couple was said to be "patrilocal" if they established a household with or in the area of the husband's parents, and "matrilocal" if they established the household with or in the area of the wife's parents.

Several serious objections have been put forward to this mode of classification. First of all, the two adjectives were often attached to the noun "marriage" instead of to "residence." Secondly, someone asked, "What about modern Westerners?" Are we "matrilocal" or "patrilocal"? The answer, uncomfortably enough, tended to be, "We are civilized." Obviously, thus, there were some instances that did not fit the dual classification. Third, the terms did not distinguish between those instances in which a newly married pair established a new household near that of the parents of one spouse, and those instances in which the pair joined the already existent household of that spouse. Last, and perhaps most unfortunate of all, the terms apply to a new residence formed at marriage from the standpoint of the potential *children* of that marriage, not from the standpoint of the spouses. The confusion was complete.[1]

---

[1] In fact, the confusion got to the point that the sixth edition of *Notes and Queries in Anthropology* (Royal Anthropological Institute, 1961) dismissed the whole problem in a footnote: "Inquiries should be made as to the residential location, temporary and permanent, of married couples. The definition of marriage as patrilocal when the couple lives in the locality of the husband's parents, and matrilocal when the couple lives in the locality of the wife's parents, is misleading and should be avoided."

It was in the 1940s that a wholesale attack on the problem was begun. In fact, there were several attacks, and they are still going on. They were not and are not now coordinated attacks.

One of the earliest thrusts came from a German anthropologist turned Australian, Leonhard Adam (1948), who suggested that the terms matrilocal and patrilocal should be replaced by the terms "uxorilocal" and "virilocal"—thus getting rid of the confusion of generations. A few persons, notably some British anthropologists, have followed Adam's suggestion, but most have discovered that once the new terms had been introduced both the new and the old became indispensable, for they do not have reference to the same phenomenon. Murdock (1959) says correctly enough that the term "virilocal" does not distinguish residence with the husband's father, residence with the husband's mother's brother, and residence in a new household established by the husband himself. One need not, however, agree with his recommendation to abandon the term.

A further thrust came from Professor Mischa Titiev (1943) who attacked another weakness: the confusion between a new household in the area of the parents of one spouse and entrance of the married pair into an already existing household. The important point, he noted, was whether the newlyweds established an independent household of their own or merged with an already existing residential unit. There is obviously a fundamental difference in the content of relationships among kinsmen, especially affines, if the couple merely move to the quarter in the village of either the groom or the bride, or if the newlyweds are expected to move into a household already occupied by kinsmen of one or the other.

To allay this objection, Titiev enunciated a new principle: that of "unilocal" residence. Unilocal residence means that the married pair moves into the already existing household of one spouse or the other. Thus, there is what Titiev calls unilocal matrilocal and unilocal patrilocal, as well as "neat" matri- and patrilocal residence, which means the newly married couple establishes residence merely in the vicinity of the parents of one or the other.

Titiev points out that if unilocal-patrilocal residence is consistently practiced, the result is inevitably the formation of local groups containing a man, his sons, grandsons, and so on, together with their respective wives and unmarried daughters. Men form a permanent group; women leave their groups.

Some rather serious difficulties remain however: When is a residence a new residence and when is it an extension of the old residence? Among the Tiv, for example, the first time a man marries, he establishes an unconditionally unilocal-virilocal residence; that is, he brings his wife into his mother's hut, which is a part of the cluster of huts in his father's homestead. The wife joins the production and consumption unit: she farms with the husband's mother and cooks with her. Except that the men usually eat separately, the group also forms a commensal unit. More realistically, the bride and her mother-in-law certainly form a single cooking unit—this practice is unilocal residence with a vengeance.

However, when the wife has been present for a year or two, or at least when she bears a child, her husband builds her a hut, usually behind that of his mother. It may be at the same time, it may be later, that the young wife begins to cook separately. But the separation does occur—especially if another wife is brought into the husband's mother's hut—either the wife of the husband's brother or a second wife of the husband himself. Now, the question arises, are they still unilocal? They are very close together, there is always very close cooperation—points that make the question even more pertinent. Obviously, it is necessary to set up some very specific set of criteria: some suggestions might be commensality, common food preparation, a common house. A scale of "unilocality" might, thus, be established, although so far it has not been.

Still another attack on the problem of residence came from Murdock (1949). His egress from *cul de sac* was by a ladder of terminology: a term for every different sort of residence he could isolate. He rejected uxorilocal and virilocal, and accepted and retained the terms (1) matrilocal and (2) patrilocal. He added further that some societies permit a married couple to live near the parents of either spouse. The choice is usually made on such factors as the relative wealth or status of the two families or on mere personal preferences. Such a situation Murdock calls (3) bilocal.

He uses the term (4) neolocal for those situations in which a newly married couple forms its own household independent of the parents of either. Murdock notes that this rule is often confused with patrilocal residence in the literature; it can be added that the confusion is undoubtedly due to the undesirable generation skip in the terminology.

A fifth alternative is (5) avunculocal residence. In this instance the newly married couple go to live with the groom's mother's brother. The Trobriand Islanders are the best recorded example of avunculocal residence. Here both man and woman live with their parents until marriage, at which time they go to live with the husband's mother's brother. Since the boy's mother went to live with *her* husband's mother's brother, and since only Trobriander chiefs practice cross-cousin marriage, their residence can only be described as avunculocal. If there were cross-cousin marriage with the mother's brother's daughter, avunculocal residence and matrilocal residence could not be distinguished, obviously.

Murdock then points out that there are some instances in which the residence rules cannot be fitted into these five categories. The most common is that instance in which the couple lives with the parents of the bride until a child is born, after which they move to the home of the parents of the groom. Murdock calls this form (6) matri-patrilocal. He has also included the peculiar residence form of the Dobuans—annual movement from the area of the wife to that of the husband, and back—as matri-patrilocal. These six forms of residence are, in Murdock's scheme, one of the major dimensions of social organization. He has not exhausted them, however. We might, on his basis, call the Tiv situation patri-neolocal: the changes can be rung widely.

ETHNOGRAPHICAL UTILITY OF RESIDENCE TERMS

The Murdock terms—and a few others that can be made in analogy to them, such as amitalocal meaning residence with the husband's father's sister—are of considerable utility in carrying out comparative studies. However, their utility in ethnographies was very cogently questioned by Ward Goodenough and John Fischer in the middle 1950s. These two anthropologists (one from Yale, one from Harvard) both worked on the tiny island and Romonum, in Truk, independently but within three years of each other. Both took censuses, and both classified households and married couples on the basis of residence. To their consternation, they came out with very different analyses of what was to all intents and purposes the same situation (Table 6).

TABLE 6 RESIDENCE PROBLEMS IN TRUK

	GOODENOUGH		FISCHER	
TYPE OF RESIDENCE	CASES	PERCENT	CASES	PERCENT
Matrilocal	46	71	36	58
Patrilocal	1	1.5	20	32
Avunculocal	10	15	0	—
Neolocal	4	6	6	10
Other arrangement	3	5	0	—
Ambiguous	1	1.5	0	—
TOTAL	65	100	62	100

Both men were shocked that two fully trained and highly competent anthropologists could come out with such basically different answers to the same situation—in which fewer than 300 people were involved. Goodenough classified the Trukese as matrilocal; Fischer as ambilocal. The shock was sufficient to send both of them into a detailed study of residence, to the lasting benefit of the entire science of social anthropology.

Goodenough and Fischer compared their censuses; the changes that took place in the three years elapsing between their periods of fieldwork accounted for only a minor portion of the differences in recording. Obviously, the discrepancies arose "from an honest difference in how to interpret the data." They found two possible reasons for the differences: (1) "The established definitions of residence forms are so phrased as to make unclear how they should be applied to the enumeration of individual residences." (2) The two investigators both used census material, and each used other material in addition in order to arrive at his selection and assignments to a category. This "other material" differed between the two.

It is Goodenough's claim (1956) that terms like matrilocal and patrilocal are of a very high order of abstraction. He compares them to such linguistic terms as "agglutinating" or "inflecting" that are used in making gross distinctions, but that cannot be used intelligently until the grammatical processes have first been fully analyzed. He continues the analogy with linguistics and shows that linguistics was loosened from the bonds of *a priori* assumption only when it realized that the terms satisfactory for comparative purposes did little but bind the hands and minds of students of specific languages. Every individual language must first be handled theoretically, and then this theory—rather than the so-called "facts"—could be used in creating comparative theory. In other words, to go into a society with a ready-made set of categories, or one derived from comparative studies, and try to force that society into one or more of the *a priori* pigeonholes may seriously distort the information. In the case of residence, it will at best be an oversimplification and may create serious distortion. Goodenough concludes that the ethnographer must discover what actual choices a member of the society can make, in his own terms.

That is to say, in doing fieldwork, the ethnographer must ask the local people what determines their residence choices, and he must understand the situation in their terms. "Patrilocal" is, thus, a term in an analytical system. No matter what its effectiveness in comparative studies, it is clearly not a sufficiently effective framework to allow one to do careful reporting of field research. Goodenough's charges lead to a conclusion we have already encountered—that a useful analytical category may not be, in itself, sufficient to describe the usages of a single culture, because in order to be sufficiently broad to allow meaningful comparison, too much of the folk evaluation may have to be stripped away.

In re-evaluating residence on Truk, Goodenough noted that when a married Trukese man and woman make up their minds where they are going to live, they do not even consider setting up a new household for themselves, but rather always assume they will join a household already in existence. The sort of households found there are those based on the extended family, itself with a matrilineal lineage at its core. The point, then, is to ask "Whose lineage do we live with"?

However, some lineages are recognized that are not the core of recognized extended families, and hence some people do not belong directly to a village community based ultimately on lineage. Since a couple can live in the lineage-based community of either spouse, if one of the two belongs to a lineage without a community, the issue is settled out of hand. But if the lineages of both are associated with communities, they must make a choice. There are, moreover, two "second choices" that can be made in appropriate circumstances: the husband's own father's lineage, or his wife's father's lineage. Goodenough found these rules to apply: (1) "Other things being equal, as long as one party to the marriage belongs to a lineage which is localized, this lineage will be chosen before joining the other's father's lineage. Resort to a father's lineage of either spouse is, therefore, a fairly rare occurrence. Other things being equal, moreover, a couple will regularly choose to live with the extended family associated with the wife's lineage rather than that associated with the husband's" (p. 31). In short, residence with the wife's extended family is the first choice, with the husband's second, with the wife's father's next, and with the husband's father's last. Goodenough then gives a detailed account of some circumstances that can upset this choice pattern (p. 32). Most importantly, however, he has pointed out that when Trukese decide where they are going to live, they do it on the basis of distance from the families of the spouses, the amount of land available in the communities of the husband's and wife's lineages, and similar practical considerations. They distinctly do not make it by choosing whether they will live with the parents of one or the other. Therefore, he concludes, the categories of the comparative, analytical system are inadequate for the exigencies of ethnographic description and theory.

OTHER CONTRIBUTIONS TO RESIDENCE THEORY

To give another example of a set of principles by means of which the people of a society make up their minds where they will live, Goodenough took his fieldwork from the Nakanai of New Britain, and found that again there was a commonly recognized pattern, plus some factors that obscured it (Goodenough, 1961). The pattern was fairly simple though not an easy one to discover: in spite of the fact that the society is matrilineal, every man takes his wife to live in the village in which his father is living, so long as the father is living. After the father's death, the couple may stay on where they are, particularly if the father was without sister's sons. More often, however, the couple moves to join the husband's immediate matrilineal lineage where he has heredity land rights.

There are several forces that bring about exceptions to the general rule in Nakanai: if a man's father dies before he marries, he will move to the village of whatever kinsman carried out the father's duties at the time of his marriage. Again, it may also be that dead kinsmen may be as important as living kinsmen in determining where one decides to live.

As a result of the mix-up in interpretation between Goodenough and Fischer, Goodenough turned back to the material and established the point once and for all that the ethnographer must interpret his data in the light of the folk image before it is possible to compare. The best way to make a comparison, then, is to correlate lists of residence principles such as those elicited for Truk and Nakanai, with other aspects of the societies. Few ethnographers have followed this suggestion, for unfortunately few of them have adequate data to determine the bases of choice as Goodenough did.

Fischer (1958), too, has made an important contribution to residence theory as a result of the disagreement. His suggestion was that anthropologists apply the locality terms to individuals rather than to married couples. Fischer suggested that every person has a sponsor in the household, and it is his relationship to his sponsor that determines the type of residence in which he lives. Thus, when a woman moves in with her husband, the husband is her sponsor, and she is living in virilocal residence; if the husband is himself living in the compound of his father, he is living in patrilocal residence. The ethnographer must, in order to determine the residence, take a census of the population and determine the residence mode of each individual. The possible types are given in the following table:[2]

TABLE 7

TYPE	KIN SPONSOR
I. Neolocal	Self
II. Consanguineolocal	Any consanguine
A. Patrilocal	Fa or male agnate of ascending generation
B. Matrilocal	Mo or female uterine kinsman of ascending generation
C. Filiolocal	Son or son's son
D. Filialocal	Daughter or daughter's daughter

[2] This table is reprinted from J. L. Fischer (1958, p. 513). I have modified the order slightly from Fischer's original and have changed the terminology on two points: Fischer consistently used "patrilineal relative" to mean "agnate" and "matrilineal relative" to mean "uterine kinsman."

TABLE 7 (Continued)

TYPE		KIN SPONSOR
	E. Avunculocal	MoBr or male uterine kinsman of ascending generation
	F. Amitalocal	FaSi or female agnate of ascending generation
	G. Fratrilocal	Br or male parallel cousin of own generation
	H. Sororilocal	Si or female parallel cousin of own generation
	I. Nepotilocal	SiSo or other male uterine kinsman of descending generation
	J. Heterolocal	Any other consanguine
III. Affinolocal		An affinal relative (almost invariably spouse)
	A. Virilocal	Husband
	B. Uxorilocal	Wife

In short, Fischer's question is: "Who lives in the household now and what was his reason for joining it?" That is, which is his closest kinsman in the household, and what are the kinship ties that brought him there? It has the disadvantage that the question must be asked separately for which relationship brought the person there and which ones keep him there —a source of possible misunderstanding.

A somewhat simpler and more inclusive classification can be made if the distinction between family and household and the eight basic family relationships are kept in mind. We can then ask another question altogether: In the formation of households, which of the basic relationships is considered the most fundamental?

We can put the question operationally: If two or more different kinship relationships within the household come into conflict, which is the last to be broken in a statistically significant number of cases? That is to say, if a man's father and his wife cannot get on, and he must, for purposes of residence, break one relationship or the other, which one survives? That relationship can be called the pivotal family relationship for domestic grouping in that society.

It is possible to find, in various societies recorded in the literature, households built on five of the eight basic relationships. I have not discovered— but see no reason that there should not be—a society that stresses the mother-son link in the creation of households. Households based on brother-brother relationships are usually (but not necessarily) indistinguishable from those based on father-son relationships, and similarly those based on sister-sister relationships are indistinguishable from those based on mother-daughter relationships. Both are, in any case, possible of inclusion in the category of households based on a more general classification of sibling relationships.

The five basic situations,[3] then are:

1. Societies in which the households are based predominantly on the husband-wife relationship
2. Those based on the father-son relationship
3. Those based on the mother-daughter relationship
4. Those based on the father-daughter relationship
5. Those based on the sibling relationship

HOUSEHOLDS BASED ON THE HUSBAND-WIFE RELATIONSHIP

According to this classification, the residence patterns of Western civilization are overwhelmingly based on the husband-wife relationship. In the popular lore and beliefs of Western culture, little but difficulty awaits the married couple "unfortunate" enough to have to live with the parents of one or the other spouse. Westerners are predominantly "neolocal." Further, it is the norm that in a dispute between a person's spouse and parent, he must take the side of the spouse. Further, parents, in determining modes of action for raising their children, try to work out methods and techniques for presenting a solid front. Among Westerners, the husband-wife relationship forms the basis of household grouping, and in almost all classes the "normal" mode of living is for the married partners to live together, with no one save their young children.

Yet, not all of the societies whose values incline them to households based on the husband-wife relationship can be classed so decisively as "neolocal." The Hausa of Northern Nigeria are an example (Smith, 1954, p. 21; Dry, 1950). Here marriage is virilocal, the woman coming to live with the man. Usually it is also patrilocal—the couple lives in the husband's father's compound, especially if it is the man's first marriage. Thus the core of the residential unit is a group of males linked by agnatic kinship ties. However, in middle-class Hausa society, a man soon after marriage, seeks to set up a household of his own. His reasons are usually expressed in terms of women: the wives of the household head look on a daughter-in-law as someone who will now do all the work for them; this attitude is resented by the new wife. The husband then has the unenviable task of resolving the quarrels between his wife and his mother. Therefore, he is anxious to take the first opportunity to keep them apart. Yet, because *purdah* is extreme in this stratum of Hausa society, the young man need move only a short distance to accomplish his purpose. From the standpoint of the village or quarter, the marriage can still be regarded as "patrilocal," even though different households have been established. The man and his father still

---

[3] It is also possible to base households on secondary relationships, particularly the mother's brother–sister's son relationship, and less commonly the father's sister–brother's daughter relationship.

cooperate in agricultural activities, even though each is nominally independent and a new "domestic group" is established.

HOUSEHOLDS BASED ON THE FATHER-SON RELATIONSHIP

The Tiv of central Nigeria can also be described as "virilocal and usually patrilocal": all wives move to their husbands' compounds at marriage, and in the case of about 83 percent of males, that compound is in the husband's agnatic lineage area, and the men in it are principally his agnates. In twenty-six months' fieldwork among the Tiv, we found only three instances of uxorilocal marriage (one of those in official records of a murder trial in which a man killed someone for jeering at him for living uxorilocally). Moreover Tiv men seldom—almost never—move into compounds of their own while their fathers are still alive. The Tiv compound, spatially based, like the Hausa compounds, on the genealogy of the polygynous family (Bohannan, 1954, Appendix A) normally splits a year or so after the death of the compound head, or occasionally following disputes between brothers or other nonlineal kinsmen. The difference from the Hausa becomes apparent when we realize that it never occurs to most Tiv to leave their fathers' compounds should their wives dispute with other members of the compound. In Hausa society, if mother-in-law and daughter-in-law cannot get along, a new household is established. In Tiv society, if a wife cannot get along with her husband's mother or kinsmen, her marriage is dissolved. Tiv say that you can get a new wife any time but you have only one set of parents; they hold that the gravest fault a wife can commit is to split brothers. The Tiv father (and, after him, the mother) is always right; a man almost always takes his parents' side against his wife. These facts have a profound effect on the settlement pattern of the two societies.

HOUSEHOLDS BASED ON THE MOTHER-DAUGHTER RELATIONSHIP

One of the best-known and best documented examples of a society whose residence norms stress the mother-daughter relationship is that of the Hopi of Arizona (Eggan, 1950; Titiev, 1944). Here the houses, or pueblo rooms, are owned by women and handed down from mother to daughter. Men, though they build them, do not own houses. A man considers his sister's house his real home and he leaves his ritual objects there when he takes his mundane property to the house of his wife. He is peripheral to both his sister's and his wife's household.

HOUSEHOLDS BASED ON THE FATHER-DAUGHTER RELATIONSHIP

This type is the most ephemeral of all, and may be found to depend on some other basic relationship, when more research is done. Like domestic groups based on the mother-daughter relationship, those based on a father-daughter relationship tend to be associated with uxorilocality or matrilocality or both. However, societies that stress the father-daughter relationship for establishing residence seem always to be characterized by a strong economic or subsistence relationship between the father-in-law and son-in-law. Opler (1941) notes that among the Apache the bride and her kinswomen build the new house near the home of her parents. One of the fundamental ideas behind the organization of economy assumes the close cooperation of the sons-in-law. Because of a man's economic obligations to his wife's father it is almost necessary for him to live in the vicinity of his wife's parents. Sometimes, also, a man's kinsmen follow him and establish their homes with his affines. Classification of this instance will obviously vary with the definition of "household" and we are nowhere given the Apache definition.

HOUSEHOLDS BASED ON A SIBLING RELATIONSHIP

Finally, there are those comparatively rare societies in which the household group tends to be based primarily on a sibling relationship. Professor Fortes found an example in Ashanti. When he was working there, he noticed that in Ashanti villages about an hour before dusk, girls were to be seen hurrying in all directions, carrying large pots of cooked food. One child often carried food out of one house, and a few minutes later another carried an equivalent amount of food into it. The food, Professor Fortes found, was being taken from houses where the childrens' mothers lived to those where their fathers lived. Husband and wife, obviously, need not live in the same household group; the children usually divide their time between these two households. Although modern educated Ashanti live in households that differ little from those of Europe and America, the Ashanti of the villages still live in these sibling households. Dr. Fortes' analysis of his extensive genealogies shows that the norm in the villages is for the dwelling group to be a single cognatic group with a few affines: most often, a group of brothers and sisters, with perhaps the sons and daughters of the sisters (Fortes, Steel, and Ady, 1947).

Another example, even more complex, of households formed on the basis of sibling groups is provided by the "predominantly matrilocal" Yao of Nyasaland, studied by Professor Clyde Mitchell. Here the women of matrilineage form a localized group whereas men are dispersed. Within any matrilineage group, groups of uterine sisters are differentiated from each other, *"but always in reference to a man who is usually their eldest brother"* (Mitchell, 1951; italics added). It is around this relationship of a man to his sisters that domestic groups are organized—the groups Dr. Mitchell calls "sorority groups." Most men (all except those acting as caretakers of their group of sisters) live matrilocally, even though only a small portion of their time is spent in the village into which they are married. Men caring for "sorority groups" (composed of their sisters and sisters' husbands and children) take their wives to live with such groups. The domestic group, or hamlet of four or five huts, is thus based primarily on the sibling relationship of sisters to an elder brother. Dr. Mitchell says specifically that "the bonds between brother and sister are much stronger than those between husband and wife," and cites a dispute in which a woman took her brother's side against her husband, "though she must have known that this might lead to divorce" (1951, pp. 330-331).

Just as it is often difficult—indeed, undesirable—to categorize a society as being "patrilocal" or "matrilocal," it is also sometimes difficult to categorize a society as building its domestic groups on a specific relationship. The Nuer form a special and interesting case. They are what, in the Murdock classification, would be called "matri-patrilocal." In the early stages of a marriage, the father-daughter relationship is stressed, and the bride stays at the home of her father. Then, when the first-born has been weaned the husband builds his wife a hut in his father's homestead (Evans-Pritchard, 1951, p. 73). It is now the husband-wife relationship that becomes dominant. Husband and wife often live with the husband's father, but may move about, living with the kinsmen of either. In other words, the household is established on weaning the first child, not at marriage.

The distinction to be drawn is clear: the family is a social group that may or may not be a local, spatial group. If it is, it will almost of necessity choose one or the other relationship as the primary or basic one on which to build households. It is possible to make a supplementary classification of residence patterns by determining the values and norms for residence in this regard, and the proportion of households within the society which conform to it.

FUNCTIONS OF THE HOUSEHOLD

It should be repeated that the household usually functions as the unit that fulfills the specific physical needs of the human organism: the provision of food and shelter. It is, moreover, the household that assumes almost everywhere the responsibility for bringing up the children, and implanting in them the values, ideas, and techniques of the culture. The household is, in short, the primary institution of education. Both consumption and education, obviously, may be carried out by supplementary institutions as well. And, most importantly, the household can assume any function. The household can be the producer as well as the consumer; it can be the basic political unit, the religious congregation, or whatever.

The household is well-nigh universal, and everywhere it bears the greatest load—one might even say that it is the residual unit. Every function necessary for people or for society that is not performed by some special institution is performed by the household.

The relationships that go into forming households also go into forming all sorts of attitudes toward life. Hsu (1963) has illustrated that Americans not merely build their households on the husband-wife relationship, but build their whole value system and morality on it. Similarly, what gave traditional Chinese social organization its stability—and it may be that the Communist Revolution in China will prove in the long run to be less drastic than is thought, because of this very stability—was that the father-son relationships not merely formed the heart of the household, but also the central idea of the religion, the core of the outlook and the basic premise in the evaluation of all social activities. Indian civilization, he found, is rent precisely because such great prominence is given morally to the mother-son relationship when the household is father-son dominated.

The household, divorced from family considerations, is an inadequately studied institution. It may well be that a classification of societies on the basis of how many and which functions are carried out by the household, and the moral dimensions given to the basic family relationships that lie behind each would provide a sensible scale for the complexity of society.

7

Extended families and polygamous families

THE NUCLEAR FAMILY is in most societies a unit in itself, but it may also be a building block for more complex family arrangements. These arrangements are of two types: extended families created by increasing the number of roles in a syndrome of kinship roles, and polygamous families created by recognizing roles of shared sexuality, therefore increasing the number of roles recognized.

EXTENDED FAMILIES

A man is, in a nuclear family, either the husband/father or the son/brother. Obviously, however, most men during their lifetimes play out both of these syndromes of roles, just as most women are wives and mothers as well as daughters and sisters. Thus, any given person is likely to link two nuclear families, in one of which he is spouse/parent and in the other of which he is child/sibling.

The overlapping of two primary syndromes in a single person, to create a secondary syndrome of husband/father/son/brother (or its feminine equivalent), is the basis of the group that is called the extended family or grandfamily.

The English phrase "starting one's own family" is sometimes used of marriage, sometimes of the first pregnancy. However, "starting one's own family " does not make one any the less a member of one's parents' family. In order to keep these two aspects of any individual's family relationships distinct, anthropologists traditionally use the label "natal family" for that nuclear family into which one is born and in which one is child and brother. The family in which one is spouse and parent is called the "conjugal family."

Obviously, every family is *somebody's* natal family and somebody else's conjugal family. If one thinks of the two families in the first person no confusion can exist: my natal family is the one in which I am child; my conjugal family is the one in which I am spouse. My natal family is my father's conjugal family, and my conjugal family is my child's natal family[1] The term "nuclear" family is an analytical term, which does not require any "ego"—a personal viewpoint or place to start in describing a genealogical system. The terms "natal" and "conjugal" family refer to the same family, seen from the standpoint of the roleplayers within it. The

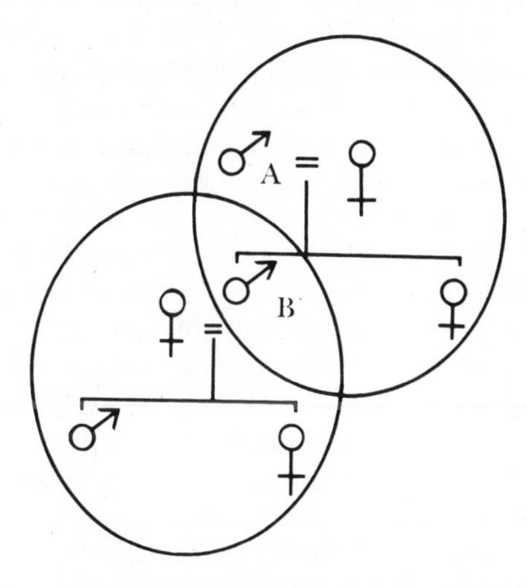

FIGURE 6 Extended Families

nuclear family illustrated in Figure 6 is A's conjugal family and B's natal family.

The ego in computing kinship groups is similar to the ego in describing kinship terms—it is a reference point to which all relationships are referred. "Nuclear" family has no ego. "Natal" family is a nuclear family with an ego.

The extended family shown in Figure 6 is an "agnatic" extended family because the linking of the two nuclear families is through a male. That is to say, two of the direct descent relationships—those of father-child—are called "agnatic" because of the sex of the parent in the relationship is male. The feminine equivalent is the "uterine" link—that between mother and child. Both are postulated on the sex of the parent. Thus, an extended family can be based on uterine links, agnatic links, or both (the latter usually called "bilateral").

---

[1] It is common, particularly in the older literature, to encounter the term "family of orientation" for the natal family and "family of procreation" for the conjugal family. These terms are difficult because they harbor a change of mode: one is passive, the other active. The family of orientation is passive—it is the one in which I am oriented; the family of procreation is active—it is the family I procreate. The two are easily confused by transposing the mode. I have experienced so much difficulty in teaching these terms that I have given up trying; they should, however, be recognized.

AFFINAL SECONDARY RELATIONSHIPS

The grandfamily adds a third generation to the nuclear family, through the device of compounding syndromes of roles in the middle generation. The result is also, however, that a large new group of secondary relationships is added—these relationships depend on a combination or chain of primary links. Some of these new secondary relationships are affinal—those between parents-in law and children-in-law. Others of the new secondary relationships are lineal—those between grandparents and grandchildren. Still others of the new relationships are collateral —those between cousins, who are children of siblings.

First to be considered among these new relationships are the additional affines. The grandfamily creates new sets of affinal relationships based on combinations of relationships of descent and sexuality:

WiMo–DaHu	HuMo–SoWi
WiFa–DaHu	HuFa–SoWi

The so-called "in-law" relationships are almost universally acknowledged as difficult; their content is usually hedged about with formalized joking, respect, or avoidance.

There is, for example, potential strain in the relationship between a woman and her mother-in-law. American society solves this problem—insofar as it does solve it—in the same way it handles other tricky relationships between adults: by personalization. The roles to the relationship are given a minimal definition, and the two women are required to create a satisfactory personal relationship on the basis of their good will and their own personalities. In the cases in which this solution works at all, it tends to work well. In many cases, however, it does not work at all, and the relationship becomes one of total avoidance. Lack of any ideal role content leaves nothing else to fall back on. At the other extreme is the highly codified relationship between mother-in-law and daughter-in-law as it occurs in most patriarchal families: the prerevolutionary Chinese family or the patriarchal family of the Old Testament both provide vivid examples. Ruth's cleaving to her mother-in-law is a case in point; it is also one difficult to understand in modern America without special background in the culture with which Ruth and Naomi lived. Modern American interpretation of the story is usually based on the supposed relationship between Ruth and her dead husband; when Ruth's "thy people shall be my people" is quoted, it is almost always quoted in a context of husband-wife relationship or as a hymn to everlasting sexual love. Ruth's personal regard for her dead husband was beside the point in the original story—she was being a good daughter-in-law in a society in which the role of daughter-in-law was minutely surveyed.

Similarly, a woman's relationship with her father-in-law is subject to strain because of the fear most peoples either express or rigidly do not express that some mention or action concerning sex will come between them. This situation, in which the specific absence of sex is important, is considered artificial and certainly presents more of a strain than the approved presence of sex or its being beside the point. The situation is most often met by one of two patterns: physical avoidance between the two persons playing the roles of father-in-law and daughter-in-law, or else a relationship hedged round by very precise requirements and very minute regulations of behavior.

Similar avoidance or carefully controlled behavior obtains in many societies between a man and his wife's mother. The old anthropological term "mother-in-law avoidance" has percolated deep into the modern Western cultures because it is immediately pertinent to some of the West's most deep-seated personal problems. Any anthropologist from outside would note the pronounced mother-in-law avoidance patterns of American society; the alternatives are formalization (never very comfortable for Americans) or personalization. The terms of address used by American men toward their mothers-in-law (what proportion use the given name?) reveal much in this matter.

The wife's mother is the butt of jokes in most societies. Certainly, she provides some of the West's most stalwart bromides. The Tiv of West Africa sing bawdy songs about mothers-in-law while working in groups of men; but in the presence of his mother-in-law every Tiv practices very precise and curtailed deportment.

The relationship between a man and his father-in-law is seldom so difficult, and is not recognized so widely by especially prescribed behavior.

These adjacent generation affinal relationships are important everywhere that the extended family is recognized—even if, as among ourselves, they are given little or no functional importance. In societies in which the extended family becomes the basis for household formation, these relationships may become pivotal in the workings of the household. The difficulties experienced by a bride with her mother-in-law in the Orient or in parts of Africa form the basis both of drama and novel. Indeed, such difficulties may lie behind a high proportion of female suicides in those countries.

LINEAL SECONDARY RELATIONSHIPS

The secondary relationships between lineal kinsmen of alternate generations is of a completely different sort; there are few relationships possible within the extended family in which so little tension is generated. The possible alternate generation lineal relationships are the following:

SoSo–FaFa	DaSo–MoFa
SoSo–FaMo	DaDa–MoFa

SoDa–FaFa DaSo–MoMo
SoDa–FaMo DaDa–MoMo

The changes in cultural content that can be rung on these eight relationships are, of course, tremendous.

Grandparents can be mentors without being disciplinarians, so long as parents are present. For this reason, the grandparents and grandchildren are often found in league against the members of the intermediate generation. It is further true that to have grandchildren rounds off a life, as it is envisioned in most societies. Being a grandparent allows a person to see the life cycle from three points of view within it: his own advanced age, the parenthood of his child (which he has himself experienced), and the childhood of his grandchild (which he experienced himself, then guided his child through, and now at one remove is seeing his grandchild through). Grandparenthood is a living opportunity to sum up life as it is seen in any culture. The "merging of the alternate generations" comes from a grandparent's realization of the meaning of his culture, and of the child's opportunity to see adult roles without interfering authority patterns. Even in patriarchal families, where the grandfather is the authority over all, he is not the direct socializing authority on the child, even though he may later come to represent it.

A word should be said about the relationship of children to great grandparents, but only a word because it is seldom important in actual fact. The Ashanti of West Africa call the great grandchild "grand-child-don't-touch-my-ear," for if a person's ear is touched by a great grandchild, it is said, he will die. This relationship is seldom given cultural importance, however, because it is rarely found in any statistically predominant number of cases.

It is not until we get into the matter of shared descent, however, that the complexity of the grandfamily becomes truly awesome. In a three-generational system, there are collaterals of the same generation and collaterals of adjacent generations. The possible secondary relationships between collaterals of adjacent generations are:

MoBr–SiSo FaBr–BrSo
MoBr–SiDa FaBr–BrDa
MoSi–BrSo FaSi–SiSo
MoSi–BrDa FaSi–SiDa

It is seldom that all of these possible relationships within a grandfamily are in fact found to be of importance. The difference again derives from whether the agnatic or the uterine links are emphasized, or whether there are nonkinship criteria such as residence for limiting the behavior patterns.

Within the junior generation of a grandfamily, there are ten possible secondary relationships that can be divided into two overall groups:

Parallel Cousins	*Cross Cousins*
FaBrSo–FaBrSo	FaSiSo–MoBrSo
FaBrSo–FaBrDa	FaSiDa–MoBrDa
FaBrDa–FaBrDa	FaSiSo–MoBrDa
MoSiSo–MoSiSo	FaSiDa–MoBrSo
MoSiSo–MoSiDa	
MoSiDa–MoSiDa	

Grandfamilies, when they form the basis for social grouping, particularly when they form households, are extremely complex forms of social organization and allow enormous cultural variety in behavioral content.

It would be possible to add an additional generation or even two generations to this pattern; to do so would create a model of even greater complexity, but fortunately one that would not be very helpful for analytical purposes at the present time.

POLYGAMOUS FAMILIES

Whereas extended families are created by the addition of syndromes to one another, polygamous families are created by the concurrent repetition of the same roles by the same person. An extended family is based on the fact that one man is both son/brother and spouse/father. A polygamous family is based on the fact that he may be spouse/father in two nuclear families at the same time.

Obviously, it is not possible to be a son or daughter or a brother or sister in more than one family. (Half siblings complicate the matter, as we shall see below, but do not affect the generalization.) It is, however, possible to be spouse and parent to two or more families at the same time. That statement is unequivocally true for males—it is possible for a man to have two or more wives and father two or more sets of children. Women can equally easily have two or more husbands—but women cannot in the same way as men have two separate sets of children (unless it be serially).

There are two sorts of polygamy (the word means plural marriage in Greek). The situation in which a man may, according to the rules of his society, have more than one wife at a time is known as polygyny (plural women). That which results when a woman may have two or more husbands is called polyandry (plural men).

POLYGYNY

There are two common ways of viewing a situation of polygyny: one is to say that two matricentric families are attached to the same male (A in Figure 7); the other is to say that two nuclear families share husband/father (B in Figure 7). A "polygynous family" results when two nuclear

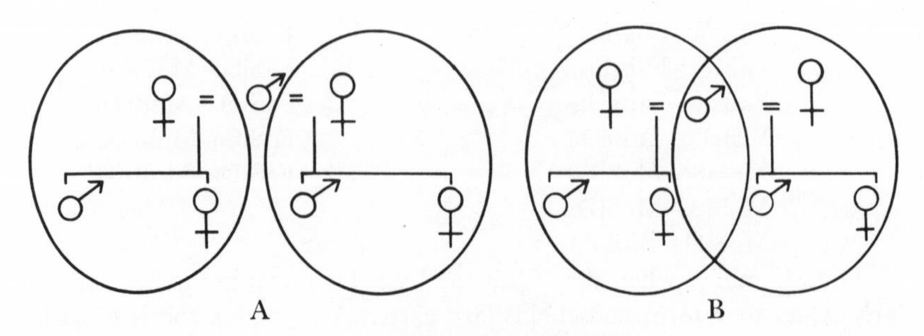

FIGURE 7 Polygynous Families

families are conjoined by one man's being husband/father in each.Besides containing all the relationships of the nuclear family (repeated as many times as there are wives), the polygynous family exhibits some new types of relationships: first and most obvious is a relationship based on shared sexuality—the relationship of co-wives. Second, and perhaps most troublesome, is the relationship of limited shared descent—the relationships of half siblings. Third, and usually of limited significance, there is a secondary relationship between a man's children and those of his wives who are not their mothers.

If a polygynous family is to work, there must be some sort of a relationship between the two women who are wives of the husband. In those societies that have been most successful in institutionalizing polygyny, the roles of this relationship have come to have a very precise content. That is to say, the behavior expected of a good co-wife is known to all. Women do not leave it to chance to get on with their co-wives; rather, a set of rules comes to be the norm of the relationship. Then, if a woman lives up to those rules, she is a good co-wife; whether she likes her husband's other wives is beside the point. If she does not live up to the rules, she is not a good co-wife.

The sort of adjustment that is made between co-wives varies widely from one society to another. In some there is an institutionalized relationship of hostility. In others there is one of cooperation and friendliness. Among the Tiv, for example, a woman takes over all of her co-wife's duties, including farming and sometimes cooking, during the last month or two of the latter's pregnancy; she acts as assistant to the midwife when the child is born, and helps to care for her co-wife for a few days or even weeks after confinement. To have any sort of overt difficulty with a co-wife is in the very worst possible taste; it also cuts off a major source of cooperation. However, if a co-wife does not live up to the required patterns, *then* it is possible to fight and argue with her—not because she is a co-wife but because she is a *bad* co-wife. Westerners with whom one discusses polygyny almost always assume—merely assume—that jealousy, particularly sexual jealousy, would make such a relationship as that of co-wives abominable. "Having that other woman around the house" would also be a bore, because nobody wants to share her kitchen. And the least informed of all associate polygyny with the lechery of the male. All these points show a basic misunderstanding.

Co-wives are, as a matter of fact, usually jealous of one another unless they have a good husband: a man who treats all his wives equally or at least equably in whatever respects are considered important by them. The division of labor in a polygynous household is such that in most polygynous societies women desire co-wives in order to lighten their own labors. The choice may become, in a situation in which industries and agriculture are not highly developed, "Do I want a co-wife or do I want to work myself half to death for inadequate return?" Secondly, especially in Africa which is largely polygynous, there is in all places a very strong belief that a woman should not have a second child until the first is at least two years old. This spacing of children is achieved, in Africa, because women do not have sexual relations with their husbands for as much as two years after each child is born. Under the circumstances, most women prefer another wife or two in the compound. At least the husbands are occupied and attend to their share of the farming. I have known African women, and many others have been reported from various tribes, who made the initial arrangements for a congenial girl and brought her home to be her husband's new wife because they wanted the companionship and help of a good co-wife. Most tribes think it is a good idea for a man's wives to vet his new wives, but everywhere some egoists refuse to consider their opinions. The wisest are not, for no matter how much a woman likes a man, she is not likely to stay with him if she does not like his other women. If she finds a congenial group of women, she may put up with a lot from a husband.

Secondly, women in polygynous societies do not share kitchens or houses. In almost all African societies, each woman has her own hut or rooms, and each her own kitchen. Each cooks separately, and this is especially important after she has children. The husband either divides his mealtimes among his wives, or eats a little of the food from each. Each has a sphere of her own. She can reduce the co-wife relationship to a formal one if it becomes necessary. They can stay out of one another's way if they don't like each other.

It is the more necessary to make these statements about polygyny and polygynous households because of the fact that the only time it has been tried on any large scale in the modern West—the Mormon experiment—it did not work.

Mormons—and more especially their critics—confused polygyny with the position of women. Or, to put it another way, in the middle and late nineteenth century when Mormon polygyny flourished, the position of women was very low. Some Mormon women and all non-Mormon women saw the fact of polygyny as the ultimate persecution of women: a final injustice that they had either to bear or fight. It was not enough that they had no property or legal rights; they had, it was held, been deprived even of domestic rights. There was some truth in what was said; however, the truth lay not in polygyny but in the clumsy way the Mormons practiced it. All the contemporary critics of Mormon polygyny, including some Mormon women who bolted, seem to have centered on the fact that it is impossible to multiply the number of similar relationships and retain the quality or content of the relationship. Story after tearjerking story was told of old women who, after thirty years of devoted married life and thirteen children, had to die alone and be buried without the balmful presence of a weeping husband, who was off cavorting with his younger wives. Such events, if they occurred, were instances of failure to practice polygyny sensibly, not necessary concomitants of polygyny.

In short, polygyny was viewed as if it had been multiple monogamy. No allowance was made for change in content of the relationships. Such pologyny was no better than monogamy when it is seen, as many Africans today see it, as maimed polygyny—again because they do not consider the change in content of the relationships. Mormon women, though many of them doubtless worked out satisfactory individual relations with their co-wives, had no generally recognized rules for playing the role of co-wife. The role of co-wife had inadequate ideal content.

In fact, the lot of the polygynist husband, even in societies in which polygyny is a working part of the social structure, is not a happy one. If one women can henpeck a husband, think what three women in league can do. Many men in polygynous societies look forward with only dread to the polygynous state and make the same jokes about it as Americans or Europeans make about the married state itself. But where the only sure way for an old man to be secure is with his children, and when the only sure way to get followers is, as one African elder put it, to beget them, polygyny becomes a necessity for the successful man.

In some societies that practice extensive polygyny, special means are sought to maintain stability among co-wives. Assuming that women who are already related to one another in one way or another will make better co-wives than those who are not, they have instituted "sororal polygyny," in which a man marries two or more sisters. However, for every tribe which has found sororal polygyny an adequate mode of controlling the relations among co-wives, it is possible to cite another which expresses shock that anyone could let the possibilities of conflict inherent in the co-wife relationship affect the amity of sisters.

Polygyny does not mean that there are more women than men in the society. Much nonsense has been written on this subject, in which "authorities" presumed, without counting them, that men were rarer beasts than women in societies with prescientific cultures. Noting the slightly higher femininity rate in Western countries—though more boys are born than girls, boys die more readily in childhood and early adulthood than do girls—they assumed that this state of affairs was universally true, which it is not. They also assumed that the differential of males and females was increased by the dangerous occupations of war and hunting, in which young men of primitive societies were assumed to engage. When somebody went to examine the situation, most of the assumptions were discovered to be false. In many African polygynous groups, there is actually a *masculinity* rate—that is, more adult men than women are present in the society. They also discovered that (some ill-informed gynaecologists to the contrary) there is no more dangerous occupation in the world than childbearing under primitive conditions.

The answer is, obviously, that in a polygynous society lacking a large femininity rate, a greater portion of women are married than men. Women usually marry at a much earlier age than men. If there are approximately equal numbers of men and women, and women marry when they are fifteen, men when they are twenty-five, there are obviously many more marriageable women than marriageable men. Where polygyny is the rule, there are more married women than men, but need not be more women than men in the total population.

Polygyny is most tenacious in a society in which economic rights in women can both be acquired and have some meaning. In American society, the whole subject is misunderstood—even if a man acquired economic rights in his wife, her economic potential is low during her childbearing period. Wives are an expense in Western society. The number of men who could afford more than one is limited. In a place like indigenous Africa, where women are valuable economically and invaluable domestically, having more than one wife becomes a desideratum for all. As Western industrial economy spreads, the utility of polygyny declines.

Besides the relationship of co-wives, which must be realized and institutionalized, there are other relationships in the polygynous family that add to its complexity. The most vital relationships of all are those between half siblings, especially when the content of that relationship is considered to differ from the content of the relationship between full siblings. This relationship creates major problems in most recorded societies in which extensive polygyny is practiced. As we have seen, most women can get along with their co-wives—but the task becomes considerably greater when their children begin to fight, as brothers do. A man always should side with his full sibling against his half sibling, if they dispute. Any woman sides with her children against the children of her co-wives. Precise rules of inheritance and of the ranking of children, by age or by social status of the mother or some other means, may ameliorate the struggle, but they seldom banish it.

Who gets the "South 40"—that most fertile piece of land? Who gets father's best shotgun, and who gets the second-best bed? The polygynous family contains the seeds of its own dissolution. The seeds may germinate when the center of interest of any individual turns from his natal family to his conjugal family. That particular dissolution can be stemmed for a few generations by property rights and other jural rights. But within the polygynous family, there is a double pull: the newly developing conjugal families, and—strengthening the tendency to fission—the fact that "we have different mothers," and hence different sets of matrilateral kinsmen.

Every society practicing institutionalized polygynous marriage must overcome these two problems: (1) How do co-wives get along? (2) How do half siblings behave toward one another? The most successful instances are those in which the content of both sets of relationships is firmly structured and where only a minimum is left for the individuals playing the roles to work out on a personal basis. A satisfactory structural relationship to fall back on if the personal relationship fails seems to be vital.

POLYANDRY

The family resulting from the plural marriage of women is much more complex than that resulting from the plural marriage of men. Polyandry, perhaps because it is difficult for actors as well as for analysts, is rare. Fewer than ten adequately authenticated instances are to be found in the literature, and the documentation of most of *them* is inadequate. Polyandry is no mere inversion of polygyny as was once supposed.

The most difficult problem, for the analyst certainly and for the actors probably, arises because there is only one matricentric family in the polyandrous situation, and therefore the polyandrous family cannot be seen as mere multiplication of nuclear families. Several problems emerge: (1) What is the relationship of co-husbands? (2) What are the relationships of "half siblings" in the polyandrous situation? (3) What is the relationship between a person and the mother's husbands who are not his "father"? It is evident that all these problems may be more difficult for polyandry than the equivalent problems were found to be for polygyny.

Co-husbands can get along perfectly well if there is a recognized standard to which each must comply: if there is a customarily stated set of rights and duties for each husband to follow. The differences between the

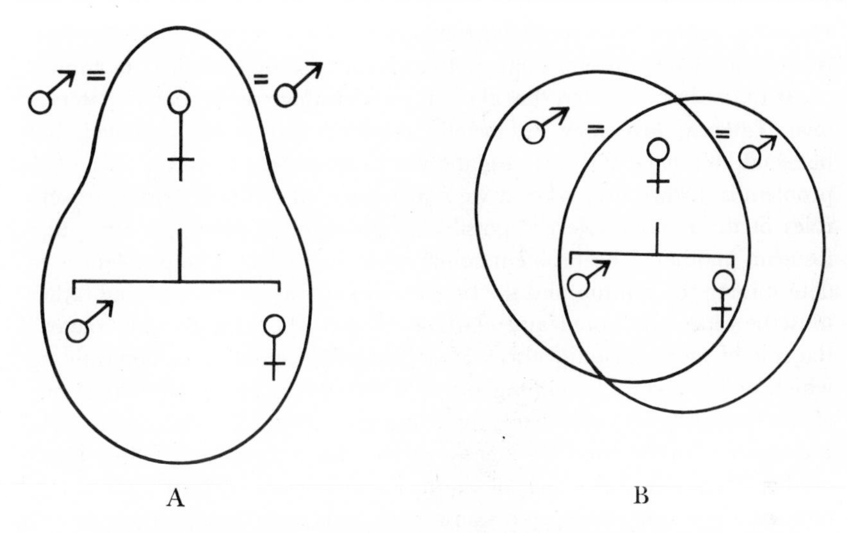

FIGURE 8 Polyandrous Families: *(a)* The polyandrous family seen in terms of matricentric families and males; *(b)* the polyandrous family seen in terms of combined nuclear families.

adjustment of co-husbands and that of co-wives arises from the fact that men have, in almost all societies, a wider range of social relationships than do women. The interests of men do not, because they cannot, center in the family. Whereas a woman who is a co-wife can focus on her children and recognize a realm in which her life is worthwhile and her responsibility is supreme, a man who is co-husband cannot do the same. He therefore is driven either outside the family altogether, or else into a more intense relationship *not* with the wife and children, but with the very co-husbands.

Thus, it is no accident that in most recorded cases of polyandry, there is a relationship among the co-husbands other than the mere fact of their being co-husbands. Most commonly the co-husbands are brothers—"fraternal polyandry" or "adelphic polyandry" is the family in which a group of brothers share a wife. Polyandry among the Toda of Southern India is usually of this type, and so are the Tibetan forms. However, the co-husbands may be trading partners. In such a situation, the husbands may take long trips, one at a time; both he who travels and he who stays at home with the family—to keep the shop—are benefiting from what is both a business and a kinship partnership.

It is in the aspects of paternity rather than of the husband roles of the male-parent syndrome that polyandry becomes most difficult.

Since a woman will not bear any more children in polyandrous union than in a monogamous one, the problem of determining paternity becomes crucial in polyandrous societies; furtherfore, the problem of half brothers is of a completely different nature than is the case in a polygynous family.

It has been postulated that there is no such thing as "natural" paternal love. Paternal love may be socially required and hence achieved, but paternal love does not have a glandular basis as does maternal love. The problem is thrown into relief if we remember that all three aspects or subroles of the mother role are possible in polyandry: mater, genetrix, and fostering mother. The problem comes with the males: The problem is in determining the genitor, and the subroles of pater and even fostering father must be especially noted and clarified. The Toda, who do not "factor" the role of father in quite this way, still see the necessity for determining which of the several possible genitors is the child's pater. He is that one of the husbands who most recently before the birth of the child performed a ceremony called the "Ceremony of the Small Bow" with the child's mother. Regardless of which of the husbands actually begets the child (a fact usually unknowable, and considered beside the point), the pater is known by this or similar means. Among the Tibetans, the pater would seem always to have been the eldest brother, or the senior of the group of husbands.

Obviously, sibling rivalry in the junior generations of the polyandrous family is probably not going to be much different from that in the nuclear monogamous family. Sibling rivalry is however the primary problem in polygyny. In an analogous way, the father-child relationship need not be much different in the polygynous family from that in the monogamous family. In the polyandrous family, it is the father-children relationships that create the problems.

To sum up the point of this chapter, the form of the family may vary widely and it varies on several scores: the number and sex of the spouses, and the way in which overlapping familes are extended to form active social groups on the basis of the obvious principle that almost all people are members of two nuclear families—natal families and conjugal families —thus providing an overlap from one generation into the next.

8

Divorce, widowhood, and remarriage

MARRIAGES ARE NOT only made in every society, but in every society they are also terminated. All societies must deal with the problem of widowhood. Most societies must also deal with the problem of divorce.

DIVORCE

Divorce does not merely undo a marriage. Rather it turns a husband-wife relationship into an exhusband-exwife relationship.

Some aspects of marriage are contractual—those are the aspects that can be broken. But some other aspects of marriage are the weft of kinship —indeed, the very source of kinship. Once established, these aspects cannot be broken, any more than any other kind of kinship. They can, at most, be repudiated.

The contractual aspects of marriage that can be broken by divorce can furthermore all be broken without divorce. Every society may indeed be characterized by a "divorce rate." But to correlate a divorce rate with a rate of "unsuccessful" marriage is, even in Western society, farcical.

In Chapter 5, it was noted that the role of wife can be divided into four subroles, as can the role of husband. It was also noted that three of the subroles for husband and wife have ramifications in the roles of father and mother. Here we must add to these statements by noting that the subroles of consort and the subroles of householder and housewife are fundamentally contractual in nature, whereas the subroles of bearer and begetter of children and of child's pater and child's mater are of a kinship nature. Similarly, the roles of fostering parents are contractual. The subroles of genitor and genetrix are of the essence of kinship, whereas those of pater and mater may be viewed as either kinship or contract.

Goode (1956) points out that there are at least four possible ways to cope with marital conflict: (1) to prevent tensions by external forces—that is, forces external to the marriage or the family give ready-made answers to family tensions; (2) to alleviate or deflect marital conflict into some other cultural field; (3) to increase or decrease the definitions of what is bearable; (4) to remove the forces of marital conflict by removing the people who create them—that is, by divorce.

In a society that has chosen to institutionalize one of the first three means of coping with marital conflict, divorce will obviously be statistically rarer than in a society in which the accepted mode of coping with marital conflict is to change the structure of the relationships.

Thus, divorce is an institutionalized element in some kinship systems, and is not always pathological. The "pathology" is, in any case, in the folk evaluation of divorce; it cannot be so in the analytical evaluation.

Divorce is relevant, obviously, to the husband-wife relationship and to the household, as well as to the content of the family relationships that are not affected by it. It is not so obvious, however, that there is a role "divorcée" in the total society that must be given content. The roles of married persons or single persons are, in American society, fairly well understood and fairly well charted. The roles of divorcées are not: there is little standardization of the cultural content of the role "divorcée." Whereas a man is exhusband to his exwife, he is divorcé to much of the rest of the society. Being divorced is a "civil state," as the French call it, comparable to being single, married, or widowed. As such, the divorcée is subject to an overall code of behavior relevant not merely to the family, but to the greater society. In most societies this behavior is more or less structured and predictable.

Probably no subject dealing with kinship is so difficult to regard dispassionately as is the subject of divorce. The American folk evaluation of divorce is constantly interfering with a scientific examination of it—in the reader even if not in the writer of reports on the subject. Therefore, the American attitude must be made somewhat overt so as to reduce the moral dimension of the scientific problem.

In American society, divorce is always considered, in one sense or another, an admission of failure (Goode, 1956). Therefore, two assumptions follow: first, that divorce is an index of "social disorganization" and, second, that experiences of divorce are destructive of personality and character.

It is not merely scholars studying American divorce who have been blinded by such ethnocentric considerations—anthropologists themselves have been so blinded. Anthropologists, with a few exceptions (Murdock, 1950), have tended to search for "divorce rates" on the one hand (Barnes, 1949), and merely to list the "grounds" for divorce on the other. They have in almost no instance sought to evaluate the different social situations in different societies in which divorce is the answer to unsatisfactory marriages. There is almost no documentation on the folk evaluation of the processes of divorce, or even the full examination of what divorce entails in various societies.

The fact that Western European cultures recognize almost no norms for the role of divorcé has created not merely personal problems in the West, but analytical problems for Western social science. There is, for example, absolutely no ethical imperative on a divorcé's natal family. What position should father or mother or siblings take in the matter? If the divorcé is friendly with his family, they will probably support him. But once a person has become a householder or housewife, it is not very likely that he will be accepted back into the household of his parents. The "agony" columns of the popular press stress the point day after day.

Neither is there a generally accepted way in which friends or relatives can give emotional support during the period of divorce. By personalizing the relationships, it can be done. But the role situation being what it is, there is no way in modern society for the natal family of a female divorcée to supply her with a firm background of support.

Another serious gap in our own society is that there is no institutionalized way to move divorcées into new families (Goode, 1956). Initial marriages and courtships are highly institutionalized, but subsequent marriages and courtships are not.

Obviously, the difficulties may not result from the practice of divorce, but rather from lack of concern with the divorcées. Our mills for creating divorcées run smoothly; our mills for dealing with them once they have been created have scarcely begun to turn. If our culture had an institutionalized means of getting divorcées back into new families so that none, save those who so chose, stayed single in the status "divorcée," marking time, the problem of divorce in our society would be very much less critical.

Finally, there is in our society no recognized behavior pattern by which it is obvious to all either that a divorcée is either being a good, successful, and moral divorcée or else is not. It is this lack more than any other that creates the divorcée's difficulty. It is also this lack that has created the anthropologist's attitude toward the study of divorce. All this is not the case in many preliterate societies, and we need very badly a series of studies investigating whether the experience of divorce need be either traumatic or pathological.

Thus, every time an anthropologist approaches a new culture, he must search for roles and the cultural content of roles. He must examine the content of the roles of spouses and exspouses. He must, moreover, determine the content of the roles of divorcées in the society, and the ways in which divorcées either are or are not reintegrated into family groups.

Another distinction must be made in order to understand divorce in a comparative context: grounds for divorce must be distinguished from causes of divorce. The first is legal; the second familial.

Grounds for divorce can always be traced to nonfulfillment of rights or obligations assumed at marriage. So incisive a thinker as Rebecca West has argued, in a newspaper piece, that societies recognizing no legal grounds for divorce cannot set a legal minimum requirement for spouses. Some grounds for divorce are those involving the nonfulfillment of the obligations of the housewife or householder; and still others for nonfulfillment of the obligations of bearer or begetter of children. Adultery is commonly, but by no means universally, a ground for divorce; it is a flagrant violation of the role of consort—at least female consort—as it is defined almost everywhere. Failure to allow sexual access to the spouse is ground for divorce in many societies—again, it is failure in the role of consort. In many societies, refusal of the spouse to bear or beget children is grounds for divorce. In some societies, a man can even acquire a divorce if his wife is barren. In American society, there appears to be some question as to whether the woman's failure to carry out the role of housewife is grounds for divorce. Among most peoples of the world, it unequivocally is so.

Causes of divorce are more varied and much more difficult to examine than grounds for divorce. Divorce by mutual consent, for example, means that the cause for divorce has not been inquired into and that grounds are not necessary in order to have the marriage legally dissolved. Yet it seems that even in societies where divorce by mutual consent is recognized, only comparatively few marriages are dissolved by this means.

Before an adequate cross-cultural study of divorce can be made—and one has not been made as of the present writing—several important factors must be investigated. Divorce must be evaluated in a context of the other ways in which unsuccessful marriages may be treated. Divorce must be studied in relation to its mechanics (that is, who first wants the divorce, who sues for it, what are the means of achieving it, and so on). The status of divorcée must be studied, in connection with the number of reasonable alternatives a society provides to the roles of husband and wife. Finally, it is necessary to go into the overall problem of the children of divorced parents.

Here only a few comments can be made on these important questions. In American society, most divorces are first desired by husbands but first suggested by wives (Goode, 1956). The husband, thus, must determine a way in which he can make himself so obnoxious that his wife will suggest a divorce. His alimony may be lower. Certainly, overwhelmingly divorce suits are filed with the wife as the plaintiff. The plaintiff is usually confused, in American thinking, with the "innocent partner." Wives begin most American divorce actions, whoever might have been responsible for the cause or the ultimate idea of the divorce. On the other hand, in Islamic societies women almost never sue for divorces; divorces are undertaken by men. Women in Islam have few grounds for divorce. Among the Tiv, where divorce is common, I know of only two cases in which husbands actually began divorce action. In both of these cases, the cause was inability on the part of the wife to get along in the husband's compound with his agnatic kinsmen and their wives. All other divorces among Tiv are initiated by women.

What proportions of divorcées remarry and what periods of time elapse between divorce and remarriage? What proportion of a population are divorcées at any one time? Such questions are impossible to answer with the state of the present data. Among Tiv, for example, almost all female divorcées remarry. As a matter of fact most of them "remarry," so to speak, before the dissolution of their marriages. There is a linguistic term for a female divorcée and specific definite ways in which she is to be treated. And yet there are not very many divorcées at any one time, although a very great portion of Tiv women—probably most—have at one time or another in their lives been divorced.

It is obvious that the form of the household may have important bearings on the degree of trauma experienced by the children of divorcing parents. In American society, with its monogamous marriage and with its domestic group based on the nuclear family, the trauma is considerable. Where households are based on extended families, the trauma is less devastating; so it is among polygynous families. And it can be relatively slight in large extended polygamous families.

ANNULMENT

Divorce is only one means of canceling a marriage. Another is what is called "annulment" in our own society. An annulment is a legal or ritual recognition of the fact that no actual marriage ever occurred. In every culture there would seem to be a point before which a marriage can be called off or annulled and after which it must be broken by divorce.

In the West, sexual consummation of the marriage is such a point. Before it, any marriage can be annulled; after it, annulment can occur only in very special cases. This rule was brought out in a case in the United States several years ago. A woman, whose husband was not capable of consummating their marriage, was artificially inseminated with his sperm and bore a child. Two years later, she sought an annulment on the grounds that the marriage had not been consummated. The judge told her that, under ordinary circumstances, she had grounds for annulment, but that since the annulment would amount to bastardizing the child, she must seek a divorce.

Ethnographic literature abounds in examples in which acceptance of a specific payment marks the watershed between annulment and divorce. In Dahomey, for example, a groom's lineage must, among other bridewealth payments, pay a castrated goat and a bag of salt to the lineage head of the bride. This payment, which is not returnable in case of dissolution of the marriage, is accompanied by a ritual notification of the ancestors of the girl that she has married so-and-so. It may even be that it is the ritual that makes the difference.

Most East African Bantu tribes have one specific cow in the cattle bridewealth which, when accepted by the father of the bride, marks the marriage as complete. It does *not* mean that a debt may not exist in addition to the marriage. Rather, it means that the marriage cannot be broken merely by return of the bridewealth. Grounds for divorce are demanded in addition.

A ritual may mark the point at which divorce becomes necessary. Among the Tiv, there is a ritual in which a goat is killed, its blood smeared on the doorstep of the bride's new house in her groom's compound. After this rite, the bride's people can sue for nonpayment of bridewealth or exchange, but they cannot remove their child in what is known to Tiv as "the woman breaking down" (*kwase bunde*) rather than by divorce (*mpav*).

WIDOWHOOD

Divorce is only one way to break up a marriage: everywhere, it would seem, more marriages are ended by death than by divorce. The syndromes of widowed persons are similar to, but different from, the syndromes of divorced persons.

First of all, when a marriage is dissolved by death, only one of the two syndromes remains—therefore, a basically simpler situation remains. Secondly, the "breaking" of the husband-wife relationship by death need not be culturally recognized; even if it is, there can be less of blame or of uncertainty attached to the role of widow or widower.

The syndrome of wife/mother is not appreciably changed by the death of the husband/father—content may be drastically changed, but none of the subroles in the syndrome is specifically repudiated. Therefore, the role of widow in the larger society is added, and the various subroles are given new content. For all that death of a spouse/parent may create personal tragedy, it is not a social tragedy in any sense.

This being the case, the investigator can see that the role of widow (or widower) affects subroles of the spouse/parent syndromes. But the effect is mainly a qualitative one. There are, both rationally and actually, two precisely opposite ways in which the content can be restructured: no change of content may be recognized, or a complete change of content may be recognized. Obviously, neither extreme will be found in empirical situations.

If no change in content, or only minimal change, is recognized, the widow may not be allowed to remarry. That is to say, none of the rights in the woman are considered to have lapsed on the death of the husband. A greater change results with recognition that some of the rights, but not others, may be inherited—such a situation is involved with what anthropologists usually call "inheritance of widows." Greatest change comes when, as in the West, all rights are considered to have lapsed with death.

A norm prohibiting remarriage is taken to its ultimate conclusion in the institution known as *suttee*, which comes from the Indian word for the immolation of widows on the pyres of their dead husbands. This institution is found a few places outside of India—notably in Fiji where widows were strangled, and in a few South American tribes. It has been the subject of some specialist studies, mainly by feminists aimed at reform who have sought the most extreme examples of "degradation" of the female.

TABLE 8

WIFE/MOTHER/WIDOW SYNDROME

MOTHER (ego is child)	WIFE (ego is living pro-husband)	WIDOW (ego is dead husband)
Fosterer ♀	Housewife	
—	Consort ♀	
Genetrix	Bearer of subsequent children	Bearer of children
Mater	Child's mater	Child's mater

Enforced remarriage of widows creates a situation in which the wife/mother syndrome is made the object of three egos rather than two (see Table 8). When a woman is inherited, she becomes housewife to her new husband's "householder," and she becomes his consort. So much is unequivocal. It is in the roles of bearer of children and of child's mater that the dead husband may still be relevant.

Inheritance of widows is usually associated with the institution known as the levirate. The levirate properly so called is the institution in which the dead man is said to retain rights *in genetricem:* all of the children born by the widow after his death continue to be legally filiated to the dead husband. These children are begotten by the man who inherits sexual and domestic rights in the widow. These inheritors are called the levirs. The leviratic family, then, is made up of a man who is genitor and fostering male to his children, but who is not their pater. The wife, on the other hand, is consort and housewife to the levir but child bearer and child's mater to the dead husband.

Purists insist that only when a man inherits all rights, including rights *in genetricem* in his brothers' wives, do we have true inheritance of widows. Thus, "inheritance of widows," in a narrower sense, is not to be confused with the levirate, in which the man does not inherit rights *in genetricem* but merely raises up seed to his dead brother.

At the other extreme, in American society, the widow's role is given a very different content. All of her wife roles are put into the past tense, as it were, though none is broken. She is free to remarry, and the new husband acquires total rights in her. Widow's roles are, obviously thus, more clearly defined than are divorcée's roles. It is an interesting historical fact that as the divorce rate grew, divorcées began to acquire, in the popular imagination, all of the libidinous traits formerly associated with widows: men today tell the same stories about the gay divorcée that their fathers told about the merry widow.

The position of a widowed or divorced person is difficult for one other reason: a widow or divorcée is likely to be the head of a matricentric family that is not attached to a male. Even where it is the norm, such situations are difficult. Even more difficult is the situation in which a widower or divorced man is left with dependent children. A man and his dependent children, lacking wife/mother, is nowhere considered to be a normal situation. It inspires pity, disgust, or both.

REMARRIAGE

The notion of a "remarriageable population" is of use to sociologists interested in interpreting the customs of Western civilization, and good use has been made of it (Bernard, 1956). However, the idea of a remarriageable population changes with the institutions of the society in question. Among ourselves, only persons who have been divorced or widowed are of the remarriageable population. In a polygamous society, many other people may be constantly in the remarriageable population. In a polygynous society, theoretically at least, all males who are married or have once been married are part of the remarriageable population. Sociologists of our own society have been able to ask the question this way: "What sort of person is divorced?" "What sort of person is widowed?" These questions can of course be asked in any society, but, like the idea of a remarriageable population, they must be carefully evaluated for every change in cultural norm.

In many societies, divorce follows a new alliance instead of preceding it. In such a situation, it might even be said that all people are constantly in the remarriageable population. In short, if there is not a highly legalized mechanism and stipulated waiting period, or both, one may not be able to speak sensibly of a remarriageable population at all. If a widow's husband is, so to speak, "built-in"—that is to say, if she is expected to marry one of her late husband's kinsmen—she can scarcely be considered part of the remarriageable population even after her husband's death. A social category made up of people eligible for remarriage changes so drastically as one proceeds from one society to the next that statistics concerning it are scarcely meaningful.

One of the best books written by a family sociologist in recent years is Jessie Bernard's *Remarriage* (1956). Dr. Bernard has pointed out several ways in which remarriages differ from initial marriages. Remarriages have all of the problems of first marriages, but most of them seem to be even more intense. Moreover, they have their own problems as well, especially if there were children of the first marriage. This brings us to Dr. Bernard's second point: only two generations, in our society, are involved in an initial marriage—the generation of the marrying couple and that of their parents. In remarriages there are often three generations concerned, because children by former marriages are to a greater or lesser degree concerned in the new marriage. Probably the most important difference is that remarriage is not a *rite de passage* so much as it is a change of personnel.

Every culture follows certain rules that should be observed in order for remarriage to be seemly. In America it is sometimes said that a year should elapse between a divorce or the death of a spouse and remarriage. Emily Post has used the term "the year of respect." Most people merely say you should wait a "decent interval." Moreover, in America the divorced or widowed person usually has to change social groups on remarriage. People who are friends of both divorced persons prefer not to take sides; they are hesitant about meeting the new spouse when they were friends of the former spouse or when they had known the former couple together. Therefore, it is usually easier for the new couple to move into completely new surroundings. This is one of many situations Americans meet by moving into new communities. Other societies demand very short waiting periods, or even demand that any waiting period be foregone.

In cases of remarriage of divorced parents, the structure of the family becomes very complicated. To take the maximally complex situation—one in which husband and wife, with children, are divorced and each remarries a spouse who already has children—there are nineteen relationships (some of which occur twice) to be juggled, and among which a *modus vivendi* of sorts must be found (see Table 9).

TABLE 9 THE FAMILY OF REMARRIED DIVORCEES

	DIRECT	SHARED
SEXUALITY	Hu–Wi exHu–exWi	Wi exHu–ExWi Hu Hu exWi–ExHu Wi
DESCENT	Fa–So Fa–Da Mo–So Mo–Da stepMo–stepSo stepMo–stepDa stepFa–stepSo stepFa–stepDa	Br–Br Si–Si Br–Si half Br–half Br half Si–half Si half Br–half Si stepBr–stepSi stepBr–stepBr stepSi–stepSi

Of these new roles found in families of monogamous remarriage, far and away the most important and the most widely recognized is that of stepmother. It cannot be overemphasized that the stepmother-stepchild relationship is one about which a mythology has grown up in most societies. It would seem every place to be the prototype of the relationship of cruelty. William Carlson Smith, a sociologist who published in 1952 a study called *The Stepchild,* points out that the term "stepchild" in English is applied to anything mistreated, neglected, or mismanaged. The concomitant notion of the cruel stepmother is found in all folk literatures of the world, apparently. We have here, in short, something almost as ubiquitous as the prohibition of incest. However, as Dr. Bernard points out, cruel stepmother stories are toned down in cultures that have a system such as the levirate to protect the child against the contingency of the death of a parent. In such a system, the child's new parent is a kinsman to him already and probably someone he has known all his life. Therefore, the most traumatic aspects of stepparent experience are minimized.

Although cruel stepmothers are probably rarer than good ones, there must be a kernel of truth in the stepmother myth. The question arises, Why is it always the stepmother who is cruel instead of the stepfather? Jessie Bernard (1956) has found an answer in the difference between the roles played by men and women: men are, she claims, more willing to sacrifice their children to happy and peaceful spouse relationships in the remarriage than are women. Therefore, the stepmother, by working through the child's father, can usually get her way about how to deal with the child. Women, on the other hand, will not so sacrifice their children for their new husbands. Therefore, stepfathers cannot be "cruel" to the same extent, even if they want to be so.

Bernard says that many children, at some time during their early youth, accuse their mothers of being stepmothers. These children say that nobody who is their real mother could possibly be as cruel as this woman is being; therefore, she must be a stepmother. It would seem, then, that the natural mother may be accused of being the stepmother whenever she must be stern or frustrating, but that only when the fostering female is indeed the stepmother does such a charge become a lasting problem, for the child is enabled to separate the source of discipline from the source of love.

In addition to the complication of the adjacent generational relationships, there are complications in each of the generations. Not only is there a new husband-wife relationship, but there may be a relationship between the husband and his exwife, the wife and the exhusband. There may, further, be a relationship between the husband and exhusband, the wife and the exwife, or both. Thus, there are five new relationship types (see Table 9) and as many as nine relationships involved here. The difficulties inherent in these relationships are well attested in popular literature and drama.

It is not, however, until one gets into the junior generation that the full range of the difficulty appears. Among the children of the new spouses there may be as many as nine relationships, among siblings, stepsiblings, and half-siblings. Written out they appear as brother-brother, stepbrother-stepbrother, and halfbrother-halfbrother; brother-sister, stepbrother-stepsister, halfbrother-halfsister; sister-sister, stepsister-stepsister, and halfsister-halfsister. That makes nine. One can only say that it is small wonder families of remarriage present more difficulties than families of initial marriages.

The number of relationships that might be factored out of polygynous remarriages becomes almost astronomical. To attempt to do so would serve little purpose here. The whole matter of divorce, widowhood, and remarriage demands extensive thought, research, and analysis. We are only just beginning to understand enough about it to make such research possible or profitable.

9

Consanguine kinship groups

NO MATTER HOW COMPLEX the ramifications brought to light by study of the family, the simple facts about families must never be forgotten: a family contains people who are linked by sexual and affinal relationships as well as those linked by descent and collateral relationships; all families larger than a nuclear family contain people who are linked by secondary relationships; that is, by chains of primary relationships.

The English word "family" is, in popular usage, extended to include any group of kinsmen. "Family business," "family council," and "family picnic" are examples in which the word is used for any group of people, tracing kinship links to one another, who carry out some activity. "Family" groups of this sort are limited by nonkinship factors—personal interest and propinquity being the secondary limiting factors after the primary criterion of kinship itself. They are groups of kinsmen, but they are not kinship groups—membership may be restricted, but it is not compulsory. Kinship, in such a group, is a criterion for admission, not an organizing principle.

In Western societies, families are the only recognized kinship groups. Therefore, any group of kinsmen, garnered for whatever purpose and with whatever secondary qualifications, is called "family" for sheer lack of any other term. In comparative studies, however, the word should be used with care, and usually should be preceded by a precise adjective.

NONFAMILIAL KINSHIP GROUPS

Many societies make use of structured kinship groups other than families. Such groups are limited by kinship criteria rather than merely by nonkinship criteria, such as propinquity, personal interest, or inheritance of property. A person is as irrevocably a member of some of these kinship groups as he is irrevocably a member of his natal family.

Such "nonfamilial" kinship groups have in common that they exclude all affines; they are, therefore, often called consanguine kinship groups. The simplest but rarest forms include *all* consanguines; more complex but more common forms exclude some consanguines.

It would at first seem to be possible to cut out either lineal kinsmen or collaterals and create groups from those who are left. However, a moment's reflection shows that a group made up of no one except lineal kinsmen would of necessity be very small. Moreover, such a group must somehow be limited to one member of each generation, otherwise collaterals will necessarily appear. Any group containing all of one man's lineal descendants will, if he has more than one child or more than one grandchild, necessarily contain collaterals. Therefore, a sort of kinship group containing only lineal kinsmen can have very little cultural content.

On the other hand, a collateral kinship group would be one in which all lineal links were outlawed. Such a group must be limited to all the members of a single generation, in order to avoid including at least some lineal kinsmen. A few such groups appear as residence units in such societies as the Nyakyusa in Tanganyika (Wilson, 1951), but this type is extremely rare in actual fact.

In order to examine nonfamilial kinship groups, it is necessary to do so on two quite different axes: whether or not all consanguines are included, and on the position of the ego.

EXCLUSION AND INCLUSION

There are two biological principles on which consanguine kinsmen can be excluded from groups. Both occur as a result of refinement in the definition of the lineal links: the sex of the parent, or the sameness or oppositeness of sex of parent and child. That is to say, the children of men can be included in the group whereas those of women are excluded, or else the children of women can be included whereas those of men are excluded. Such a situation leads to the sort of group usually called a "unilineal descent group," though it will be necessary to refine this term below. On the other hand, same-sex lineal links such as mother-daughter and father-son may be excluded or included, and opposite-sex lineal links such as mother-son and father-daughter may be included or excluded; this arrangement leads to what is generally called a "rope," a term which translates the term in the New Guinean language of the tribe among whom such groups were first adequately described.

POSITION OF EGO

When we were investigating families, we discerned that the structure of a kinship group could be examined either with or without introduction of the concept of the ego. The same is true in consanguine kinship groups, with the difference that one position of the referent ego may be recognized culturally, whereas another position is either disregarded or denied. With nuclear families, the introduction of ego spelled the difference between a natal and a conjugal family. With consanguine kinship groups, similar distinctions are created on the basis of whether the ego is an ancestor of all the members, or only a contemporary representative of the group.

The ego in a consanguine kinship group can occur in two places within the genealogy, and the difference is essential in discerning the way the group works. On the one hand, the ego may be contemporary—leading to an emphasis on collaterality. All kinsmen who are members of such a group trace a relationship, through a chain of selected primary relationships, to some person now living. A kinship group can be created if an ego traces all his kinsmen in every line out through a given number of degrees. The ego may, on the other hand, be an ancestor to all the members of the group. The important factor in such a group is descent, not collateral kinship with a living person. It is the ancestor himself and the lineal links from him to the living persons that are essential.

It is a little startling, nevertheless, to realize that every descent group is in point of fact made up of a group of collateral kinsmen, whereas every collateral group in fact involves computation of descent.

As with any other logical arrangement that requires distinction on two axes, it is well to create a four-square so that the categories can be kept clearly separated (see Table 10). The two axes are, of course, the position of ego and the inclusion or exclusion of consanguine kinsmen. Two more

TABLE 10 NONFAMILIAL KINSHIP GROUPS

	Ancestral Ego	*vs.*	Contemporaneous Ego
Inclusive of all consanguines	Omnilineal descent group	Cognatic groups (↔)	Omnilateral group
vs. (↑↓)	Descent groups (↑↓)		Collateral groups (↑↓)
Exclusive of some consanguines	Unilineal descent group (lineage) Ropes	Exclusive groups (↔)	Agnatic and uterine collateral groups

sets of terms are necessary: descent groups and collateral groups are both inclusive and exclusive groups deriving from an ancestral and a collateral ego, respectively. Cognatic and exclusive groups are those that are both inclusive of all consanguine kin or of only a systematically selected part of them.

COGNATIC KINSHIP GROUPS

Cognatic kinship groups include all of the descendants of an ancestor or ancestress (the omnilineal descent group) or else they include all the kinsmen, on all sides, of a contemporary ego, limited only by degree of kinship. We shall examine the former with an example from Truk, the latter with an example from the Anglo-Saxon tribes.

OMNILATERAL GROUP

Probably the best-known example of the omnilateral kinship group is the Anglo-Saxon "sib."[1] It was a group of consanguines computed from a contemporary ego, limited by degree.

In computing my "sib," I am the central point. My full brothers and sisters (or double cousins) and I share a "sib." They and no others share *all* of my "sib" mates. My half brothers share only half of my "sib," unless the parents we do not share are full siblings. To these Anglo-Saxons, one's sib contained all cognates computed to specific degrees. Radcliffe-Brown (1950) reviews the ways in which computations of kinship degrees were made by using the parts of the body. Kinsmen of the first degree—the father and the mother—were said to be kinsmen of the head. Those of the next degree (one's full brothers and sisters) were neck kinsmen. First cousins are in the shoulders, second cousins in the elbows, third cousins in the wrists. The next lot of cousins—fourth, fifth, and sixth cousins—at the joints of the fingers. Finally come the fingernails at which stand the seventh cousins "nail brothers." This term is still used in German, *"Nagelbrüder,"* to mean distant kinsmen.

The original Anglo-Saxon sib included sixth cousins but did not include the "nail kinsmen," or seventh cousins. The computation went from the self, through all lines, through both men and women.

Another way of viewing the sib was to divide it into several concentric "circles": the "innermost circle of the sib of an individual included his father and mother, his brother and sister, and his son and daughter—the 'six limbs of the sib' " (Radcliffe-Brown, 1950, p. 16). Another circle was that recognized as the "relatives within the elbow"—that is, all my kinsmen

[1] It is a great pity that latter-day term mongers have reintroduced the word "sib" and some of its variants such as "sept" into the literature so many times, and with a different meaning each time, so that the terms have become almost meaningless. Lowie (1920) used the term "sib" to signify a unilineal descent group—a "misusage" of the original term, because the original "sib" was not unilineal. Murdock (1949) circumscribed Lowie's usage. To use this sort of word as a scientific term requires *ex cathedra* definition and, inevitably, leads to futile partisan sniping and, worse, to the idea that social anthropology is less developed and more inexact than is actually the case.

through second cousins (all the descendants of my eight great grandparents). The entire sib, which went through sixth cousins, included all the descendants of my sixty-four great-great-great-great grandparents.[2]

The Anglo-Saxons themselves appear to have assigned different functions to different circles of kin. One circle included all those with whom marriage was forbidden. It is difficult among the Anglo-Saxon tribes to determine just exactly which kinsmen such a circle included—even when the Teutonic and Welsh records say that the limitation was carried to the fifth degree, there is some dispute about whether they meant to include third cousins or fifth cousins. The lack of clarity comes in part from the state of the records, but also in part from inadequate research in them.

The difference between the sib and any given man's "kindred" is that on some occasions, the sib actually was called into action and performed as an organization with at least a tentative system. Although such group action was rare, it did occur: at a man's marriage, and at any time when he killed another man or was killed. There is more information about sibs in connection with the institution of *wergild,* or blood money, than in any other context.

If you killed a man, all of the members of your sib, to the sixth degree, contributed a share of the blood money to give to the sib of the victim. The various kinsmen contributed according to the distance of their relationship to you. When the sum was made up and handed over to the sib of the dead man, it was divided out again more or less on the same principles as those on which it was collected: the closest kinsmen got most, and the more distant members of the sib, further out in the circles or down the joints of the arm, increasingly less.

In those parts of the United States in which kinship is recognized beyond the confines of the grandfamily, it is almost always figured in much the same way the sib was computed, with the notable difference that groups are not formed. In parts of the South, notably Virginia, and in a few New England cultural enclaves, "quartering" is still important. A quartering is a statement delineating in all lines the ancestors of a given individual. When computing kinship for the purposes of suitability for marriage or for any other purpose, it is traced from the contemporary ego back in all lines, and then insofar as it is relevant down again to contemporaries.

It must be remembered, however, that First Families of Virginia and Boston Brahmins, for all that kindred and quartering are of great importance, never call all the kindred into an active, social unit. Therefore, they have nothing resembling the sib in all its details. It is not possible for a Virginian, say, to get all of the people to whom he traces a socially

[2] It is interesting that in an article on family structure, Talcott Parsons (1959) without reference to the Anglo-Saxon institution, uses a system of circles to explain modern Western family organization.

important kinship link to form a group on his behalf. Indeed, there is no social situation in which it is desirable for them to do so. One's kinship position ratifies one's social position; but one's kinsmen as an organized group do not defend it.

The omnilateral group—the cognatic kinship group based on a contemporary ego—is rare. In an attempt to increase the number of examples, a subterfuge is usually resorted to: groups made up of cognatic kinsmen often appear when they are associated with a village or with some other local group. In such instances, as we have seen, the organizing principle of the groups is likely to be propinquity or locality, whereas kinship is merely a criterion of eligibility, the "kinship group" may be an epiphenomenon of the facts that residence with kinsmen is the norm and that local groups act as units.

OMNILINEAL DESCENT GROUP

The second type of cognatic group is the omnilineal descent group—the cognatic group computed from an ancestral ego. This sort of descent group, in part because it is obvious and therefore not easy to see, was discovered very late in the development of kinship studies. Goodenough (1955), who called this group an "unlimited descent group," is the first to give an adequate analysis of it. He found, while working in the Gilbert Islands, that the criteria for limiting membership in descent groups were not kinship criteria, and therefore the usual modes of describing descent groups did not apply. Goodenough found three descent groups in the Gilbert Islands, none of them unilineal.

First of the three is the unlimited descent group from any ancestor, which the Gilbertese called on *ooi*. This group is an entity and functions in relation to the property that was owned by the founder. This group can be limited by the application of a nonkinship criterion of eligibility: when the inheritance of certain seats in the community meeting house is considered, only the holders of certain lands are eligible and such a group is called a *bwoti* by the Gilbertese. A third group is the *kainga:* it is made up of those members of an *ooi* that form a residential or local unit. Thus, the primary criterion of all three of these groups is descent. Secondary criteria of a nonkinship nature limit the membership of two of the groups. The *ooi* contains all the people who have a right to inherit land from a single ancestor or ancestress, whether they have actually taken it up or not. Some people take up the inherited land from one of their ancestors, whereas others take it up from another. Therefore, only a relatively small portion of a person's descendants will actually inherit his land. Nevertheless, the fact that they do not inherit does not remove their right to inherit, because residual rights in land (if a person dies without heirs) revert to the other members of the *ooi* of the original holder of the land. Thus, the *ooi* is a group determined by land rights, and it is also an unrestricted descent group.

The *bwoti* is quite a different group, but all of its members are members of the *ooi.* However, instead of being based on the possibility of inheriting land rights, it is based on the allocation of positions in the community meeting-house organization. Each position goes to the *bwòti* of the person who first held the position. The *bwoti* are those kinsmen or members of the *ooi* descended from the original position holder, who actually have inherited specific plots of land. It differs from the *ooi* in that the *ooi* is an unlimited descent group all of whom may inherit, and the *bwoti* is a limited descent group—limited to those members who have actually inherited. *Bwoti,* thus, has two criteria of membership: (1) membership in the *ooi,* and (2) actual inheritance of land that belonged to the ancestor of the *ooi.* A man is potentially a member of as many *bwotis* as *oois* to which he belongs. But he can activate only one *bwoti* membership at any one time. Thus, although the *bwoti* is a descent group, full brothers may belong to different *bwoti,* since the secondary criterion of membership is not kinship-based: one brother has taken the land that came to them from one ancestor, whereas the other took the land that came to them from quite a different ancestor.

The third type of descent group is the *kainga,* which is a residence group. A man and woman, when they marry, move into the area in which they will inherit land. Since either is entitled to inherit land, they will probably move into that area in which the larger holdings will be available. In most cases, residence is patrilocal: however, the exceptions are critical in understanding the principles. A person belongs to the *kainga* associated with the land that was associated with the ancestor of that *ooi* in which his parents have decided to reside. Thus, all the members of an *ooi* have a right to reside on the lands of the original ancestor, until they move away. Thereupon, their children, although remaining members of the *ooi,* no longer have the right to live on the land of the *ooi* and are said to lose membership in the *kainga.* The *kainga* are those descendants, members of the *ooi,* who have actually lived in the area originally associated with the ancestor of the *ooi.*

Goodenough sums the situation up:

> All three descent groups are somehow connected with the land. An ancestor having established ownership of a tract was the founder of all three. All of his descendants form an *ooi.* Those in actual possession of a share in the land are eligible to membership in a *bwoti.* Those whose parents resided on it form a *kainga.* None of these groups is unilineal [1955, p. 75].

Thus, the point to be made here is that an unlimited descent group is a type of kinship group containing the seven consanguine relationships and is focused on an ancestor. It can be limited only by nonkinship principles.

EXCLUSIVE KINSHIP GROUPS

When some of the seven basic relationships of consanguinity are excluded for the purposes of forming social groups, it is obviously necessary that a new criterion be adduced. The most commonly recognized biological kinship criterion for limiting consanguine groups is the sex of the parent in parent-child relationships. Mother-child links may be considered by the people to be of a different nature from father-child links; one or both may be used to the exclusion of the other for creating viable and important social groups.

The link of a father to his children is called an agnatic descent link;[3] that of a mother to her children is a uterine descent link. Either of these links can be formed into chains: the father's father's father is a secondary agnatic kinsman; so is the father's father's brother's son's child. In exactly the same way, the mother's mother's mother or the mother's sister's child is a uterine kinsman. However, the mother's father is neither a uterine nor an agnatic kinsman, because there is a combination of one agnatic and one uterine link. A male, obviously, has no uterine descendants, a female no agnatic descendants.

Exclusive kinship groups, therefore, include only five of the seven possible basic consanguine relationships. The agnatic group is made up of the Fa–So, Fa–Da, Br–Br, Br–Si, and Si–Si links, the uterine group of the Mo–So, Mo–Da, Br–Br, Br–Si, and Si–Si links. Seen in diagrammatic form, the exclusive kinship groups appear as in Table 11.

TABLE 11 UTERINE AND AGNATIC DESCENT GROUPS

	DIRECT	SHARED
SEXUALITY	Excluded from all	consanguine groups
DESCENT	Agnatic: Fa–So Fa–Da	Br–Br Si–Si Br–Si
	Uterine: Mo–So Mo–Da	

[3] Many anthropologists use the terms "patrilineal" and "matrilineal" to extend to what are called here agnatic and uterine links. I prefer to use the former words only when they apply specifically to unilineal descent groups.

To review: the husband-wife relationship was eliminated in forming the consanguine kinship groups; some consanguine groups, those we have called cognatic groups, contain all the other seven basic relationships. When an agnatic group is formed, the mother-son and mother-daughter relationships are further eliminated. If you take the members of your kin and strike out all the persons related to you through a marriage, you have all the potential members of your consanguine kinship group. If then you strike out all those consanguines who are related to you through a uterine link (save any with whom you also have an agnatic link, such as full siblings), you have the potential members of your agnatic group. Similarly, if you strike out all kinsmen who are related to you through an agnatic link, but retain those through uterine links, you have the potential members of your uterine group.

UNILINEAL DESCENT GROUPS

It is an interesting fact that any group of agnates or of uterine kinsmen will, if they trace their ascendants far enough, reach a single ancestor or ancestress. There is, thus, an element of descent in every agnatic or uterine group. Conversely, the agnatic or uterine descendants of a given ancestor are obviously collaterals, so that such groups also have an element of collaterality. Some cultures emphasize the descent aspect in their image of the group; others, the aspect of collaterality.

A unilineal descent group is, then, a group of agnatic *or* uterine kinsmen based on an ancestral ego—a group in which descent is considered by the members to be the essential point. Such groups of kinsmen are often called "lineages." The agnatic lineage is called patrilineal, the uterine lineage matrilineal, because from any contemporary member, the line back to the founding ancestor is through a line of fathers or a line of mothers.[4] It behooves us to examine closely the idea of descent so that we can realize its importance when it is present in a culture, as well as recognize its absence when the descent aspects of uterine or agnatic groups are not stressed or even culturally recognized.

The word "descent" has several meanings. Biological descent commonly forms a cultural image on which jural descent is based. Jural descent comprehends both inheritance of property and succession to social positions. It is the mechanism by means of which rank and property are handed from one generation to the next. Systems of jural descent often select some

[4] The common substitution of the terms "matrilineal" and "patrilineal" for uterine and agnatic, so that one says "patrilineal kinsman" for what is here called an agnatic kinsman, has been instrumental in hiding the fact that the unilineal aspect of agnatic or uterine groups may be epiphenomenal in the culture concerned.

criteria of biological descent in determining suitability for inheritance and succession.

Obviously, there is no need whatever for biological and jural descent to overlap. That I am my father's son is biological descent. That I am his heir is jural descent. However, my father's brother may be his heir; or I may be the heir of my mother's brother. Biological descent and jural descent are phenomena in different spheres, but may sometimes be brought together in the folk image of biology and society.

Thus, in patrilineal lineages, the physical descent is paralleled by or closely associated with jural descent. However, in matrilineal lineages, such is not the case: the biological descent line runs from mother to child. But since men are the primary holders of property and status in all societies, including matrilineal societies, the jural descent runs from a man to his closest uterine kinsman in the junior generation—his sister's son. The jural line of descent in matrilineal societies might be called "avunculineal"—a barbarism, perhaps, but a vivid one. Only when the lines of jural descent are confused with those of biological descent does matriliny appear difficult to understand.

Ideas in the folk evaluation of biological descent often have repercussions in the institutions of jural descent. It would be surprising if they did not. We have all read about the fact that a European woman could, in some historical eras, commit adultery with impunity only when she was pregnant by her husband, because that is the only time, in European folk evaluation of reproduction, that she cannot possibly conceive a child in adultery. In short, the "blood tie" between a man and his son is extremely important in assigning the legal right of that son to take over his father's offices and wealth. Many cultures are noted for the correlation between ideas of what Malinowski called the "doctrine of procreation" (1929, p. 158), and the jural relationship between parents and children.

The question to be answered for every culture about ideas of physiological descent is: How does this people see the physiological relationship between sire and dam? Between sire and offspring? Dam and offspring? What do they believe about the physiology and chemistry of procreation? What is the linguistic idiom they use?

DOCTRINES OF PROCREATION

Obviously, the range of beliefs about procreation is varied. At one end of the scale are those peoples who are said to have no knowledge of the function of the male in procreation. The Trobriand Islanders are said to be ignorant of a male role. Malinowski (1929, Chapter VII) reported that this point was proved by the fact that they apply the notion to their livestock; they castrate all male hogs, he says, and adds that if there were no wild boars on the island, there would be no pigs at all. But since there are wild boars, the Trobrianders do not make a connection: in fact, they deny the connection vociferously. Trobriand statements in these matters seem convincing within Trobriand culture: sexual activity serves to enlarge the vagina and hence to make pregnancy possible, but the seminal fluid itself is not concerned in creation of a child. Most copulation does not result in children. Rather, impregnation occurs when a spirit enters into the body of a woman: most of Malinowski's informants said that such a spirit was implanted by another spirit (a close matrilateral kinsman of the woman, or occasionally her father). From the hair of a woman's head, the spirit entered into the blood of her head and descended into the belly. The spirit, which was already associated with the woman's clan and subclan before conception, takes on body from her blood when menstruation ceases and hence is in both spirit and body of the matrilineal descent group.

There are even some patrilineal people who, it has been claimed, have no knowledge of insemination—in spite of the fact that they follow the patrilineal principle. Mischa Titiev has, in fact, argued that patriliny among at least some of these people is an epiphenomenon of residence: they are patrilocal and unilocal. For years the Aranda of Australia have served as an arguing point for both sides—those scientists who say the Aranda do know, and those who say they do not know, "the facts of life." Apparently, this is not a simple statement. There is a difference between considering sexual intercourse a necessary prerequisite to pregnancy and considering it the precipitating cause of pregnancy. Strehlow (1908) has pointed out that in the mythology of Australian tribes in this area, either sex was, in the beginning, capable of producing children alone, unaided by the other. The Aranda say (but how equivocally their mythopoeic statements are to be interpreted is not an easy question) that a married woman, while out on her daily search for food, feels a sudden sensation in her body and recognizes it as the first stages of pregnancy. This "sensation" may or may not be the quickening of the child in the womb. She tells her husband of her experience, and of the exact spot where it occurred. He consults the men of his clan, who search clan history in an effort to discover which totemic ancestor is associated with that spot. When the ancestor is discovered, he becomes the child's totemic ancestor. If the spot is well known, the ancestor is easily determined. But if it is not so well known, reference must sometimes be had to the stories of wanderings and exploits of some ancestor. It is then assumed that at this site he lost a *churunga*—a piece of down from the ceremonial decorations of his body. This *churunga* passed into the ground, but still had a mystical connection with its former owner, so that he could, by this means, "cause" the pregnancy. What it "caused," of course, was the jural descent and filiation of the child.

Among other Aranda tribes, the totem may be discovered by determining which food first caused the expectant mother to suffer from morning sickness. Inheritance of a totem or a *churunga* may run from father to son; just as often, it runs from ancestor to distant descendant, on the basis of conception sites or some other such consideration.

There have been many—and futile—arguments about whether the Australians "really" understood the function of seminal fluid. Such arguments are "really" beside the point, for the fact is that the doctrine of procreation, whether it be "true" or "false" in the scientific, biological sense, does affect *jural* descent.

Among the Trobrianders the father of a child is not considered to be biologically connected, but he is more or less a kinsman of the child. The term for father means, if literally and carefully translated, the mother's husband. Trobriand society is uncompromisingly matrilineal; to maintain their lineal social practices they have refuted out of hand some convincing arguments from missionaries, administrative officers, traders, Dobuans, and Bronislaw Malinowski. The Australians, on the other hand, are patrilineal in some regards, but a third element enters: there may be three sources of the "elements" of a new child—the mother, the father, and the totem. Obviously, any sort of social relationship can be attached to any one of these biological and/or mystical relationships. The Australians utilize the father-son relationship as well as the totem master-totem child relationship for religious and many other social purposes.

Thus the specific doctrine of procreation, which is the indigenous belief about the content of the uterine biological link or the agnatic biological link, is not associated in a one-to-one way with matrilineal descent or patrilineal descent. Matriliny and patriliny are modes of jural descent, *not* of biological descent, which is better described as agnatic and uterine. Kinship may be only an idiom in which the connections are expressed in the folk evaluation.

Certainly we cannot say that matriliny (or patriliny) enables us to "predict" a specific sort of doctrine, any more than it enables us to predict anything else not covered in the definition. However, when so close a relationship exists between a view of biological facts and an idiom of social relationships, it would be a little odd if there were not some interconnection in the folk image manifest in the mythology and pseudoscience of a people. That association should not be confused with the more or less logical propositions of the scientific image of anthropology.

The Ashanti provide a well-recorded example. Ashanti believed in the past—and the vast majority of the uneducated still believe—that two elements go to make up a child: blood from the mother, and spirit from the father. The word for the human spirit and the word for semen is the same word in the Ashanti language. Ashanti say that the important physical characteristics are passed by the blood—note the idiom similar to our own, denoting something quite different.

Important social characteristics are made to coincide with this so-called "passage of blood" and are given ethical and pseudoscientific reason by the Ashanti. All inheritance of goods and status takes place, following the "blood"—in this case, the maternal line—*because* certain enabling physical characteristics are said to descend in that line.

However, the Ashanti consider that the father's spirit is also important in the psychic and religious spheres of one's life. Capacities such as clairvoyance, talents for divination, or aptitudes for the priesthood are thought to pass through the father. Witchcraft ability, although it was not terribly important among the Ashanti, follows the paternal line—the line of the spirit as opposed to the line of the blood. Characteristics such as cheerfulness or temper are said to be attributes of one's spirit, and hence acquired from the father.

Such ideas about procreation and inheritance of physical traits from the parents play a large part in the intellectual doctrine that underlies most unilineal descent groups. The whole situation is summed up in an argument overheard by an anthropologist in northern Rhodesia. In this area there are many matrilineal peoples living near patrilineal peoples; both come to work in the mines of the Copper Belt. Many aspects of their cultures and languages are similar, but they have long arguments about the correctness of their doctrines of procreation. The conversation in point was a sort of bull session among men of different tribes. One from a matrilineal tribe told the others: the important thing is the woman; a man adds no blood, he adds no bones. He does nothing except start the process that produces a child. The woman he likened to a sack that created its own contents, needing only initial stimulation. One of the men from a patrilineal society, who had listened with ill-concealed contempt to these remarks, asked him seriously, "If you have a leather bag, and you put a shilling in it, whose shilling is it, yours or the bag's?" He had stated the doctrine of procreation of his patrilineal tribe.

FUNCTIONS OF DESCENT GROUPS

If unilineal descent groups are found, they are found for the most part in societies of medium size that have fairly adequate means of exploitation of their environments. Although the size and economic condition ranges from the small and primitive Australian tribes to large (several million people) and technologically advanced African kingdoms, there are no unilineal descent groups found in the very smallest-scale societies, such as the Eskimo, or among the largest-scale societies, such as the modern West.

Descent groups or lineages can fulfill many functions adequately—political, economic, familial. Their usefulness stems from two facts: first of all, they can utilize a kinship morality at the same time that they include large numbers of people; secondly, there are no automatic functions of descent groups in the sense that recruitment of society's members is a function of the family or education and training is a function of the household. A descent group does not take on any specific jobs simply because it exists; conversely, it can be assigned almost any job. It is undoubtedly the most supple of all kinship groups.

Descent groups can regulate jural descent, control marriage, or form mutual aid societies. They can be of great importance in political activities, supplying groups within which political offices must be inherited; they may even take over all the functions of government, creating a viable polity in the absence of a state.

LINEAGE SYSTEMS

Lineages have another characteristic. Since they stem from ancestors that may have been related to one another, they can be linked, as groups, to one another while still utilizing the ethic and sanctions of kinship. Such systems of linked lineages are called "lineage systems"; at least two principles are known on which lineages can be linked into systems. There is no reason to believe that there are not other principles, although I do not know them if there are. One of the known principles of lineage grouping is called the principle of segmental opposition; the other can be called the principle of the spinal cord.

Although the principle of segmental opposition has been known for many centuries (political theorists, dealing with different sorts of social groups, call it "balance of power"), it was not made an anthropological principle until the work of Professor E. E. Evans-Pritchard (1940) among the Nuer brought it to the fore. The principle, in agnatic groups, is an extremely simple one. It is a projection of the idea that my brother and I are antagonistic to each other only so long as there is no person more distantly related to us who is antagonistic to both of us. I join my brother against my half brothers. My half brothers join me and my full brothers against the group of our father's brother's sons. They join us, again, against our father's father's brother's sons' sons.

A simple diagram illustrates the point. Let us say that A on the chart is a group of agnates, descended from a common grandfather. B is the group of descendants of his brother. A and B, however, are all sons of 1, the great grandfather. In fighting and in other sorts of political action, A stands against B *unless* 2 gets into the fight. In that case, A and B join,

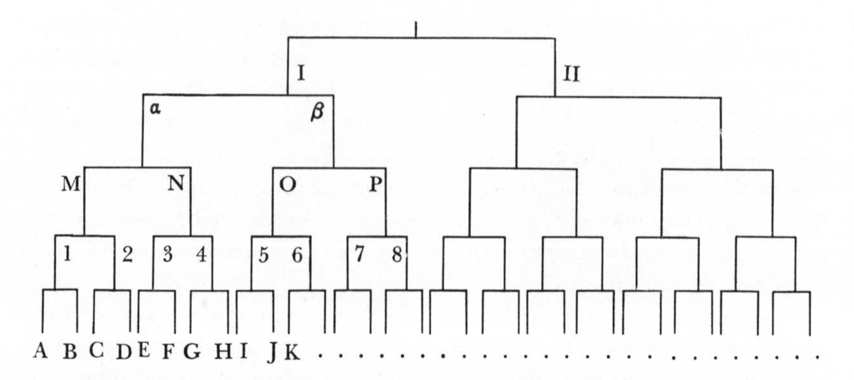

FIGURE 9 Lineage System Based on the Principle of Segmental Opposition

as group 1—they swallow their differences and form a single group. This situation continues until N comes into the matter, whereupon 1 and 2 sink their differences and become group M, as opposed to group N. Group N and M join as group Alpha, against group Beta. This process can be carried on for as many generations as it takes to include all of the members of the most inclusive lineage.

In a group of this sort, which is carefully structured internally, the same principle separates the subgroups at one level as joins them at another level of the structure. This is an extremely economical form of social organization and is found widespread in Melanesia and Africa. The variants range from Tikopia to the Nuer, from the Tallensi to the Bedouin Arabs.

The other form of lineage organization—that on the principle of the spinal cord—centers around a specific piece of property. It forms a single line with various sublineages tying in at various points of the line, rather than utilizing a system of segmental opposition. The organization usually centers around a kingship or around some other piece of indivisible heritable property. In such a system of unilineal descent groups, there is a dominant line associated with the property. It is continually "sloughing off" collateral lineages. The entire descent group is organized in terms of the kingship, as can be seen in Figure 10. In this diagram, which can also be read as a genealogical chart, C is the person or group that is directly descended from the king, via a line of kings. At each generation, there may be one or several collateral lineages. Each one ties in not by the principles of segmental opposition, because the presence of the indivisible inheritance renders equality among the segments impossible. Rather, the tie is found in the relationship of each collateral lineage to the main line at the point in the genealogy at which it branches off. In the lineage system based on segmental opposition, all of the branches, at every level, are equal. In the

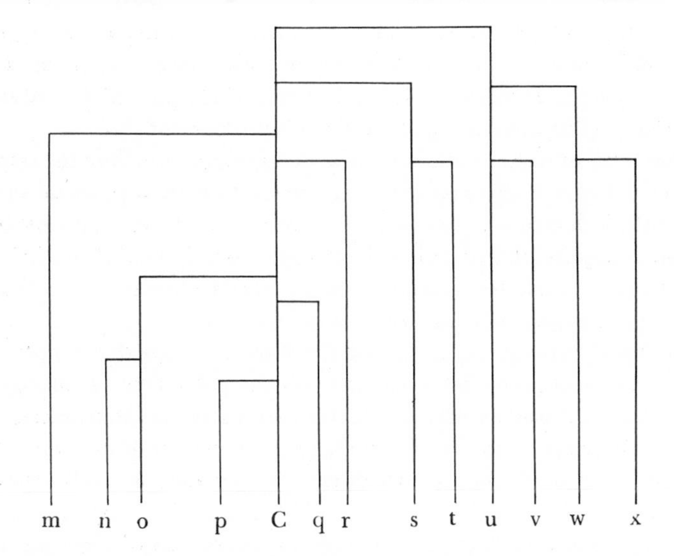

FIGURE 10 Lineage System Based on the Principle of the Spinal Cord

lineage system of the spinal-cord type, built around an office or a piece of property, one lineage is senior in wealth, status, and rank, and the others hook into the main line of descent.

DOUBLE DESCENT

Many societies, such as our own, recognize neither agnatic nor uterine lineages. Many societies recognize one or the other. A few recognize both. Those situations in which both matrilineal and patrilineal lineages are recognized are called "double descent" or "double unilineal descent."

Recognition of the existence of double unilineal systems became fairly general about 1940, although indications of them go back several decades. The first adequate treatment was an analysis by Forde (1939) of the Yakö society of eastern Nigeria. Here patrilineal groups are recognized and form the primarily political units and units of landholding. Matrilineal groups are also recognized, and they form chief units within which inheritance of movable property takes place; they also provide a set of priests of shrines to the founding ancestresses—the priests act as an organized check on the political activities of the officeholders determined by membership in patrilineal groups. A neat balance is worked out between the two sets of unilineal descent groups.

About the same time as Forde, Lawrence (1937) made a major contribution to one of the problems that had haunted anthropology for decades: some of the so-called "marriage classes" in Australia turned out to be groups formed by the interaction of the matrilineal and patrilineal groups in a double unilineal system. The Ashanti also have a form of double unilineal system (Herskovits, 1937; Rattray, 1923, pp. 45 ff.), although patrilineal groups there are given little cultural content.

Even some preponderantly unilineal peoples may recognize the opposite line, but not give it any content or use it for formation of social groups. Fortes (1945) has shown that even so vigorously patrilineal a people as the Tallensi recognize the matrilineal principle, which he called the "submerged line." It has been found in many places since this time that the submerged line may be recognized but not utilized.

A word of warning should be inserted about a danger that is not always avoided. In societies in which one line—say the patrilineal—is strongly institutionalized, it usually happens that a man's mother's patrilineage is of very great importance to him. Thus, the primary descent groups with which he is associated will be his own patrilineal lineage and, on a different jural basis, his mother's patrilineal lineage. This association may be extended to the patrilineal descent groups of his two grandmothers. These patrilineal descent groups to which one is associated through uterine ties show a recognition of kinship—this is *not,* however, the basis for a matrilineal descent group. Hence such a situation cannot be analyzed in terms of double descent. Double descent means that two principles are at work in group formation. It does *not* mean that a single principle leads to several groups, to which an individual can be connected through different sorts of jural or kinship links. Among the Tiv, for example, one's agnatic lineage is one's *ityô*. One's mother's agnatic lineage is one's *igba.* Tiv do not have any word or any institutionalized recognition of any uterine group. Every person is associated with several agnatic lineages. He is agnate in one, "sister's child" in three others.

AGNATIC AND UTERINE COLLATERAL GROUPS

Whereas the lineage is a group of agnates or of uterine kinsmen who see the basis of their organization as descent from a given ancestor or ancestress, the same people might see the basis of their organization somewhat differently. Instead of descent, they might emphasize collaterality. Indeed, many agnatic or uterine groups claim to be ignorant of even the name of their founding ancestor, let alone the genealogical links between the ancestor and themselves. Many American Indian societies present this characteristic. In the past, such groups have been analyzed more or less as if they were the same thing as unilineal descent groups. We here call them agnatic and uterine collateral groups, and note that they have not been well studied comparatively and certainly have not been adequately separated conceptually from unilineal descent groups.

ROPES

Finally, we must deal briefly with a type of descent group that results when consanguines are excluded not on the basis of the sex of the parent alone, but on the basis of same-sex or opposite-sex links between parent and child. The "rope" exists, so far as is known, only in New Guinea. It was described briefly but adequately for the Mundugumor by Margaret Mead (1935, pp. 126-144), and at length but incompletely for the Banaro by Thurnwald (1916).

A rope is a descent group that mixes agnatic and uterine links, but does it in a regular way. An agnatic link depends on the sex of the parent only; that is, the father-son and the father-daughter relationships are both agnatic. "Ropes" are not made by counting agnatic or uterine links in this way. Rather, they are the product of considering the four relationships Fa-So, Fa-Da, Mo-So, Mo-Da from a different point of view: there are two same-sex relationships (Fa-So and Mo-Da) and two cross-sex relationships (Mo-So and Fa-Da). A rope is a descent group made up of cross-sex parent-child relationships. Therefore, within a rope we have only four relationships: Mo-So, Br-Br, Fa-Da, and Si-Si.

The descent group that starts with a man has, thus, a Fa-Da relationship, but in the next generation, it has a Mo-So relationship from the woman who was daughter to the original founder. In the third generation, the son is a member, with his daughter, her sons, and so on. Therefore, a rope cannot contain brother-sister links. It is a descent group represented by only four of the nuclear relationships.

THE TERMINOLOGY OF KINSHIP GROUPS

The naming of kinship groups shows wide variation in the literature, making necessary a warning that every ethnography must be carefully perused for the definitions that are operative for that work, and every comparative work carefully searched for the different aspects of definition which the scholar has chosen to use as his basis of generalization.

Variation and lack of agreement in terminology of kinship groups is commonly held by the noninitiate to indicate a weak point in social anthropology. Actually, the lack of terminological agreement is inevitable at one stage. It arises from the fact that many comparative studies of the past have generalized terms that have narrower meanings in specific ethnographies. The word "clan" is a case in point. If one were to try to determine "the" meaning of the word clan by examining the many ways it has in fact been used, he would be able to say no more than that a clan is a kinship group of a sort that does not appear in the modern West. The Chinese "clan" is an extended family because it includes the wives of its members; an African "clan" is a unilineal descent group; a North American Indian "clan" is likely to be an agnatic or uterine collateral group. It is possible, moreover, to cite many *ex cathedra* definitions for comparative work of the word "clan" (which was originally the term for the old Irish matrilineal descent group). The most widespread is probably the definition of Murdock (1949), to whom a clan is a unilineal descent group which is also localized.

Various other general terms have appeared from time to time: *gens* was at one time used for a patrilineal descent group (with clan being reserved in this system for the matrilineal group). *Sib* was any unilineal group, whether patrilineal or matrilineal (in its original ethnographic meaning a sib was a nonunilineal collateral group, with a contemporary ego). These terms, whenever they are encountered, must always be specifically investigated in the context of whatever book one is reading. To ask what a clan "really" is, is to misunderstand the nature of the word because it has been sensibly used in many ways.

Two more terms should be mentioned, both of which have been somewhat less subject to the vicissitudes of the term mongers. A *phratry* is a collection of clans (whatever that may mean) joined, usually on nonkinship principles. Phratries are typical of many American Indian societies. A *moiety* is any group, based on any principle, so long as there are only two such groups in the total society. Moieties are found in the New World and in Melanesia; in fact, the "dual organization of society" is very widespread.

The primary task facing the student of kinship groups is to keep straight a great deal of variation in the use of terminology, much of which is poorly chosen, to describe groups based on a few distinctions and fewer principles of organization. The task can be accomplished if the scholar keeps in mind the distinctions and categories represented in Table 10, and if he follows two rules: (1) examine carefully what the writer of any specific work means by the terms, and (2) in doing one's own comparisons, use *only* self-explanatory terms.

The network of agreements

part 3

10

Contracts and associations

FAMILY LIFE IS NOT the only aspect of human social life fixed by the central fact that man exhibits those characteristics that led him to classify himself a mammal. Indeed, most other aspects of man's social life take their basis from other dimensions and ramifications of the same situation.

Mammalian reproduction requires two sexes. It also requires of one sex a great deal more time and energy than it requires of the other. The mammalian male has to do something the rest of the time—even if it is loaf. Like most other mammalian males, human males have turned their attention on one another. In some situations they have tried to outshout one another as howler monkeys do. In many they have found excuses, often good excuses, to outfight one another. In some, they have formed agreements to what each apparently believes to be his own benefit. It may or may not be true that the human male fights instinctively, whatever may be meant by that (Ardrey, 1962). It is certainly empirically true, however, that one of the characteristic modes of behavior between men is fighting. Yet, it is equally true that one of the characteristic modes of behavior between men is reaching agreement.

In the late nineteenth century, a highly original German ethnologist named Heinrich Schürtz wrote a book, *Altersklassen und Männerbunde* (1902), that has since that time been either ignored or misunderstood. Schürtz' basic proposition was that women had no organizing and little social ability. The timing of his publication was wretched, for within a few years the suffragette movement was to prove overtly how wrong his proposition was. He claimed, concomitantly, that males had in abundance the very social capacity that women lacked, and that therefore they deserted the females from time to time and formed social groups on bases and principles other than kinship.

Schürtz—like Freud, who, under the influence of nineteenth-century evolutionist dogma, had to put the truths of *Totem und Tabu* into an outlandish, not to say silly, guise—was required by the best thinking of his time to put his proposition into developmental, evolutionary terms. He therefore stated (mistakenly in all probability, but the question has become one of purely speculative interest) that males, responding to the needs of their "superior" natures, which included social talent, first utilized this social talent to form groups based on other criteria.

Schürtz' statement of his propositions made it appear that he really believed males had greater social ability than females. Today, we are aware that a term like "social ability" has little meaning, because it is impossible to define and hence impossible to measure and compare. One can measure social activity, but not social potential. Males are not superior to females as Schürtz would have us believe, nor are they inferior to females as Montagu claims (for some purposes at least) to believe. Rather, the fact is merely that they are *not* females. Male and female are not comparable in terms of "superiority." They are, however, comparable in another regard: females as a category have to spend more hours, calories, and reveries on childbearing and nurturing than males have to spend on child begetting and provisioning. The involvement of the female, during her early adult years, in the reproductive process may be reduced a little; her longer-term involvement in the nutritive processes may presumably be reduced to naught, but such is nowhere the actual case. Many cultures have "emancipated" women, at least some women. As many or more have "imprisoned" men by vastly expanding the involvement of the male in the nutritive and cozzening processes.

The fact remains that men have more time on their hands and uncommitted energy in their bodies than are usually vouchsafed to women. They use their time and energy not merely to provide for their women and children, as most men in most cultures do in some degree, but also to create situations that are as satisfying to themselves as the domestic positions of women (which they cannot emulate in any save a few superficial regards) can be made for most women in most societies.

What males do when they are driven outward by their very irrelevance in some of the basic functions of birth and nourishment can be studied in analogy to the activities of birds and the so-called "lesser" mammals if we are careful neither to anthropomorphize the birds or to ornithomorphize (if the term be permitted) the men. Most male birds, and among some species the females as well, spend their time fighting either for territory or for position in a hierarchy or for both. So do chimpanzees. So, presumably, do some men—at least some men in some societies. And so, worse luck, do some women. It is wrong, however, to assume that just because the national state can be analyzed as a human form of territoriality or a rank system as a human form of dominance, that man can't help "fighting for real estate" (Ardrey, 1962) or dominating his neighbor.

Some form of territoriality is a necessary corollary of the fact that human beings, like birds, take up space and must exploit their environment; some form of control of social power is necessary to achieve order. Tyranny may result from either. Man's capacity for different types of territorial and dominance control seems to be greater than that of any other species. Leslie White (1948) is correct to say that man has not made himself by will alone. But mankind would be very different from what it is if the will—indeed, wilfulness—were not a human attribute.

KINSHIP AND NONKINSHIP GROUPS

Mankind, by his nature and by his *soma,* is driven to form nonkinship groups just as surely, if not as strongly, as he is driven to form kinship groups. The difference is that the very existence of the species depends on kinship groups—and kinship groups can fulfill all of the social needs of mankind. In that sense, the kinship group is the least "specialized" of all human groups. Students of biological evolution assure us that the least specialized organism—that which can adapt itself most readily to the widest variety of demands in the widest variety of environments—has the greatest chance of survival. Kinship groups are nonspecialized in that sense: all social tasks *can* be assigned to them, and in some places will be found assigned to them.

Thus, kinship groups are not merely basic; they are also simple. They are basic because they and they alone (by definition, if you like) control reproduction. They are simple because a single event—birth—is fundamental to all. Kinship groups, no matter how small they may be writ, automatically envelope everyone who does not perish.

In spite of these qualities in kinship groups, however, and of their universal and fundamental nature, there are limitations on the scale of society and on the complexity of the culture of any group based solely on principles of kinship. In the first place, the optimal size of a kinship group is small. Even unilineal descent groups (which may contain hundreds of thousands of people), or the Chinese extended families called "clans" in the English literature (which may be even bigger), become unwieldy in fulfilling *some* of the necessary social requirements. Beyond a certain number, the ethic of kinship is not always an adequate sanction to control behavior. In the second place, and even more restrictive, is the fact that relationships *between* kinship groups are difficult to solve in kinship terms. The means are, in fact, limited to intermarriage of members with concomitant creation of kinship links.

Thus, kinship groups are limited in their scope, for all that they are fundamental and ubiquitous and that they form the core social organizations of all known human societies. In only the smallest of societies with the rudest of cultures are they the only social groups to be found. Such societies as the Eskimo and the Bushman prove both points: that with only kinship groups, human society is possible but its scale is limited. To break the limitations means creation of nonkinship groups by the very people, usually men, who are on at least some occasions peripheral to some kinship activities. The formation of such groups necessitates creating more specialized social forms than the generalized kinship groups.

There are, obviously, nonkinship groups to be found in most societies. Indeed, in our own society, all kinship groups except the nuclear family have either been obliterated or assigned peripheral tasks. Nonkinship groups have all but swamped the kinship groups. Anthropology—and, indeed, sociology—has not been signally successful in dealing with these more specialized nonkinship groups, and it is instructive to inquire into some of the reasons for lack of progress at the same time that we examine the nature of the groups themselves.

It has been the practice of some anthropologists to consider all nonkinship groups as a single sort, suppressing the realization that they form a residual category and a very mixed bag. The first person in Anglo-American anthropology to insist with any degree of stress on the importance of nonkinship groups was Lowie. Lowie, in fact, tried to find a theory of nonkinship groups. In *Primitive Society* (1920) he was struggling with the fact that it is erroneous to force the data on all exotic societies into a kinship formula, as he claimed Morgan had done; at the same time he knew that it was wrong to force it, as he claimed Schürtz had done, into an equally unyielding formula based on the untenable proposition that men have greater social capacity than women. Lowie put in a plea for *not* making any clear analyses of nonkinship groups for fear that such an analysis would cause the analyst to miss the important points about them. Lowie was fighting even in those days for the view that folk images should not be submerged in the commanding oversimplifications of facile theorizing. Unfortunately, however, his *modus operandi* and his advice can be—and to this day sometimes is—warped into a denigration of theory.

Lowie won a complete victory on his main points: no one since he wrote (unless bemused by the dogma of Marxism) has seriously tried to force all social organization into the Morganian mold. Likewise, those who have considered him at all have not taken Schürtz too literally. So much is all to the good. However, Lowie also won a complete victory on his second point: conceptualization of nonkinship organizations has remained extremely fuzzy or has been silently dismissed. The most influential book of the 1940s to deal with these matters—Murdock's *Social Structure* (1949)—deals only with kinship groups, saying nothing about any other sort of grouping.

One reason that Lowie's concern with these problems has never been adequately taken up is the very good reason that Lowie made them almost unstudiable by insisting that all nonkinship groups be studied together and by giving them a name. In fact, during his professional life, he gave them two names. In his early book, *Primitve Society* (1920), he used the word "associations" to cover all nonkinship groups. Later, with his book *Social Organization* (1948), he adopted another term: "sodalities." Happily, he has had no followers in the later usage and comparatively few in the earlier. Effective terminology can never be achieved by taking words from the common language and restricting or changing their meanings in technical contexts. A sodality is (by dictionary definition) a religious brotherhood, and membership is based on training and initiation. To expand the meaning of this word is to leave us without a good term for a religious brotherhood at the same time that it leaves us without an unequivocal word for a general group based on organizational principles other than kinship; most damning, the word is not self-explanatory.

Lowie's worry that "a logical classification might easily lead to a separation of these related institutions" can be dismissed today as groundless, because modern anthropologists no longer search for exclusive classes of groups, but rather for principles of organization.

In working with the ideas of process and principle, it is wise to begin with a brief examination of some of the characteristics of all social groups, including kinship groups, and a consideration of their social purposes and the cultural idioms in which they are expressed. The best starting place is to be found in Malinowski's concept of the "institution" (1945). An institution, according to his definition, is a group of people who are united for a purpose. They have the material culture and the technical knowledge to carry out the purpose, or make a reasonable stab at it. And they have a "charter," which assures them that the purpose is worth carrying out. We shall, in later chapters, add descriptions of several other characteristics of institutions that Malinowski did not stress—their characteristic event sequences, and their more or less complex philosophies, which go beyond the mere charter. The immediate point is that there is a definite mode of recruitment of members into every ongoing institution, that it has a power structure (dominance pattern or even "pecking order," if you prefer the language of the student of birds' behavior), and that there is an ethic that motivates the members.

Kinship institutions are, as we have seen, simple, because they center around the fact of birth. Birth, and the activities that precede and follow it, are the essence of family. Birth is the purpose, which is to say that reproduction is the function, of the group. Birth is the mode of recruitment (with more or fewer secondary criteria, as we have seen) of all kinship groups. Birth and the relationships created by it are at the base of the ethic and the charter of all kinship groups.

Out of these several institutional characteristics, one alone has been repeatedly chosen for comparative purposes: mode of recruitment of members. For better or for worse, the "principle" of a nonkinship group has been confused with criteria for membership. So long as it proves adequate, and so long as we do not confuse mode of recruitment with the structural principle of its organization, we can follow tradition. We shall examine social groups in which the principle of recruitment is age, in which it is sex (as distinct from sexuality), in which it is agreement. Agreement, which is the form of social relationship opposed to fighting (itself a social relationship, of course), is the class that includes contract. Obviously, such a list is not exhaustive—any anthropologist can add others, and any people can make up new modes of recruitment. No such list can be exhaustive because the modes of recruitment are in folk images, and folk images are closed systems only by cultural fiat and for relatively brief periods of time.

SOCIAL GROUPING BY AGE

Probably most cultures in the world have linguistic categories into which they classify people according to age and position in the life cycle: boys, youths, middle-aged men, decrepits, or some such series of descriptive terms. In Africa, the list usually runs something like this: newly born infant, child on the lap, uninitiated boy, initiated bachelor, married man, elder, retired elder. Shakespeare, it will be recalled, reported eight such grades. Each of these descriptive terms represents a stage or position recognized by the culture. The people in that position—who play the roles implied—represent a category in the total population. These categories are usually referred to in the modern literature as "age grades."

Age grades are categories of people in the same general position in the life cycle. They are, in some ways, like the categories of kinsmen recognized by terminological tags; they can vary almost as much from one system to another.

Age grades are not to be confused with age sets any more than a category of kinsmen, marked by a single term, is to be confused with a kinship group. Age sets are corporate groups composed of people belonging to the same age grade, or to a specific part of them. Being classed in the category "old man" is very different, obviously, from being a member of a social group for which the criterion of membership is age.

Age grades are of interest to anthropology because of the fact that differing conceptualizations of the potentialities of peoples in different age spans can have great influence on behavior and expectations. Age grades are of importance to the study of social organizations, however, in only two situations: first, if there is a specific age set organization, and the various members of a set pass through the age grades together, with greater or lesser ritual or other recognition of passing from one to the other; and, secondly, if age is a criterion for membership in either formal or informal social groups.

The home par excellence of age sets is East Africa, although they are found in one form or another all over the world. In Africa, however, this form of grouping has been particularly exploited, especially on the eastern half of the continent.

In East Africa, and in most other places, boys and men usually enter age sets as a result of initiation. Such is not the case everywhere, however. We must, therefore, keep in mind during our examination of some examples that initiation, unlike birth, does not occur everywhere—it does not even occur everywhere there are age sets. Therefore, the act of initiation stands in a different kind of relationship to age sets from that in which birth stands to kinship groups. In fact, there is no other instance in which so positive a correlation between a focal event and a principle of organization will be found.

The Nuer offer a case in point in which initiation is important. Nuer youths are initiated into manhood and formed into age sets when they are about sixteen years old. The initiation comprises a ceremony that culminates in the operation of cutting deep incised lines on the boys' foreheads. Such lines are tribal marks signifying adult status. The boy goes to an age mate of his father and gets the simple ceremonial blessing of that set, and then proceeds, with some of his contemporaries, to the home of an operator. Usually from four to a dozen boys pass through the initiation at the same time. After the operation, the boys are members of the same age set. The initiates from six or seven consecutive years are formed into a group by the fact that a ritual officeholder of the tribe, called the "Man of the Cattle," will, after some six years, declare that the operation must not be performed for about four years. Thereafter, a new set is formed, hence the span of each age set is approximately ten years.

Age sets among the Nuer—and indeed every place else—are also limited spatially. When an age set is closed, and given a name, the closing first takes place in the immediate area of the Man of the Cattle. It then spreads to the other communities within the subtribe. The sets are named by Nuer, and the names tend to be different from one subtribe to the next; however, they are correlated by the members, so that if a man goes on a visit to another subtribe, he can always determine with ease which age set is correlated with his own at home, and can readily identify himself with it.

In some East African societies, the names of age sets are repeated at regular intervals, giving what is called a cyclical system; such a system is usually associated with a specific pattern of time concepts, and a view of time as basically cyclical and repetitive. Other societies do not repeat age-set names, but each one has its own, with the progression conceived as having no beginning and no ending. This form also is associated with a characteristic time notion, which more nearly resembles our own. Such sets are usually called "progressive."

A cyclical age-set structure has the same effect as would our naming the decades of a century, then seeing each century as a repetition of the last. The classical Chinese system of time reckoning, in repeated cycles of sixty-four years, gives a similar sort of cyclical structure, though in China literacy and the monarchy led to other forms of time reckoning as well. In East Africa, time reckoning is more consonant with that built into the age-set structure. A "cycle of time," so to speak, is the length of time that it takes for an age set to go through all the age grades: from birth, initiation, warriorhood, marriage, elderhood, and death. There may be—and in some tribes it is thought that there must be—members of both the young and the old alive at the same time: thus, age set X is made up of very old men, but associated with it are the very young boys who will be members of that age set when they are initiated.

In both these situations, whether the age set is cyclical as among the Masai, for example, or whether it is noncyclical as among the Nuer, all of the men of the set go through the various age grades together, and these changes in social position are marked by more or less formalized acts. Initiation is the first. Commonly, initiation turns boys into young men.

FUNCTIONS OF THE AGE SET

After initiation, the uses to which the age set may be put are many and varied. Initiation does not, like birth, imply any specific tasks to be fulfilled, functions to be satisfied. The question becomes: What does an organized group of young men do? Obviously, the variation can be considerable, in spite of the fact that the tasks they can be assigned are limited. The Zulu provide a good example. After initiation, the Zulu sets—that is, all the members of an age set from a given community—proceed to the king's village, and there become part of the active army. The set in which they were initiated becomes a unit in a regiment, so-called, of men of approximately the same age. These men live in groups numbering up to several thousand. Each member has brought a younger kinsman to act as his cook and bat boy. During the time that their set is in the regiment, they form the active army of the nation. They were given training, and they were sent out to police the nation, to collect tribute, to conquer neighboring tribes. At the apex of Zulu achievement, the whole army organization was based on local age sets.

After a certain period—apparently about ten years—the men could return to their native villages, marry, and raise families. Their entire set, in other words, was demobilized at one time: the men now, by a ceremony of retirement from active duty, passed as a group from their positions as warriors to positions as elders. As elders, which here means men of from twenty-five to sixty or so, they were the backbone of the community. They were the chief producers of agricultural goods and they were the owners of the herds. They were also involved in local government and politics. After about sixty or so, the entire set, which still existed as a social group, retired from active participation in community affairs—they "became ancestors." This retirement of the group was apparently almost as horrible an experience as is retiring in American society. The men, as a group, ceremonially handed over the reins of government to the sets that had more recently returned from military service.

Such a group, during the years of its existence, can obviously perform a great many functions: first of all, it marks the progression of its members through the life stages. When its members are young, it provides a basis for education and training, and hence shares with the household the function of enculturating and socializing the young. Next, it acts as a military organization, and as such it has political function in the control of power relationships within the nation and between nations. Then, upon its dismissal from active service, it becomes an organ of local government, and hence takes on another political function: that of controlling the power decisions made within the local group. Finally, the set is retired and given a religious function in society—upholding the supernatural welfare.

In one tribe in southwestern Tanganyika age sets are even used as a basis for village grouping. Because of the fact that these people—the Nyakyusa—impose a very severe avoidance relationship on a woman and her parents-in-law, it has become customary for the members of an age set, at the time they marry, to set up a new village some quarter of a mile or so from the village of their parents. This means that their wives will have a certain amount of freedom of movement, but will still be able to fulfill the requirements of the avoidance relationship. In ten or fifteen years, after the wives have borne their children, the avoidance is relaxed somewhat, and the age set nature of the villages disappears. By that time, however, there are younger age sets who have their own age villages. Therefore, a Nyakyusa community always has some age set subvillages on its periphery (Wilson, 1951).

In other parts of Africa, age sets tend to be more informal, and in some areas formation of sets is not accompanied by initiation. In West Africa, sets, where they exist, are usually used as labor groups. Among the Ibo, for example, the elders of a community would decide that they needed a new shrine, or some work done on the marketplace. They would thereupon call out three or four age sets. The sets were much shallower, covering only about three years, and hence there were more of them. Each age set comprised some twenty or thirty men. The members would get together and organize themselves to do the job pointed out by the elders. They would bring the wood or the mudbricks needed for a building, and their leader would organize them into gangs. They worked together easily and well; in this way community works were accomplished quickly and with a minimum of administration.

It is recorded that when early European administrators first discovered that the Ibo worked in age sets for communal labor, they began to call out age sets for the enforced work of road building and carrying. Almost immediately the age set organization withered and died. Within a few years, the Ibo could truthfully say that they did not belong to age sets or have any sort of age set organization. Therefore, a new type of group had to be discovered for the required communal work. It was, in fact, usually an *ad hoc* group composed of whatever men the government-recognized chiefs could cow into appearing and working.

Still other functions that an age set may perform include acting as assistant in the protection of one's rights, particularly when they are infringed by one's kinsmen. In a society with strong kinship groups, it is often necessary to have some other sort of group especially to protect people from being exploited by their kinsmen; the age set is a fairly common answer to this need. The Tiv provide an example: here a man can be bewitched only by his agnatic kinsmen; therefore, he must have someone to protect him from them if they decide to bewitch him. That "someone" is his age set (Bohannan, 1957; 1960). The Tiv age set backs up a man when he needs help against his kinsmen. It also protects his reputation, and protects his family after his death. A man may, if his agnates are bewitching him and killing his children, flee from them to the home of an age mate, who will protect him, give him farmland and a home for as much as several years. Tiv also call up their age sets to do farm work.

An association of contemporaries is an obvious basis for social grouping and in many widespread areas it is utilized. However, there is no single focal event that serves as criterion for admission to age sets everywhere: initiation is not universal, and there is no reason whatever that it should be. Moreover, the functions of sets are disparate precisely because there are no specific functions that are logically inseparable from the criteria of eligibility. Because young men tend to do whatever offensive fighting is done, age is a criterion in most societies for membership in military organizations. The statement cannot be reversed, however: military organization does not imply age organizations, let alone age sets.

SOCIAL GROUPING BY SEX

Lowie is one of the few modern theorists to have discussed groupings by sex. He even claimed that some societies grouped peoples into three—bachelors, spinsters, and married people. Lowie's difficulty provides a vivid warning that most nonkinship groups—and, indeed, many kinship groups—have not one but *several* criteria for admission. Today we can see that two criteria of grouping are applied in Lowie's example: sex and marital state. The initial grouping is into one category of married persons and one of unmarried persons; the latter category is further subdivided by a secondary distinction between males (bachelors) and females (spinsters).

Social groupings based on sex alone are rare. Combined with other criteria, sex is fairly commonly found as a criterion of admission to groups. In most societies, there are some social groups and some activities from which women are barred; others from which men are barred. Our own culture provides examples: lodges, altar guilds, and indeed some commercial firms that are closed to one sex or the other. Probably nowhere is the separation of the sexes so adamantly maintained as in Melanesia. One of the most careful descriptions is that made of the Siuai of Bougainville by Douglas Oliver (1955, pp. 329 *ff*.). Here many villages have men's societies, the main function of which is the social one of providing feasts, although the members may owe one another labor and some goods. The membership is limited locally, as well as limited to men; not all men are required to be members, and not all localities have active men's societies. There is an informal and variable hierarchy within the clubs; the more powerful the leaders, the more active the men's club is likely to be.

In examining descriptions of groups composed of one sex or the other it is apparent that such groups may be assigned a wide variety of tasks, but that in every empirical case those actually assigned are limited to a few. The purpose of the group may be economic and provide welfare for its members; it may be religious; it may be the organizer of entertainment. In all cases, however, if the leadership or membership is inactive, or if the task is performed badly, there is no panic and no serious social maladjustment. The tasks performed by such groups tend to be either peripheral to the basic tasks of society or else to be fairly easily taken over by kinship groups or some other.

SOCIAL GROUPING BY AGREEMENT

One of the gravest difficulties in the study of social organization is to be found with groups formed on the basis of no more than mutual agreement of members. The difficulty takes several forms. In the first place, such groups can vary widely in the form their organization takes. They can, moreover, be organized to achieve any purpose whatever, although the legality of their purpose and activity affects both form and membership criteria. The form of the organization may, except for the criteria by which members are admitted, differ not a whit from an age organization, a one-sex organization, or some other organization. Moreover, since kinship groups can perform all the necessary functional requisites of society, and since almost all groups lend themselves to more than one purpose, to study social groups based on mutual agreement by investigating the purpose each is meant to serve can be of use only before comparative studies are essayed, or if we require a catalogue of the ways a single task can be performed.

A further difficulty is evident: the principle of agreement of members has been analyzed largely in terms of contract, which is a peculiar type of agreement that has been of especial interest to Western law since Roman times. Moreover, latter-day social science has often approached such groups in terms of "voluntary association," equating that notion with contract, forgetting that so far as voluntarism is concerned, there is a fundamental anomaly in contract: formation of a contract may be a voluntary act, but once the contract has been made, the element of volition has necessarily to be foregone.

The confusion has been deepened by a failure to distinguish the lawyer's opposition of contract to status with the sociologist's opposition of "voluntary" to "involuntary." "Status" means, to lawyers, a set of rights and obligations that are inherent in social positions (achieved by any means other than contract), whereas contract means a set of rights and duties initially assumed volitionally by the parties to the contract. To lawyers, "status" is the residual category, whereas to social scientists, "contract" has been the residual category. The content of the former is largely confined to a narrow radius; the content of the latter is of a much wider sort and, within the canons of law, can be dictated by the agreeing parties.

The basic technique of the four-square can straighten out at least some of the confusion (see Table 12).

TABLE 12 VOLUNTARISM AND CONTRACT

	STATUS	CONTRACT
VOLUNTARY	?	"Free" contract with consideration 1. casual 2. durable
NONVOLUNTARY	Kinship groups Ranks One-sex groups Etc.	"Social" or commonweal contract

Logically—and we shall find it also to be true empirically—there may be nonvoluntary contracts as well as voluntary contracts. We shall investigate the problem of contract and social groups formed on the basis of agreement first by explaining the network of contracts. We shall then, just as we did when we studied kinship systems, show how some contracts can be made durable, and hence provide the basis for relationships that can be linked, by means of syndromes, into stable social groups.

Contract, as the word is usually understood, is an initially voluntary agreement between two or more people to carry out certain obligations and gain certain rights, when these obligations are not part of any other relationship in which the contracting parties stand to one another. Kinsmen can (but usually do not) make contracts with one another if the rights and duties implied by the contract are separable, and definable as different, from their kinship rights and obligations. The same, obviously, can be said for age mates. Contract, thus, is a principle for creating a bond between two roles, with overtly stated obligations and rights—called a "consideration" by lawyers—being the determining characteristic.

FREE CONTRACT

"Free" contract, with consideration, may imply only a minimal relationship. I go into a drugstore and exchange some coins for a pack of cigarets. I have made a contract and engaged in a social relationship. The relationship is, however, casual—the duration is extremely short, its content minimal; I may never again go into that same drug store.

The market system of economy, which we will investigate in some detail in a later chapter, provides a network of social relationships of this casual, nondurable sort. There is a statistically discoverable rate of interaction; there is a passage of goods and the cultural symbol called money, so that many parts of the culture work well with no more than such casual relationships. The proportion of the relationships that are of this casual sort is one of the most diagnostic features of any society.

No society, however, can depend solely on casual contractual relationships, because the number of necessary tasks that such relationships can perform is limited—probably limited to distribution of physical necessities and some "services," which economists see in analogy to "goods." Indeed, it is probably true that the greater the proportion of casual relationships, the more rigid the noncasual relationships have to be made. Even some of the contractual relationships must be given permanency and security.

The duration of many contractual relationships is extended by the nature of the consideration. Some achieve a permanency similar to that of kinship groups. The permanency is brought about by a sort of division of the relationship into two phases. When I go into the drugstore to buy cigarets, the roles directly involved are salesperson and customer. The cultural content of that role is minimal, and the number of relationships is multiplied manyfold. I am not a "professional customer," as it were. But the role of the salesperson is part of a syndrome— he *is* a professional, which is to say that the role of salesperson is linked in a syndrome with the role of employee. In short, the salesperson, by an agreement he as an individual has made, has assumed a role of "employee" in a large-scale social group the roles of which are independent of the persons in them precisely as the roles of father and son are independent of any particular father and son. Thus, the personal contract, made volitionally, has had the effect of putting a man in a role, or many roles, which are parts of social structures that exist over time. The "free contract," in short, may be used to bind oneself to role behavior that, once bound, does not allow of free content.

The voluntary aspect of contract, therefore, tends to disappear before analysis. It is of very great importance in the folk system that contracts are thought to be formed in such and such a way and broken in such a way. It is of somewhat less importance in the analytical system precisely because the mode of entry into the role may be unimportant in many contexts, and moreover the "freedom" may be illusory.

Therefore, the totality of the network of casual contracts that underlies modern Western society does not supply stable social groups—rather, it supplies a network along which goods can move. But in order for *people* to move, there must be, in addition, other contracts that *do* create stable social groups. In the process the element of contract has ceased to be voluntary in any sense save that one may presumably be free to engage or not to engage at all in any particular contractual relationship.

In order to keep these two types of contract strictly separate, it is well to give each a distinguishing adjective. We can say that there is "free" contract on the one hand, but that the stable contracts which lead to formal social groups are "social" or "commonweal" contracts.

COMMONWEAL CONTRACT

The second type of contract, based on the common weal, has for centuries been discussed only in a political context. The word "commonweal" is given in the *Shorter Oxford English Dictionary* as (1) "common well-being"; (2) "commonwealth," which is (under the next entry) defined as "public welfare" and "the body politic." The apparently inextricable mixture of commonweal contract and political organization has lead many European philosophers down some blind alleys that we would be wise to avoid. We are, for the moment, interested in stable social groups which are held together by agreement among members to cooperate for common well-being. We are specifically not interested, at the moment, in how these groups are formed. It was failure to make such a distinction which misled Hobbes, Rousseau, and the rest of the "social-contract" philosophers, just as it was failure to distinguish sufficiently between functions and origins that misled the early anthropologists.

People "agree" to band together for a common purpose, not just the casual complementary purposes that are served by sales of packs of cigarets. Social groups based on internal cooperation focused on achieving an end considered to be beneficial to all can be said to be based on "commonweal" contract. The social groups so constituted may be as simple as a cooperative credit institution in Japan or as complex as General Motors or the AFL-CIO. The point is that they have ceased to be voluntary, but have not ceased to be contractual.

It was noted above that when administrative officers began to use Ibo age sets to do communal labor, the age sets quickly disappeared. The purposes Ibo had achieved through age sets continued to be achieved, however. It is instructive to see what organizations replaced the age set. Besides being a work group, the Ibo age set was a protective association; and economically very important in the provision of mutual aid to its members. Obviously, this purpose can be fulfilled by any number of other types of social groups. What the Ibo did was to adopt a new sort of grouping that has come to be called a "meeting"—the English word is used.

These meetings are not well reported, but the outlines can be clearly perceived in even a short conversation with Ibo informants. They say that meetings have permanent memberships, and are of two kinds: those meetings whose main purpose is mutual aid, and those whose main purpose is drinking and prestige. In the former kind, meetings are convened, usually on Sunday afternoons, and each person brings a certain amount of money and makes a deposit, which is marked by the treasurer and other officers in a book. Any member of the meeting can withdraw his money and can borrow money from the fund—to be repaid in more or less stated terms. I believe that there is a vote required for borrowing and perhaps even for withdrawing one's balance, but this matter undoubtedly varies from one group to the next. The meeting usually is a social function as well, the host providing beer or food. The other sort of meeting is sometimes called a "dinner club," again in English. This is a small group of friends who entertain one another—usually quite lavishly—once a month, sometimes twice a month. The membership is constant, although members sometimes invite outsiders when it is their own turn to entertain.

Such "meetings," especially as they function as mutual-aid societies, are spreading through Nigeria. When I worked in southern Tivland in 1949-1950, the Tiv vastly mistrusted the meetings of the Udam, a people between themselves and the Ibo. The Udam meetings were, originally, carried out by age sets. Tiv, who say that Udam age sets in the old days were made responsible for obtaining Tiv victims for human sacrifices, were sure that this method for collecting money at each meeting was a ruse for getting enough to buy Tiv heads to resuscitate the practice—they were unsure just who would be the sellers, but convinced that the world is full of corruptible people who might be.

When I returned to this area late in 1952, meetings were in full swing among Tiv. They had not yet "replaced" age sets, which were still functioning as they had been before; but neither had Tiv made use of age sets as the "meeting" membership unit, as the Udam had. When I inquired about the evil practices of meeting memberships, I was told either that only the Udam did that but that for Tiv the meeting was merely a mutual-aid group, or else that Tiv had misunderstood the Udam originally.

Thus, among the Udam, an existing social group—the age set—was given a new function (that of savings association) and a new name. The Tiv, observing the new function, did not adapt an existing organization, but created a new one on the basis of commonweal contract, to carry it out.

Mutual aid or social security can be carried out by great varieties of social organizations, especially by kinship groups and age sets. It is common, however, that groups for this specific purpose are created on the principle of commonweal contract. Wherever they appear, they show many of the same characteristics that we have already noted for West African "meetings." One of the best recorded is that called *ko,* found in prewar rural Japan. This cooperative credit club has been vividly described by John Embree. (1939, pp. 103 *ff.*)

Any man who needed money was free to form a *ko* to raise it, if he could find other members. He asked several friends to help organize it. They, in turn, asked others to become members. On a given day, the *ko* would meet, the amount of obligation of each would be decided upon, rules made, and officers chosen.

Embree gives as an example a man who needs 160 (prewar) yen and gets a group of twenty of his friends to form a *ko,* each giving him ¥ 8. The amount is repaid, with interest, at ¥ 10 per meeting until each man has received his investment plus interest. The original borrower had, obviously, paid ¥ 40 interest; but without an additional element, some men would have earned quicker repayment (and hence greater interest) than others; the added elements were a form of bidding for position on the repayment roster and a payment to be made by each member at each meeting, to go to the person whose turn it was on the roster.

The *ko,* after its first meeting, usually met twice a year. At each meeting, each man made a bid, written on a piece of paper. The man with the lowest bid received ¥ 10 from the original borrower and from any other member who had already won, plus the amount of the bid, say ¥ 4, from each of the other members. People who had won and collected could bet at later meetings, but had to pay ¥ 10 each time. Obviously, the man who can hold out longest before he needs money badly enough to make a bid that will allow him to collect gets the most return. Thus, usually people bid high at first, not desiring to win, but reduce their bids toward the end of the *ko*. Here is Embree's example:

First meeting:	everyone (twenty people) pays ¥ 8 to the man in need. Total—¥160.
Second meeting:	the original organizer pays ¥10; everyone else pays the lowest sum bid, say, ¥6. Total—¥126.
Sixth meeting:	the five men who have won the bid, plus the original organizer, all pay ¥10. Everyone else pays ¥5. Total —¥125.
Twentieth meeting:	nineteen men pay ¥10 each, and the others the lowest sum bid, say, zero. Total—¥190.
Final meeting:	all twenty members each pay ¥10, the last automatically getting ¥200.

Ko payments were sometimes made in rice rather than in money; obviously, they could be established in any form of wealth. Sometimes *ko* are formed for labor; each member can call the group once during its lifetime. Although interest rates are high, and skill is involved in bidding, no one in the *ko* is ever required to put out any large sum at one time—yet each member at some time receives a large sum all at once.

The important point is that an organization of this sort, based on commonweal contract, might last as much as twenty years if there were forty or fifty members. During that time, some members are likely to die; if that is the case, a member's heir—usually his eldest son—inherits his rights and obligations of membership. Here, then, is an example in which not even entry into a social group based on contract can be said to be voluntary. The social group, once it has been created, once its obligations and rights become established, has a sort of life of its own, and its members come into and pass out of it. Although its original members entered the *ko* on the basis of commonweal contract, they created an organization of long-term roles and relationships that superseded the mere contract: the obligations of the positions were incumbent on the man's heirs. Contract had, in short, created an institution that went beyond itself: the "contract" had become "anomalous."

Another widespread type of long-lived organization that is based on commonweal contract is the guild. Guilds are usually associated with medieval cities, but in fact they have been discovered and studied in many ages and on many continents. Some of the best studies have been those of West Africa.

Traditional Yoruba crafts were associated with certain lineages, and control of quality, production, and other features was in the hands of the same men who were the lineage elders and the lineage head. However, in the 1920s and 1930s the Yoruba learned a great many new crafts. Bicycles were introduced, and had to be repaired. Chairs and tables came to be requirements, and carpenters arose to make them: the first carpenters were trained by missionaries, but soon they came to be trained by one another in a system of apprenticeships. Tailored clothing became fashionable, and with it came the specialist who learned to operate sewing machines and to make clothes to measure. Such clothing had not only to be washed, but to be ironed; and ironing clothes is a highly specialized technique, especially where imported charcoal irons are major capital investments and not part of the accoutrements of every household. Therefore, the number of jobs for which craftsmen were needed increased rapidly. The craftsmen soon came together to form organizations.

The first craft guild known to have been set up by the Yoruba was, Dr. Peter Lloyd (1953) tells us, founded in 1925 in the town of Iwo; it was an organization of carpenters. The local goldsmiths followed the next year, and within a few years the number of guilds increased tremendously. The initiative for forming the guild always came from the craftsmen themselves: one of their number would invite the others to meet at his compound or his shop, and a guild was born.

Yoruba craft guilds have officers who are usually elected: the headman, known as the *Bale* or the *Baba Egbe,* is often the oldest man of the guild, in keeping with the lineage tradition of looking to the oldest male member for guidance. There is also a secretary, who must be literate—and indeed may be the only literate member of the guild. The guilds assess dues and are strong enough that every practitioner of the craft finds it in his interest —indeed, he may even be coerced—to join the guild and keep his dues current. In some situations just before Nigerian independence, the local government of Yoruba towns cooperated with the guilds by threatening to deport any practitioner who did not join, and by allowing the guild to confiscate the tools of the offender.

The guild serves several purposes, not the least of which is the training of craftsmen. When boys—usually at about age sixteen—show an interest in a craft, they are apprenticed to one of the members of the guild, and are recognized by all the members of the guild. The father of the youth usually pays a small annual fee for his son's training, which may require two or three years. During that time, the master craftsman furnishes the apprentice his food, but nothing else. One of the tasks of the guild is to standardize the apprenticeship rate and see to it that the fees are paid. When a man has finished his apprenticeship, he can set himself up as a master if he can get the tools and attract customers. If he manages to do so, he becomes a regular member of the guild. If he does not, he may become a wage-earning laborer for some master—a journeyman. The guild fixes wages according to the type of work done.

The guild also undertakes to maintain standards among members. Such a job is difficult and not always well carried out, but the attempt is made. The guild censures members about whom complaints are received. The guild settles disputes among masters and apprentices, and will not allow apprentices to run willy-nilly from one master to another. The guild fixes prices on workmanship and also undertakes to protect the customer who may make an initial payment for an item and then not get the job completed. Most guilds levy a weekly contribution on each member to cover expenses—both the head and the secretary are, however, unpaid.

The guild has become an important group in the local government of the town. Recognized by the king of the town, or by whatever other local government official may be present, the guild undertakes to make its members pay their taxes as a group, and to enforce professional sanctions on them when they do not comply with the law. The guild has not, however, replaced the lineage—it is the lineage that takes care of its members in sickness and old age, and that carries out most of the other functions of social security.

The study of groups based on commonweal contracts extends in a continuous line to the firms and the unions that form the subject matter of industrial sociology. The principle of contract and the manifold variety of the types of group that can be based on this principle have permeated modern society. In fact, they have been characteristic of modern society that has allowed—indeed, demanded—the sort of technological development that has taken place. Contractual groups do not have the limitations of kinship groups, though they undoubtedly have many others. As a glance at modern bureaucracies will show, they are capable of including very much larger numbers of people than are kinship groups or those based on any other principle. The study by anthropologists of contractual grouping and of the principle of organization by agreement has only begun.

Contract is the most pervasive and compelling of the modes of agreement that lead to social grouping. It is, however, not the only one. Friendship is only one of the difficult and anomalous types of social relationships, based on agreement but specifically not on contract, that have received little attention from social scientists. We have no cross-culture study of friendship.[1] We have, indeed only begun the unraveling of social relationships based on one or more types of agreement. It may be that the difficulty is not merely the complexity of the social forms that may be raised on this foundation; it may be that the difficulty arises from the fact that we have scarcely begun the systematic investigation of the foundation itself.

Thus, we have seen that the human male is not merely social in forming permanent and repetitive types of kinship group. He is gregarious because, driven out of the kinship group on some occasions, he was enabled to create a second or third or fourth reference group in which he can find comfort, friends, enemies, and status. And it is to status that we must now turn—one of the most misunderstood of all social phenomena, because it is one of about which our moral attitudes are undecided and our activities often covert.

---

[1] Probably the closest thing to it is a study by Tegnaeus (1952) of blood brotherhood.

11

Inequality

IT IS ONE of the best known facts of animal sociology that such birds as chickens and reed buntings peck at one another to establish a scale of social privilege, and that any group of such birds can be reduced to a "pecking order." It is one of the best known metaphors of human sociology to ornithomorphize men and say they form "pecking orders" just as chickens do. Recently, the proposition has tended to become even more generalized. One of the dimensions of society in the nonhuman animal world is "dominance": apes do it (except gorillas), birds do it (except ducks), and even fish (except guppies and carp) do it. The generalization about dominance turns out to be that most familiar of all social science "laws": some do and some don't.

"Dominance behavior" is indeed exhibited by many animals. On the other hand, many other animals fail to show dominance behavior. Within human groups, any of several types of human dominance may be shown—yet in some cases, a society may go to ridiculous extremes to avoid recognition of any sort of dominance. In short, it is as scientifically shortsighted to say that human beings are dominance ridden, engaging constantly in peck orders and "status seeking," as it is to say that they are the opposite. The state of grace, it must be remembered, can be interpreted as a situation in which everyone knows his place and takes eternal joy in it—a peculiarly static sort of social dominance.

RANK

What is true is that when the attentions of men are turned outward from the focal kinship groups, one type of social activity that may appear can be summed up under the notion of "rank." Rank can be seen as a summary of human modes of dominance, but rank is a neutral word. It means relative distance, usually considered "vertically," among several sets of two objects. In human cultures many things can be ranked: roles can be ranked, social groups can be ranked, social categories can be ranked, culture traits can be ranked. And each of these rankings gives rise to a peculiar type of "rank system" that characterizes at least some societies.

In this chapter, we shall examine several schemes for ranking social characteristics. In the next, we will take as our subject one particular mode of ranking—the pariah groups based on race.

When the phenomena of rank were first given serious scientific study in the middle of the nineteenth century, no effort was made—it could scarcely have been made at the time—to distinguish folk evaluation from scientific evaluation, and still less to distinguish theory from policy. Marx, the first great modern thinker to tackle the subject of rank, worked entirely with data from western and central Europe. From his observations, and his humane principles, he made generalized statements that his followers (Marx, in his later life, is quoted as remarking "I am not a Marxist") interpreted as generalized and proved theory. Max Weber, the next great mind to work in the field, has been repeatedly summarized by later writers —with some truly amazing misinterpretations—but has never had a worthy successor in this branch of his work.

The bulk of social scientists today discuss institutions of inequality either in terms of "status," a word of extraordinarily difficult ambiguity, or else in terms of "stratification." Thereby, as we shall see, they load the dice. These two notions must be examined in some detail so that the obscurities they harbor can be illuminated.

The term "stratification"—the easier of the two to dispense with—implies not merely a ranked hierarchy, but also a homogeneous quality within each of the various strata. This quality, present in some class and estate systems, is certainly absent in what have been called "situs" systems (see below) and minimal in caste systems.

The word "status," used in studies of inequality (and, in some American work, notably Linton's [1936] [1] also in static studies of social structure), is more difficult. It is a Greek word, but it entered social science as a translation of the German word *Stand. Stand* means in German more or less what in English we would call "rank"; but it also was applied to the medieval European institutions the English language discusses with a French word, "estate" (*état*). The whole has, in the twentieth century, been further confused by the erosion of the word "estate" and its increasing use to mean "old family home," and its ultimate degradation to lower-middle-class housing developments.

In this situation, two types of ranking systems were missed—the medieval estate system (the first to be rediscovered by modern sociology; see Barber, 1957) and the American type of rank system for which sociologists have coined another new barbarism, "situs." It is the nadir of irony that the

[1] Linton meant by this term no more than "a collection of rights and duties." Yet, since he selected the word "status" to express his meaning, he has been badly misunderstood. Such is, in fact, the point of the following paragraphs.

sociologists, missing the type of system that was dominant in the United States until about the time of the 1929 crash and the Great Depression, have popularized another notion—that of "class"—as the basis of American ranking, therefore making it all but impossible for Americans to appreciate any earlier type of class system and its characteristics.

Anthropologists, let me hasten to add, have created an even greater melee in this field than have sociologists; the latter merely misunderstood their own institutions (a common failing), whereas the anthropologists by giving their own institutions general validity (the professional sin of ethnocentrism) have made ethnographic descriptions of rank more or less unintelligible. They have talked about "social classes" and then added that in some places there are both social classes and "economic classes." (Some turned it around, implying that the major distinction of "class" is economic, but that there are also other determinants which perturb such a distinction.) Probably no range of social phenomena (unless it be the economy) has been so badly observed cross culturally as that of the institutions of inequality.

One of the most lucid of several efforts among modern writers to bring sense out of the chaos is that of Kingsley Davis (1948, Chapter XIV). His most telling point is that kinship relationships and hierarchal rank relationships can never be fitted into the same context without doing violence to, and ultimately changing, one or the other. There is differential power within the family, but as a general rule rank structures do not break through families—the exceptions are to be found in pariah situations. This hypothesis has been considered by Steiner (1950) in another guise: that of the range of the status of inequality. Inequality may be relevant within the family but not outside, as in some forms of domestic slavery; or may be relevant outside it but not within it, as in an aristocracy based on primogeniture. Davis' point is that rank determined outside the family and of wide social range is seldom given importance in the internal structuring of the family. Put another way, families share rank, at least so long as they form households. Rank is in a sense the epitome of nonkinship.

Here, however, this analysis will go in another direction: the question will be "What is ranked?" Some of the answers have already been mentioned: (1) roles, (2) social groups, (3) social categories, (4) culture traits.

SITUS: THE RANKING OF ROLES

The most widespread type of rank system is one in which the various roles within an institution are ranked according to some fairly overt principle. An army organization is perhaps the most obvious case in point.

Armies are—and must be if they are to function—organized hierarchically, and the positions in the hierarchy must have a total range within the army. The general is the general. He ranks highest. The various generals under him may be ranked; the colonels and the lieutenants form still lower ranks. Then, an abrupt break marks "officers" from "enlisted men"—what in the British army are called "other ranks." Within the enlisted men there is a firm, indeed a rigid, hierachy.

However, the army organization also best demonstrates that the rank within an institution may not have total social range. An enlisted man in the army, with a low rank, may have a very high rank in the business or professional or theatrical world. The general may have a low rank or none at all among the self-appointed "400." Moreover, the general and the corporal may mix on more or less equal terms or even inverted terms at a house party where army rank is not the criterion for superiority. In short, the military organization has a highly organized rank system, but in America that rank system does not have a total social range.

American sociologists (Benoit-Smullyan, 1944; Hatt, 1950; Morris and Murphy, 1959) have used the term "situs" to describe the ranked positions within a social organization that have this limited social range. They have reserved the word "status" for ranked positions that have a total or at least very wide social range. The situs of general and the situs of "company executive" are not necessarily bunched into a social stratum—there is a tendency in this direction, more pronounced since 1929 or so. But all generals are not of one "class" and to create priorities in seating arrangements demands special protocol officers because the "status" of any "situs" may not be generally known or agreed upon. In fact, situs is relevant only within a given, small-scale framework. The ranking of any situs outside its context may provide practical difficulty to the people of the society concerned. America, especially as it existed at the end of the nineteenth century, was marked by pronounced interest in situs, as it is to this day. Americans of that time gave relatively little attention to "status," in the sociologist's sense as explained here, until the middle of the twentieth century. Melanesia is the home of a complex situs system in which only a minimal broad-scale stratification of situses has been introduced. In the Trobriand Islands, there is an extensive situs system within each clan; the clans are ranked on the basis of religious myths, some clans being given certain prerequisites. There is not, however, an "upper class" among the Trobrianders. In nearby Manus, there is also a highly developed situs system; but rank in Manus depends primarily on gaining wealth in an involved economic and prestige system, and the prestige is not of total social range (Mead, 1930).

The unit in such a system is an individual office or social position. The occupant of that position automatically has the "situs" ; a man may occupy many situses, some high and some low, and these not be necessarily brought together into a syndrome that signifies "status" of broader range.

CASTE: THE RANKING OF SOCIAL GROUPS

At the other extreme from a situs system of rank is the caste system, where the social range of the rank is total; that is, an individual's caste position affects every aspect of his life, and he occupies the same rank in all the intercaste organizations to which he belongs. Whereas the unit to be ranked in the situs system is the role, in a caste it is the social group.

A caste, as it existed in preindependence India, is a corporate group composed of extended families. It is made corporate by the fact that it has organization—a head, and a council called a *panchayat*. Thus, the units in a caste system are not individuals holding positions or playing roles. Rather, the units of a caste system are social groups. Theoretically at least, the organization of each individual caste is beside the point. It is the systematization that is important. The Indian caste system was a ranked hierarchy of groups made manifest on the basis of the sacrificial requirements of the Hindu religion.

Because a caste is a corporate group, it must also be a fairly circumscribed group spatially. Brahmins existed all over India. But a man belonged only to his local caste of Brahmins. A Brahmin from the South who went to the North did not become a member of the local Brahmin caste in North India, but rather still had to associate with his own. Another reading of the situation would be that the caste has local chapters, and that one cannot transfer from one to another of the chapters. Each local caste had its headman and *panchayat*. Independently of it, there were village and state *panchayats* as well. Obviously, it is as necessary to control the disputes and relationships that exist between members of different castes who form the same village or general local area as it is to settle those within the caste. This is the task of the village *panchayat,* whereas the caste *panchayat* controls the difficulties and disputes only of its own members. The *panchayat* was the guardian of the rules of the caste, and it expelled or outcasted members who refused to live up to these rules. Being outcasted was a very serious affair in India; if one had no caste membership, one had no social position. One did not belong to a group in a society in which belonging to a group was everything. The *panchayat* could readmit members whom they had outcasted if those members paid penalties and went through a set of purification ceremonies.

One of the most important developments in the caste system in the days immediately preceding independence (whereupon caste was declared illegal) was the vast increase in range of organization of any specific caste. That is to say, in the old days when transport and communication facilities were limited, a caste had to be of a more or less restricted local nature in order for its organization to work. However, as education and communication facilities increased, caste members could and did communicate with members of associated castes over a very much wider area. Particularly, the low-ranking castes were highly organized and just before independence and the outlawing of the caste system, were becoming more so. The whole caste might form an association and have branches all over India; there was even, in some cases, a central headquarters.

Caste, in other words, must be defined structurally. The key to the sort of definition we need is found in a sentence in Hutton's book, *Caste in India* (1946). He says: "A caste is a social unit in a quasi-organic system of society and throughout India is consistent enough to be immediately identifiable, [but] the nature of the unit is variable enough to make a concise definition difficult" (p. 44). The important point here, in spite of the fact that the metaphor is dated, is that caste is a unit in a functional *system* of such units.

One of the most important characteristics of an Indian caste, then, is that it contains all the members of several extended families. The caste is an agglomeration of kinship groups—kinship groups both interrelated by marriage and blood, but also joined together on nonkinship bases into an organization.

A class, as we shall see, is not only *not* joined together in an organized way, but it has no kinship basis. Westerners see this very lack of a kinship base in a class society as "opportunity" for individual movement from one class to another. Family interests and class interests *may* clash, but in India family and caste interests are always and necessarily conjoined.

The caste *system* provides the principle that has united Indian society, welding the various competing if not incompatible groups composing it into a single community. India, one apologist has remarked, "has developed a system of castes which, as a scheme of social adjustment, compares rather favorably with the European system of warring territorial nationalities" (Gilbert, 1944, p. 82).

Caste in India has its whole mythological charter and its whole logical model set forth in the Hindu religion. The caste system is not only a political system, it is also a religious system. The basis of the system is twofold: it is based first on descent and second on sacrifice (Hocart, 1950). Descent determines the membership in a specific caste; sacrifice is the essential determinant for ranking the castes.

The castes, in addition to being ranked in accordance with the particular Hindu religious customs they follow, are also each marked by specific offices that are important in the political sphere. Hocart (1950) has compared the situation to a combination of the church and the state of which the head is both the king and the high priest. He is the head of the ritual, he is also the political leader. The various officials in both the kingdom and the clergy then hold positions that are vested in specific castes. Often within the caste, it is a specific kinship group that must supply the incumbent of the position. The various local *panchayats*, and indeed the caste *panchayats*, are organized on very much the same basis as is the king's court.

From the Western point of view—it may be the necessary point of view for an industrial society—perhaps the most important thing about a caste is the epiphenomenon that social mobility of individuals is difficult or impossible within the system. The unit of mobility, like the unit of organization, is the caste itself. In the situs system the unit of mobility is the individual because the unit of the system is the role. The lack of individual mobility in caste has been the primary characteristic considered by sociologists in their interpretations. Seen in another way, however, this lack of mobility can be viewed as social insurance providing a group of associates that can be counted on in all situations, so long as an individual lives up even moderately well to the requirements placed upon him by his position. A man's caste

> canalizes his choice in marriage, acts as his trade union, his friendly or benefit society, his slate club and his orphanage; it takes the place for him of health insurance, and if need be provides for his funeral. It frequently determines his occupation, often positively, for in many castes the occupational tradition is very strong indeed, commonly negatively, since there are many pursuits, at any rate in the case of all but the lowest castes, which he cannot follow, or can follow only at the cost of excommunication from the society to which he belongs. It must often happen that membership of a caste will take the place of attachment to a political party, since in such cases as disputes between castes in the Right Hand or of the Left his views of the merits of a dispute and the side he is to support are predetermined for him by his caste membership [Hutton, 1946, p. 97].

To sum up caste briefly: a caste is a social group; a caste system is a hierarchically organized arrangement of such social groups. The individual is not the unit of ranking; neither is the role. Indeed, neither is the social category, which we shall investigate in the next section on estates. In India, every caste was a part of a far-flung caste system, and that system was manifest not merely in economic, occupational, and legal norms; even more important, it was at the basis of the Hindu religion.

Each caste had a certain place in the religious hierarchy, and it is this aspect that gave caste its immutable quality, even though as a matter of fact the position of the castes vis-a-vis one another was *not* fixed—there was considerable movement of castes up and down in the scale (Weber, 1958).

A caste in the Indian system represents a subculture. Not merely does it have an association with one of the techniques of production, and a purchasing power that gives it a certain standard of living, and more or less comparable tastes; but it also has a common set of religious observances and religious prohibitions, which mark it off from all the other castes.

Caste, in brief, is a ranked system of corporate groups, each having a different subculture, the religious aspects of that subculture going to make up one link in the ritual of Hinduism. As we shall see, classes and estates are also marked by differing subcultures, but they are not corporate groups.

ESTATES: THE RANKING OF SOCIAL CATEGORIES

One of the most widespread institutions of inequality is the estate system, which is commonly—and often mistakenly—analyzed in terms of one of its typical manifestations, the feudal system of medieval Europe. Estate systems have just enough in common with caste systems that they can be easily confused. An estate in an estate system is something like the four "colors" or *varna* into which each caste is placed in the Indian system; estate membership is, within the terms of the system, sometimes considered to be immutable, so that there are similarities in the difficulties of personal mobility.

The differences between estate and caste, however, are overriding. Whereas a caste is, as we have seen, a structured and organized group, given expression and organization in the religious system, an estate is a category of people who are not organized but take their position from the fact that they share legal rights and obligations specifically different from the legal rights and obligations of people in the other estates.

In feudal Europe an estate was defined in the folk system by rights and duties concerning land. There were three primary estates. There were the landowners or nobility; there was the yeomanry, who owed certain types of allegiance—including defense of the land and landlord—to the landowners in return for certain specific rights in space and its economic produce. At the bottom of the three categories—that is, the lowest of the estates—were the serfs. Serfs had limited, but precise, rights in land. We often confuse serfs with slaves because they could not leave the land—the criterion of individual mobility, which Westerners always invoke because it is primary in a situs system and a class system. Serfs were not slaves—

as we shall see, they had almost nothing in common with slaves. It was a fact that serfs could not leave the land—it was also a fact that yeomen and nobles could not leave the land.

The estate, however, was not organized as a caste was organized. Every manor contained people of every estate, and the organization was found in the manor or in the principality. The basic idiom of organization in the feudal estate was land tenure and land rights—it might, of course, be almost anything. The estate had very wide ramifications outside the political and economic area, and the range of one's rank was all but total—there were a few urban craftsmen and traders who were outside the system, organized in guilds. The social category was ranked—noble, yeoman, serf. There were scores of roles within each category; but there was no group, because the estate was not organized—there were no officers and no formally structured relationships.

CLASS: THE RANKING OF CULTURE TRAITS

We have so far discussed a situation of ranked roles (situs system), a situation of ranked social groups (a caste system), and a situation of ranked categories defined by jural rights (an estate system). We now come to a completely different situation: one that is usually called class, but is in fact a cultural ranking not of roles, groups, or categories, but of culture traits. In a true class system, what is ranked are the culture traits. Then, one takes one's position by what culture traits one either practices, demonstrates, or stands for. It leads to a system based primarily on education and sophistication.

MARX'S ANALYSIS OF CLASS

The earliest good analysis of class is that of Marx, and yet today it appears, at least to this observer, that Marx analyzed the class system of Europe as it was emerging from feudalism in terms of analogy to estate. Instead of taking the land as the primary referent, Marx generalized and took the entire institutionalization of the production of wealth. Instead of one's rights in the land being the determining factor of one's estate as was true under feudalism, the rights that one had in the means of production became in Marx's system the determining factor in one's "class." Society had changed considerably between the time of feudalism and the time of the Industrial Revolution of which Marx wrote. To sum it up briefly, it had ceased to be a landed society and had become a market society. The basic principle of organization had ceased to revolve about rights in land; it became the necessity for everybody to sell something in the market. Ultimately, the Marxian classification depends on just what it was that the individuals concerned sold in the market; and on the basis of what they sold, they were grouped into classes by Marx.

Marx took the overall production process and broke it down this way: there were the "owners" of the factors of production, who were the aristocracy and, newly emerging, the capitalist bourgeoisie, who provided land and capital. Then, there was the great mass of workers whom Marx called the proletariat, who provided the labor. Now, most of Marx's empirical data were accurate for mid-nineteenth-century western Europe where he was doing his sociological analysis. At that time, firms were by and large owned by the people who were their officers: the capitalist bourgeoisie. The proletariat was a group of workers thrust into the labor market by the Corn Laws and the Speenhamland Act in England, and by similar legislation on the continent. It was in the late eighteenth and early nineteenth century that the dictum "work or you don't eat" was changed to "put your labor on the market and get and hold a job or you don't eat." Before that time, the parish supplied relief for the unemployed. Yet, as the Industrial Revolution proceeded, it became obvious that so long as a capitalist could pay a man less than a living wage, with the difference made up by the parish, the parishes were soon going to be impoverished. Therefore, laws were passed that the parish relief must stop and that if a man was going to eat and feed his family, the only way he could do it was to sell his labor or his brains at the best available price. This creation of a forced labor market in Europe at the end of the eighteenth century caused widespread poverty and misery. Dostoevsky reports what happened (somewhat later) in Russia. DeFoe's *Moll Flanders* shows the effect on the common people of Great Britain. Probably at no time in the history of Europe has suffering existed on so wide a scale.

What had happened is that the type of society had changed, and adjustment to change always brings some misery. Vast change brought vast misery. Whereas formerly the economy had been a combination of a subsistence economy with household or cottage industry to supply money, it became—in the course of a few decades—a full-fledged market economy. This means that if you want to eat, you have to sell labor, rights in land, entrepreneurial daring, capital, or goods. That is all there is to sell in a market system—so far, at least.

Karl Marx saw the human suffering about him—especially that in Great Britain, where the Industrial Revolution took place first, and where it probably was at its most acute. He interpreted this new industrial market society developing in Britain in terms redolent of late continental feudalism. Whereas estate in feudal society was determined by land in a subsistence economy, Marx generalized and postulated that the position of every "class" must be determined by its place in the processes of production, determined by what it sold on the market. He read this proposition as a "law" of general applicability.

Marx, in short, noted that there were several important factors here: the first is that people are ranked. The second is that there are easily discernible categories of people, and that in nineteenth-century Europe these categories were given names and called classes: there were the aristocracy, whose position still came from their entailed land; there were the capitalists, whose position came from the fact that they put entrepreneurial know-how and monetary capital into the production mill; there were, at the other extreme, the workers who had nothing to sell but the strength of their backs and the sweat of their brows.

Now, so much of Karl Marx's sociology is impeccable reporting and analysis of the nineteenth-century situation. Marx did not, however, stop there. He sought to rebuild the society and the class structure on what he considered a more equable basis—indeed, on what he considered the "correct" basis. The first thing that Marx noticed is that the classes of nineteenth-century Europe were not organized. Such is, as we have seen, the basic difference from Indian castes. He made an error of judgment when he thought that the aristocracy and the capitalists *were* organized, but that the petit bourgeoisie and the workers were not. It is true that the aristocrats tended to know one another and marry one another's daughters. They were a small category, and they were a closed sector to the rest of the society. Marx mistook this solidarity for organization. In the same way, capitalists were few in number, tended to know one another, and to join the same clubs. Marx said that the clubs and the informal alliances such as friendships and marriages among them led to—indeed, that they constituted—an organization. Marx was wrong on this point: the classes were not organized; rather there were some organizations into which one could get only if one could be categorized as of a certain "class." Criteria of eligibility are not the same thing as principles of social organization.

Marx's ideas were now converging: on the one hand, you take widespread misery among the workers while they changed over from one type of society to another. On the other hand, you take the illusion that the upper classes, so-called, were organized. Finally, you interpret both in terms of a model derived from the medieval estate system, and throw in the economist's desire to effect policy. Marx's reaction could have been foretold: "Workers of the world, unite! You have nothing to lose but your chains!"

Marx called an unorganized class an "incomplete class." He urged the workers to *become* a class, as he had defined it. However, a glance at some of the other class systems of the world, including the mid-century American one, has by this time shown us that a class is never organized. A society may be marked by a number of institutions and organizations that draw their members from specific classes, but the class itself is *not* an organized social group. It is not even a single category; no more is it a collection of situses. Even in Communist countries, in which the so-called "Revolution" has been completed, the workers are not organized: it is merely that there are a series of recognized "classes" and a great many organizations that they can join. The viewpoint of the working classes can, through organizations such as the Union or perhaps cells of the Communist Party, be expressed. But the class remains at most a very diverse category; never a group. For all that class may be a criterion for admission to a group, it does not itself constitute a group.

In recent years, Professor Sorokin of Harvard has restated a part of Marx's theory about a class becoming self-aware, in less dogmatic and hence more acceptable terms. He points out that

> Persons having essentially similar occupations, economic position, and rights and duties cannot fail to become similar in a great many other ways, physical, mental, moral or behavioral. The similarity of the objective bonds and conditions renders them "mutually assimilable"...and possessed of consciousness of kind....The objective basis of all these similarities is the similar occupation, economic and legal position of the members [Sorokin, 1935, p. 90].

Either Marx's or Sorokin's accounts can be restated in cultural terms. If classes are composed of people who have different occupational experience and knowledge, different economic incomes, purchasing power, and the like, and sometimes even different rights before the law, they must obviously form different subcultures within an overall culture. It follows, then, that they *may* have different ideas of child rearing, courting, food habits, recreation, and all the rest. Kinsey (1948) if his report accomplished nothing else, showed that sexual behavior varied with class, as determined by occupation and income. Voting behavior and many other areas of life also vary widely with class, determined by these two criteria. Criminologists are discovering, moreover, that there are actually criminal subcultures, and that delinquents usually learn to be delinquents and to participate in this particular type of subculture, in which criminality is the norm (Sutherland, 1960). The fear of TV reformers is that television may be used to disseminate criminal subcultures to "noncriminal classes."

Therefore, to an anthropologist, a class system becomes a system of ranked culture traits, and insofar as a person shows these culture traits he can be "classified." Indeed, this is what all the recent popular accounts have claimed—Nancy Mitford's (1956) "U" and "non-U" is no more than a hierarchal ranking of culture traits. In fact, Lloyd Warner's (1941) whole approach is his generalizations about a classification of culture traits. It is necessary, however, to follow through the history of the subject in order to arrive at two points: (1) the social structures that accompany a culture-trait ranking of the sort we today associate with class; (2) the sense in which caste and estate systems are also systems of ranked subcultures and the ways in which they differ from class and from one another, in cultural terms.

WEBER'S ANALYSIS OF CLASS

After Marx the next great thinker about the matter of rank was Max Weber. It was he who first distinguished class from caste on the criterion of the corporate group. Weber said that classes were not structured units (*Gemeinschaften*—a word he used much differently from Tönnies), whereas castes *are* structured units. In other words, classes are, for Weber, made up roles that have identical or easily identifiable ranks in the society of widest range, and common cultural experience. They are not organized like castes; they are not of merely limited social range, like situses.

Max Weber was not, however, able to tear himself away from the nineteenth-century *Zeitgeist,* as it is typified in Marx. He, therefore, clung to the production processes as the primary referent of all ranking and stratification phenomena.

AMERICAN STUDIES OF CLASS

American studies of "stratification" have been of a completely different order. They have been influenced, often to too great an extent, by the European studies, but they do not find their point of departure in the production process. The early American sociologists—those who worked before 1925 or so—showed little or no interest in problems of stratification, undoubtedly for the good reason that in a situs system it did not impinge on their lives. Then, in the 1930s, sociologists realized with something of a start that American society not only ranked people, but the ranks were divided into strata, and that here was a phenomenon worthy of thorough study. They (Lloyd Warner was the most important of them) mistook the fact that there is a rank system in the United States by calling it a "class" system, which is only one type of rank system. Since it had never been studied—since, in fact it was only emerging—nobody knew precisely what it was. The Europeans had studied their systems. And Warner and the others took over all the determinants of "class" in Europe—even those that were peculiarly European. American thinking about rank would be very different had they taken a Melanesian model—not a fantasy, because Warner was fully aware of Pacific ethnography having himself made what is one of the most important single twentieth-century contributions to it.

Like the good American sociologists they were, they started to work with statistical techniques. Such techniques are utterly irreplaceable for studying casual and largely unstructured social relationships. They are, however, useless without hypotheses, and without something to count. The hypothesis they used was that most Americans are "middle class," thus supposing anything that has a middle has two ends and thus assuming a tripartite division; the objects they counted were the cultural concomitants of the classes so determined. The result was obviously that they could give us long lists of culture traits that divided the "classes" from one another, at the same time that they provided the original books which Nancy Mitford and her collaborators have parodied so ravishingly.

Warner, following his initial tripartition, subdivided the upper, middle, and lower classes into three each: upper-upper, middle-upper, lower-upper, and so on. The process started over. It could go on indefinitely if anyone cared to carry it further.

Today it is hard to distinguish how analytically successful the Warner studies were from the possibility that they fed back into the general culture and "seeded" the chaos of rapid change into a system. Americans are, in fact, forming a class system; the situs system may be no weaker, but the class system is certainly becoming stronger. Americans are well on the way to filing various situses, of narrow range, into classes of much wider social range.

EUROPEAN CONCEPTS OF CLASS

Continental European systems of rank are still taken much more from positions in the means of production, writ wide in social range. Americans have not to the same degree widened out the range of the situs associated with the task in the production processes. They have, rather, utilized association with culture traits in creating their wide-scale stratifications. Therefore, Europe has a "working class" and a "bourgeoisie," whereas America has a "lower class" and a "middle class."

England has always been a sort of halfway house between the Continent and America in this matter, as in many others. You say "upper classes" (in the plural) in common British speech, but not "lower classes" unless you are being facetious—in which case "lower orders" marks the facetiousness more safely. Rather, the correct term is "working classes." The people in between are called by a large number of subclass names, such as professional classes, university classes, small shopkeepers. They may, however, also be lumped together with almost everybody else and called the "middle class." Middle class in Britain has a meaning something of this sort: it is a category of people who have fairly good educations, who make fairly prosperous livings in business or in the professions, who have full political rights of commoners but not political privileges of peers. There are, thus, economic, occupational, and legal characteristics definitive of the so-called "middle" class.

When, in the formerly British colonies in Africa, Malaya, and elsewhere, people emerged who showed these same qualifications—politically aware entrepreneurs, teachers, and clerks with some education—the British called them an emergent middle class. Yet, in the African situation, they are not middle—they are far and away on the top. They are only questionably a class, for they had, before independence, comparatively little recognition of common interests or experience.

We have noted that class systems are a hierarchy of culture traits and that, therefore, "classes" are really little more than concatenations of culture traits as marked by the people who practice them. We have also noted that castes are subcultures within a cultural system, at the same time that they are organized, structured social groups marked by religious function and practice. The various estates in medieval Europe certainly displayed different cultures. The question before us, then, is to investigate these systems in terms of culture to see whether or not the problems can be further unlocked from this point of view.

American culture is, from an anthropological point of view, made up of many subcultures, some of which are primarily associated with what we call "class." If one wants to change classes, one must first learn the new culture; afterwards one can, with greater or lesser fluency, move with that class and "be" that class. These culture traits include many subtle items—even mode of walking, certainly of speaking (although it is likely to be grammar, vocabulary, and voice quality rather than "accent" which change), modes of behavior and especially of evaluation of behavior. American class position is "achieved" in this sense, even though one takes the class position of one's family at least until one's education is well under way.

Preindependence Indian society was also a hierarchically ranked series of subcultures, but there were important differences. The first one is that culture was "ascribed" rather than achieved, just as was the position of an individual within the system. Secondly, however, the subcultures of caste India were unified into a single simplistic system by religion. Subcultures in a class situation are concatenations of traits; the traits make up the whole culture, but no single concatenation forms a central key. There is no unitary "upper-class culture" in American society that fits together with a unitary "lower-class culture" to make up the entire culture, as there were Brahmin culture, warrior caste culture, farmer caste cultures, and the like, which together made the whole of preindependence Indian culture. We are saying, in cultural terms (in which it is clumsy), that castes are corporate groups whereas classes are not.

Thus, although it is true that culture is ascribed to certain castes in India, and it is achieved by some people in America, it is also necessary to point out that the problem goes deeper: there are social positions in a caste system that must be filled—like quotas in a centralized production system. In a class system, on the other hand, classes result from the thousands and million of choices made by the citizens who practice the culture. There is no necessary position "upper class" in the fabric of American society. There is only an epiphenomenon "upper class," which results from the workings of American society and culture. The class system is, therefore, of the same logical nature as the economist's "market." It shows regularities and can be studied with analytical techniques, and there is a regularity about it that makes it predictable. The caste system is different in that maintaining it is one of the purposes within the society. It is in no sense epiphenomenal. It can be learned by acculturation rather than by scientific analysis. A class system, on the other hand, consists only in disparate traits minimally recognized, and a scientific analysis.

SERVILITY

In addition to the institutions of inequality based on rank, there is another set of institutions that grow out of relationships of servility. A servile relationship can be said to exist when one person or individual has legal rights in another, if these rights are held to the exclusion of other persons and are not derived from either contractual or kinship obligations. The rights of the master in the slave are legal rights, derivable neither from kinship nor from contract, and they exclude all other people from similar rights. Conversely, the rights of the slave in the master—and they are as binding as their counterpart—are likewise nonkinship, noncontractual, but nevertheless legal rights, and they can be exercised against only one master and only by his recognized slaves.

In the modern West, our legal rights are based either on kinship, citizenship, or contract. We have no recognized institutions of servility at the present time. For this reason, and perhaps some others, it has been difficult for us to discover the essential aspects of the master-slave relationship. We have tried to analyze it in economic terms, because the plantation slavery of the South is regarded (whether correctly or not) as primarily economic. The slave is considered in our folk evaluation to be a "chattel" of economic worth rather than a person related to a master by legal means that are based neither on kinship nor on contract. There is, undoubtedly, an "economic aspect" to such a relationship—there is an economic aspect to many kinship relationships—but such may not be the essential quality. We have combined this economic criterion with that other favorite Western criterion, the mobility of the individual, and have lumped slavery and serfdom into a category in which we think it would have been preferable to be a serf (but not much preferable)—and so have failed to understand either institution.

THREE ASPECTS OF SERVILITY

There are three aspects of the servile relationship that must be examined here. First of all, servile relationships are what we might call "antikinship" in analogy to antimatter. They are not merely *non*kinship (in analogy to nonmaterial), as are relationships based on contract or those established by rank. They are, rather, actively antikinship in that a slave can have no kinsmen and is connected with kinship groups by nonkinship criteria. The exceptions are those instances in which the "master" is a nonkinship group that nevertheless performs some obligations of kinsmen for the slave. Secondly, there is the matter of the range of servility; this problem can be examined much as we examined the social range of rank. Third, servility is often masked by rank systems such as class and caste in the societies in which it occurs, and it must be separated from them.

Slaves are essentially kinless people; kinlessness is an essential of slavery wherever it is found and whatever else may accompany and mark it. Everyone who has read *Uncle Tom's Cabin* remembers that one of Mrs. Stowe's criteria for a good master was that he did not break up the elementary families of his slaves for whim or profit—he always "left families together." However, he had a right to break them up. Moreover, the kinship system was seldom extended beyond the nuclear family, and the fact that many of these families were broken up—or never properly formed—has made the matricentric family the focal aspect of kinship among the slave population, which to this day is still reflected in lower-class Negro culture.

In Africa, where slavery existed in many forms including but not stressing the form of plantation slavery which is the only one the New World has ever known, there were two ways for a man to become a slave: he could be captured by slave raiders, or he could be sold by his kinship group. A man who was a thoroughly bad lot could, by the agreement of the authorities of the group and through the performance of a simple ritual by his kinsmen, be "unkinned" if we may put it so. Such a ritual stripped all of his kinship rights. He had literally no position in society when the major determinant of position was kinship affiliation. He necessarily became either a hermit or a slave.

Becoming a slave meant that he associated himself on an antikinship basis with kinship groups not his own. Therefore, complementary to the slave's kinlessness is his immediate legal dependence on his master. The dependence of slave on master is similar to dependence among kinsmen: the obligations are legal on both sides and do not develop out of contractual arrangements or the rights of citizens. Even the plantation slaves of the New World were attached to the kinship groups of their masters, although the content of the relationships may have been largely economic. The only exceptions to such a generalization are to be found in those areas in which slaves are attached to temples or to courts that fulfill for them the requirements of kinship groups.

The content of the master-slave relationship may vary greatly. One or the other aspect may be emphasized: economic, domestic, religious, sexual, or whatever. Any attempt to classify systems of servility in terms of the economic obligations and positions of the slave is to assume that this one point provides an index for the rest, when in fact such a situation must be shown empirically to exist or not to exist. The division of labor between master and slave is of importance on the same scale as division of labor between husband and wife; there are a few constants, but many more differentials.

The slave is his master's man in a sense very like a son is his father's man. A man cannot change fathers—but he can be renounced, and in some places even sold. With a few exceptions, a slave cannot change masters—but he can be sold. For such a reason, a man's slave is trustworthy—like a son, the slave has no place to go if he engages in double-dealing with his master. Slaves are more to be trusted than are age mates or contractual partners, and certainly more to be trusted than employees.

This situation gives rise to the fact that slaves often enjoy very high status within a domestic group of the master or within the court if the master is a chief or a king. It has often been wondered at that slaves, whose social rank in the totality of society is low and who are always legally deprived, can rise to such heights of eminence and power. The reason is that slaves, by definition, occupy two hierarchal positions that are differentiated on the basis of range. Within the total social structure, the rank of the slave is low; within limited structures, such as domestic or political groups, it may be very high indeed. Thus, the range of inequality is similar in servile institutions to that found in institutions of rank, with the important difference that there are always two ranges. The servile institution itself insures the rank of the slave in total social range; his position may be high within a kinship group or some other.

From the standpoint of the greater society, rank within family or household is always beside the point. It is a commonplace that the sons of a man may rank according to their seniority for purposes of distribution of tasks within the household, or for purposes of inheritance, or some other. Such a ranking does not imply a higher social status for the elder brother outside the immediate family, even in artistocratic inheritances. There is no instance on record, Steiner (1950) tells us, in which a higher *wergild* is paid for an elder brother than for one of the younger brothers: the principle of the equivalence of siblings—one brother being the same as another—holds outside the sibling group, but scarcely within it. A minor within the family may be and usually is completely under the *potestas* of the paterfamilias, but nevertheless he is, from the outside, of the same rank as its other members.

It is possible, therefore, for a nonslave to have a low rank inside the family; it is just as possible for a person who is a slave to have a high rank inside the family. As an illustration of the first instance, we can point to Schapera's account of the Tswana who, in former days, killed illegitimate children, but have since ceased to do so (1941, p. 225). Today an illegitimate child grows up in the home of his mother's father. Here the child mixes with the other children, but is regarded as inferior. He or she has to do the most unpleasant work, and is treated with contempt by the other minors. However, on reaching maturity this person, if a girl, is married off in the same way as the other girls of the ward, the same customary bridewealth being paid for her. Such could not be the case if she were indeed of an inferior status in the range of the total society.

But a slave occupies, by definition, a degraded position in the total society. He may or may not do so in the family group of his master. Greece and Rome both had slaves of great learning and high domestic position. These slaves enjoyed positions of authority and great intimacy within the household. The same was true of the king of Ashanti in the nineteenth century, whose slaves were his most highly trusted army officers, precisely because they could not be usurpers. There is, thus, often a great resentment by both slave and master when the former is referred to by his overall social position of "slave," if his position in terms of the household is a high one. The literature abounds with examples in which it is bad taste or even criminal to call a man by his true status of slave.

Servility is further complicated by the fact that servile institutions appear in many different types of society. There may be servile institutions within a class society; they are also to be found in caste societies and in estate societies. These institutions can be distinguished by whether or not the servility is to a role or even to a social group, or whether it is to an individual. Only in the latter case—in situs and class systems—does servility approach the "ownership" idea that Westerners commonly associate with it.

CLIENTAGE

One other type of servility should be mentioned: that which exists when a whole social group is servile to another whole social group. "Clientage" is the term usually given to such an arrangement, but the term is taken from medieval feudalism and has been inadequately analyzed as yet. Some of the clearest examples are to be found among the Bedouin Arabs of Cyrenaica, whose kinship groups are divided into those that are considered to be descendants of the prophet, and therefore owners of the countryside, and those "client groups" who do not own pasture lands, wells, or other important cultural items and who therefore attach themselves, as a group, in a servile relationship to the descendants of the prophet. Similarly, on the northwest coast of North America, there were some clans who had lost or never had the boats and fishing tackle that were basic to the production of livelihood. They therefore attached themselves in a quasipermanent bondage to groups who did own the means of production in order to acquire their use under certain fixed and limited circumstances.

PARIAHS

We have now noted that rank is a matter of classification of persons in terms of roles, groups, tasks, or the culture items they manipulate. We have further noted that servility is a legal type of relationship, based on antikinship and noncontract, and is to be kept distinct from rank (in spite of the fact that the total social ranking of servile persons is low). There is one further type of relationship of inequality to be considered: that of the pariah. Pariah is an Indian word for an unowned scavenger dog. It is applied, in analogy, to the "untouchables" or "outcastes." Pariahs are people who are neither part of the accepted rank system nor occupants of servile positions. They are "outsiders" in the true sense.

Pariahs may perform certain vital tasks for the community: the *eta* of feudal Japan, for example, were the only people allowed to touch dead animals. Therefore, they provided the butchers, the tanners, and the candlestick makers for the entire society. The only relationship with the "in group" was an economic one. Aside from this economic task, they did not exist. Similarly, untouchables in India carried out some of the necessary jobs, particularly those of scavenging and keeping the community cleaned up. But their range of interaction with the major community was minimal. As a look at twentieth-century America will show, even class and situs systems have pariah groups.

Slaves are not pariahs. They are an integral part of the social structure.

Pariahs are, by definition, kept outside the recognized major institutions of the social structure, although they usually have an economic link with them. One of the most far-reaching movements of the last century in America has been the turning of slaves into a pariah group, and the extension of the pariah status to all persons who can be categorized by the scientifically shaky concept of "race." It is to racism—the social aspects of race—that we now turn. We are in all truth examining one of largest scale examples of pariahism known to man.

12

The chimera of race

THE PURPOSE OF THIS chapter is to examine material concerning a scientific concept of race, to see how the word "race" is used in the English language, to examine the practices and institutions associated with race, and to question whether or not there is any rational connection between the physiology of race differences and the social institutions associated with race.

There are four problems that must be tackled in association with "race"—and often they are confused with one another. First, there are genetic, heritable physical differences found in various groups of human beings, all or some of which may be indicative of a "race." Second, there are various assessments of these physical differences in the folk evaluation of various cultures. Third, there are some social organizations and categories that have entrance requirements based on these folk assessments of race. Fourth, there is doctrine for maintaining or changing the status quo of racially determined groups or categories in any society by linking the evaluated physical differences and some aspects of social organization. The first of these problems can be called "the science of race" from the standpoint of the physical anthropologist. The second can be called the folk stereotype of race. The third is a problem in social inequality. The fourth is what Ruth Benedict (1950) analyzed as "racism."

RACE: THE PHYSICAL ANTHROPOLOGIST'S PROBLEM

As Professor Howells of Harvard has pointed out there is no such thing as "plain" *Homo sapiens* (1959, p. 213). In order to imagine man at all, it is necessary to give him some qualities that today are associated with race. The problem is simple: there is no standard type man from which all the others are deviations. To ask the question in its most peurile terms, "What color was Adam?" "What is the texture of the beard of God in whose image we are made—frizzy, wavy, or lank?"

In short, genetic physical differences among peoples exist. Social problems between classes and culture groups made up of some of these peoples exist. And our question again: Do "race" and "racism" provide a good enough answer for the manner in which the two are connected? For the way physical differences are related to social problems? Ashley Montagu, an accomplished and honest physical anthropologist, has pointed out that everybody seems to know what race is and, more seriously, that

> all but a few persons take it completely for granted that scientists have established the "facts" about "race" and that they have long ago recognized and classified the "races" of mankind. Scientists do little to discourage this view and, indeed, many of them are quite as deluded as most laymen are concerning the subject.... It is not difficult to see, therefore, why most of us continue to believe that "race" really corresponds to something which exists [1942, p. 1].

Now note, Dr. Ashley Montagu did *not* say that physical differences do not exist, because obviously they do. We can all see them. What he did say is that "race" is a classification of human beings, and that it is imposed by theorizers of one sort or another as a way of looking at these differences. "Race" does not exist as anything except an ideal classification of empirical biological differences. Race is, in short, not part of the data, but it is a way of looking at the data.

Race is like gravity. Gravity is not a thing or a phenomenon. It is an explanation of phenomena and the activities of things. We *explain* the movement of bodies by the theory of gravity. Race, in the same sense, exists as a theory to explain certain observable phenomena.

Physical anthropologists have attempted, by more or less scientific methods, to classify and fit the varieties of mankind into definite groups, the so-called "races." They have never, as far as I know, been able wholly to agree on their results. Every generation, the brightest or most ambitious physical anthropologists set forth new classifications of race. Every generation, everybody else disagrees—almost as if on principle. Physical anthropologists even claim that racial classification is older than anthropology. "The wall paintings of ancient Egyptians used four pigments for the complexions of the four races they knew: red for themselves, yellow for their enemies in Asia, white for people from the north, and black for Negroes. This classification has been reduced by one and given a Greek terminology" (Benedict, 1940, p. 37). A social anthropologist is bound to ask whether here is in fact a "classification of race" *per se* or merely an artistic tradition based on observable differences: the two are not the same, and the distinction is of considerable importance.

Aristotle had some things to say about barbarians, which latter-day savants and Aristotle-baiters have sometimes interpreted in terms of race. The Greeks and the Romans were both singularly free of racial prejudice or even of any developed racial ideas. Almost all authorities agree on this point.

Dr. Ashley Montagu has stated, with *ex cathedra* finality that is unwise to say the least, that there were only five documents dealing with race published in the seventeenth century. His point is, however, well taken: comments on race were rare and did not catch on. He notes that Leibnitz read one of them and found it logically unsatisfying, and that

> Physical differences were, of course, known to exist between groups of mankind, but what was unfamiliar was the notion that the differences exhibited by such peoples represented anything fundamental. Such differences, it was believed, could all be explained as due to the action of differing climatic and similar physiographic factors [Montagu, 1942, p. 18].

Race did not, as a matter of fact, really become an issue until late in the eighteenth century. It was in the second half of that century that the term was first given a technical meaning—it is an old root in most of the Latin languages, meaning "root"—modern French *racine* comes from the same Latin original.

In 1775, there was a book published in Latin by a German, called *On the Natural Variety of Mankind*. The author was Johann Friederich Blumenbach. Blumenbach, as an intellectual exercise, set out to classify the varieties of mankind and to discover whether any significance was to be attached to the differences. He claimed from the beginning that no clear distinctions could be made between races:

> Although there seems to be so great a difference between widely separated nations, that you might easily take the inhabitants of the Cape of Good Hope, the Greenlanders and the Circassians for so many different species of man, yet when the matter is thoroughly considered, you see that all do so run into one another, and that one variety of mankind does so sensibly pass into the other, that you cannot mark out the limits between them [quoted in Montagu, 1952, pp. 15-16].

Obviously, from the start, a grave difficulty in defining race was felt. And as recently as 1931, Hooton could write: "Even the term 'race' as applied to man is commonly employed with no accurate and well-defined meaning" (pp. 395-396). In common English, it can refer to skin color, religion, nationality, linguistic distinctions, geographical space. Indeed, all these items have been confused with race and often, in public thought, still are. But Hooton, like men 150 years before him, was undaunted by the difficulty. Instead of asking "Does what I am defining correspond to something real?" he made a definition and forced his data into compliance. He defined race as:

> a great division of mankind, the members of which, though individually varying, are characterized as a group by a certain combination of morphological and metrical features, principally non-adaptive, which have been derived from their common descent [1931, p. 397].

As common-sense definition it is superb. The question is, Can it be made the basis of scientific research? Only within the last few years has anyone asked whether or not race *can be* defined scientifically at all (Livingstone, 1962).

Blumenbach's book did not begin a tide of racism. Blumenbach died in 1840—a very old man—sixty-five years after his book had been first published. During all that time, he consistently upheld his views: that boundaries between races were not determinable because of the plethora of criteria to be considered.

But by 1840 the intellectual ferment in Europe and the waning power of Christian dogma over scientific thought had been felt in many fields. Linnaeus' classification of animals had long been accepted in principle. A classification of man could not be far behind, and it was Darwin's brilliant synthesis that brought the matter to the fore. Before the expansion of Europe, which we can consider for convenience to have begun with the explorations of Prince Henry of Portugal, the Church was the arbiter in all such matters and the position taken was that all men had sprung from the loins of Adam, and hence were all of a single line. With the voyages of discovery, however, when the full variety of the cultures of *Homo sapiens* began to be known and the full variety of human types to be considered, another possibility became apparent. Could it be, as one of the documents of the time expressed it, that each of these different human types was a "separate thought of God"? Could one account for the differences among red men and black men and the inaccurately labeled white men in terms of different acts of creation? The argument became a more or less theological one of the rectitude of monogenesis or polygenesis (Benedict, 1940, p. 33).

Into this arena, Darwin's thought entered in the form of a compromise. One could eat one's cake and accord with Scripture in the idea of monogenesis, but could also have one's cake and accord with the polygenesists by saying that different races had been "selected" and grown toward independent species.

Throughout this time, men such as the great jurist Montesquieu denied that the variations in mankind could be accounted for genetically at all, and said rather that they had to be seen in terms of climate. Indeed, as Benedict has so convincingly pointed out, the first great physical anthropologist, Theodore Waitz, was convinced by the monogenetic position as a result of physical measurements that he made on peoples of different races, showing that racial stereotypes failed to correspond to the facts. And Darwin's book, published the same year as Waitz's, made it possible to claim not merely that all men were the result of monogenesis and growing disparateness, but that all primates—the men and the apes—had been created in such a fashion.

DARWIN'S CONTRIBUTION

Since Darwin, all racial studies have had a totally different set of background ideas from those that were made before him. As we have noted elsewhere, it may be extremely difficult for people to realize what social attitudes and cultural evaluations may have been before the advent of a great and simplifying idea. In order to investigate the problem, we must strip Darwin's contribution of its specific details to see the sort of argument that he put forward. Darwin and the year 1859 are the center point through which all considerations of race and racism must pass.

There are, in both physical and biological science, as well as in social science, two sorts of explanation (you may make it six or even eighty-three if you wish, but for our purposes these two are relevant). One of these ways is analysis, which means breaking a subject into its parts. The explanation then consists in telling you how the parts fit together and how they work. Its basic analogy is to a system, conceived mechanically or organically or some other way.

Another, and very different, mode of explanation is the genetic explanation; that is, to tell the genesis of something: how something was made. Its basic analogy is not to system, but "growth." In mathematics, and in most physical science, genetic explanation may be the more elegant sort. The definition of a circle is the classic example of successful genetic explanation: a circle is a line which connects all the points equidistant from a given point. That definition, or explanation, tells you how to *make* a circle. It does not break a circle into arcs and tell you how they fit together.

Genetic explanations had been used in European sciences for some time before Darwin. The pseudoscience of philology provides an example. Many decades before Darwin, the philologists were explaining the relationship of one language to another by a genetic method: one language, they said, grew out of another and hence many languages evolved. They traced them back and made up ancient languages that were, they claimed, similar to the long-dead parent language. Languages could be related to one another in a treelike analogy, with trunks, branches, and twigs. As language grew, languages became more differentiated. Philologists encountered no difficulty. The Bible had said that people had spoken many languages ever since Babel; it was not even considered daring to seek a genetic explanation for classification of languages. Even in our own day, such a classification has scarcely been questioned. Other aspects of philology, which *were* questioned, gave way to a new science called "linguistics," which resulted from application of the analytical method rather than the genetic method to language.

What Darwin did was to apply the method of genetic explanation to biology, and particularly to geology and palaeontology. In this field, it was new. It tromped on all sorts of vested interests and hence encountered severe opposition and censure from almost everybody. And yet, its victory was amazingly quick. It has since been surprisingly difficult to question, not because it supplies all the answers (for it does not), but because of the fact that the educated public clings to it with the same ferocity that an educated public a century earlier clung to the religion-oriented opinions of outdated scholastics. Darwin, it seems, provided not merely a scientific theory. He also provided a *credo*—the faith for an age that needed it badly. Today our problem is to accept (and test) the theory without making obeisance to the creed.

Darwin's daring genetic explanation was applied in the one field, where, perhaps, more than in any other, it is valid; for biology does indeed *deal* with units that are demonstrably related genetically. It became the rage. Genetic explanation—actually, in the form of analogy to Darwin's biological theories—was applied to everything, including culture and society. Only in our own day have we begun to free "culture evolution" of the organic metaphor.

In the social and historical sciences, and this includes palaeontology, the method of genetic explanation contains a very knotty difficulty. It is easily confused with history. Genetic explanation is, if it is properly performed, a logical method for stating relationships. History is what has *actually* happened at some time or another. Genetic explanations are merely what *must* have happened, and usually cannot be accurately reported in terms of historical events.

In the field of palaeontology, genetic theory and history reinforce each other. The fossils and the ruins are points that can be used to pin theory to the empirical world. But in most other subjects the two methods do *not* reinforce each other in this way. Almost anything cultural or social provides an example of the difficulty. Indeed, the difficulty even goes back to race, which should deal in inherited characteristics, and hence be subject to solution by a genetic explanation. If a scientist gives a genetic explanation of race, his explanation almost invariably carries the implication—and he might even have intended it to do so—that races actually were created in this way.

Take an example from Hooton. Hooton (1931) said that the Dinaric subrace of the Caucasian group of races is a mixture of the Nordic race and the Armenoid race. To give him his due, he says it "may" have been. This "may" should be an indication that what he really meant is that the Dinaric stereotype has some of the features of the Nordic stereotype and some of those of the Armenoid steretotype. Whether or not Nordics and Armenoids ever had any actual contact is another, and historical, matter. The history of the thing is unknown, and it cannot be inferred from skull shape and hair color, even when such data be well attested.

To say that the Dinaric is a "mixture" of the Nordic and Armenoid groups is to offer a genetic explanation. To assume that this genetic explanation is in fact historically true, and that the Dinaric race was produced by the crossing of Nordics with Armenoids can be argued only on an historical basis, which requires historical evidence, not somatometric evidence. Genetic explanation is, thus, extremely tricky in biology—which, of course includes problems of race—specifically because of the nature of sexual reproduction.

The distinction between genetic explanations and history seems to be a difficult point. It *must* be a difficult point to have baffled so many generations of scholars. Irrevocable circumstantial evidence that something has happened does not in itself give us license to say when or how it happened. Racial characteristics are inherited. Some source must be postulated. However, to postulate it in *historical* terms is quite erroneous and quite unprovable—*unless* there is evidence in palaeontology or archaeology. The postulation, on the evidence solely of the genes, can be made logically, but *not* historically. The confusion of genetic explanations and history has been, more or less, cleared out of academic ethnography and social anthropology. It lingers in linguistics—indeed, glottochronology has given it a new lease on life—and runs rampant in physical anthropology.

It will be the science of genetics that finally will straighten out this difficulty altogether. For we can see that taking Hooten's explanation of the Dinaric race literally by confusing logic with history leads to an even greater confusion: it confuses possibility with actuality. The intermediate position of the Dinaric between Armenoid and Nordic *may* represent a cross. But the only provable *fact* is that in some regards the type called Dinaric is intermediate. Now, perhaps some day this problem can be solved by genetics—are the genes such that a cross can be said necessarily to have occurred? What is certain is that we can never say for certain on the evidence of what is known as the phenotype.

PHENOTYPES AND GENOTYPES

This difference between phenotypes and genotypes is the one on which the genetics revolution in racial theory has been based. Phenotypes are types of individuals—races, if you will—which are described in terms of external characteristics. Genotypes are types—races, if you will—which are described in terms of the composition of genes and chromosomes in their cells. Physical anthropologists are fast forsaking the phenotype and becoming qualified geneticists. To do otherwise would be to reduce their science to the level of alchemy.

The arch criterion of race in the phenotype is skin color, supported by more or fewer of the following: eye form, nose form, chin form, hair types, lip eversion, and the like. Indeed, if one goes to the *Encyclopaedia Britannica,* one can still find an old article by Dudly Buxton in which hair is the major classifying criterion and the races come out as leiotrichous (straight haired), ulotrichous (woolly haired) and cymotrichous (curly haired). However, skin color is usually the primary criterion.

The color of the skin is dependent on three factors: the thickness of the skin, the amount of pigment in it, and the degree to which the blood shows through it. Professor Hooton playfully adds a fourth—the amount of dirt on the skin (1931, p. 440). Color pigment is to be found in the dermis, and is a substance called *melanin.* Melanin is usually black, although some granules of it are as light as bright yellow. The color of the skin is determined not by the color of the pigment so much as by the quantity of it—the same coloring matter, in different amounts, colors the skin of all the races. The same pigments also color the eye and the hair.

As Professor Hooton has pointed out, studies in albinism have led us to the belief that pigmentation results from interaction of an oxidizing ferment with a color-producing substance. Both these substances are secreted by the tissues of all normal human animals. The action of sun upon the skin tends to produce additional pigmentation. The amount of pigment itself is, however, inherited and has little or nothing to do with environmental conditions beyond the fact that sunlight causes darkening or "tanning" in all races.

Classifiers of races on the basis of color can now do one of two things: they can either subscribe to the beverage classification (Negroes are chocolate or *cafe au lait,* Europeans milky white, Mongolians the color of weak tea), or they can introduce a phony scientism and match skin tone to a chart. These charts used to be supplied to all anthropologists going to the field. They consisted of about a dozen cards, some three inches wide by fifteen inches long. On each there were patches of perhaps half a dozen colors printed. In the center of each color patch there was a hole about the size of a quarter. The anthropologist got out his pack of cards, and then caught a subject. He made him take off his shirt (if he had one on) and lift his arm, because he wanted a patch of skin where the sun had never shone. He ran the cards along the patch of skin until he found a match—when the color of the skin through the quarter-sized hole was the same as that on the printed card surrounding it. That gave him a number, which he wrote down. When he got all his subjects measured, he added up the numbers, divided by the number of subjects, and got what can only be called a "mean shade." I never owned a set of these cards—their heyday was, in fact, before my time. But I did once use them in an anthropological laboratory in which all of the students typed each other. The difficulty was that in all of the shades of pink, white, and beige on the cards—and the colors ranged from Rubens to Rembrandt—not one of them came anywhere near matching any of the subjects. When we tried to judge which color patch was nearest, we all came out with different judgments: one man judged on the pink tones, another on the tan tones—and don't forget that white skin has green tones in it (as any painter can tell you) and black skin has a phenomenally wide range of tones. In the end, we proved more or less conclusively by our charts that all of us, including one Japanese-American, were Caucasians.

Pigmentation is quantitatively different in different individuals but qualitatively alike in all. The quantities are inherited by a sort of skewed Mendelian law. But if we try to pin down the external color more closely—is that science? Is mathematical description more scientific than the beverage description? Of course it is not. Until we indicate that such a color scheme is relevant to something, we have just been doodling.

There is one other phenotypical character that old-fashioned physical anthropologists have worked with *ad nauseum*. That is head shape. They all claimed that the genetics of head shape are very important, but few ever discussed it further. Is head shape inherited? In a general way, yes—with some modifications. How? The genetics of the thing would seem to be completely unknown. That fact, however, does not stop the phenotypers.

One of the earliest computations that physical anthropologists learned to make was the cephalic index. The cephalic index is the ratio of head breadth to head length. It is a particularly handy figure, because few people object to having their heads measured but most do object to being measured almost anywhere else. You can measure skulls that go back for many millenia. It would be very nice for anthropologists if the cephalic index were indeed indicative of something. Nobody has ever proved that it is not, but so far as I know nobody ever proved that it is. We know that with an increase in height without an increase in brain weight, we got more long-headed, and vice versa. We know also that our brains are not growing bigger with the passage of generations. Anthrologists have in the past so wanted cephalic index to mean something that they did not seriously ask whether it in fact did.

Hooton (1931, pp. 407-409) has provided an able summary of some of the experiments and situations that have a bearing on this point. As early as 1923, Boas showed that children born in America of foreign parentage had different cephalic indices than their parents. Round-headed Polish Jews were producing mesocephalic children. So were long-headed Italians. Boas postulated that intermarriage and admixture of many racial strains were responsible; Hooton suggested that perhaps nutritionally the American-born children are better off and hence their heads could attain their normal shape. Another experiment was that of Professor Alexis Ivanovsky, who measured a sample of people every few weeks during a severe famine in Russia. As they got hungrier, they got more long-headed. When normal diet was restored, their heads regained their normal shape.

It is just such criteria as these—color, hair type, head shape—that led to the phenotype race classifications. And these classifications—for all that they comply with the externals—are of the same sort as classifying whales with fish because they swim. Swimming has, in fact, been found to be a relatively poor basis of classification. So has gross color.

TRAIT CLUSTERS AND "PURE" RACE

There were two things that physical anthropologists could do when they had reached the point we have now described. One of these was to work with the cluster of traits. This they did, with the result that they were led to say, over and over again, that there is no such thing as a pure race. The other was to apply a new scientific method: to leave off the phenotypical explanation of "race," and turn to an analytical explanation of human genetics. This is the triumph of modern genetics, just as surely as Darwin's first application of the genetic method to inheritance problems was the triumph of the mid-nineteenth century.

Let us take the two positions up one at a time: first, the matter of trait clusters and "pure race." Hooton assures us that "no single bodily character exhibits a sufficient range of variation to enable us to assign to each of the great human groups which require racial classification a distinct and exclusive development of that feature. There are not enough variations of any one feature to go around, unless we confine ourselves to two or three primary and well-nigh hypothetical races" (1931, p. 398). However, he does not so confine himself. I mean no disrespect to the memory of a very fine scientist when I say that if he had confined himself in this way, he would have had nothing to do. Had he been twenty-five years younger, he would have become a geneticist. He decided instead that a race "implies the common possession of certain variations as a result of the same ancestry" (1931, p. 398). He further noted that, since all races have survived, the differences among them must not have anything to do with survival value. And he ended up with the idea that "significant racial criteria should be based principally on nonadaptive bodily characters" (1931, p. 398). Race for Hooton, as for Blumenbach, was determined by a set of physical criteria that made no difference to anything.

Physical anthropologists have set up stereotypes of groupings of the same old criteria—skin color, eye color, and all the rest of the nonessentials. Some have said that there are seven races, some that there are fourteen. Hooton, in his book, gives detailed descriptions of twenty-six; Weidenreich (1946, p. 67) says that the number ranges from five to thirty-eight, but he does not give references and I cannot find another book that lists precisely either five or thirty-eight.

Measurement after measurement has been made, and average after average struck by honest men. And they have come to the conclusion that if you take a racial stereotype, almost nobody lives up to it. In a study of Swedish army recruits of forty years ago, for example, five "Nordic traits" were taken, and it was discovered that less than ten percent of the recruits had all the traits. The assumption was not to question the stereotype, but rather to question the actions and morals of the ancestors of their subjects. Similar studies were made in Switzerland. Six percent of the Swiss were "pure" Alpine racial types. No more than six percent fitted the stereotype—but nobody threw out the stereotype, which would be the scientific course. They only said the Swiss were a mixed lot racially.

However, the men who did these studies and who interpreted them *were* honest men. They merely failed to question their premises. They got out of their difficulty with the conclusion that there are two types of races: primary races, which are achieved only by evolutionary means, and secondary races, which are achieved by the mixing of primary races. The difference is, to say the least, a little confusing. Yet their honesty shows through in passages such as this one from Hooton:

> The criteria by which race classifications are established are for the most part of secondary races and primary races are represented only by inbred peoples within areas where little race contact is known to have taken place. Of such inbred people only a small fraction represent primary racial types either because they are absolutely unmixed or because pure racial types have been segregated out in relatively few individuals [1931, p. 398].

Weidenreich makes the same point in an analogy to dogs:

> If the overwhelming majority of present mankind consists of "hybrids"

> for the reason that very few individuals correspond to the demands of a detailed racial scheme regarded as indispensable, one may ask: Where are the "pure" individuals who produce the hybrids anew each day? Every dog show exhibits "pure" breeds of the Doberman pinscher and makes us acquainted, at the same time, with the "impurities" of this breed. Although the Doberman itself produces marked mongrels when crossed with other races, the history of its race tells us that it was first bred, in 1865, by crossing Manchester terriers, Great Danes, sheep dogs and setters. Nevertheless, today the notoriously hybrid Doberman pinscher is generally acknowledged as a "pure" race. What, then, makes the difference between hybrids and "pure" types, regardless of whether we are dealing with dogs or human beings? [1946, p. 91]

Faced with such insuperable obstacles, of their own creation, it is the more amazing that physical anthropologists have been so reluctant to throw out the concept of "race." Weidenreich comes closest—and I believe that almost all physical anthropologists since his time agree with him on these points— when he says that races are not stable in any time view except the very short one of Western civilization. The "races" of the world are today interbreeding, and if for any reason large groups of people are in the future again geographically blocked off from one another as they have been in the past, a new set of more or less true-breeding races will be formed. That is, our present set of secondary races will interbreed, disappear, and then, with isolation, produce new sets of secondary races. All this, of course, takes many millenia. But the races that we recognize are passing phases, not eternal entities. Dixon put the same point long ago: "Race is not a permanent entity, something static. . . . It is dynamic and is slowly developing and changing" (Quoted by Weidenreich 1946, p. 91.)

Many people, of many races, find this a saddening thought. I venture that there are Freudian explanations—concerned with narcissism—for their downheartedness. Social and economic reasons also spring to mind.

BLOOD STUDIES AND "PURE" RACE

The first deadly blow to phenotype racial classification came in blood studies. Blood is something about which most laymen in the West know little, and about which they have many superstitions. Ashley Montagu has written persuasively about blood. He points out (1952, pp. 210*ff*.) that "blood" and "race" are two of the most emotion-laden words in English, though the emotional attitude toward "blood" is very much older. Many of the points we made in the context of kinship, Ashley Montagu makes in a context of race: blood is thought in the Western myth to be the quintessence of the body, and the characteristics of a stock are carried in it. Thus, kinsmen are of the same "blood," and therefore races or nations may also see their similarities and their genetic connection in an idiom of blood. Dobzhansky, one of the great biologists and geneticists of our time, has written of it in this way:

> Before the rediscovery of Mendel's work the transmission of heredity was thought of in terms of inheritance of "blood." Parental "bloods" mix and give rise to the "blood" of the child which is a compromise between those of the parents. In a sexually reproducing population the available variety of "bloods" mingle owing to intermarriage. If such a population is left undisturbed, the continuous mixing process will result in an uniform solution which will represent the "blood" of a race or a variety. When a complete or near complete uniformity is reached, you will have a "pure race"—a group of individuals with identical germ plasma. If two races mingle, a mixed race arises; if race miscegenation ceases, a new "pure race" will eventually result. It is most unfortunate . . . that the theory of "blood" though invalidated decades ago still colors not merely the thinking of laymen but finds its way explicitly or implicitly into text books [quoted in Montagu, 1942, p. 211].

Today, in all the vernaculars of Western civilization, race and "blood" have become more or less synonymous. There are such terms as "blue blood," "blood royal," "German blood," "Negro blood," and all the rest of them. Look at the terms "fullblood" and "halfblood" and the pejorative uses to which the latter has always been put. And look out for "bad blood." Ashley Montagu has pointed out that bad blood very often occurs between people of good blood. We might add that bad blood that occurs over good blood too often draws blood.

Blood is, in short, believed to be equivalent to heredity, and in some mystical way to determine the quality of a person. By extension, his social status as well as his biological status have come to be discussed in terms of "blood"—and many people take the metaphor quite literally. During World War II the plasma of Negro blood was stored separately from that of Caucasian blood, although the two are chemically and every other way identical. The separation was made on the basis of social prejudice, not on the basis of scientific fact. I have found, in the North, a human milk bank in which milk from Negro mothers is stored separately from Caucasian milk—even the Southerners who are most adamant about blood find this incident amusing.

Today we know, of course, that it is the genes and not the blood that are the transmitters of hereditary characteristics. We know that no blood passes from mother to child—indeed, they are often of different blood types—any more than from father to child.

There are many types of blood, based on small differences, all of which are heritable by Mendelian principles. Save for AB type, which seems to be absent among American Indians, all the major types are found among all races. Many of these characteristics, but not all, are also shared by the great apes.

GENETICS AND "PURE" RACE

Those physical anthropologists who have learned genetics and listened to the geneticists know that no two human beings save identical twins have the same genetic characteristics—even full brother and sister inherit different combinations of genes from their parents. Blumenbach was right. Except statistically, there is no way genetically to distinguish one race from the next because members of different races differ from one another by the same characteristics as members of a single race. To equate "pure race" with shared germ plasm becomes absurd: Hans Kalmus (1948, p. 44), the noted British geneticist, has remarked that with mice it would take thirty generations of mating fathers with daughters or sons with mothers for a group to become genetically homogenous. Using brother-sister matings, the number rises to fifty or sixty. Such "pure races" have been artificially produced in a few laboratory animals. Certainly they never occurred in nonlaboratory conditions.

Therefore, even if we assume that a human being is genetically no more complex than a mouse, it would take sixteen centuries of full-sibling incestuous unions to produce a genetically pure race. It could be done in thirty generations, or 850 years (counting twenty-five years per generation), by mother-son or father-daughter incest. The moment that you increase either the genetic complexity or the size of the breeding population, you *ipso facto* vastly increase the length of time that would be required to produce a genetically primary race.

The impact of genetics on pregenetic race studies has been, obviously, to reduce them to prescientific hodgepodge.

We must now review a little to see some of the things we have *not* done. We have not denied the physical differences among the so-called races. The physical differences are there and can be seen with the naked eye, even if they disappear before more delicate instruments. We have, however, questioned the idea that "race" means anything—the notion that it refers to anything that can be scientifically defined. Next, we have not said that race is unimportant, for so long as it remains the basis of pariah group behavior anywhere in the world, it is of professional interest to the social anthropologist. We have said, rather, that races are socially recognized categories into which people are thrust on the basis of socially recognized physiological criteria.

We have not denied that the races are mixing—but we have claimed that even the idea of a "pure race" is either cant or nonsense. There exist more or less exclusive (and *ipso facto* more or less overlapping) gene pools. Not all of the genes in one are to be found in any other single pool. But what the pool is considered to be changes with every mating.

We have not denied that each of the gross traits that goes to make up a classification of racial phenotypes is inherited—it may be. But each of the gross traits that goes to make up a racial phenotype is independently inherited; the so-called cluster of traits for determining a race is not therefore stable unless the size and content of the gene pool is maintained.

The gene combinations that result in what we call races are unstable, and they change in time. Thus race is a function, in part, of geography; it is a function of history and of social structure. It has sometimes been said that social considerations can also maintain races separate, but probably this is not true: if races are in contact, miscegenation will result. At least, it always has. Curiosity can sometimes be a stronger motivating force than narcissism. Thus, the gene pools are constantly flowing into one another, and changes thus occur in the gene pools with every generation.

Race is a social problem, not a scientific problem. Races exist in the modern world. But we must study them historically, not merely physiologically. Analytically, we study genetics. Historically, we can study the interaction of "races," in this new sense. The true existence that races have is in the folk analysis of culture and civilization. They are real because we "know" that they are real and because they figure as forces in our life. But they are subject to scientific investigation only in terms of genetics, before which the concept of "race", as it is known to laymen, disappears.

Our next question must obviously be: What are the folk beliefs about race? This problem is best handled by first investigating the history of "racism" in the Western world, and following it with an ethnographic survey of concepts of race among other peoples and other cultures.

RACISM: THE SOCIAL ANTHROPOLOGIST'S PROBLEM

We have determined that the facts concerning the physical differences among peoples are best studied by the science of genetics. We are left, however, with facts of a different order: social and cultural facts, which need explaining in social and cultural terms. Groups or categories of persons labeled "races" are a social fact, whatever the view of geneticists and physical anthropologists. They can, hence, be studied by the methods of social anthropology and by history. Negroes and whites exist in the United States in the same way that Republicans and Democrats exist, or Catholics, Protestants, and Jews exist. They are social categories that influence action.

Sociologists and geneticists are not, obviously, studying the same thing. Sociologists are studying culturally defined groups and categories in interaction, and the resultant social structures. Geneticists are studying genes and chromosomes in interaction, and the resultant organisms.

Now, how are the two brought together? If they are at all, it has too often been by a notion of "race." This phenomenon has been investigated by many anthropologists and sociologists, but for clarity of argument and eloquence none has reached the same pitch as did Ruth Benedict (1940). She distinguished the genetic studies of physical anthropology from the sociological studies of socially defined "races" and their interaction, and both from what she called "racism." "Racism" she defined as the dogma that one race (assuming the stereotypical folk definition) is superior to another. Racism, she claimed, can be studied only by the historical method —in which she would, of course, include current history—for the simple reason that there is no other kind of data.

Racism, Benedict assures us, must be studied just as religion is studied. Like any belief that goes beyond the scope of scientific knowledge, it must be judged "by its fruits, and by its votaries and by its ulterior purposes" (Benedict, 1940, p. 153). If it uses, or misuses, facts, such is a concern of science— and "the literature of racism is extraordinarily inept and contradictory in its use of facts" (Benedict, 1940, p. 154). One can, in fact, assume that the facts are of no interest in racist matters—anything but. And that charge can be applied to both sides. Benedict summed up the essence of racism in a five-word proposition: "I belong to the elect." The formula, obviously, has a much longer history than have the doctrines of racism.

DEVELOPMENT OF RACIST THEORY

"The elect" is a category in which almost everybody puts himself, but his grounds for so doing may be almost infinitely varied: kinship, nationality, religion, or politics. It was of late occurrence in the West that "elect" came to be defined by "race," for at least some purposes. As with Marxist sociology, racist sociology grew up in the shadow of a feudalism still inadequately analyzed. The breakdown of feudal estates had left the Western world without a firm image for its institutions of rank. The sense of the differentness of peoples was vastly augmented by the discovery of the New World, and by the explorations of Africa and the Pacific. The "noble savage" became a piece of standard equipment in the popular literature of the time: Chateaubriand's *Atala,* or *Paul et Virginie* and *Les Natches* are cases in point. Rousseau's "noble savage" was a traditional figure even before Rousseau.

The romantic spirit of the literature was not, however, found on the frontiers, where Westerners were slaying and enslaving the very noble savage their kinsfolk at home were romanticizing. Even the official policies of the various governments were flouted by the people on the spot who wanted cheap labor and captive markets, or who wanted land and enough slaves to work it. "Natives" were scarcely human beings—the Spanish church and crown held a conference to determine whether or not they had immortal souls; Australians and North Americans decided on one occasion or another that they had not, and hence could be hunted as "animals"—the terms are contemporary, not latter-day tearjerking.

The interesting point, however, is that even with the romantic literature and the frontier disregard for indigenous peoples, it took a dogma of racism some three centuries to develop. These people justified their actions not on the basis of race but on that of religion—non-Christians were fair game. It will undoubtedly be as difficult some day for people to understand the distinctions we make on the basis of race as it is for us to to understand the distinctions the sixteenth and seventeenth centuries made on the basis of religion.

What Benedict calls "the unbeliever theory of native inferiority"—which was in fact a combination of ethnocentrism and opportunism—dominated the contact of peoples for several centuries. The original work of missionaries was, thus, humanitarian as well as evangelistic, for when a "native" professed Christianity, he was at least theoretically no longer fair game. Thus, the activities of missionaries were greatly hampering to settlers and slave traders. Hence, before long the practice of freeing slaves who became Christians ceased, for the new form of society established its vested interests very soon. Benedict dates the demise of the theory of the division of the world into two camps of believers and unbelievers as about the beginning of the nineteenth century in South Africa, and rather earlier in much of the rest of the world.

Racism grew out of a situation of conflict among the classes—the overthrow of the aristocrats by the populace. The racist theory began in France, as an explanation and apology for the old system of feudal security in a rapidly changing revolutionary situation.

The Count de Boulainvilliers was the prime spokesman for the aristocrats who had been the feudal lords. These old nobles, of whom he can be counted typical if *nouveau arrivé*, wanted to reassert their rights against the State, and to throw off the increasing burden of taxes, which was threatening their whole existence as a group. The English, faced with this situation, presented King John with the Magna Charta. But the French procedure was less direct. One of these indirect procedures was Boulainvilliers' invocation of what we today would call racism. "The nobles," he said, "were of the blood of the Germani, the Teutonic barbarians who had overrun the Roman Empire" (quoted in Benedict, 1940, p. 175).

According to Boulainvilliers' argument, the "aristocratic freedom" of these Teutonic tribes was the heritage of the Frankish nobles of the eighteenth century. The quality of their blood, he reasoned, demanded that the aristocratic leadership which was theirs by right be maintained. The way to maintain it was to end the absolute monarchy whose kings were of Roman descent and hence not of the "true" blood, and to keep the populace in their place—the populace, the doctrine finished, were also not Teutonics, but rather were descended from the Celts and Mediterranean types of the conquered. "Race" became what it has remained—a determinant of role ascription.

By 1791 and the French Revolution, the political situation had changed—and Boulainvilliers' pronouncement had become racist dogma. And, as it follows from the argument, the Alpine and Mediterranean populace admitted the dogma but claimed that they instead of the Teutons were superior. They were obviously "right"—on the same grounds as were the Teutons. The racist dogma has the practical advantage that it can be perverted to any group's advantage. Since it has no basis in fact, no claim is too extravagant to make for it.

Racism did not really get going full speed, however, until the middle of the 1850's—the same decade as saw publication of Darwin's *Origin of Species* and of Waitz's *Anthropology*. In that same fateful decade, the Count de Gobineau published (from 1853-1857) the racist classic, ***Essay** on the Inequality of the Human Races*.Gobineau used the word "Aryan" of the superior blond race. In our time, the same group has been called Nordics.

It is important—and difficult—to realize that when Gobineau wrote, he was not writing as a nationalist. Like Boulainvilliers, he was representative of a category that, with the destruction of feudalism, had ceased to be an estate. Racism became associated with nationalism only in the twentieth century: before that time, it was still a tool in the jostling for power and position that accompanied the great changes following the French Revolution.

Gobineau divided the human species into black, yellow, and white. But he was not talking about Negroes, Mongolians, and Caucasians—that did not come until years later. He was rather talking about three Caucasoid subraces: the Alpines were yellow, the Mediterraneans black. Whites were the group today called Nordic. He was not concerned with the nationalist struggle of the twentieth century, but with the rank struggle of the nineteenth.

Gobineau was not interested in the purity of race, except for the Aryans: he urged that all civilizations needed all races, as he defined them, but that civilization would perish without the Aryans (read "aristocrats") who were the carriers of civilization.

Gobineau wrote at the same time as Darwin. His book was published before *Origin of Species.* He certainly could not have known the geographical distribution of racial traits as we know it today, for that was discovered only later; he certainly could not have known the laws of genetics, which were discovered much later.

However, Gobineau's successors did add the Darwinian notion of the survival of the fittest to the racist doctrines, developing his theories in two directions. The first was that they brought Gobineau's ideas to bear on the anthropometric measurements that were taken by the successors of Waitz, and, second, they made the assumption that "survival of the fittest" gave the power structure of society the stamp of scientific law.

The nineteenth century, for all that it is known as a period of great peace and prosperity in some parts of the world, notably Europe, was one of the most heartless and bloodthirsty of history. Violence was not so much engaged in—though the history of France and the story of the Crimean War indicates that there was plenty of violence—as it was enshrined as the great crucible of progress. In politics-cum-sociology, Herbert Spencer proposed the origin of the State in violence and warfare. The nineteenth century believed it all. In biology and politics, as we have just seen, the doctrine of the survival of the fittest raised dog-eat-dog to the level of a scientific morality—it is small wonder that Darwin was considered by many of his contemporaries to be the anti-Christ. In economics, forms arose that allowed, theoretically at least, of no interference with the price-making market.

Anthropometric measurements were perfected in France during the second half of the nineteenth century. Such scientists as Broca, Lapouge, and Ammon, like those before them, were not interested in national differences, but rather in class differences. French and Germans worked together amicably describing the "two Germanies" and the "two Frances" one of each made up of Nordics, the other of round-headed Alpines. They were attempting, however, to determine specifically which was "superior" —or, rather, to find grounds for saying that the one they considered superior was actually so. Out of their ratiocinations came Lapouge's famous statement that "the narrow-heads are the hunting pack and the broad-heads the marauded sheep." This interpretation was, of course, in line with the Darwinism of the day.

MODERN ATTITUDES ABOUT RACE

It was not until the eve of the twentieth century that racism was brought to the aid of warring nationalist states. In America, it never became such but remained a doctrine for underwriting the maintenance of the social *status quo*: the "superiority," meaning better social position and education, of the northern Europeans over the central and southern Europeans who arrived later, and the superiority of both over the Negroes who had been slaves. Racist activities along these lines led to the immigration policy of the United States and to the racist attitudes of many social groups such as clubs and labor unions.

The arguments of the American racists were taken from Gobineau and from Houston Chamberlain, who had in turn adapted Gobineau to nationalistic uses in a book called *Die Grundlagen des Neunzenten Jahrhunderts.* He claimed that "the amount of Nordic blood in each nation is a very fair measure of its strength in war and standing in civilization" (quoted in Benedict, 1940, p. 193.)

Americans, in short, dredged up these Nordic myths and used them politically, primarily as a tool for changing the immigration laws.

> American temper had changed since the days when our motto was "No distinction of race, creed or color" and we offered "an asylum for the oppressed" and wrote enthusiastically about the "the Melting Pot". . . . Because of social conditions in the U. S. there was no doubt that immigration could no longer be left wide open. The only point at issue was the basis on which choice could be made. Madison Grant's *Passing of the Great Race* was an adaptation of Gobineau that led to the Quota Act in 1921 [Benedict, 1940, p. 196].

Probably the most amazing fact that Ruth Benedict's study turned up —at least it is amazing when read in the 1960s—is that what we consider our major racial problem, the conflict between Negroes and Caucasians, was of minor importance in the literature of racism until the 1930s.[1] At that time, immigration had ceased to be a pressing problem; the emergence of Negroes with education and mobility was becoming apparent.

Fascism in Europe took on alarming proportions during the first four decades of the twentieth century. That doctrine was built on Gobineau, reinterpreted as nationalism and held together by nonsequiturs. We are already far enough away from it to see that we would no longer make quite the same mistakes—even though our newspapers are full every day of stories about equally foolish and equally sickening mistakes the world is making.

Ruth Benedict's book *Race: Science and Politics* (1940) on which I have leaned heavily in this summary, ends by comparing the Nazi race policy with the Inquisition and with the situation that developed around the Albigensian heresy. It was her opinion that "in order to understand

[1] Since this paragraph was written I have seen drafts of a forthcoming, as yet untitled, history of Africa by Philip Curtin, which may require that this statement, adapted from Benedict (1940), be revised.

race persecution, we do not need to investigate race; we need to investigate persecution. Persecution was an old, old story before racism was thought of" (p. 230).

RACE AND PARIAH GROUPS

In the modern West, certain physiological characteristics have been selected as diagnostic and people who bear sufficient of these characteristics are set aside as a special group, called a "race." It was only in 1951 that the last of the federal laws restricting the legal rights of Negroes in the United States was altered. Every September rearguard actions are being fought in the states themselves, where legal rights of Negroes are not equivalent of those of non-Negroes. There are a few areas in the United States that still have laws restricting the rights of all non-Caucasians.

"Race" is or has recently been a concept used by some societies in the modern world to create and maintain pariah stiuations. Scientific men of good will have spent many hours and many words trying to determine whether racial differences are in fact accompanied by differences in intellect, cultural capacity, and the like. They might have saved much of that effort had they mustered the courage to face squarely the fact that "race" is not scientifically definable. They could have saved it all if they had refused to care whether it is so or not. The issue of importance is not whether 4 of 100 Caucasians and only 2 of 100 Negroes are"outstanding."It is rather whether the country and the culture can afford to forego as many outstanding citizens as that (or any other) figure could amount to.

Race is a folk concept, not an analytical concept. Like most folk concepts, its scientific validity is beside the point of its power to move people. Science can be used and misused to "prove" anything at all about the matter—yet science stands aloof because the only thing it has proved is that "race" is not a useable scientific category or concept.

Races, however, exist. Races are social categories based on observable physical differences. The differences are observable anywhere, by all normal people—even though "race" as a concept is not widespread.

"Race" in modern Europe—right down to the Nazi era—has had to do with class. During the Nazi era, it was perverted to create or prolong a pariah situation. Race in North America has been used to create a pariah situation out of a particular form of institutionalized servility, the Southern plantation system. The pariah group in the United States has often, and I think mistakenly, been analyzed as a caste situation, mainly on criteria of individual mobility and endogamy, or epiphenomena of pariah rank.

Pariahs are persons who are not admitted to the rank systems or even the servile institutions of a society. Rather they exist outside that system and may even, within their own group, maintain rank organizations that reflect those of the major society. Pariah groups may be outcastes as in India, economically underprivileged kinship groups as on the Northwest Coast, or races in the modern United States. "Race" is the modern Western idiom for pariah groups.

The concept of race, interestingly and alarmingly enough, has never, so far as I know, been the subject matter of ethnographic surveys or cross-cultural analysis. Our own ideas of race have been so firm that we have not been able to question them in the light of someone else's ideas about physical differences. It is time we discovered what some of the non-Western peoples make of this situation. It is time we took race out of the analytical system and began investigating, comparatively, folk images of it.

I have called this chapter the "chimera" of race. A chimera is a mythical beast: "A fire-breathing female monster, reported to be of divine origin. . . . According to the description of her given in the Homeric poems, the fore part of her body was that of a lion, the middle like that of a goat, and the hind that of a dragon. She laid waste the fields of Lycia and all the country round. Hesiod says she had three heads, one for each of the three animal parts composing her body. She was destroyed by Bellerophon with the help of Pegasus" (Bulfinch, n.d., p. 103).

Space and things

part 4

13

Ecology, work, and production

THE ANIMAL NATURE of man lies not only behind kinship systems and organizations based on age, sex, rank, and race. The requirements of the human body for nourishment and a limited temperature range dictate that man must exploit his environment to satisfy these needs on a daily repetitive basis. Being material, the human body must also exist in a space already filled with other men and with other animals. Thus, all men must organize themselves in order to adjust to one another in space and to exploit the environment to provide their daily needs. The two purposes can never be wholly separated.

ECOLOGY

These two axioms—that man exploits his environment culturally, and that he and his society and culture must have a spatial dimension—are at the basis of the science of ecology. Ecology studies the interrelationships in a given area of the animal and plant populations—including, of course, man. Ecology came of age in the middle nineteenth century and formed one of the foundations of Darwin's biological studies. Although the subject has made vast strides since Darwin's time, few succinct statements of the fundamentals of ecology are so exciting as are some of those made in *The Origin of Species.*

The ecological principle is the same as the basic principle of evolution: "the survival of the fittest." In the struggle for nutriment, those organisms that exploit their environments more efficiently than do either others of their own kind, or organisms of other species, live and breed. Those that are less efficient die. Evolutionary theory studies the effect of this state of affairs on genetic development of species. Ecology stops at an earlier stage and studies the interaccommodation of organisms and species on the earth's surface.

Darwin's ecological studies were minute but highly informative. He recounts (1859, p. 49) that on a piece of cleared and turned ground three feet by two feet in dimension, he recorded every weed that came up. During the season, 357 plants sprouted in those six square feet. Of that number, 295 were destroyed as seedlings, most of them by insects and slugs. In another experiment, on a piece of mown turf three by four feet, he found that twenty species of plant and weed germinated; of that number nine species perished merely because all the other species were allowed to grow freely.

Darwin discovered on a piece of heath owned by one of his kinsmen in Staffordshire that some twenty years after enclosure, when one section was planted to evergreens and another not, there were different species of insectiverous birds in the plantations from those on the unplanted heath; there were at least twelve wild plants in the plantations that were not to be found on the heath. In another part of England, he found (1859, pp. 51-52) that after enclosure and exclusion of cattle from an area that had once been common land used for grazing, large numbers of fir trees sprang up. He was concerned about the manner in which such large colonies of firs could develop from the minute quantities of seed that he could trace to a source. On close investigation, he found that the fir trees had been present all the time, but had been cropped by cattle. Some of the tiny, stumped firs had as many as twenty-six rings, but the browsing and grazing of cattle had prevented their growing above the level of the heath grasses. When the cattle were removed, the ecological conditions favored the firs.

The discipline of ecology, which has been illustrated with these simple observations of Darwin, is the study of the way that plants and animals live together in space, exploiting and hence creating the natural environment that *is* terrestrial space.

Man is one of the most potent forces in creating any specific environment: man enclosed or did not enclose the common, and allowed or did not allow cattle to graze in a certain area. Man created the plantations that led to the change in insect, plant, and bird life on the heaths. Indeed, Darwin himself roped off the piece of turf in which he counted the growing species.

No other animal can change and bend the environment to its own needs to the same extent as man. The changes that man works are brought about by the same instruments as he uses for every other purpose of living —cultural instruments. It is possible to establish a crude equation about the relative effects of nature and culture in creating the environment:

$$\text{Nature} \times \text{Culture} = \text{Environment}$$

If the natural features of an area change, and there is no compensating cultural change, then a new environmental balance comes into being. Similarly, if new cultural inventions or ways of doing things are instituted, and there is no change in the natural aspects of the area, then a new environment has been created. This equation quickly breaks down, because it soon becomes impossible to distinguish nature from culture on any but the most pedantic of definitions. Culture, indeed, is natural, from the standpoint of the ecologist. Few landscapes in the world have escaped the mark of human culture.

Nevertheless the simple—indeed, oversimple—formula allows us to examine some fundamental examples of the human condition, and to do away once and for all with one of the most persistent of errors haunting social science: the error of environmental determinism.

It stands to reason that the simpler the culture, the more directly dependent man is on the noncultural elements of the environment. Probably the most dramatic example is to be found with the Eskimo who have a simple but effective culture and a limited and harsh natural environment. Eskimo are hunters and fishermen and are almost entirely dependent on the migrations of game animals and fish. At some times of the year they follow herds of caribou, at other times they hunt polar bears, seals, and other arctic animals, at still other times they live on fish. Their lives are a constant reaction to the migratory movements of the game and fish. Their culture has institutionalized the resultant migrations of the people themselves. The Eskimo form, at a primitive level, an ecological balance with bears, seals, fish, caribou, moss, and lichens. Even the introduction of firearms had only relatively little effect on the ecological balance.

However, the Eskimo—and probably any other people who live by hunting and gathering—are toward the "nature" end of the continuum: that is, the noncultural elements loom large. Within the last ten or fifteen thousand years, human culture has vastly reduced the part that raw nature plays in creating the immediate environment of human beings. The geophysical environment, in other words, is replaced with a cultural and social environment; more complex cultures limit the degree to which man is dependent on the natural aspects of the environment. It does not, however, reduce the primacy of *total* environment. The error in environmental determinism is the assumption that the natural—noncultural—part of the environment *determines* the cultural part of it. Actually it merely places a limitation on the human social group—there is probably a corner in every environment that is impervious to culture.

Thus, the idea of an ecological system concerns itself with the balance of life in a certain area. When there is only plant life and the life of lower animals and insects, an area reaches a sort of "brute balance," as it were, dependent on who gets the food. Limited food determines that not all organisms can survive. Survival of some individuals and some species and the disappearance of others creates the ecological environment, as well as the history of the evolution of species.

There is one important change that results when man is introduced as a factor in the ecological picture. Man manipulates his environment instead of "merely" exploiting it. His aim is not mere survival, or even comfortable survival. Man, indeed, has introduced the illusion that he controls his environment. Although ultimately his control may be illusory, and the human cultural mode of creating environment a totally natural one, and although cultural control proves merely to be an epiphenomenon of (or even the way of expressing) the will to survive, nevertheless culture creates great complexity in the ecological chain.

Thus, environment may *limit* a culture, but it cannot determine it. Indeed, the whole economic history of the modern West—or of any other civilization, no matter how rude—is a struggle against environmental limitation.

The point of "human ecology" is a simple one. The condition of human society and culture is affected by, but not determined by, the qualities of its geographical and nonhuman space. A culture, which has ways of exploiting an environment, must be congruent with the area concerned. At the same time, the very act of exploitation changes the characteristics of the area.

ECONOMY

Early anthropologists had a tendency to confuse ecology with economy, and to confuse both those topics with technology. They recognized that in order to insure the necessary goods for the maintenance of human life and society on a daily, weekly, and repetitive basis, people must perform some activities to exploit their environments. They investigated these activities under the rubric of "work" or even "labor." They then classified the type of "work" and, erroneously, called their categories types of ecological adjustment and of "economy."

Investigating the economy, it is well to be somewhat more detailed. Economy is a result not merely of interaction of environment and culture, as is ecology. Rather, it is a result of the interaction of those portions of the environment that are utilized by the culture in the form of resources, and those aspects of the culture that are techniques for utilizing the resources and transforming them into products. The factors important in economic analysis are some of the same factors that are important in ecological analysis, but the purpose of the analyses is vastly different, and hence the theoretical ends and methodological means are different.

The way in which resources, technology, and work are combined to satisfy the material requirements of human beings and of social groups can be called an economy. As we shall see later, the science of economics deals with this triumvirate in its own way for its special purposes. Anthropologists may, of course, deal with it in quite a different way for the purposes of their own discipline.

RESOURCES

It is probably true to say that every land environment in the world, and many of the sea environments, can be made to yield a living if the technology of the people is adequate. Resources, in short, do not exist except insofar as they can be exploited by the technology of the people who control the territory in which the raw materials exist. The coal in Pennsylvania was not a resource for the Indians who lived there, yet modern Americans have based an industrial culture on it. The seed-bearing grasses of the Great Basin country of Utah, Nevada, and Idaho are not resources to the modern Americans who live there today, yet they once dominated the way of life of the Shoshone and Paiute Indians who lived there. The Nuer of the southern Sudan live in an area rich in wild game which they, being a herding people, do not exploit; therefore, the game is not for them an important resource. For other peoples with other technologies, the game might be a resource or even the staff of life.

TECHNOLOGY

Economists have often, and justly, accused anthropologists of confusing technology with economy. The basis of their charge lies in the fact that anthropologists have often, in the past, used technology as the basis for classifying economies (as well as ecologies). Anthropology, or at least early anthropology, used the basic technique for getting subsistence as the index for its classifications.

According to the traditional anthropological classification there are five basic forms of technology or—what was in those days thought to be the same thing—five basic types of economy. The first of these is hunting and gathering; the second is herding; the third, horticulture; the fourth, agriculture (with or without cottage industries); and the fifth, industrial mass production of goods in factories.

HUNTING AND GATHERING

Societies that depend on hunting and gathering for their basic subsistence were fairly common as late as the early twentieth century. Australia was represented by little else. The Western half of North America was, a little earlier than that, the preserve of people who gained their livings by hunting and gathering. The Northwest Coast depended on fishing and berries, the California Indians on acorns, the Indians of the Great

Basin country of Nevada and Idaho on grass seeds and game. Plains Indian culture depended almost solely on the buffalo as the basis of subsistence. In Africa the hunters and gatherers range from the Pygmies of the Ituri Forest to the Bushmen of the Kalahari Desert. Most South American Indians depended on hunting, though in many areas also grew manioc.

Although the number of societies that get a living by hunting and gathering is large, the number of people involved in each of these societies is small. No environment can support very many people on the basis of wildlife and wild plants. One of the major exceptions is the area from Puget Sound north along the northwest coast of North America. The fantastically plentiful wildlife of this area supported a relatively large Indian population by techniques of hunting, gathering, and fishing. The whole Arctic area of the New World, however, supports only a few thousand Eskimos. The Kalihari Desert supports only a few hundred Bushmen, and the great deserts of Australia and America supported at most a few thousand aborigines or Indians.

Probably the most important single feature about a hunting and gathering society is that the economy of the society and the economy of the domestic group are largely undifferentiated from each other. In every society there is a basic household or domestic unit in which food and other items of primary consumption are prepared. As we shall see, there is within each of these domestic units a basic division of tasks. In hunting and gathering societies—and in a few others—the basic consumption unit, which is the domestic group, is also the production unit.

Hunting and gathering as a technology will support comparatively few people on the land. In many areas where it is practiced it also provides minimal return for the effort expended, although as we have seen, the Northwest Coast with its fish, deer, and wild plants was an exception, and the coastal areas of California with its munificence of acorns provided another exception.

HERDING

Throughout the world there are to be found peoples whose basic technique for exploiting the environment is to keep animals. These animals may be reindeer among the Lapps or nothern Siberians; they may be goats in Morocco and along the northern edges of the Sahara; they may be the cattle of the Near East or of much of Africa; they may be the camels that are found in Arabia and the Sahara; they may be horses as was the case in the Great Plains area of North America; they may be pigs in Melanesia; and in South America there are herds of llama.

The number of peoples who live solely off their herds is, of course, very much smaller than the number of peoples who carry on some herding activities while depending on farming. Nevertheless, it is not a negligible one. Herding is generally considered to be a somewhat more secure way of exploiting the environment than is hunting, and most herding peoples, even though they may live in an area replete with wild game, do not make much use of it. Whereas the insecurities of hunting peoples focus around scarcity of game, the insecurities of herders are bound up with the welfare of their beasts. The damage that an epizootic such as rinderpest can create may leave a whole society in a tenuous condition for some years.

Herding usually allows greater density of population than does an economy based on hunting and gathering. However, it also gives rise to the necessity for movement. The people must see to it that their animals move from one area of pasturage and water to another, from one season to the next. Therefore, most herding peoples are either nomadic or transhumant.

Nomads, following the demands of their animals for pasture and water, move in careful response to those needs. Nomads, however, do not "wander." Even if they wanted to wander at random, other people who live around them would not allow them to do so. Rather, they have definite routes along which they proceed, and they go over the same routes in a sort of circle again and again. They may take shortcuts in the route, and they may take some areas in a different order on one occasion than on another. However, the nomad "route" is a known one, requiring from three or four to as many as fifty years to complete.

Nomadism enforces certain limitations on the material possessions and demands of the people who practice it: nomads must live either in movable houses such as the skin tipis of the American Indians or the camel-hair tents of the Bedouin Arabs, else rude and hastily constructable shelters that are made anew for each camp site and abandoned when camp is moved.

Transhumance differs from nomadism in that the cycle of movement is an annual one and follows the seasons, rather than a longer one requiring several years. Some Lapps are transhumant, moving their reindeer herds between coastal areas where they can provide food in the winter time and the mountain recesses where the pasturage is best in summer. Many Pakistani and Indian peoples move their herds to the mountains in the summer and back in the winter. The cattle-herding peoples of the upper Nile are almost all transhumant. During the wet season they live in villages with fixed huts and herd their cattle in nearby areas on the higher hummocks, which are not flooded by the great Nile plain. Then, as the dry season proceeds and the water recedes, they are forced to take their cattle ever further away, sometimes to live in cattle camps at some distance from their permanent villages in smaller (or sometimes larger) groups than the villages themselves provide. This annual movement between village and cattle camp is the most striking characteristic of the technology of societies that practice transhumance, just as temporary, movable shelters are characteristic of nomads.

Herding peoples throughout the world are said to be of a noble and independent frame of mind. Without exception, they are said to scorn settled life and agriculture pursuits even when they, or at least their women, engage in agriculture to a limited degree. It is probably safe to say that herding peoples have had a more difficult time than any other adjusting to life in a modern world on the fringes of an industrial economy. Certainly they have held out longest against it.

HORTICULTURE OR GARDENING

It is traditional in anthropology, but the tradition is by no means accepted without question, that the presence of the plow differentiates horticulture from agriculture. Horticulture consists in gardening with hand tools, such as the digging stick and the hoe. A very large variety of crops can be grown with this technique. Grains such as corn, millet, or sorghum, and roots such as manioc, yams, or potatoes are the staple foods of horticulturists everywhere.

Gardening allows a very much more dense population than does either herding or gathering. It is often said that gardening allows a population to become sedentary or stable. Such, however, is seldom the case because most people who depend on gardening usually do not have an adequate technology to maintain the fertility of the soil if it is used year after year. Therefore, they must move their gardens every year or every few years, allowing the old gardens to return to fallow, either bush or jungle, so that fertility may be regained by the natural means that built it up in the first place. Nevertheless, horticulture certainly has the effect of reducing the distance people move when compared with herding; it also restrains the time limit during which they can make specific types of moves.

Horticulture as a technique of getting a living makes very characteristic changes in the environment. Land must be cleared of grass and bush, and trees must be removed or at least thinned out. Horticulture also provides its own unique type of insecurity to the peoples who practice it. Irregularities of weather and infestations of destructive insects and birds can create hunger for an entire year. People who practice horticulture are usually dependent for their food on the crops they themselves produce, with only a minimum amount of exchange and trading.

Without exception, people who practice horticulture work hard. In most places the men do the heaviest work and if there is dangerous work, such as that involved in felling trees, it is also usually alloted to the men. In many places, however, horticultural activities, such as planting, weeding, and harvesting, are carried out by women. The place of women in horticultural societies is everywhere an extremely important one.

AGRICULTURE

The invention of the plow was undoubtedly one of the most important points of change in the history of the world, for it combined horticulture with the effective use of animals as a new source of energy that could be used in the acquisition of the necessities of life.

Agriculture also reduces the hazards, or at least substitutes a new set of hazards, in the regularity of the supply of products. Agriculture work is seasonal; therefore some periods are available in which other types of production can be carried out. New and sometimes more complex industries can be developed in agriculture situations than in horticultural or certainly in herding situations.

FACTORY INDUSTRIALISM

Factory industrialism assumes a form of energy beyond that of the human being and his domesticated animals. It is traditional to date the beginning of the Industrial Revolution from the invention of the steam engine. Like the Agricultural Revolution, the Industrial Revolution swept away old problems and presented new ones, just as compelling, to take their place.

The efficacy of factory industrialism and the society and economy that can be based on it is to be found in the small portion of the population engaged in producing basic foodstuffs, whereas in hunting and gathering, herding, and horticultural societies, the major effort of almost all of the people goes into the production of food. With agriculture the number may be reduced and with factory industrialism the percentage of people engaged in producing primary food crops may be reduced to less than ten percent—and perhaps in the future far less.

Factory industrialism is, in one sense at least, the logical opposite of hunting and gathering societies. In hunting and gathering societies there is minimal separation of domestic and community economy. In factory industrialism, the domestic economy and the economy of the community are almost totally separated. The household remains the major consuming unit, but it is no longer a basic production unit. Production is carried out by new social groups, of which business firms are representative, that are based on the principle and ethic of contract rather than on the principle and ethic of kinship. Linkage between the household, or consuming unit, and the firm or producing unit is by two means: secondary syndromes of roles link the families' husbands/fathers, as breadwinners, to the firm's technicians or executives; material items and overwhelmingly powerful ideas such as money provide the means for the movement of goods both from producer to consumer and from one producer to the next. Such a description fits the U.S.S.R. as well as it fits the United States.

It is obvious, then, that each of these forms of economy goes with a specific type or a range of types of social organization. Hunting and gathering peoples almost always live in bands, which are collections of nuclear families. Herding peoples almost all live in groups that are based on the kinship of the men among them joined by their wives—that is to say, in patrilineally extended families, in patrilocal communities. Horticulture and agriculture both coincide with village types of organization. In some types large-scale consanguine kinship groups are encountered. In advanced types, such as those found in medieval Europe, the village may contain a manor, with its involved system of stratification by estates, and towns associated with trade may grow up outside the manor. As a general rule, however, all of these types of economy are associated with social organizations based to one degree or another on principles of kinship. Factory industrialism, on the other hand, is associated with the type of society based not on kinship but rather on contract, and usually—so far at least—the adoption of factory industrialism as a form of life has gone hand in hand with the reduction of the family to the small nuclear group and to the pronounced playing down of all other kinship organizations.

The Industrial Revolution gave rise not only to a new form of society and a new form of economy, but also to a new way of thinking about economy and society—one that was summed up under the name "Political Economy." This subject, as a separate entity, focused as an organized discipline in the gigantic work of creative synthesis performed by Adam Smith, and leads directly to the economic theory of the present day.

It is of profound importance, in attempting to understand the ways in which non-Western people get a living, to realize that economics as a science grew up with the type of society it set out to analyze and investigate—factory industrialism, imbedded as it usually is in a society based on the principle of contract, with greater or lesser freedom of contract, in that the organization of work and the allotment of resources are not concordant with kinship and community, but rather are determined by the network of contract that such industrialism itself fostered.

Although it need not be so, the type of contract that lay at the back of Western development was the casual contract centering on sale, at a price determined by the law of supply and demand: so-called "market exchange." In such a situation, everything needed to supply the recurrent social and individual wants of the population comes to be subject to the same sort of contract: contract based on the market. Resources, work, land, products, skill—all became the subject of contracts.

It is common—it is, indeed, probably necessary—that when the factors of production and the products are all subject to the same sort of market contract, that all become measured in terms of one single standard—money. Such a system, with the factors and the products all commensurable in terms of money and being the subjects of contract, is called a "market system."

It is characteristic of a pervasive market system that these various elements or factors of production change hands in response to supply and demand as indicated by market activity. In such a society, resources are those items (usually called raw materials) bought by producers. The services of working men, called labor, are also bought by producers, and so is the use of land, commonly called rent. So are technology and "know how" for sale. Even money has a price and is sold on the market—the price for use of money is called interest or dividends. All of these items come together and can be equated with one another in terms of a money value.

It is this fact of modern economy—the centralizing effect of a single social principle, contract and of the single money that converts all to a single standard—that has made possible the vast strides in the science of economics and the vast growth in material production. But economics is like geometry in one respect: it will work only if certain axioms or premises are held firm. The axioms or premises of the science of economics are to be found in the institutions of the market based on exchange according to supply and demand, and the greater or lesser freedom of individuals and of social groups called "firms" to make contracts in accordance with the terms dictated by their own best material interests.

The moment that these institutions or "premises" of the economy are changed, economics must enter into a non-Euclidian universe, so to speak. In places where the principle of contract is not extended with the same freedom as among ourselves, or where contract is controlled politically rather than by free market exchange—as Americans knew in World War II's rationing and price control—the principles of economics must be supplemented.

In societies where social groups such as family or lineage, based firmly on kinship rather than contract, are granted highest regard, then land, work, resources, and ingenuity are institutionalized very differently and different concepts and exercises are involved in the analysis. In such societies—and they vary from the factory industrialism of the Soviets where contract is largely by government fiat, to the horticultural societies of Africa or South America—the principles of economic and social organization form such a non-Euclidian universe. The market, if it is present at all, may become of only peripheral significance. The modes for organizing the factors of production in such a way that production can take place to meet the recurrent needs may become strange enough to Westerners as to seem irrational until they are understood. For the anthropologist these exotic circumstances are as interesting and as worthy of attention as are those of the factory industrialism and the market system in which we are experienced. And the apparent irrationality disappears before comprehension and, eventually, understanding.

FACTORS OF PRODUCTION AND THEIR INSTITUTIONALIZATION

It is not difficult to see that in the absence of markets for labor, markets for land, markets for resources, even the absence of markets for products, production must be institutionalized in a way very different from that of mid-twentieth-century Western society. This matter is of equal importance with a further factor—the absence of machines. What remains constant, however, is the need for raw materials, for land, for work, for ingenuity, and for tools. Economists call these things the "factors of production." It is most instructive to examine ways in which the factors of production can be institutionalized in the absence of the type of system familiar in the Western world.

WORK

It has been pointed out by a famous Dutch historian (Huizinga, 1944) that all people may not work, but all people do play. It is nevertheless true that most people work. The very dichotomy between work and play is one which most people of the world fail to draw; at least they draw it in very different ways from the common ones we know. In the past, Westerners have assumed that work is painful and that play gives pleasure, when they actually should know (if they would examine the situation critically) that work is sometimes painful and sometimes gives pleasure, and play is sometimes pleasant and sometimes unpleasant.

It is not surprising that the pleasure-pain principle and the play-work dichotomy became involved or even confused. As social reformers never tire of telling us, the Industrial Revolution created new work conditions that were not merely unpleasant or even arduous in themselves, but new conditions in which the rewards and the pleasures had no direct connection with the work that made them possible. Even today we contrast "work" with "fun."

Most peoples of the world contrast "work" with "laziness." They see work not as an unpleasant necessity, but as an integrative activity. That is to say, it is the activities that a person performs so that some other member of the community will perform another and complementary action. Both of these actions are required for the well-being of the individuals and of society. Play, on the other hand, takes place in a more restricted scale. In playing, one is not making a required contribution to the functioning of society. Playing and having fun are two different things. It is possible to have fun working as well as playing. Work and displeasure are also separate—it is possible to be more bored the harder one plays. Play occurs in the restricted field of art; work occurs in the total field of society.

Work is universal, at least it is so in the sense that we have defined it. The activities of artists, of priests, of farmers, and of professional ball players are all work. Their products and acts are all reciprocated in some form. It is, however, not uncommon in the popular mores of our own society to draw distinctions between "productive" labor and "nonproductive" labor. The former we say is that which is required for the basic "economic products" without which we would perish—the common difference between "luxuries" and "necessities." We have shown a lamentable tendency to exclude from productive work activities leading to products that maintain a way of life itself. A distinction between products established on this basis can be found only if we sell our culture short.

The idea of work has become blurred in our culture with another idea—that of labor. The economist deals only with that work which is sold on the market and therefore goes into the processes of production and distribution. The work of a housewife, which is not recompensed directly, is not considered labor by economists. It is not computed as part of the national income. For all that, however, a housewife performs work, which if it were sold on the market as labor, would bring between $3000 and $5000 a year—approximately the amount of the average national income. No one denies that a housewife's activities are work. No one denies that they are productive.

Everywhere in the world there is a domestic economy made up of the interlocking tasks of the members of the household. The most basic division of labor or division of tasks, to use a better word, is that between a man and a woman who are usually husband and wife. Tasks of these two persons, each of which depends on satisfactory performance by the other, are the basis of what is called the sexual division of labor.

There are certain tasks everywhere said to be the work of men and others said to be the work of women. Some societies adhere to their principles of the sexual division of tasks more firmly than do others, and certainly the sexual division of tasks assigns work to men in some societies that it assigns to women in others. Potmaking, for example, is a task assigned almost indiscriminately to men and to women and yet is one which most societies feel very strongly should be a prerogative of one sex or the other.

The sexual division of tasks does not follow lines Americans or other Westerners would consider to be "natural." Men do not always do the "heavy" work and women the "light" work. We carry this particular distinction to phenomenal, and indeed silly, lengths on occasion. It is illegal in America for the federal government to hire women to do manual labor. For this reason all female archeologists, whatever their degree of competence or skill, must either be excluded from projects financed by the government or else must be bootlegged in under their initials or under the cover of a man who does no more than collect their pay for them.

It often happens, furthermore, that different tasks are assigned to the young and to the old, to the noble and the commoner, to the priest and to the layman. Division of tasks and complementary allotment of work is of very widespread occurrence. Obviously—and yet, it was for centuries not obvious—every place where there is a division of tasks, there automatically comes into exsistence a relationship of dependence between the people who perform the tasks. If I do everything necessary for my existence, I depend on no one. I am, in fact that hypothetical character the economists invented—that man who is not dependent on his fellows for any of his needs—and then mislabeled Robinson Crusoe. They invented him merely to make a point by contrast—we must not believe it any more than do economists themselves.

If I allow my wife to cook the food I bring home, she becomes dependent upon me and I upon her. As Adam Smith detailed, division of tasks can continue to the point where the whole world is dependent upon the rest of the world. The more complex the division of tasks, the more complex must be the organization that ties together the people who perform the various individualized tasks.

The division and organization of tasks are ultimately dependent upon the nature of the work to be performed; some tasks lend themselves to division and organization more readily than others. Hunting and gathering, for example, depend upon several people all doing roughly the same task, although the hunting itself may be divided up into several complementary tasks among several hunters, and organized systematically. Agriculture requires, or at least allows, a much more complex division of tasks. However, industrial manufacturing requires a division of tasks almost unbelievably complex, and with it an organization of work and of society so involved, extended, and complex as almost to baffle analysis.

LAND

There are many parts of the world in which land as a factor of production is not in short supply. Like air or water, it is available to all and resembles what economists used to call a "free good." However, even when land is not scarce for means of production, there tends to be another matter that makes people value it and demarcate it. That is its value as a site.

Land is useful to human beings in two ways. One of these ways is that it is a necessary dimension of society. Human beings are material and they must exist in space. For this reason all social relationships and all social groups have a spatial element or dimension. Individuals and groups demand space not only in order to produce their material needs, but to maintain privacy or cultural exclusiveness and integrity.

In modern Western society land, both as a factor in production and as a domestic site, has entered into market exchange. It can do so only in a contract-dominated society. In a society dominated by any other principle the social group, which has dimensions in space, exists apart from the contracts people make with one another and with their governments to occupy, live, and work in such-and such places. In a market-oriented society one buys one's piece of earth on which to live. That is not true in any other type of society. Second, land is valued for what it can produce and therefore it enters the market as a factor of production as well as a site. It is an amazing fact that among ourselves the ethnocentric view of land has followed the second rather than the first principle—the principle of site has been expressed in terms of the principle of production.

Whenever one begins to think or write about land, the word that immediately comes to mind is "tenure." Thereupon, the discussion goes almost immediately into a legalistic disquisition on land-tenure practices in the societies concerned, and an economic analysis of the results. Just as labor suggests "organization," land suggests "tenure." Both can be explained by the fact that in our own society land and labor enter the market.

Once we have made the distinction between land as site and land as factor of production, it quickly becomes possible to examine these two matters independently in our own society as well as any other. In a society based on principles other than contract, some existing social groups live together and so make a community. In a society based on contract, on the other hand, local groups result from a large number of individual contracts. Since contracts can be made and broken at a much faster rate than other types of social relationship, the membership of spatial groups so organized tends to be less permanent.

It is usual for the two aspects of land occupation—production and site—to go together. It is also usual for the dominant one to be the site aspect. One exploits that land on which one finds onself as a member of a localized social group. Only in a contract society, where land enters the market, do we have the opposite situation, in which local groups come into existence because land has been parceled out in a certain set of ways in order to maximize production, and then sold.

The land, one way or another, does produce the subsistence that keeps alive the members of the social group at the same time that it is the spatial milieu in which they move. For these reasons, territorial or group integrity is often confused with rights to exploit certain pieces of land. Such a confusion—or rather lack of distinction—on the folk level is understandable, but on the analytical level the spatial distribution of people must be handled under a heading the geographers call *chorology*. Exploitation, on the other hand, is irrevocably a matter of economy.

Our immediate purpose here is to examine the way land is viewed and institutionalized in the absence of a market system for its distribution and allocation. In order to do so, it is first necessary to ask some questions about how people who live in nonmarket societies view the spatial dimension of their societies, and also, but separately, view their exploitation of the land. Such a task is most easily accomplished if we subject our own views of this matter to intense scrutiny.

Every people, including ourselves, must have some view or opinion about the physical milieu in which it lives. That is to say, they have a folk geography of the world and their place in it. For the last few centuries Westerners have viewed the world as a sphere covered with a grid. The grid can be manipulated in scale from the size of the earth itself down to the size of the classroom globe. It can even be reduced to two dimensions and reproduced on a flat piece of paper. The next step is to take a position on the earth and, by use of an instrument called a sextant (which was invented only in 1723), locate this position vis-a-vis the stars so that it can be checked by the next person. This position is then given an arbitrary but culturally accepted position on the grid. The piece of land is then further marked off by lines extending from the point checked with the sextant, by use of another instrument called a transit, and by precise measurement. In this way it is possible to make lines on maps that do not correlate with any marks on the earth but that will outlast any specific terrestrial landmarks. It is obvious that the grid must be completely rigid. To achieve precision, it is defined astrally, with overtly assigned relationships to quite arbitrary points on the earth's surface. It is specifically *not* defined terrestrially by earthly landmarks, except as such landmarks have first been located astrally.

We Westerners have taken a seafarer's map, and with the aid of precision instruments, applied it to the measurement and delineation of land. These measured pieces of land become, for purposes of legal and economic activity, precise, identifiable things that can be held and transferred according to the market system and the dominant legal mode which has culminated in the principle of contract, securely enforced.

Thus, culturally, land—whatever else it may also be—is a measurable entity divisible into thinglike "parcels" by means of the mathematical and technical processes of surveying and cartography. We live on some of these parcels and produce food on others. This complex notion of "land," with its accompanying technology, is an absolute essential to the Western system of land tenure. Legally recognized rights can be held in such a parcel of land and these rights can be sold or exchanged for money at a market price.

In other societies there are other kinds of maps and other kinds of rights held in accordance with different principles of organization and in different contexts. A few of these different kinds of maps and different kinds of rights will be investigated here.

The Tiv of central Nigeria see geography in the same image as they see social organization. The idiom of descent and genealogy provides not only the basis for lineage grouping, but also of territorial grouping. Tiv group themselves according to a lineage system based on the principle of segmental opposition. Eighty-three percent of the adult males living in the territory are agnatic members of the lineage. This minimal lineage, made up of men descended from a single ancestor, plus their wives and daughters, is located spatially beside another of precisely the same sort, descended from the first ancestor's brother. In reference to the father of the two apical ancestors of minimal lineages, the two minimal lineages form an inclusive lineage, and their territories form a spatial unit. This process continues genealogically for several generations, until all Tiv are included; it continues geographically until the entirety of Tivland is seen as a lineage area, segmenting into increasingly smaller lineage areas. Tiv have place names for streams and hills. Otherwise, their only place names are the names of lineages living in certain areas.

This "genealogical map" of Tivland moves about the surface of the earth, in sensitive response to the demands of individual farmers as their needs change from year to year. The "map" is a genealogical map, and its association with specific pieces of ground is of only very brief duration—a man or woman has precise rights to a farm during the time it is in cultivation, but when the farm returns to fallow after two or three years, the rights lapse. However, a man always has rights in the "genealogical map" of his agnatic lineage, wherever that lineage may happen to be in space. These rights, which are part of his birthright, can never lapse. Whereas the Western map, based on surveys, resembles geometry, the Tiv mode of viewing geography resembles topology, which has been called "geometry on a rubber sheet." Whereas the Western map is rigid and precise, the Tiv map is constantly changing both in reference to itself and in its correlation with the earth.

The Tiv concepts for discussing the spatial aspect of their social organization are simple ones: the term *tar* means the "map on a rubber sheet"—*tar* is the people, the compounds, and most particularly the juxtaposition of people and compounds. This is quite different from the earth, or *nya*. The *tar* changes its position on the *nya*, which is itself immutable. Every Tiv has a right to an adequate farm whatever earth holds his *tar*. This is a right to a *farm*, not to a specific piece of land. A farm lasts only for two or three years, then reverts to fallow and the specific right lapses. However, the right to *some* farm in the *tar* never lapses. Thus, the position of a man's farm varies from one season to the next, but his juxtaposition with his agnatic kinsmen and his rights do not change. Tiv might be said to have "farm tenure," but they do not have "land tenure."

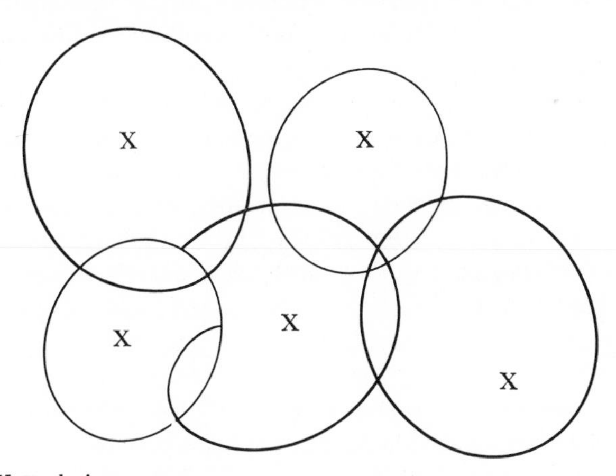

FIGURE 11 Tonga Rain Shrines and surrounding village and farm areas

The Plateau Tonga of northern Rhodesia (Colson, 1948; 1951; 1954; 1958) supply another variant. Their "map" is a series of points, each representing a rain shrine. Rain shrines are of two sorts: either natural features that have been made sacred, or specially built small huts. A rain shrine never changes geographical location, though it may and probably will be forgotten after a generation or so. In former times, if a man lived within the area associated with a rain shrine, he was required to participate in its ritual. Rain-shrine neighborhoods were the basic territorial grouping, and they changed constantly as allegiances shifted with the creation of new shrines or the shifting efficacy of old ones, as well as with people moving in and out of the area.

The rain-shrine area composes usually from four to six villages. A village is a group of people, each owing some sort of allegiance to the headman. That allegiance may be based on kinship, on affinity, or on friendship. People change the villages of their residence with great alacrity and frequency, so that there is a constant movement from one village to another. Concomitantly, but in longer time span, the villages themselves change locations.

Residence in a village carries with it rights to clear farms in the vicinity. The headman can show a newcomer the land that is already claimed, but does not have authority to allot him rights in any unclaimed land. Rather, every man selects his own site and works it. Once he has cleared it, he has rights there until he abandons the site to fallow or moves to another village. If he moves, he may assign it to someone else. Like the Tiv, Tonga have "farm tenure" rather than "land tenure."

The village is not a territorially contained unit: it has a spatial dimension but is not a territorial unit. Farms of members of different villages may be intermixed.

In sum, Tonga country is hooked to the social organization at a series of rallying points marked by shrines. Villages move about in this country, and villagers are subject to the rain shrines of their area so long as the shrines are efficacious. Whenever they are not, new shrines are created. Members of villages have rights to farm near the momentary site of the village, and once they have worked on the field retain farming rights in it as long as they want them.

INGENUITY

In every society a real amount of ingenuity has to go into the serious business of making a living. The greater the knowledge of the environment and the efficiency with which it is used, the higher the standard of living is going to be. The ingenuity that can be utilized toward this end is usually cut up by economists into two or more ideas, which must be considered. First of all, there is the notion of maximization. It is a postulate of economics that the ordinary man, given the opportunity, will improve his lot. Of course, it is well known that certain social values will hem in any individual man's capacity or even his desire for self-aggrandizement, beyond a certain point. Kinship, requirements of the sacred, ideas of stratification, notions about the seemliness of possessions of men of different stations—all are important in determining the actual degree of aggrandizement. Much ingenuity, in short, goes into manipulating the system, whatever it may be.

A specific kind of ingenuity, when it is exercised by a people in a free market economy, is called entrepreneurial activity, or managerial skill. Another kind is technological skill, or "know how." Like labor and land, ingenuity in the form of entrepreneurship, or "know how," commands a market price. Analogous ingenuity may be rewarded by quite other means in other cultural situations.

Every society puts definite limitations on the kinds of activities it allows its entrepreneurs and its technicians. No society, including our own, is completely permissive in this matter. Some encourage risk taking and maximization and the social differentiation that goes with it. These are the societies in which goods and affluence are ranked and are there to be achieved by anyone who has the proper amount of ingenuity. Other societies limit their entrepreneurs. They are specifically the ones in which social position is ascribed by criteria other than possession of goods, achievement, or the ingenuity that one shows. In such societies, to show too much ingenuity and to attempt to achieve a social position or a quantity or quality of goods not in accordance with one's status, may lead to very severe sanctions. One finds oneself whittled down to the size of the social position that has been ascribed to one.

Another type of ingenuity is that which is required to change a culture, including that part of it which deals with the production of annual requirements of food, lodging, and security. It can safely be said that people are willing to change the direction and reward of this sort of ingenuity only in situations in which they are convinced that their new position will be materially better and physically more secure than their old position. It is land and work and the ways in which ingenuity is used that should indicate the degree of economic growth in any given society.

Yet merely maintaining the constant fight against the elements to get a living by use of labor and land is in itself demanding in ingenuity. Without the constant renewal of the ingenuity of human beings it would be, of course, quite impossible for society to continue to exist or for economies to function.

CAPITAL

Outside of the Western world, or of a capitalistic system, there is some doubt about the advisability of using the word capital without understanding thoroughly that it is used only as a metaphor. Capital is a working tradition plus a set of tools. In the Western world the word capital is used in yet another way: in a society marked by the presence of general-purpose money, that money itself enters the market and becomes itself a tool—the means for acquiring all the other factors and for financing production. The tools used in production are called capital goods or producer's capital. Long-term consumption items such as houses, automobiles, and refrigerators, which enable people to live and produce the better, are sometimes called consumer's capital. It should be noted, however, that a washing machine is "consumer's capital" only because a housewife is by definition not a producer. The same machine in a laundromat is producer's capital.

Every culture, seen from this point of view, is marked by a set of tools and a set of houses or utensils that can be considered as producer's and consumer's capital. In most nonmanufacturing societies, however, the value of the capital goods is limited and does not represent the same amount of investment of work and ingenuity, and indeed of resources, which it represents in the industrial world. Nevertheless, capital of some sort, no matter how elementary, is necessary to carry out the production processes, whatever their degree of complexity.

Like land, capital is subject to ownership, and in Western society capital and capital equipment (like land) enter the market and change hands in accordance with the market principle of supply and demand. The number of societies in which this statement holds true is, however, very small.

The basic "economic facts" have now been placed before us. People require a constantly renewed source of consumers' products. In order to get them, it is necessary to organize certain elements of the environment and the society, which economists call the factors of production. These factors include, among others, people and their work, land and its fertility, ingenuity and its motivation, and capital and its ownership. Most important of all, these various factors of production must be integrated into a system in order that the requirements of society be dependably produced and allocated. It is to such modes of integration and to allocation that we must now turn.

14

The economic integration of society

ECONOMIC ANTHROPOLOGY is probably the most difficult branch of the subject to teach to Western students. The reason is twofold: Westerners take their economy very seriously and regard it as "right" because it has been technologically successful and because they find difficulty in creating fantasies about its absence or change. Moreover, among Westerners production is complex, utilizing many technological principles, whereas allocation is simple, using primarily a single principle. Among most of the peoples of the world, production is simple but allocation may be almost unbelievably complex, even when it is not excessive. The complexity of allocation, moreover, lies not so much in quantity as in the diversity of principles employed.

In the last chapter it was noted that early anthropologists had studied and classified economies on the basis of technical processes employed in production. Such classifications are still enlightening, although we no longer believe that they are in fact classifications of "economies." Anthropologists were not the only people to make these classifications in the eighteenth and nineteenth centuries—early economists did precisely the same thing. The best-known example is probably the famous labor theory of value, which attempted to solve the problem of how items acquired value. It was postulated that they were valuable because people had expended time and effort—that is, labor—upon them. The mistake of Smith and Ricardo was that they sought the idea of value in the production process. They raised one of the factors of production, labor, to the position of cause.

There is a sense in which the labor theory of value was right and another in which it is extremely useful. One must either agree with it or do one of two things. The simplest of these two things is to say that the stronghold had been erected on the wrong factor. Some economists, notably Henry George, created a land theory of value, others a resource theory of value. Each is as sensible—and as limited—as the labor theory of value.

The other and more difficult road—it must have been difficult because it was almost a century before it was discovered—is to question the whole premise on which Smith and Ricardo were working. One can deny that value arises out of either any individual factor of production or out of the juxtaposition of factors. It was not until the end of the nineteenth century that economists solved this problem. It was not until well into the twentieth that they were able fully to understand just how the solution worked. What had happened is that the point of focus had changed from production to allocation.

One of the major insights that provided a basis for sophisticated development of economic theory came in the work of Karl Menger and Alfred Marshall when they, separately, elaborated supply-and-demand theory and the crucial role of price in the market-organized economy. Like all great ideas, this one is extremely simple. By the time a generation had grown up with it, it had become "obvious." As with all "obvious" discoveries, it is somewhat difficult to give the originators of the idea the credit that they in fact deserve. Menger and Marshall discovered that the important factor is not "value" but rather "price." The market value of an item is the price it will bring. They also discovered that price varied not with the labor expended on an item or the land involved in its creation, but rather with its total cost of production and the demand for it. Given the free market and the principle of contract, an item will change hands only in those instances in which its value to a consumer is greater than the price he must pay for it, and its value to the producer less than the price he can get for it. Here was the basis of so-called "classical" economics. Once given such a premise, economic science has never looked back from its successful course.

It is well for the anthropologist, however, to point out that what happened is that the focus had changed from concern merely with factors of production to concern with allocation of goods, services, and end products in society. That is to say, the central or focal point in the economy lay in the way that goods and products and factors moved and changed hands.

The shift in attention could have occurred unnoticed only in a market-dominated society. Only when production is primarily for the market, and the market the chief instrument for acquiring goods and services, is a common element present: the market. The market provided, in short, a bridge between the problems of the nineteenth-century economists and those of twentieth-century economists. The path the interest of the economists followed from production to allocation is a straight and narrow one, leading through the market place. In an industrial, market-dominated economy, set within a society whose integration is based primarily on the principles of contract, all the factors of production as well as the products themselves change hands according to the principle of contract at a price determined by the law of supply and demand.

In assimilating this tremendous stride forward—the shift from value to price as the dominant theme of economists—it is easy to make a mistake similar to the one that led to acceptance of Adam Smith's premises for so many decades before they were finally questioned. We continue to assume that Menger and Marshall had discovered the market and therefore put economics on the right road, when as a matter of fact they had, by discovering the market, put economics on the right road by turning away from primary concern with production and toward the study of the principles of allocation.

RECIPROCITY, REDISTRIBUTION, AND MARKET EXCHANGE

It is only in our own day that a daring and original economic historian, Karl Polanyi, has made it possible to study allocation cross culturally without disrupting the science of economics and without becoming its slave. Polanyi has not been popular with most economists, probably because he chose guns instead of butter in planning his scholarly armory. Yet he can in the long run only add to their glory because he has given us the beginning of a theory of allocation and a classification of institutions of allocation that includes the market but is not limited by it. Although comparative studies of production are of reasonable antiquity, comparative studies of allocation of goods are in their infancy.

According to Polanyi, there are three basic modes of allocation. He does not say that there are not more, but only that he has isolated three. He has given them names: reciprocity, redistribution, and market exchange. Every empirical economy exhibits at least one of these principles of distribution; most economies exhibit two; many are characterized by all three.

Market exchange is the exchange of goods at prices determined by the law of supply and demand. Its essence is free and casual contract. Only in a society in which there is an enforceable contract law can the market gain any great predominance. As we shall see, markets are present in many societies where they affect daily life only little, unlike our own society in which the market is central. In examining the other forms, it should be recognized that both supply and demand are probably present in all cases of exchange, but only in some cases is the institutionalization such that they are instrumental in determining price.

Redistribution is defined by Polanyi as a systematic movement of goods toward an administrative center and their reallotment by the authorities at the center. The limiting cases are modern tax institutions, which (even at their most Tory) redistribute wealth in society, and at the other extreme the head of a band or compound, whose followers must put their subsistence into a common store under the surveillance of its head. Just as market exchange depends on a workable and enforcable law of contract, so redistribution depends on a socially recognized hierarchal rank system, with sufficient sanctions to be effective.

Reciprocity involves exchange of goods between people who are bound in nonmarket, nonhierarchial relationships with one another. The exchange does not create the relationship, but rather is part of the behavior that gives it content. The most vivid systems of reciprocity are those based on kinship obligations, but there are many other bases to which reciprocal transfer of goods is essential.

The name that Polanyi has given to these three forms of institutionalization of exchange leave a good deal to be desired, because they do not form exclusive categories. We have already seen that supply and demand may be operative even in nonmarket exchange, but may not be primary forces in determining price. Certainly goods are redistributed in society whenever any kind of exchange, on any allocative principle, takes place. Just as certainly, all exchanges are reciprocal in some sense—reciprocity is the essense of contractual exchange, and there are reciprocal obligations of the central authority when redistribution is examined. It must be remembered, in using them, that the terms are not to be applied as if each is an exclusive phenomenon, but rather as each is a central principle in a situation in which it may be possible to discover peripheral principles.

Most empirical economies, as we have noted, display more than one of the principles of allocation. American economy of the middle twentieth century can be taken as an initial illustration of this point. American economy is dominated by the market principle. Not merely products but the factors of production themselves all enter the market. The market is at the very core of American society, and if it were to disappear, American society would either collapse or in some other way change its nature utterly. Nevertheless, there is a large area of American economy that is controlled by redistribution—taxes and fines are cases in point. Economists sometimes go to great pains to explain taxes by market principles. They try to make us think that we are buying the services of the government, on the theory that we have made a "social contract" (choice, they could say) of living under such a government, part of which choice is agreeing to pay for it. To see such a state of affairs in terms of market morality may not be wrong, but is putting the cart before the horse. It is a case of confusing allocation by the market principle with the totality of allocation.

Similarly, there is a small corner of the American economy that is dominated by the principle of reciprocity, in the form of gift exchange. The fact that Americans buy on the market most of the gifts they give does not mean that there is not a nonmarket aspect to the allocation involved in the actual giving. In fact, we are highly critical, even indignant, of the person who computes the market value of reciprocal gifts.

In the American economy, redistribution and reciprocity as principles of distribution are peripheral, whereas the market principle is central. There are other societies in which this situation is different: in which some other principle is central, and the market, if it is present at all, is peripheral. In general, the mode in which the factors of production are allocated —especially land and labor—is the central mode, whereas any others are peripheral.

TROBRIAND ECONOMY

One of the best recorded of the "primitive" economies is that of the Trobriand Islands. All of the principles of allocation are apparent there, but it is the principle of reciprocity that is central, whereas market and redistribution are both peripheral.

The economy of the Trobriand Islands appears complex, but the appearance is deceptive and derives from the fact that if this economy is to be simply explained, it must be analyzed in terms different from those used to explain Western economy. It is necessary, to explain Trobriand economy, to examine six institutions found in that culture, in order to see how allocation and production take place. It would seem, on the basis of Malinowski's descriptions (1922), that the Trobrianders themselves do not interlink these institutions, and some of them are specifically entrenched behind moral battlements so that members of the society will not interlink them. These institutions must be given their Trobriand names, for there are no English translations of the terms. They are: (1) *kula*; (2) *urigubu*, which is counterbalanced within a single institution by *youla*; (3) *gim wali*; (4) *pokala* ("tribute" is an adequate translation); (5) *wasi* (exchange at fixed rates, between permanent partners, of yams and fish that Polanyi has playfully called fish-and-chips reciprocity); and (6) *sagali*, (a type of giveaway feast).

WASI

There are, in the Trobriand Islands, villages in the interior that do not have fishing rights either on the lagoon or the sea. There are also seaside villages that do not have access to adequate farmland. The exchange of necessary commodities between these two sets of villages is based on a series of standing partnerships and is done at a fixed rate of exchange. At harvest time members of an inland village will bring quantities of yams to their partners in a lagoon village. Every man will set his yams in front of his partner's house. This act constitutes an indemnification on the man of the lagoon village to return an equivalent amount in fish. As soon after such a visit as can be reasonably arranged, the men of the lagoon village give notice to the inland people that they are going out on a fishing expedition. By the time they return, the people from the inland village have arrived on the beach. The haul of fish is taken directly from the canoes and carried to the inland village. The equivalence between yams and fish is not measured precisely. A bunch of taro, of what Malinowski calls "the standard size," or an "ordinary" bunch of yams is given in return for a bundle of fish that weighs between three and five kilograms.

When large hauls of fish arrive in the inland villages, they are often distributed in accordance with the institution known as *sagali.* Fish is the only commodity that can be used in *sagali* giveaways in the inland villages. Conversely, the yams enter into the giveaway economy of the coastal areas, whether it be in *sagali* or in that form of giving to the sister's husband known as *urigubu.*

Wasi exchanges more or less follow the supply and undoubtedly in a good year for fishing one gets more fish per yams than in a bad year, which is to say that the bundles will be heavier in a good year than in a bad year. However, there is still a strict one-to-one equivalence between the number of bundles of yams and the number of bundles of fish. Such a situation resembles what modern merchants call packaging to price. What is important, however, is not that there may be a fluctuation in quantity and hence a change in "price." Rather, it is that "price" does not appear at all in the Trobriand evaluation of the institution. Moreover, such exchanges cannot be made with just anybody—there is no "freedom of contract." Rather, *wasi* is carried on with partners who have been "properly" come by—either through inheritance or religious pledges.

Wasi, therefore, represents a kind of reciprocal giving and receiving that is based on a special type of contract. Such a situation, if it is not adequately explained—and it is not in this case—is usually handled by anthropologists with the word "ceremonial," and Malinowski indeed speaks of *wasi* as ceremonial trade.

One further factor should be noted: *wasi* creates a debt structure among the various villages of the islands. It would be erroneous, however, to analyze this debt structure in terms of credit. Rather, it is a matter of indemnification. Although credit and indemnification provide a superficially similar debt structure, the rights and obligations—and more specifically the tone—of all such exchanges are very different.

KULA

Very similar to *wasi* but dealing in very different goods is the institution known as *kula. Kula* is the exchange between permanent contractual partners, and no one else, of treasure items—never of subsistence items such as the fish and food in *wasi* exchanges. Treasures are of several types in the Trobriand Islands. The most exclusive and highly valued type is called *vaygua,* which Malinowski translated as "valuables." By no means do all Trobrianders engage in the *kula.* In some of the villages anyone may engage, but in others the right to take part in the *kula* is a carefully guarded prerogative of rank. As with *wasi,* a man has a set of partners to whom he gives one thing and from whom he receives another—in this case, both are *vaygua.* But the further rule is added that those people to whom he gives one class of *vaygua*—large white arm shells called *mwali*—all live in the same direction from him, whereas his partners to whom he gives the spondylous shell necklaces all live in the other direction.

As is the case in *wasi,* a man cannot keep what he gets by *kula* exchanges. Whereas in *wasi* he may consume part of it but must give the rest of it away through the institution of *sagali,* in the kula there is no way by consumption to get the *vaygua* out of the system and no moral sanction or prestige attached to keeping it, but only to getting it and giving it. Therefore, what a man must do in order to make the system work is to give away again what he has received. In so doing, he gives away to his partner to the north what he received from his partner to the south and vice versa. His own reward is in the pleasure of having had the valuable and in the reputation as a generous and powerful man, which will accrue to him.

The participants in the *kula* are located in such a way that they form a rough ring, several hundred miles in circumference. The necklaces go around the ring from one person to another in one direction whereas the arm rings go around in the other direction.[1]

With such a bald description it is difficult for Americans to realize what motivates men to participate in this particular kind of trading of treasure. The answer is to be found not in any kind of system of economic production or exchange, but rather in the social system of ranking and prestige. Thorstein Veblen (1899) has long since proved that desire for rank and prestige is one of the most moving elements in our own economy. It is certainly no less so in Melanesian economy.

As the *kula* treasures circulated around the ring, stories become attached to them—stories about the great men who had owned the treasures. The aplomb with which these men received and handed them on, and the excitement of the travel and expeditions undertaken in order to receive them. In this way the particularly handsome or fine treasures acquire not merely a patina of use, but a patina of myth and history; and every time that one of these historical pieces changes hands it is as if another chapter were added to the significant story of the valuable.

[1] Other and similar rings have been described; see, for example, Thomson (1949).

This game is complicated by the fact that every man has several *kula* partners. A commoner will have five or six in either direction along the ring. A chief may have as many as seventy or eighty. The trick is to find a way to be sure your partner gives you his newly acquired treasure instead of giving it to someone else. This may be achieved in a number of ways, the most common of which is presentation to that partner of what one might call second-grade treasures. Malinowski (1922, p. 512) refers to these second-grade treasures as "permanent *vaygua*"; they are stone blades, a certain type of belt, and pendants made from boars' tusks.[1] These second-grade treasures indemnify the owner of the treasure that is sought; he must return it with equivalent or better second-grade treasure. But more importantly, such a gift of second-grade treasure serves as "bait" to indicate your interest in your partner's *vaygua* and a public statement of your belief in your capacity to match it with an equivalent gift if he gives it to you rather than to another partner. It is interesting that the name for such a gift, given to solicit a particular gift in *kula,* is *pokala*—the same word as for tribute given to a chief. It might be assumed that in so doing a man acknowledges his partner's outranking him and solicits his good will and generosity.

The entry of valuables into the ring after their manufacture and the way in which they are removed from the ring is, of course, of primary importance to understanding it. Only two villages have adequate magical protection for making the arm shells. The shell from which the arm shell is manufactured exists all over the area, but the magic is limited to the two villages. It is also important that the "manufacture" continues as the valuables move along the *kula* ring. They may, for example, get into the *kula* when a man who finds a particularly valuable shell gives it to his brother-in-law as a return gift in the *urigubu* institution. The brother-in-law may then knock off the excess part of the shell and give it to a *kula* partner as small change, so to speak. The man who receives it may polish it and add decorative items. So begins the concomitant creation of the myth, which ultimately may make the arm shell of great value. Somewhere along the route of exchange it will get a name.

The important thing about the *kula* is not economic in any sense of providing livelihood; rather, it points up the fact that exchange, even of treasures having no practical use, can be a great motivating force. This kind of exchange, further, can be analyzed with the same set of tools as those with which *wasi* can be analyzed.

Like *wasi,* the *kula* takes place as a reciprocal giving and taking

[1] Mrs. Kennedy gave the President a whale's tooth incised with his portrait for Christmas, 1962. It makes a valuable addition, according to the press, to his collection of scrimshaw.

between partners who are contractual allies of permanent standing. One's prestige in the society, at least in part, depends upon the *kula* valuables one is able to receive and give away. Thus, the luck in inheriting partners and the wisdom with which one selects one's new partners are of great importance. The *kula* is done with a decorum and a seriousness that resembles modern stamp auctions, where, too, people trade for treasures of no intrinsic worth. The difference is, of course, that the stamp auction is associated with the market principle whereas the *kula* is associated with reciprocity.

The *kula* is far and away the most romantic of the Trobriand exchange spheres because it involves long and dangerous overseas voyages to collect the presents that one has a right to receive. The *kula* is an extremely important mechanism of communication and social organization, as well as a quasieconomic institution, as Malinowski has shown.

GIM WALI

Accompanying the *kula* expeditions, but certainly not limited to them, is another form of exchange that is very much more understandable to modern Westerners. This exchange, known as *gim wali,* is the moneyless exchange of nontreasure goods according to a market principle. Just as behavior in *kula* exchange must be decorous and "ceremonial," the accepted behavior in *gim wali* was the higgling and haggling common to the marketplace. The morality of the *kula* is to attract to oneself, and then to give away with generosity but some show of regret, the most notable of the treasures. The morality of *gim wali* is that of getting a bargain.

Too much can be made of the fact that *kula* expeditions both overseas and inland take large supplies of *gim wali* trade goods to exchange for other such goods. A man can never perform *gim wali* with his *kula* partner. However, he can perform *gim wali* with the *kula* partners of all the other members of the expedition. Therefore, during the visits it is the *kula* exchanges or gifts that get all the attention. *Gim wali,* very often noisy *gim wali,* takes place at the same time as, but at some short distance removed from, the *kula* exchanges.

There has been a tendency in the past for anthropologists to say that the *kula* was just an excuse for carrying out *gim wali.* The fact that they go together does not prove the one is the cover for the other, and to say that such is the case is not merely to put the entire institution of the *kula* into the crass terms of money and market economy, but to assume that *gim wali* needs a cover. The *kula* is an institution dealing in prestige items for the enhancement of one's personality and rank. *Gim wali* is trade of pedestrian household items.

There is another type of exchange related to *gim wali* called *laga.*

Malinowski notes that this term means a big and important transaction. He says that if a small pig is exchanged for food or minor objects, it is called *gim wali;* but if a large pig is exchanged for treasure (*vaygua*), it is called *laga*. *Laga* is also the term used when certain tasks are "purchased" or when garden plots are transferred. Malinowski does not say what the tasks may be, but only calls *laga* a "ceremonial purchase" (1922, p. 186).

POKALA

We have already met the term *pokala* as the word for a solicitory gift to one's *kula* partner. We noted at that time that it had something to do with relative rank. *Pokala* is also a general term for the tribute paid to a chief (Malinowski, 1922, p. 181). The word *pokala* is also used for gifts given between affines, particularly those given in exchange for the items or rights one would have eventually inherited from one's mother's brother. Malinowski states specifically that the two meanings of this word are distinguished and that the two are homonyms and not a single concept (1922, p. 186). However, he postulates that they developed out of a single concept. Perhaps the most important point that can be made about the *pokala* to the chief is that it seems to be almost indistinguishable, except by name, from the *urigubu* paid to a chief. The gifts to the chief in *pokala* are, insofar as it can be determined from the literature, subsistence goods. It is not at all clear what the chief does with them, but presumably he gives them all away again in a series of feasts similar to *sagali*. Since the Trobrianders produce an excess of food, however, it may be of little practical importance. It is also very difficult to make out the sort of gift the chief gives in return, if any, for the *pokala* he receives. It may be "services" of a political or religious sort. From some passages in Malinowski it would seem that he may return *kula* treasures; in others, there seems to be no return.

URIGUBU

Urigubu is the custom in which the man makes annual contributions of food to his sister's husband. Malinowski never gives an adequate description of the *urigubu* institution, but notes only that it would be so complex as to necessitate a preliminary account of the kinship system (which he never wrote). He does say, however, that as much as three quarters of a man's crops go either as tribute to a chief or to his sister's or mother's husband and family as *urigubu*. Thus, a man is dependent for his subsistence not on himself (his own crops go to his sister's husband) but on his wife's brother.

Malinowski's greatest interest was in the points where *urigubu* and *pokala* overlap—that is, where a chief married women who were the sisters of the headmen of the various villages and thereby received from them *urigubu* in amounts that were equivalent to tribute. He seems to have received *pokala,* tribute, from many areas as well. From these combined scources of income, then, he was expected to make huge feasts and also to pay for the many services to which he had a right but for which he was nevertheless obliged to pay. Thus, turning *pokala* into *urigubu*—turning a particular type of political association into kinship ties—was the surest way for a chief to maintain his position and his capacity to demand tribute.

The gifts a chief returned to the people who gave him *urigubu* were called *youla.* It is of interest that they were never of the same type as the goods he received. *Youla* consisted primarily of small or unimportant or secondary *kula* valuables. It is difficult to discover whether or not the chief received *kula* valuables, or even the secondary ones, as *urigubu* gifts. Certainly, however, he gave them away in return.

The function, thus, of the *urigubu* is to shunt *kula* valuables among various people by means of non*kula* transactions. It is also a way to shunt these valuables down the rank order of the society.

In summary, the Trobriand Islands exhibit a set of institutions each one of which is based on its own combination of ranked goods and a mode of transaction. *Kula,* properly so-called, is a sphere limited to two types of treasure. *Gim wali* is a sphere limited to subsistence produce. *Wasi* is a sphere limited to certain specific types of food.

There is another kind of institution, however, in which spheres are crossed. In the *urigubu,* which is based on a form of redistribution, the initial indemnifying payment is in subsistence goods. The return, or *youla,* is or may be in terms of treasure. Thus, the better *urigubu* that a man can make, the more likely he is to be given a treasure in return. In the same way *pokala* is payment of food to the chief or headman and seems to be returned in the form of treasure. What is lacking in *pokala* that is present in *urigubu* is the kinship rationale. Finally, we have examined *sagali,* which is the big giveaway feast—what the American Indians would have called a "blowout." Thus, whereas the chief receives food in the *urigubu* and returns *kula* valuables, he also returns the food in the form of feasts, although he may use it to make further *urigubu* or *pokala* payments.

There are contractual reciprocities in the area of *kula* and *wasi;* the market principle is at work in the *gim wali;* and there are definite institutions based on rank and the redistribution from recognized centers in the *urigubu, pokala,* and *sagali* institutions.

Trobriand economy is, in short, like our own in that a series of institutions are brought together by linked transactional principles. In America, the bonhommie of gift exchange is carried out on the basis of reciprocity, the task of financing political organization is carried out by the institutions of taxation on the principle of redistribution, and the production of substantive needs (and some other things that we have learned to see in analogy to the substantive needs) are transacted by the market principle. In the Trobriand economy, similarly, there are six interrelated institutions. The difference in the two economies lies primarily in the fact that several economic institutions of the Americans are amalgamated into a single entity by general-purpose currency and by the concept of price, whereas the amalgamation of the Trobriand institutions is of a sort that is foreign to Americans and indeed to the science of economics. The nonmonetary mode of amalgamation of the various economic institutions is the subject of the next chapter.

It remains for this chapter to carry to conclusion the idea that in every society there are dominant modes of transactions and peripheral modes of transaction, and that these modes vary from one culture to the next.

PERIPHERAL MARKETS

American society is marked by the fact that it is economically dominated by the market principle of transaction. Such a statement means that, with negligible exceptions, it is vital for at least one member of every nuclear family to "sell" one of the factors of production on the market. He must either sell his work as labor, rights in his land as rents, rights to use his money in return for interest or dividends, or else an idea, a capacity to take risks, or a managerial skill. If he fails to do so, or is unable to do so, he (and probably some of his family as well) will starve—except, of course, insofar as the government or some other body ameliorates this harsh epiphenomenon of market by "giving" him the necessities of life, which is no more than to say that relief institutions are part of the redistributive rather than the market operations of Western economy. If the combined market for factors and produce were to disappear, American society would be unrecognizable.

The market may be present, however, in many societies that it does not dominate in the way that it dominates the societies of the twentieth-century Western world. It is usual for Westerners to oppose the market society and economy to what they know as the "subsistence economy."

There has in the past been a common error in defining a subsistence economy. That error is to assume that a situation in which a people produces largely what they themselves consume is the same thing as the absence of a market. The Trobriand situation belies such an assumption.

Trobrianders do not, as individuals, consume their own produce—there is extensive shifting of produce, and a family subsists on the produce grown by the brother of the wife/mother. It is not, however, a market that intervenes between the producer and the consumer. There are, moreover, other situations, such as those found in traditional West Africa, in which there is an active market, but nevertheless almost every family produces its own food, clothing, and shelter. What, then, is a "subsistence economy"?

A "subsistence economy" is one in which the factors of production are not transacted by the market mechanism. In a subsistence economy, some produce may enter the market—such a situation can be called a "peripheral market." It does not follow that simply because the factors are not transacted in the market that there are no transactions of the factors of production—we have created only a negative, residual category: the absence of market transaction of the factors of production. We have already seen that factors of production can be institutionalized in the absence of a market. It remains here to examine ways in which markets work if they do not apply to factors of production, which is to say, if factors of production are transacted by other mechanisms. Logically, of course, the institution of the market may or may not be present in a society. If it is present, it may be dominant (as in the twentieth-century West) or it may be peripheral in the sense that it is peripheral in the Trobriand institution of *gim wali*. It may indeed still be peripheral, yet be one of the most noticeable culture traits a society possesses. Such is the case in West Africa.

THE EXAMPLE OF WEST AFRICA

Market places are numerous and colorful in West Africa. They are easily appreciated by even the most amateur observer, and therefore have been described, at least superficially, over and over again. These market places do not, however, occupy the same position in African society as "the market" occupies in the West. Analyzing the difference necessitates distinguishing the market place from the market principle. As we have already established, the market principle is the determination of price by free working of the forces that create supply and demand. As any economics text testifies, *the site of the market is irrelevant to the working of the principle*. Therefore, the "market place" must be studied in analytical separation from the "market principle" and the two conjoined only where there is a good empirical basis for so doing.

The market place thrives in most of West Africa and the Congo. But until after World War II, the market was largely peripheral, because the number of people who actually derived their livings primarily from the market was small. West Africa has had a few professional traders for centuries. Most West Africans, however, would suffer little change in their way of life were the market to disappear. Unlike the situation in the United States or in Europe, their society and culture would not be totally unrecognizable, totally changed, if the market principle were to disappear. What, then, does the market place do for West Africans?

Market places provide regular meetings of fairly large numbers of people. The attendants at markets are usually cross sections of the population. It is to be expected, therefore—and it is certainly found—that the market place is utilized for purposes far beyond those for which nominally it was established. Market places can be utilized for almost every conceivable purpose that requires a large number of people brought together in a controlled situation.

Probably the most common—because it is the most basic—noneconomic function of market places is their function as nodes in the network of communication. Undoubtedly, one of the most important points for the dissemination of information is the market place, and that dissemination can take place either on an informal, more or less unrecognized basis, or on a formal one. Chiefs, priests, administrative officers and many others make announcements in the market. In most areas, to make an announcement requires the permission of the market authorities, and it may even require that the announcement be made by one of them to signify his approval.

Of even greater importance, perhaps, is that market places provide a place to meet one's friends and kinsmen, and exchange news and gossip. Women, in particular (most of Africa is virilocal even when it is matrilineal), meet their kinsmen at markets and keep in remarkably close touch with their natal villages by this means. Although it would be difficult to carry out, a study of markets (and perhaps other institutions) in their role of communications nodes would be extremely interesting.

The people at market provide not only listeners and gossip mongers, but also provide a ready-gathered audience. Performances of dancers and entertainers often occur in the market places. The festival aspect of markets is first pointed up by its frequent use as the place to drink beer. The market day usually falls off into a beer drink.

In a more organized fashion, the market place can be of political relevance. The reasons, obviously, are twofold: it can be politically advantageous to control the market place itself, and hence to some degree the people in it. On the other hand, it can be politically advantageous to control, in whatever degree, the produce that goes through the market place. Thus control of market places is usually in the hands of political authorities. In those parts of East and Central Africa where markets were introduced by the colonial administration, it continued to control them: the size and shape of the market place, the type and arrangement of buildings, the conditions for selling, and the composition of the sales force and the selection of goods were all to a greater or lesser degree dictated by that administration. In West Africa, on the other hand, or anywhere else that the markets antedate European control, the market places remained in the hands of indigenous authorities throughout the colonial period. Control of a market put a man at the hub of communications, where he could have immediate contact with people. It also gave him a recognized and approved *raison d'être* behind which he could hide any political chicanery that was to his advantage to hide.

In return, the political authorities in control of market places provide a "market peace," to use the old English term. This means that the markets are policed and the safety of traders and customers more or less assured. It may even be that the market place, or a portion of it, is used as a point of political asylum.

Obviously, also—this point has been made many times with reference to old European market places—it is necessary, if the economic functions of a market are to be performed, for the market peace to be observed. Successful trade demands at least a minimal degree of political stability. The man who is responsible for the market peace thus must have a police force of some description at his disposal, and he must control sufficient power actually to maintain the peace. West African market officials can either call on their families, members of their clans or other social groups, or on the police forces of their governments to police their markets.

An extremely important political consideration is the fact that the market is often used as the center of legal activities—in some areas the chiefs or other judges actually establish themselves as courts in or near the market place; in others their presence assures that when one finds one's adversary (easier at a market than any other place), the case can be laid before the officials informally. No African chief can refuse to hear a case brought to his attention at market (though he may postpone it until a regular court hearing). These courts may be the same as—but are often different from—the arbitrating facilities for settling disputes that arise among sellers and customers within the market place itself.

Markets are also often accompanied by religious activities, some of which may be connected with the market peace. The peace of Ibo markets (Ottenberg and Ottenberg, 1962) and Tiv markets (Bohannan, 1963) is kept primarily in the name of and with the sanction of certain shrines and the forces they symbolize. Some African market places—particularly in those areas in which the market is indigenous—are founded with a religious ceremonial.

In summary, market places—particularly in areas in which the market is economically peripheral—fulfill many social and cultural needs of the population. Indeed, some markets are not regarded as primarily "economic" institutions by the people. They provide a meeting place where a certain minimum, at least, of security is assured and hence they can be used for political, religious, social, and personal purposes. In a society in which collections of people on nonkinship bases may prove difficult, the market place provides the setting for a wide range of social activities.

Market places are in most instances, however, primarily places for trade. Even people who produce most of their own foodstuffs are likely to respond, if they are given the opportunity, by growing extra foodstuffs to sell so that they can purchase imported articles. In such a situation a market grows up that may be of very extensive proportions, but it may nevertheless not affect the basic fact: that the family produces most of the basic subsistence it needs. West Africans, for example, produce quantities of cocoa, soybeans, peanuts, sesame, and other crops, which they sell for money. They use this money to buy imported cloth, imported dishes, hardware, and many other imported items. If the market for their produce expands sufficiently, they may in fact begin even to buy some of their food on the market. Ghanaian and Nigerian cocoa farmers, for example, obtain large portions of their food on the market. However, they have by and large not yet reached the point of no return—the individual cocoa farmer can step up food production and weather a bad year. When disease wiped out part of the cocoa plantations of Ghana, the Ghanaians did not move away and they did not starve: they adjusted to the lower cash income by growing more of their own food. The market was peripheral—they were not dependent for their subsistence on selling factors of production on the market.

Today, the factor market is gaining in importance in West Africa. It will undoubtedly continue to do so. However, there are still large areas —and there will continue to be—in which the markets are peripheral.

Prices in a peripheral market are formed in precisely the same way as in any other market: by the silent and invisible working of forces of supply and demand, and by multiplex decisions on the part of sellers and buyers. They are different only in the position the market holds in the total society. Peripheral markets are decorations on, not bulwarks of, the social organization.

A few words should also be said about the way in which the African markets are fitted together into systems or "rings" of markets. African markets do not meet every day, but rather only every four, five, or seven days. A market "ring," then, is a series of market places where meetings are held on successive days. Among the Ibo of eastern Nigeria, the market rings are made up of four markets, each meeting every fourth day. Among the Tiv to their north, the rings contain five markets, each meeting every fifth day. The phenomenon of market rings has been found in widespread parts of the world; a Mexican example has been described briefly and elegantly by Moore (1951).

The ideas and institutions found in various parts of the world to fulfill man's material needs, and the nonmaterial ones such as prestige or rank maintenance that he sees in analogy to the material ones, are diverse. It is likely, too, that no set of institutions is so fragile and no set of ideas so ephemeral when they are brought into serious and overt question by the impact of new ideas. There is, in economic institutions, a very delicate balance among human motives, human institutions, and human ideas. When institutions change and motives do not, when ideas change and institutions do not, chaos is likely to spread. The "conflict of economies" is one of the most obvious problems in culture change, and it is also one of the vital characteristics that we must understand about the economy. When the balance of distribution changes, no corner of society, no reach of culture, is unaffected.

15

Multicentric economies, conversion, and the conflict of economies

THE DISCUSSION SO FAR has emphasized the fact that most empirical economies are collections of institutions based on a variety of transactional principles. Some economies nevertheless seem unitary, whereas others seem to be made up of the most diverse institutions with real difficulties of coordination.

The apparent unity in the organization of the institutions of American economy arises not wholly from a simplicity or congruity of institutions, and not merely from the fact that "market mentality" (Polanyi, 1947) pervades Western thinking. Besides all these forces there is the central fact that a single cultural trait—money—permeates the whole. Money lies at the very heart of the market. It is the means by which we pay taxes or receive relief in the redistribution system; and it is the way we acquire most of the gifts we give, and in terms of which moral miscreants even evaluate the gifts they receive.

Conversely, the apparent complexity of the organization of the Trobriand economy arises from the absence of general-purpose money. The various institutions of exchange are interconnected not by monetary means primarily, but by devices and ideas that may be foreign to us and hence seem complex, the more so since money is such a simplifying device.

This chapter sets out to do two things: to examine the nature of money and its place in the coordination of economy and society, and to examine some of the ways and means by which such coordination can take place in the absence of money.

MONEY

For the last several centuries in Western society, and in a few corners of the world for millenia, exchange and distribution have been simplified by that universal solvent called money. Money is, however, a dangerous concept for the student of comparative cultures because its very simplicity creates difficulty in analyzing those situations in which it is not part of the folk image.

Economists, in their search to understand the nature of money, have determined that it can be used for three or more purposes. We shall here examine only three. In the first place, money can be used as a means of exchange. Money allows you to exchange something you want less for something you want more without finding somebody whose situation is exactly the reverse of your own. In the absence of some sort of money, the man who has a chicken and wants a piece of cloth must find a man who has a piece of cloth and wants a chicken. Exchange in the absence of money is called "barter"—and it should be noted that barter implies nothing except lack of money in the transaction; although it is usually used with the suggestion of "price" implicit in it, such is an unnecessarily restrictive usage. Economists and savages agree that barter is a tedious and time-consuming business. *Kula*, however, is barter just as much as is *gim wali*.

In the second place, money can be used as a standard of value. Everything that can be exchanged in modern Western society can be given a money value. Money allows us to add up and to compute things of basically different sorts—items that are in their intrinsic natures incommensurable. You may add guns and butter if you do it in terms of money. No material manifestation of money is needed to utilize the idea as a standard of value: a quarter's worth of duplicates from a boy's stamp collection can be "swapped" for a quarter's worth of sea shells from another boy's collection. In most parts of the world, where extensive barter is still to be found, it is likely that this attribute of money has already been learned and tuppence worth of spinach will be bartered for tuppence worth of cooking oil.

In the third place, money is a means of payment. In fact, if money is the exchange medium, it would seem to be the perfect instrument of payment. No matter what the debt contracted, no matter what eventual product the creditor may desire, he will take money. However, payment and standard of value are not to be confused: a fine is paid in money, but the modern Western inclination to regard a standard fine, such as a two-dollar parking ticket, with the price of a misdemeanor is actively discouraged.

In the modern West, in other words, a single concept—money—with its various material manifestations (notes, coins, checks, drafts, and so on) performs all three functions. It is also noteworthy that the various manifestations of money are not distinguishable by function. In other cultures, that may not be the case: the different material items used as money *may* be distinguished by function.

Modern Western money, which performs all the functions with a single set of cultural items, can be called "general-purpose money."[1] Any cultural item that performs one or two functions, but not all three, can be called "special-purpose money."

Some economists and a few anthropologists have tried to elevate one of these money uses to a prime position in defining money—saying that anything used for payment, for example, was "money" whether any other money use was present or not. Other scholars disputed their choice and plugged for some other money use as the primary one. The result was, of course, the futile tug-of-war scholars sometimes find easier than thinking. Einzig (1949) says that means of exchange is the sure mark of "money," and fiercely denounces other scholars who venture to consider payment the primary defining characteristic. The whole problem is a semantic one that can be avoided by a distinction between special-purpose money and general-purpose money.

Two characteristics show up immediately in economies lacking general-purpose money. One is that the "commodities" valued and exchanged, whatever they may be, are separated into more or less self-contained categories, each category associated with a different institution. The other characteristic is the great effort that must be expended to bridge the categories and the institutions that demarcate them into a whole system; that is to say, the difficulties of "disengagement" of items from one institution and their incorporation into another.

Two examples will show clearly the sort of institutionalization that may occur in the absence of general-purpose money. They are taken from the Tiv of central Nigeria and the Kwakiutl of British Columbia.

TIV ECONOMY AND THE PHENOMENON OF CONVERSION

The most distinctive feature about the economy of the Tiv—and it is a feature they share with many, perhaps most, of the premonetary peoples —is what can be called a multicentric economy. Briefly, a multicentric economy is one in which a society's exchangeable goods fall into two or more mutually exclusive spheres, each marked by different institutionalization and different moral values. In some multicentric economies these spheres remain distinct, though in most there are more or less institutionalized means of converting wealth from one into wealth in another.

[1] General-purpose money may be put to other uses as well: in pre-Keynesian days, for instance, it was sometimes used as a means for storing wealth, and is still occasionally so used by the naïve. For the present analysis, however, the three functions described seem adequate.

Indigenously, there were three spheres in the multicentric economy of the Tiv. The first of these spheres is that associated with subsistence, which the Tiv called *yiagh.* The commodities in it include all locally produced foodstuffs: the staple yams and cereals, plus all the condiments, vegetable side dishes and seasonings, as well as small livestock—chickens, goats, and sheep. It also includes household utensils (mortars, grindstones, calabashes, baskets, and pots), some tools (particularly those used in agriculture), and raw materials for producing any items in the category.

Within this sphere, goods are distributed either by gift giving or through marketing. Traditionally, there was no money of any sort in this sphere—all goods changed hands by barter. There was a highly developed market organization at which people exchanged their produce for their requirements, and in which, today, traders buy produce in cheap markets and transport it to sell in dear markets. The morality of this sphere of the economy is the morality of the free and uncontrolled market.

The second sphere of the Tiv economy is one that is in no way associated with markets. The category of goods within this sphere is slaves, cattle, ritual "offices," that type of large white cloth known as *tugudu,* medicines and magics, and metal rods. One is still entitled to use the present tense in this case; Tiv still quote prices of slaves in cows and brass rods, and of cattle in brass rods and *tugudu* cloth. The price of magical rites, as it has been described in literature, was in terms of *tugudu* cloth or brass rods (though payment might be made in other items); payment for ritual office was in cows and slaves, *tugudu* cloths, and metal rods (Akiga, 1937, p. 382). None of these goods ever entered the market. Actual transfer of such goods took place at ceremonies, at more or less ritualized wealth displays, and on occasions when doctors performed rites and prescribed medicines. Tiv refer to the items and the activities within this sphere by the word *shagba,* which can be roughly translated as prestige.

Within the prestige sphere there was one item that took on all of the money uses and hence can be called a general-purpose currency, though it must be remembered that it was of only a *very limited range.* Brass rods were used as means of exchange *within the sphere;* they also served as a standard of value (though not the only one) within it, and as a means of payment. However, this sphere of the economy was tightly sealed off from the subsistence-goods sphere and its market. After European contact, brass rods occasionally entered the market, but they did so only as means of payment, not as medium of exchange or as standard of valuation. Because of the complex institutionalization and morality, no one ever sold a slave for food; no one, save in the depths of extremity, ever paid brass rods for domestic goods.

The supreme and unique sphere of exchangeable values for the Tiv contains a single item: rights in human beings other than slaves, particularly rights in women. Even twenty-five years after official abolition of exchange mariage, it was the category of exchange in which Tiv were emotionally most entangled.

Before the coming of the Europeans all "real" marriages were exchange marriages. In its simplest form, an exchange marriage involved two men exchanging sisters. Actually, this simple form seldom or never occurred. In order for every man to have a ward (*ingol*) to exchange for a wife, small localized agnatic lineages formed ward-sharing groups. There was an initial distribution of wards among the men of this group, so that each man became the guardian (*tien*) of one or more wards. The guardian, then, saw to the marriage of his ward, exchanging her with outsiders for another woman (her "partner" or *ikyar*) who became the bride of the guardian or one of his close agnatic kinsmen, or—in some situations—became a ward in the ward-sharing group and was exchanged for yet another woman who became a wife.

When an elopement occurred and a woman in exchange was not available, a debt was created in favor of the guardian's group. These debts sometimes lagged two or even three generations behind actual exchanges. The simplest way of paying them off was for the eldest daughter of the marriage to return to the ward-sharing group of her mother, as ward, thus canceling the debt.

Because of its many impracticalities, the system had to be buttressed in several ways in order to work: one way was to provide for "earnest" during the time of the lag, another was to recognize other types of marriage as binding to limited extents. These two elements are somewhat confused with each other, because of the fact that right up until the abolition of exchange marriage in 1927, the inclination was always to treat all nonexchange marriages as if they were "lags" in the completion of exchange marriages.

When lags in exchange occurred, they were filled with "earnests" made of brass rods or, occasionally, it would seem, of cattle. The brass rods or cattle in such situations were *never* exchange equivalents (*ishe*) for the woman. The only "price" of one woman is another woman.

Although Tiv decline to grant it antiquity, another type of marriage was common at the time Europeans first came to Tivland—it was called "accumulating a woman/wife" *(kem kwase)*. It is difficult to tell today just exactly what it consisted in, because the terminology of this union has been adapted to describe the bridewealth marriage that was declared by an administrative fiat of 1927 to be the only legal form. *Kem* marriage consisted in acquisition of sexual, domestic, and economic rights in a woman—but not the rights to filiate her children to the social group of her husband. Additional payments had to be made to the woman's guardians in order to filiate the children. *Kem* payments were in brass rods. However, rights in a woman certainly had no equivalent or "price" in brass rods or any other item save identical rights in another woman.

Thus, within the sphere of exchange marriage there was no item that fulfilled any of the uses of money; when second-best types of marriage were made, payment was in an item that was specifically not used as a standard of value.

That Tiv do conceptualize exchange articles as belonging to different categories, and that they rank the categories on a moral basis, and that most but not all exchanges are limited to one sphere, gives rise to the fact that two different kinds of exchanges may be recognized: exchange of items contained within a single category, and exchange of items belonging to different categories. For Tiv, these two different types of exchange are marked by separate and distinct moral attitudes.

To maintain this distinction between the two types of exchanges Tiv mark by different behavior and different values, I shall use separate words. I shall call those exchanges of items within a single category "conveyances," and those exchanges of items from one category to another "conversions" (Steiner, 1954). Roughly, conveyances are morally neutral; conversions have a strong moral quality in their rationalization.

Exchanges within a category—particularly that of subsistence, the only one intact today—excite no moral judgments. Exchanges between categories, however, do excite a moral reaction: the man who exchanges lower-category goods for higher-category goods does not brag about his market luck but about his "strong heart" and his success in life. The man who exchanges high-category goods for lower rationalizes his action in terms of high-valued motivation (most often the needs of his kinsmen).

The two institutions most intimately connected with conveyance are markets and marriage. Conveyance in the prestige sphere centers on slave dealing, on curing, and on the acquisition of status.

Conversion is a much more complex matter. Conversion depends on the fact that some items of every sphere could, on certain occasions, be used in exchanges in which the return was *not* considered equivalent (*ishe*). Obviously, given the moral ranking of the spheres, such a situation leaves one party to the exchange in a good position, and the other in a bad one. Tiv say that it is "good" to trade food for brass rods, but that it is "bad" to trade brass rods for food; that it is good to trade your cows or brass rods for a wife, but very bad to trade your marriage ward for cows or brass rods.

Seen from the individual's point of view, it is profitable and possible to invest one's wealth if one converts it into a morally superior category: to convert subsistence wealth into prestige wealth and both into women is the aim of the economic endeavor of individual Tiv.

We have already examined the marriage system by which a man could convert his brass rods to a wife: he could get a *kem* wife and *kem* her children as they were born. Her daughters, then, could be used as wards in his exchange marriages. It is the desire of every Tiv to "acquire a woman" (*ngoho kwase*) either as wife or ward in some way other than sharing in the ward-sharing group. A wife whom one acquires in any other way is not the concern of one's marriage-ward-sharing group, because the woman or other property exchanged for her did not belong to the marriage-ward group. The daughters of such a wife are not divided among the members of a man's marriage-ward group, but only among his sons. Such a wife is not only indicative of a man's ability and success financially and personally, but rights in her are the only form of property not ethically subject to the demands of his kinsmen.

Conversion from the prestige sphere to the kinship sphere was, thus, fairly common; it consisted in all the forms of marriage–save exchange marriage–usually in terms of brass rods.

Conversion from the prestige sphere to the subsistence sphere was also usually in terms of metal rods. They, on occasion, entered the market place as payment. If the owner of the brass rods required an unusually large amount of staples to give a feast, making too heavy a drain on his wives' food supplies, he might buy it with brass rods.

However, brass rods could not possibly have been a general currency. They were not divisible. One could not receive "change" from a brass rod. Moreover, a single rod was worth much more than the usual market purchase for any given day of most Tiv subsistence traders. Although it might be possible to buy chickens with brass rods, one would have to have bought a very large quantity of yams to equal one rod, and to buy an item such as pepper with rods would be laughable. Brass rods, thus, overlapped from the prestige to the subsistence sphere on some occasions, but only on special occasions and for large purchases.

Not only is conversion possible, but it is encouraged–it is, in fact, the behavior that proves a man's worth. Tiv are scornful of a man who is merely rich in subsistence goods (or, today, in money). If, having adequate subsistence, he does not seek prestige in accordance with the old counters, or if he does not strive for more wives, and hence more children, the fault must be personal inadequacy. They also note that they all try to keep a man from making conversions; jealous kinsmen of a rich man will bewitch him and his people by fetishes, in order to make him expend his wealth on sacrifices to repair the fetishes, thus maintaining economic equality. However, once a conversion has been made, demands of kinsmen are not effective–at least, they take a new form.

Therefore, the man who converts his wealth into higher categories is successful–he has a "strong heart." He is both feared and respected.

In this entire process, metal rods hold a pivotal position, and it is not surprising that early administrators considered them money. Originally imported from Europe, they were used as "currency" in some parts of southern Nigeria in the slave trade. They are dowels about a quarter of an inch in diameter and some three feet long; they can be made into jewelry, and were used as a source of metal for castings.

Whatever their use elsewhere, brass rods in Tivland had some but not all of the attributes of money. Within the prestige sphere, they were used as a standard of equivalence, and they were a medium of exchange; they were also a mode for storage of wealth, and were used as payment. In short, brass rods were a general-purpose currency *within the prestige sphere*. However, outside of the prestige sphere—markets and marriages were the most active institutions of exchange outside it—brass rods fulfilled only one of these functions of money: payment. We have examined in detail the reasons why equivalency could not exist between brass rods and rights in women, between brass rods and food.

We have, thus, in Tivland, a multicentric economy of three spheres, and we have a sort of money that was a general-purpose money in one sphere and a special-purpose money in the special transactions in which the other two spheres overlapped it.

In the Tiv economy, conversion among ranked spheres takes the place that is occupied in a monetized economy by money. Each includes the possibility that demand schedules cover all the items one wants, as well as the obligations one has to face. The Tiv demand schedule takes a different form: it is broken into discrete categories and there are two problems—first, to manipulate items within a category; and, second, to get an item disengaged from one category and into the sphere of another. A moral system pervades the practice of conversion, just as a moral system lies behind the demand schedule on the basis of which modern Americans decide how they must spend their money. Americans, however, do not have to "convert" from one category to another, because general-purpose money has entered all the categories, and hence reduced all to a common denominator.

It can be seen that Trobriand economy, too, like Tiv economy, is permeated with conversion. *Urigubu* can, for example, be seen as a mechanism for converting food into *kula* valuables.

THE KWAKIUTL ECONOMY AND THE POTLATCH

Occasionally, an economy is so bizarre as to seem unexplainable: the *potlatch* which is one of the most widely known of American Indian institutions, seems to be such. Potlatch can, however, be quite easily understood when it is seen as hyperdevelopment of conversion, and recognized that the apparent emphasis on giving away rather than on receiving may be a freakish association of Kwakiutl folk images and the European folk images of anthropologists and others, who were wont to explain it or condemn it or both.

The Kwakiutl lived on the northern shore of Vancouver Island, in British Columbia, and on the adjacent mainland, in a country with a coast line almost as long and inletted per square mile of territory as that of Norway. There were forests of giant cedar and fir; animal life abounded. The sea teemed with fish, mammals, porpoises, shellfish. Probably no other part of the world offered such riches for so little work. The Kwakiutl standard of living was among the highest the world has known. They had large amounts of material necessities, and also were the creators of an extensive and admirable art. Technology was highly developed; they had many ways of exploiting their rich environment, including adequate storage techniques. They were among the best-housed people of the New World. Their seagoing canoes held as many as fifty persons.

The Kwakiutl, even more than most peoples in the world, were obsessed with rank—indeed, in the midst of such plenty they created artificial shortages in the social system and their striving for high social position was an integral part of the economy. They were divided into about twenty-five village groups, each of which was politically autonomous. In one case as many as four groups lived in a single large village. In 1930, there were only about 1500 Kwakiutl, which meant that each "tribe" had no more than about sixty people in it. However, when European and American shipping concerns first began to trade with them, at the end of the eighteenth century, there were approximately ten times that number, so that a tribe of 600 people was a fairly reasonable number. The entire population was about 15,000. Each of the tribes was divided into from three to five subgroups, which nobody in the vast literature on the Kwakiutl seems ever to have been able to define, because of the fact that they were quasikinship groups which appeared to be formed almost by choice on the part of the members. We can call them subtribes.

In addition to this arrangement, there was an organization made up of a number of ranked but hereditary offices, each one marked by crests, ceremonial privileges, and titles. The ranking of the positions was neither automatic nor unchangeable. Rather, each position had constantly to be reaffirmed by potlatches. A potlatch (the word is from the Chinook language and means "gift") is a ceremonial occasion on which one exchanges or gives gifts to one's rival, who is a man occupying a status closest to one's own in the ranked hierarchy. The early studies of potlatch always concentrated on the fact that goods were given away. They did not linger on the more significant fact that an exchange was involved of the sort which has been called conversion. Potlatch was therefore equated with what would truly, were it actually as described, be foolhardiness. As is so often the case, however, the difficulty arose from a basic lack of understanding.

During the entire winter the Kwakiutl did little in the way of production activities, but rather turned their attention to ceremonial and potlatch. Vast feasts were common in this wealthy community, and many were accompanied by potlatching. Potlatch involves giving property by one holder of a position to the holder of another position. The former does so in order to maintain the glory of the rank he holds and of those ancestors from whom he inherited it. Potlatches were usually given on important occasions, either in the life of a person or in the activities of the community. They were frequently held in association with marriages, births, initiations. There were often potlatches in connection with winter dances or other religious rituals. A man could retire from a potlatch position and hand it down to his heir; such was an occasion for great gift giving.

The actual giving was done with vast ostentation and with vast amounts of bragging about the investment skill and the intrepidity of the position holder. The rival was openly dared to do anything half so theatrical.

Potlatching actually consisted of a whole cycle of individual potlatches, each of which was an occasion for a person ostentatiously to convert certain types of wealth into other types of wealth. However, the categories or spheres of wealth among the Kwakiutl were quite different from those involved in other economies. Because of the fact that they lived with such a vast abundance, the subsistence items themselves did not enter into the potlatching institutions. Therefore the distinction the Kwakiutl used was not one between subsistence and treasure, as the Trobriand Islanders draw it, and as indeed some of the Kwakiutl's southern neighbors, such as the Tututni, draw it. These latter make a distinction between subsistence, which is mainly food from the sea, and treasure, which was obsidion blades and large shawls made of the scalps of redheaded woodpeckers sewn together (Dubois, 1936).

Rather, among the Kwakiutl the most important potlatch counters were blankets. In the aboriginal situation, these blankets were either woven or pounded from cedar bark or else made of small animal skins sewn together. It was necessary for the potlatcher to collect as many as possible of these blankets through wise investments and precise interest rates, and then to convert the blankets into other types of goods.

In the whole potlatch literature there is only one account—Dr. Helen Codere (1950) has combed it all—of a series of transactions that can be followed through. This is a case in which a man wanted to set up his son in a potlatch position from which he himself was retiring. He arranged for several members of his tribe to give his son one hundred blankets. The boy then took the blankets and gave them to other members of his own tribe, who paid him a hundred percent interest for keeping the blankets for one year. These people also, then, at the time that they returned the hundred blankets, gave him another hundred blankets, which the boy would have eventually to return at the same hundred percent interest. Therefore, the boy on this occasion had his original one hundred blankets, his hundred blankets interest, and the hundred blankets that had been given to him. He now gave these blankets out to friends in other tribes, who returned them in a shorter time, with less interest. It gave him a total, however, of about 450 blankets. Thereupon, the father of the boy decided it was time to hold the potlatch. The boy took his 450 blankets and, amidst vast ceremonial, made his presentations. Two hundred of the blankets went to repay the original loan at one hundred percent interest. Another 200 went to repay the second loan, made when his first gifts were returned, also at a hundred percent interest. This left him with fifty blankets to give away, which seems to be the actual potlatch transaction. Giving the other blankets was a matter of repayment of debts, with interest.

Note that there are two types of exchange here. The first is among friends and tribesmen who help one to acquire large amounts of property in order that one can from the profit, so to speak, invest that property by giving it to one's rival who must return it at the same exorbitant interest rates.

However, when the rival did return the original gift, one was oneself under an obligation to make the same kind of interest payment and return. Thus, very quickly the number of blankets involved in such a series of transactions became astronomical.

As a matter of fact, there were probably nowhere near 450 actual blankets in the possession of the young man or of his people at the time the potlatch was made. In the first place, other items could be used, and their values expressed in terms of blankets. One could, for example, value a canoe at 400 blankets and give it away. Or one could even use Canadian currency as so many blankets, and give it away. Sometimes a man would receive only a tally stick, which indicated that he had already collected his blankets.

Therefore we are dealing with a situation in which all potlatch wealth is expressed in terms of blankets, not with true collections of *real* blankets. Blankets, in other words, are units of account, and whether or not they exist is beside the point. They are carrying out one of the money functions: standard of value. They are not used in exchange, and the only payment they will serve is the payment of a potlatch debt or of an investment debt leading up to potlatch. The blankets are, in short, a special-purpose money.

The question is still a very real one, however, of how such a system can persist without breaking down, without the whole economy's going to pieces. If the interest rates remained exorbitant, and if the period of time in which the investment had to double remained so relatively short, any economy would collapse. However, the system did not collapse because, through a systematic mode of conversion, the debts were cleared without actual payment. Codere (1950) had noted that if the actual blankets doubled every year, an original investment of ten blankets would, in ten years, lead to 4320 blankets[2] for purposes of potlatch. Potlatches on such scale were rare; certainly not all original loans of ten blankets led to such sums.

The whole point of Kwakiutl investment can be seen not as economic in the sense that we think of it—as dealing with subsistence goods—but with getting together, by means of blankets, sufficient purchasing power to convert out of blankets into another kind of counter or tally—the copper. Coppers were treasures of a sort similar to the *vaygua* of the Trobrianders. They were sheets of copper, slightly convex, about two and a half feet long. They were decorated with engravings of gods or crest animals of various potlatch position holders. A copper obviously had no value of its own. The value given to it depended entirely on the amount paid for it at its last transaction. Each copper was named and its history was known. Every time it was given away, its value had to increase. Boas has, probably mistakenly, compared coppers with bank notes of high denomination. High denominational bank notes are not different in quality from bank notes of small denomination; they merely represent greater purchasing power. Furthermore, there is no individual bank note given a specific name, although every copper had a given name. The coppers were also a substantially different thing from the blankets.

Thus, as the contest between rivals continued and the number of blankets increased until it became so totally out of proportion as to be impossible even to contemplate—at that time one of the owners gave a copper to his rival. With acceptance, the value of the copper became twice the number of blankets that had been given in the transaction the year before. The man who received the copper was obliged either to put that many blankets with it and give it back, or to give it to another of his rivals and get back another copper worth more than the original. A man's whole tribe would help him collect wealth in order to get a copper in this way, so that he could give it away to his rival, thereby increasing his own social position and perhaps ruining his rival completely.

Let us say that the rival, after a period of time, gave a potlatch in which he returned to you the copper plus interest. You then added interest

[2] My own computation is 5120 blankets.

to it and perhaps gave it away again to someone else who returned another that was worth more blankets. You gave that to the first rival. This process continues until one of the rivals decides that the other has extended his credit, and exhausted his resources, to the place where it was not possible for him to increase them. Then comes the coup. You destroy the copper. Amidst great ceremony, you either burn it, break it up, or throw it into the sea. However, it is important to be sure that you yourself are not too attenuated when doing this, because if the rival has reserves enough that he can destroy an equal or greater copper, then you have not won, but lost. Instead of your defeating him, you have yourself been beaten in the potlatch and your name and the name of your potlatch position covered in shame. The destruction of the copper is a means by which a symbol for computed wealth can be turned into "pure value," which itself has no symbol. It is simply glory.

The motivation of the individual Kwakiutl, then, was to get as many blankets as he could, to turn his blankets into coppers, and ultimately to destroy the coppers and turn it all into the purest value: reputation.

It was in the total destruction of the copper that the greatest misunderstanding between early European observers and the Kwakiutl is to be found. To the Europeans it was considered an utterly profitless and indeed a profligate act. Anthropologists did not recognize at this time that in the very destruction of copper, all of the debts were cleared. The debt structure that had been built up within a man's own tribe, as well as that between him and his rival, was destroyed by conversion. As Dr. Codere (1950) has put it, the Kwakiutl system, in order to exist, had to have and did have a way of destroying credit as profligate as its means of creating credit. Conversion provided such a means.

There are several other points that must be made in order fully to understand the institution of potlatch. The term "credit" is used, and used correctly, but the implications of the word are not the same as those to be found in a market-dominated economy. In a market-dominated economy, credit is initiated by the man who receives wealth to use or invest. In Kwakiutl economy, the debtor does not initiate the action—rather, it is the creditor who indemnifies the debtor. Indeed, the word indemnification might well be adopted to describe this sort of "credit," which is different in tone from the credit extended to Americans by a bank or a furniture store.

"Interest," although the word is properly used, also means something quite different in Kwakiutl economy than in capitalistic economy. In the latter, interest is the sum paid, in a market situation, for the use of the means of production or of money. In the Kwakiutl economy, "interest" is more than that: it is a reindemnification of a given partner in sparring for position. Indeed, the potlatch situation has elements of interest (the capital is repaid with a price for its use) but it also has elements of "dividends" and investment. One is improving one's own social position by a constant investment in the other positions in the system of potlatch status. The interest/dividends are reinvested, along with the capital, until they are finally disengaged from the system, and turned to pure glory: something like (but also very different from) giving to a hospital a wing that will "eternally" bear one's name.

"Potlatching" of a sort goes on in American culture. One need only read the acid prose of Veblen, describing the cast-iron deer on the lawns of the Long Island estates at the turn of the century (and note, as Veblen might have done, their degeneration at mid-twentieth century into pink plaster flamingos on the lawns of prosperous artisans, whose houses are now also called "estates"). One need only read of the coming-out parties given by the wealthy for their daughters to realize that much wealth is expended on rank rather than invested. But a great deal of wealth—more and more, Americans like to think—is turned to philanthropy, to "social causes."

The important point is that there are two (or more) means of creating a unitary system from the disparate institutions of an economy. One, which leads to a "unitary economy," is by means of a general-purpose money used to evaluate everything exchanged, and used in all transactions and for all payments. The other is conversion—a more clumsy, but basically similar, device for disengaging the material and pseudomaterial items from one institution and getting them into another institution. The difference is that general purpose money breaks down the discreteness of the institutions, whereas conversion reaffirms their discreteness. Therefore, a different morality lies behind each. It is in the conflict of these two moralities that we can find the most searching revelation of each.

CONFLICT OF ECONOMIES

No more burning question has arisen in the mid-twentieth century than the impact of a homogeneous, monetized economy geared to "development" and "growth" of capital and product, on the multicentric, unmonetized economy geared to maintenance of subsistence and the aggrandizement (growth) of social prerogative. "Economic growth" has become, besides a specialty for economists, a football for politicians and an arguing point for what Americans traditionally call cracker-barrel philosophers, even after cracker barrels have disappeared before the onslaught of modern packaging. "Economic growth" is "a good thing"—and people who do not have it are said to be "underdeveloped."

It is, sometimes, not sufficiently realized that "economic growth" can occur only in association with specific types of social organization, and that an economic revolution must always be accompanied by a social revolution: or, rather, that it indeed *is* a social revolution. We shall examine briefly what happened when Tiv economy and Kwakiutl economy were brought under the dominating influence of a monetized, growing economy.

The acceptance of general-purpose money by the Tiv was accompanied by several other changes that cannot be kept separate from it; all of them are significant in understanding economic change. A general peace was imposed by the colonial administration. Before the arrival of the British, a Tiv did not venture far beyond the area of his kinsmen or friends; to do so was to court death or enslavement. With government police systems and safety, road building was also begun. Moving about the countryside was made both safe and easy. Thus, peace and the new road network led to both increased trade and a greater number of markets. Indeed, the economic institutions of the Tiv had been put in touch with world economy. Probably none of these factors, however, was as important in the economic change of the Tiv as was the introduction of general-purpose money.

General-purpose money provided a common denominator among all the various spheres and institutions of the Tiv economy, thus making the commodities within each expressible in terms of a single standard and, hence, immediately exchangeable. This new money was misunderstood by Tiv. They used it as a standard of value in the subsistence category, even when—as was often the case—the exchange was direct barter. They used it as a means of payment of bridewealth under the new system, but still refused to admit that a woman had a "price" or could be valued in the same terms as food. At the same time, it became something formerly lacking in all save the prestige sphere of Tiv economy—a means of exchange. Tiv tried to categorize money with the other new imported goods and place them all in a fourth economic sphere, to be ranked morally below subsistence.

What in fact happened was that general-purpose money was introduced to Tivland, where formerly only special-purpose money had been known.

It is in the nature of general-purpose money that it standardizes the exchangeability value of every item to a common scale. It is precisely this function that brass rods, a "limited-purpose money" in the old system, did not perform. As we have seen, brass rods were used as a standard in some situations of conveyance in the intermediate or "prestige" category. They were also used as a means of payment (but specifically not as a standard) in some instances of conversion.

In this situation, the early administrative officers interpreted brass rods as "money," by which they meant a general-purpose money. It became a fairly easy process, in their view, to establish by fiat an exchange rate between brass rods and a new coinage, "withdraw" the rods, and hence "replace" one currency with another. The actual effect was to introduce a general-purpose currency in place of a limited-purpose money. By 1950, all conversions and most conveyances were made in terms of coinage. Yet Tiv constantly expressed their distrust of money. This fact, and another—that a single means of exchange had entered all the economic spheres—broke down the major distinctions among the spheres. Money created in Tivland a unicentric economy. Not only was the money a general-purpose money, but it applied to the full range of exchangeable goods.

Thus, when semiprofessional traders, using money, began trading in the foodstuffs marketed by women and formerly solely the province of women, the range of the market was very greatly increased and, hence, the price in Tiv markets came to be determined by supply and demand far distant from the local producer and consumer. Tiv reacted to this situation by saying that foreign traders "spoiled" their markets. The overlap of marketing and men's long-distance trade in staples also resulted in truckload after truckload of foodstuffs being exported from major markets. Food became less plentiful than in the past, even though more land was being farmed. Tiv elders deplored this situation and knew what was happening, but they did not know just where to fix the blame. In attempts to do something about it, they sometimes announced that no women should sell any food at all. But when their wives disobeyed them, men did not really feel that they were wrong to have done so. Tiv elders curse money. It is money, they said, that leads them to see their life's subsistence disappear as they produce more and more.

Of even greater concern to Tiv was the influence money has had on marriage institutions. Every woman's guardian, in accepting money as bridewealth, felt that he was converting down. Although attempts were made to spend money received in bridewealth to acquire brides for one's self and one's sons, it was most difficult to accomplish. The very nature of money makes this so. The good man still spent his bridewealth receipts for brides—but good men are not so numerous as is desirable. Tiv deplored the fact that they had to "sell" (*te*) their daughters and "buy" (*yam*) wives. There was no dignity in it since the possibility of making a bridewealth marriage into an exchange marriage had been removed.

With money, thus, the institutionalization of Tiv economy became unicentric, even though Tiv still saw it with multicentric values. The single sphere takes many of its characteristics from the market, so that the new situation can be considered a spread of the market. But throughout these changes in institutionalization, the basic Tiv value of maximization—converting one's wealth into the highest category, women and children—remained. And in this discrepancy between values and institutions, Tiv came upon what is to them a paradox, for all that Westerners understand it and are familiar with it. Today it is easy to sell subsistence goods for money to buy prestige articles and women, thereby aggrandizing one's self at a rapid rate. The food so sold is exported, decreasing the amount of subsistence goods available for consumption. On the other hand, the number of women is limited. The result is that bridewealth gets higher: rights in women have entered the market, and since the supply is fixed, the price of women has become inflated.

Because of the spread of the market and the introduction of general-purpose money, Tiv economy has become a part of the world economy, and profound changes have resulted in all the corners of Tiv culture. Tiv have had to revalue their motivations and their activities to correspond to a new reality—the market and the characteristics of general-purpose money.

The Kwakiutl experience was even more devastating because their economy and society were even further removed from the norms and principles of market and general-purpose money. The first impact, made by fur traders who came to the Pacific Northwest by sea, was to offer money in exchange for furs, and then to offer Hudson Bay blankets, as they were called, in exchange for money. The cedar-bark blankets, which had been a special-purpose money in the potlatching activities of the Kwakiutl, disappeared and were replaced by Hudson Bay blankets. For the first time, then, people began to concern themselves with money, and the whole subsistence sphere of life began, by means of the general-purpose money and the cotton blankets that were purchasable with it, to permeate the potlatch institutions. Traditionally, subsistence and potlatch were separate —potlatchers gave feasts and sometimes made ostentatious exhibitions of destroying unneeded food, but food and the necessities for clothing and shelter did not enter into actual potlatching activities. With the goal of conversion in their minds, Kwakiutl saw a new way in which conversion could be carried out and even speeded up, advancing the day of glory. They did not know that it would also break down the system and reduce them to poverty.

A second factor was important—diseases, especially measles which was brought by the white men, and increases in tuberculosis and venereal diseases, cut the population to a fraction of what it had once been. The population was reduced to the point that the number of potlatch positions was almost equal to the adult men in the tribes. Therefore, everybody began polatching whereas traditionally potlatching was limited to a comparatively few members of the society, each backed up by a number of tribesmen. Moreover, because of the influence of general-purpose money, all wealth, not just a few nonsubsistence items, began to emerge in potlatches. People began to give away their sustenance rather than their treasure. Again, the reason is obvious: general-purpose money, in league with other changes that accompanied it, created a situation in which a multicentric economy was made unicentric. Everything became exchangeable for everything else; disengagement of goods from one institution and their entry into another became simple. Money did it all. Without protection of activities that isolated or walled off the potlach institutions from the other economic institutions, the staff of life was indeed "frittered away." It is small wonder that the Canadian government made potlatching illegal —Western economy had already made it ruinous.

THE NATURE OF "TRANSITION"

There has grown up as a result of the spread of the world economy, with its basic market orientation, a belief that "underdeveloped" countries have two economies: a "traditional" and a "modern" economy. It is blithely assumed that the end result of the "transition" between the two is known: that the economy of peoples undergoing this change will come to be exactly like that of Westerners. It is becoming increasingly obvious, however, that there is a point at which the "transition" ceases and a new type of economy begins, in which there are constantly warring factors, some taken from traditional values and some from the Western world. People are in the uncomfortable position of acting in accordance with their time-honored values and having the results emerge disastrous. Institutions have changed, and values and overt motivations are among the last elements to catch up with the change.

Throughout the world that was formerly marked by multicentric economies, pressure toward a unicentric economy emerges as the spread of the market. We have seen that allocation can be done on three (perhaps more) transactional principles: market, redistribution, and reciprocity. It often happens that all the principles may be used by a single society. The true "transitional" phase is the phase in which the institutions are changing and the dominance among the principles is being redetermined. The end result is not an economy such as that in the West; it is rather one in which the market (however it may be represented) plays a bigger part than it did in the traditional situation.

What changes, then, are required for the "growth" of an economy? First of all, the folk image must change in rhythm with the institutions if chaos is not to result. New types of motivation must be fostered. But there are also certain demands of the institutionalization; two will be considered here. General-purpose money brings standard of value into prominence—therefore, precise measurement devices must be introduced concomitantly with money. Institutions must be created, which allow wealth to be invested in production rather than disengaged and "converted" into social status and "pure value."

Systems of weights and measures are part of every economy. They are not always mathematically precise, and when they are not they must be understood in terms of rank rather than in terms of mathematics. The Ashanti weights are of particular interest. One of the best-known features of Ashanti culture is the gold weights that they cast in bronze for the purpose of weighing out gold dust in making certain specific kinds of payments. These weights are small *cire perdue* castings of geometric figures, or animal and human figurines, which illustrate a proverb or are merely decorative. They were necessary possessions of all chiefs and other important men. Although there is a relative ranking of weights, there is no "true weight" in the sense of the avoirdupois that we know connected with any of them. Different weights of the same name may weigh different amounts when measured in grams. What determines price in such a case—that is, what determines the amount of gold dust that must be given to make a purchase—is the rank of the man whose weights are actually used in the transaction. In a deal between the chief and an important commoner, the chief will have heavier weights than the commoner or will at least be in a position to demand that his own weights be used. The commoner can either consent to the arrangement or decline to make the transaction. Thus, as a man becomes more and more important, he can take heavier and heavier weights, thereby getting more actual gold dust in his exchanges than he gives.

This system is almost universal in the absence of a bureau of weights and standards such as that subscribed to by modern Western nations. Without such a set of recognized standards and measures, it is all but necessary to fall back on the hierarchy of the social organization to arrive at the measurements that indicate a fair price.

Not only do rich men get more for their wares when they are sold, but frequently it is also incumbent upon them to pay more for their necessities. In such a situation it is often possible to garner considerable prestige by paying more for an item than someone else could afford to pay.

With monetization and "modernization" of the economy, the weights and measures have to be standardized. Some peoples hold out against such standardization with real zeal, because their traditional modes of bargain hunting are imperiled by the system.

The greater problem is the necessity for creating institutions by means of which wealth can be invested in production rather than converted into "noneconomic" spheres. A brief example could be discovered in Liberia as recently as 1960. In that year, because the banking facilities were inadequate, untold hundreds of thousands of dollars belonging to Liberian rubber farmers were put into American and Swiss banks at the same time that, within the country, a businessman could not borrow even modest sums of money for periods of more than a year or so. The institutions not merely discouraged "economic growth," but actually made it impossible. This situation has been changed, but there are many parts of the world in which the clash of economic institutions is such as to prevent the very "growth" that all peoples desire.

Economic "growth" results from specific types of institutionalization of man's "natural" desire to better his standard of living. It demands that investment be made more attractive than conversion to prestige items: that economic growth itself become a prestige item. Every people calls a halt to this process somewhere—a choice must be made. But, the choice is dependent in the long run on cultural values that go beyond mere economic prosperity, and on the presence of banking institutions that allow people to invest rather than to convert. The basic and fundamental idea of our own economists and politicians that we must invest is still countered with the basic and fundamental idea of our people that prestige (however defined) is worth spending money on. The anthropologist's task is to determine the balance between these factors struck by the various societies of the world.

In the last three chapters we have seen that man must exploit his environment in an organized manner—there is a specifically human set of "territorial" phenomena. There is another aspect of territoriality however, which is "dominance." Men must live together in a more or less orderly way even to be able to exploit the environment. Economy and polity can never be finally separated. And it is to political systems, the human forms of dominance, that we must now turn.

16

Politics and government

WE ARE LIVING in a political age—an age of clashing ideologies in which we tend to put our evaluations of almost all the world's ills into political terms. We argue passionately with the people we consider our allies about whether democracy is an equality of rights or of opportunity. We argue just as passionately with those we consider our enemies—and even, indeed, with some who are our friends—about whether democracy should be "economic" or what we call "political." One wonders whether the ideas generated by all this debate will hold up any better from posterity's point of view than the medieval theological arguments about the number of angels that can dance on the head of a pin. Both questions contain within them basic ideas of the nature of cosmography and society, of "free will" and determinism. Medieval terms were mystical and theological. Those of our own age are mythical—too often confused with "scientific"—and political.

THE POLITICAL ASPECTS OF SOCIETY

Every society must solve political problems, just as every society must solve the problems of reproduction and recruitment of new members, and the problems of commissariat and allocation. But what is a political problem? How are such problems solved by different cultural means?

Reduced to simplest terms, political institutions are those that control use of force within a territorial framework. Both of these factors are necessary; there is no such thing as politics without force, organized in one way or another. There is no such thing as politics divorced from territory (though not necessarily one which is bounded in the sense that a national state has boundaries). Politics is the spatial aspect of social force.

There are, furthermore, two main methods of controlling and utilizing political force—or, better, utilizing force politically. They are law enforcement and warfare. Therefore, in studying the political aspects of any society, we must recognize at least four factors: the territorial extent and organization of the society is the first. We must know somehing about the way its people are spread out on the ground, and about its ecology, as it is affected by the modes of production. We have to know whether there are so-called "natural" social units separated by geographical barriers or whether the barriers separating the different territorial or spatial units are merely social barriers. Second, we must know something about the social system through which force is allocated to different individuals playing different roles, and how that social system is seen by the people who live and work in it. Some men, obviously, occupy more strategic positions than others in the control and use of force. Third and fourth, we must know something about the two main institutional controls of force: law and warfare. Whatever units within a society go to maintain the peace and to protect each group's interest against other groups can be called legal institutions. Governments are legal institutions in that sense: they maintain the internal peace through the use or threat of force. Warfare is, on the other hand, force organized for the maintenance of territorial and cultural integrity. Of course, diplomacy can be included here: warfare is, in a sense, only the force that can be put into the field when diplomacy, its threat, fails. Such is not an idea limited to modern societies. Diplomats are to be found wherever there is organized social life and a clash of communities.

Obviously, authority behind the decisions of who will do what and to whom is the essence of law. Who has the strength or power to do what to whom is the core of diplomacy and warfare.

FORCE, POWER, AND AUTHORITY

In addition to the word force itself, two other words have been used, and they must not be confused with it: authority and power. There are, thus, three ideas to consider: force, authority, and power. First, let us take power. Bertrand Russell has contended (although I cannot find the reference) that power or "the ability to do something or to act upon a person or a thing" is the fundamental concept of all social science—indeed, he even goes so far as to suggest that it may be the fundamental concept behind all social order and even all thought. The historical development of the idea of power is an interesting and important one.

John Locke, the great seventeenth-century English philosopher, thought that power was that attribute in an object which made it capable of being a cause; that is, of producing an effect. If you can see a stone, he said, it is because of the power of the stone to be seen. Most philosophers since his time have repudiated Locke's view. Bishop Berkeley was among the first to do so, and Hume went so far as to say that all power is a purely subjective category: that power, far from being in the rock, is entirely in the eye of the seer.

A. N. Whitehead, in our own time, has labeled the sort of logical error that Locke made. He called it a subject-object confusion. The rock was not the subject of action or process—it did not initiate anything. It was, rather, the object. We are ourselves the subject. We see the rock. Saying that the rock causes our seeing is nonsense. The seeing is in us, not in the rock. Berkeley would finish up by saying that what the rock may be, in itself, can never be known, because it can never be known without a sense perception intervening between it and our knowledge of it. In that sense Whorf is a disciple of Berkeley. Today we would say that our knowledge of a rock is a sense perception, and that beyond our senses and the scientific extensions of them, its ultimate existence and nature are beside the point of science.

And yet, such a statement is not totally satisfying. We have all experienced power from outside ourselves. We are conscious of being made to do some things. If one thinks about it carefully, however, he will discover that consciousness of external power is associated with social relationships: we are made to do such and such things *because of the power of other people* who work their wills on us. Indeed, one can oneself feel the power one has over somebody or something else.

Power is obviously an attribute of social relationships. There may be electric power or mechanical power, which accrues from things and to things. But when we speak of power in a context of human beings living socially by means of culture, we are talking about the power that one human being has or wields over another. Power is, then, for the social scientist, the ability to produce intended effects, on oneself, on other human beings, and on things. Locke was right—but only about people, not about objects. Power now takes a new place in the cause-and-effect sequence. Social power produces a cause through human volition. A man is powerful insofar as he can produce *intended* results.

If this argument is followed up in philosophy, the problem of free will soon looms large. In anthropology there is no need so to follow it up. We can say merely that, by definition, a man possesses social power if, in any human relationship, he can make other people do what he wants them to do.

Therefore, it is evident that social power is an aspect of human relationships: one cannot think of social power in any sense except as an attribute of relationships. It is not so much a power inherent within individuals as it is a special kind of relationship between individuals.

In all societies at least *some* of the power relationships are institutionalized and, hence, part of the social organization. There is, in fact, a power aspect in all social relationships, whether it is exploited or not, in light of the fact that the essence of such relationships is that two or more people affect the behavior of one another. In most societies, a portion of these power relationships are given the stamp of legitimacy: they are considered right and natural, as rules of running the society successfully. When such legitimacy or right enters, the quality of the power is changed. We give the power a new name and call it authority. Authority is legitimate or rightful power.

A right, in order to exist, must obviously be acknowledged by some person or persons; it exists only in its recognition. So authority is more than the mere ability to exercise power; it implies the public acknowledgment of this ability. Authority only exists in its recognition and acceptance. The basic criterion of authority is the consensus of the community, or a major part of it, over which the authority is exercised.

Authority, of itself, does not make a situation political. If power is ubiquitous in social systems and social relationships, certainly authority is very common. There is power and authority in a family, obviously; but that fact alone does not make the family political. There is power and authority in an age set or a business firm or a university, but that does not make them political because they do not control law and warfare in a territorial framework. Although the university can enforce its bylaws on its grounds, it can do so ultimately thanks to the nation and the state, not to its power.

One other very important fact flows from this distinction between power and authority. It sometimes happens that authority is allocated in one way in a social system, but that actual power flows in a different way altogether. The social system through which the major power is allocated in a society need *not* be the same one to which authority is granted by the members of that society. Medieval Japan is a case in point. Furthermore, it may even be that the doctrine and beliefs of a people make it immoral for *anyone* to have authority in the sense that it has been discussed here: they may not grant legitimacy to any power. In short, there *may* be *no* authority structure in a society, but only a power structure.

It is, in fact, fairly common that authority in a society does not attach to any single social personality: to any single role. There is no chief, no king. Neither does it attach to any specific groups—kinship groups or any other sort of social group. There is no senate, no council of elders, no parliament, no soviet. It is in such societies that the very concept of government comes into question. There are such societies in Africa: they have been termed "ordered anarchies" by the men who first studied them adequately. Similar situations abound in New Guinea. The Eskimo are another example of ordered anarchy. No king, no headman, no formal council. In short, none of the usual organs of government.

How is it possible to study a power structure in such a situation? We certainly have the four determinants: the territorial aspect, the use of force by law and by war. Force follows the power structure, which may be independent of any authority structure.

Such, as a matter of fact, has been a primary question of interest since the days of the Greek philosophers. It entered significantly into the subject of anthropology very late: significant statements about it can be dated from the publication of *African Political Systems* in 1940. This book was a highly original contribution to anthropology in spite of the fact that it contained nothing dramatically new. Rather, its insights into what was already known gave it importance. In order to see briefly what its achievement consisted in, a review of the history of ideas about comparative politics is in order.

THE HISTORY OF POLITICAL THOUGHT

One must, in such a history, go back to Aristotle and Plato. In Aristotle's *Politics,* the first book is given over to a detailed description of the unwritten constitutions of several of the Greek city states. The descriptions are brief, but they are nevertheless competent by modern standards. We are told by Aristotle what the authority structure is and what the power structure is if the two do not coincide. Then, in the subsequent books of his *Politics,* Aristotle leaves the factual and goes into the equally fascinating and important—but certainly different—topic of justice, and what political organization *ought* to be. Until very recently nobody looked at the factual part of Aristotle's work, but merely the ethical and moral part of it—what the state ought to include. Indeed, the Oxford University Press's standard English edition even omits the empirical data. Plato was, on the other hand, perhaps the first to disregard the data that Aristotle was the first to use. In a long essay called *The Republic,* which became a sort of guide for the political philosophy of future generations, he said that a state *should include* 5040 people, and he set forth what each of them ought to do. Plato said little or nothing about the actual conditions of his time; neither did most of his followers.

The Platonic tradition, backed by the nonfactual half of Aristotle, became the tradition of the West. Nobody *investigated* politics; they merely talked about what states *ought* to do. In the days when the social idiom was a theological one, St. Augustine wrote a political tract called *The City of God.* In renaissance Italy, Machiavelli wrote a handbook for ambitious politicians called *The Prince,* which takes a very realistic view of the situation, but does not report or analyze conditions—rather, it merely provides advice on how to manipulate them. A few centuries later Thomas Hobbes perpetrated his notion of the state in analogy to an organism made up of all the people who are its members. He called it the *Leviathan*

—it is an image which, as we have seen, still haunts our thinking about social and political problems. He and Rousseau postulated the social contract—in the beginning, they said, men realized intellectually that they would be better off if they banded together and so they made a contract to live socially. Obviously, we no longer believe that the socialization or domestication of man was quite as intellectual and purposeful as that. "Social contract" is a mistaken analysis of political legitimacy in terms of contract.

It was a French contemporary of Rousseau in the middle of the eighteenth century, Montesquieu in a book called *The Spirit of the Laws,* who laid the foundations for what is today the discipline of comparative politics. But a couple of centuries passed before Montesquieu's ideas became dominant. He was a student of Roman law and of history, and he took what we would today consider a scholarly, detached, curious view of them. During the nineteenth century, Montesquieu was for the most part either ignored or forgotten, because he did not ask questions congenial to that time. The difficulty lay in the fact that the genetic method, which released the biological sciences from alchemy, merely bound the social sciences the harder to popular superstition and a narrow reading of ancient history. The nineteenth century sought the origins of all things social, and supposed that to know their origin was to understand them. Thus, political inquiry took the form of the question, "What is the origin of the state?"

Today we know that we cannot answer questions about the "origin" of the state because the factual evidence is buried deep in the unrecorded past. Even with the best of archeology, it is doubtful that ideas of such subtlety and magnitude can ever be recaptured unless they are written down or unless they survive in the oral traditions of a people.

The question of origins was crystallized in the late nineteenth century in an argument concerning the "conquest origin of the state." It was congenial to that century, which had already discovered the principle of survival of the fittest leading to evolution and biological change, to believe that the state resulted "automatically" when certain conditions of conquest and resulting rule of one people by another were met. Herbert Spencer, the British jack-of-all-philosophies, postulated that the state originated when two peoples came into conflict with each other and one of them was strong enough to subjugate the other. In order to keep the conquered people subjugated, the conquerors had to form a social organization of the sort we have come to call a state.

Whether this set of ideas is true or not—whether or not *the* state actually originated in this way—is not knowable. We can say that in some instances actual states have been formed in this way—some of these states were African, others were European—but we can also cite examples in which existing states were not so formed, and many examples in which such conquest did not lead to the formation of a state. Actually, Spencer and his followers were stating a functional hypothesis in historical terms: one of the state's functions is to control force and power. This does not necessarily mean that it originated by controlling force, and such is the assumption of the conquest theory.

Anthropologists have been investigating the political systems of primitive people since the turn of the present century. However, at first they did so with such instruments as the conquest theory, or with the difficult European concept of "sovereignty" that had evolved out of peculiar European traditions, or with the "ought" theories of the earlier philosophers. The difficulty that they had in freeing themselves from these dead concepts, and the valiancy with which they fought them, is one of the most rewarding reasons for reading the early anthropologists on comparative politics.

It was not until the late 1930s that the birth of the new comparative politics was brought to light, although excellent descriptions date from much earlier. In *African Political Systems,* social scientists reached the first important goal in the processes of freeing themselves from preconceived notions of their own polity and from the tyranny of their own language. What the authors of this book did was extremely simple. They stated the thesis that it is possible to have a stable, enduring political system, working efficiently *without* the organization known as "the state." Political order and the state are, in short, not synonymous.

Let it be insisted upon that it had long been known that some societies had organizations such as the state and others had not. The fact had, before this time, either been largely ignored, or the data had been squeezed into models derived from Western and classical notions of "the state." With this book, it became easy to note that some societies have states and some do not, but that in all societies the functions of political organization are performed. It became, indeed, obvious that we must separate the political requiremeints that must be performed in every society from any specific set of social institutions by which they are performed. Like so many of the difficult discoveries of social science, the point is "obvious."

African Political Systems did more. It claimed that in Africa there were at least three sorts of organization that performed the political functions. Several distinctions could be made. First there were those societies that had states. There were, as a residual category, those other societies that did not have states; they were "stateless societies." Logically, there is no reason to assume that all of the members of a residual category have any positive characteristic in common. It is, thus, necessary to search for principles or social forms in the residual category by means of which the functions are carried out.

It is just here that the first inadequacies in *African Political Systems* appear. The editors divided their stateless societies into those in which the political functions were taken care of by the extended family, and those in which the political functions were based on the clan or lineage. Actually, it is today possible to see that they left out a step in their analysis, because their data were not adequate. Since they wrote, we have discovered societies in Africa that do not have a state, but also do not regulate power in law or warfare by means either of extended families or of lineages. Therefore, another step can be added: stateless societies may be divided into those that control their political organization by means of kinship groups and those that do not—that is, those that control it by means of nonkinship groups. We can, then, divide the "kinship-groups" class into those utilizing extended families and those using descent groups for political purposes. In chart form, the organization of the types, made by a constant depletion of the residual category, is set forth in Figure 12.

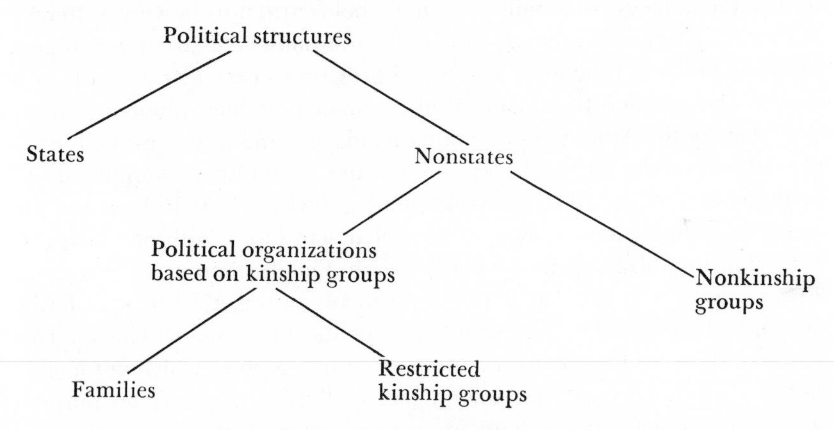

FIGURE 12 Some Types of Political Organization

A state is, in short, an organization whose primary functions are the political ones we have described. When those functions are carried out by other social groups, especially those that are kinship groups or production groups, the results are "nonstates." It is our purpose here to investigate some of the forms that the state may take, and afterwards to review some of the types of the nonstate. In the course of our discussion, it should stand revealed that there is no social group and no social institution or activity that cannot be, in some measure and by some means, politicized. Anything can become a political issue. Any group may become a political group.

THE STATE

A state is a formal organization of roles in which legal and military authority is vested and in which such authority is considered by the members of the state to be its primary purpose. The state is a special social group charged with allocating authority to use physical force in order to achieve peace and conformance with law and custom on the one hand, and to maintain territorial and cultural integrity against external threats on the other.

A state is a group of people with a purpose. They have an organization: a formal concatenation of roles and offices. They have a material and ideal culture with which to carry out the purpose, to evaluate it, and to criticize it. The officers of the state have authority to use force in order to carry out their purpose. In the first examples, it will be assumed that they also have the power to use it; there are, however, many situations in which the power system is actually different from the authority system.

The mode of organization of the state varies widely. It may be patterned on analogy to family and household structure—a very different matter from actually utilizing the family and household structures to perform the political functions. The Swazi provide an excellent example of a people who organize their political life in analogy to their family organization. Among the Ashanti, on the other hand, the army provides the fundamental folk model for the organization of the state. Other examples are to be found in the Council of Forty-four among the Cheyenne Indians and the religious organizations of some of the Polynesian states, both of which cast their state organizations into religious idiom. Finally, there is, as in western Europe and the states that derive from there, an organization specifically established to handle governmental or political functions. The modern national state is a huge network of organizations, each of which not merely serves a given purpose, but was in fact established for a given purpose within government. It does not, as a rule, make much use of organizations that are already existent and serving other purposes.

THE SWAZI STATE

The first of the African states to be described is the Swazi state enclaved within the Republic of South Africa. The Swazi are a large tribe who are not a part of South Africa, but are one of the two so-called "High Commission Territories" and come directly under the Colonial Secretary in Her Majesty's government. The present-day lives of Swazi are more or less dominated by South Africa, and they are economically a part of South Africa and subject to much the same sort of economic pressures to leave their tribal areas and go out to work in order to earn money.

The Swazi have a king—the present king, named Sobhuza, is a college graduate, who when the Swazi were studied in the late 1930s, still performed most of the traditional ceremonies his kingship imposed on him. In order to understand his kingdom, we shall investigate the territorial organization of the Swazi people, and something about their legal and military activities. (Kuper 1947).

Swazi homesteads lie scattered at irregular intervals over the hilly countryside, and contain from seven to twenty-five or more people. The plot plan of the homestead is standardized and has three key points. The first is the cattle byre, which is the central point in the homestead, where cattle are kept when they are not in pasture, and which represents symbolically the compound head. Then, there is the "great hut," which is described as typically the quarters of the mother of the compound head, but the mother may be replaced after her death by senior wife. Finally, there are the "bachelors' quarters" at the outlying areas.

The great hut is the religious center of the compound, containing the religious symbols and the altar. The "mother" or her substitute is the link between the compound head and his ancestors. The byre is the economic center of the household and it is also the center of authority. The bachelors' huts, for unmarried men and male visitors, are located at the entrance of the homestead, and the men who live there are charged with protecting the homestead from outsiders. Between the bachelors' huts and the great hut, forming an arc around the byre, are the huts of the wives and dependents of the homestead head. The compound may be spread out spatially, for Swazi consider it advisable to give co-wives plenty of room to avoid one another if they want to do so.

The domestic authority within the compound is very specifically set out. The compound head is nominally in full authority, but he is very effectively checked by the authority exercised by the headwoman. She plays a definite part in the ceremonies and sacrifices performed for the ancestors, and is the mediator of all the women's activities and all of the women's disputes in the household.

When a headman dies, his main heir must perpetuate the homestead. He must place a wife at each of the local subdivisions of the compound, "to wake the huts of his father so that they will not perish." He takes his father's place; his wives take up places in space beside his father's wives, in space.

The homestead of the king is organized in accordance with the same principles as those governing the homesteads of other important polygynists. But the homestead of the king covers not merely a space the size of a small village. Rather, the entire country is his homestead. There are two "capitals" in Swaziland: one is the king's home, and it is called "the byre" of the nation. The other, about twenty-five miles away, is the center of the queen mother and is called "the great hut." The whole nation is composed of their metaphorical family and dependents. The queen mother exercises the same sort of restraining power over the king as the headwoman of a compound exercises over a compound headman. The government cannot function unless there is rapport between the two; together they must carry out the rituals of the cult of the royal ancestors in the national religion.

There are also several "bachelor quarters" or "barracks" throughout the kingdom. In these, too, the king places members of his family. They serve as information centers—provincial capitals, as it were—and in the old days as army posts. In addition, the king sends part of his queens or other dependents to "wake the huts" in the capitals of his predecessors. The whole kingdom is indeed the homestead of the king.

The whole authority system radiates from the king. Aristocrats are graded by proximity of relationship to the ruling line of the royal clan. The king's close relatives, particularly his uncles and half brothers, wield great influence. These senior princes are consulted on all important issues. They, together with other counselors, are the king's advisers and teachers, as well as his most fearless critics. In order to avoid trouble between the king and the princes who were passed over in the inheritance, the eldest sons of most of the senior queens receive principalities as birthrights. The queens of the dead king are distributed at royal centers throughout the country; their sons become princes over the surrounding people. The position of prince in the outlying principality is usually heritable at least for several generations.

However, the king is careful not to allow too much power to his male kinsmen, and certain high posts are monopolized by commoners. These commoners are extremely important, for they link the commoner clans directly to the royal clans by links of patronage vaguely similar to those found in the European feudal past. These commoners hear court cases and give judgment, thus forming the body of judges. They look after the royal herds, organize labor, and do most of the important management jobs of running the kingdom. They can also remind a remiss king or queen mother of their duties. There are two councils of these commoner office holders that can make laws to hold the power of the king to the constitutional prerogatives of his authority.

Swazi military strength also centers on the king. Swazi men form age-set organizations of a sort that are usually called "regiments." They are organized by neighborhoods, and at certain times during their youth, the men spend several months or several years at the various "barracks," or capitals of the king, on "active duty." They provide a fighting force in wartime and a labor force in peacetime. Their allegiance is directly to the king; their officers form a council, separate from the civil councils.

The Swazi, then, see their territory organized in an analogy to the king's homestead. It is not merely the royal family writ large, however, because it has a well-defined organization made up of royal family, on the one hand, and commoner officials and councils representing specific clans. Law is administered through a civil council; warfare is taken care of by a military council. The king is the chief link between the two. Every man owes his king military service during his youth. The Swazi state is, except for the idiom of the family in which it is viewed, not so very different from our own state.

THE ASHANTI STATE

In the traditional polity of the Ashanti of present-day Ghana, the idiom of the state was quite different: it was a military one, with the army providing the most important images. The Ashanti are a nation of about a million people; their country lies mainly in the forest belt of West Africa. They divide themselves into eight uterine clans, each of which postulates a common ancestress but does not claim to know the precise line of descent from her to living persons. Within each village, representatives of most of the clans are to be found, and the clansmen within a village usually *do* know their descent from the ancestress who founded their particular lineage segment of the clan. The village contains four or five—perhaps all eight—of the clans.

Each lineage has a local head man chosen by its male members from nominations made by its senior women. In addition, a village headman is chosen from one specific clan; the headman clan varies from village to village. There are at least some areas where each of the eight clans provides the headman.

The main task of these village headmen is to settle the disputes that arise in the community. In Ashanti theory, each lineage head must, with the other elders of the lineage sitting in a sort of committee, settle disputes among the members of that lineage. The group of lineage representatives, also sitting as a committee and perhaps assisted by the elders of the village, settles disputes among the villagers who belong to different lineages. There is a formal court procedure, with pleading, witnesses, and decisions, although usually it is resorted to only after all efforts at informal reconciliation have failed. These men have powerful sanctions; they can banish a person from the community. This is not now so powerful a sanction as it once was, but before the *Pax Britannica* it was equivalent to death in the bush, without friends or assistance, or else to slavery.

These local clan heads have two or more titles. The first is the clan name followed by the word *hene,* which means "chief," the whole followed by the name of the village: "X-clan chief of Village A." The second title comes from the military organization. Each village has a closely organized military system. Though there are many variations in detail, the titles reflect the formation in which the army went into battle. The army was led into action by groups of scouts, armed with guns as well as long sticks tipped with wooden hooks for use in shaking the trees to draw enemy fire. Just behind them came the advance guard who infiltrated through the scouts as soon as the former had made contact with the enemy. They were followed by the main body of troops. At the rear of the main body marched the chief, surrounded by his personal bodyguard, of which there were two chief officers. The rearguard always faced the rear as the column went into action, maintaining this position until the enemy was routed, whereupon they, in turn, infiltrated through all the rest and took up the pursuit. On either side of the main body were the left wing and right wing, whose tactical mission was to outflank the enemy. Each wing had a commander.

The organization of the village locality, then, is fairly simple: each of the matrilineal lineages—held together internally by the reciprocal obligations of kinsmen—sends its representative to a council whose task is to maintain law and order between descent groups, where different sanctions are felt to be necessary: the relationships among these lineage representatives is expressed in military titles, reminiscent of the sanction of force.

So much for local government. Ashanti also had a type of confederacy among these village groups. When the Ashanti introduced the concept of an organization among several village localities, one of the villages of the larger unit—which can be called the division—was singled out as the capital village. The other villages were then associated by ties with the chief of the capital village, who became thus the paramount chief of the division.

If the divisional organization had been entirely consistent with the village organization, each of the chiefs of the noncapital villages would have become an elder of the chief of the capital village—that is, chiefs would have made up the council of the paramount chief. But this was precisely *not* the case. The chief of the capital village had a group of council members about him already: the heads of the various lineages domiciled in his village. When the chief of the capital village assumed the office of paramount chief of the division, he retained the same council. Thus, not only was the chief of one village elevated to a new and higher position, but his elders also took on new responsibilities and relationships. The personnel of the court of the paramount chief was the same, in skeleton, as the personnel of the chief's court in his capital village.

In order for the paramount chief to administer his division, then, each elder or councilman of the paramount chief was made the official "friend at court" for one or more of the outlying chiefs. The outlying chiefs had no direct access to the paramount chief, but had always to go through their various friends at court. Likewise, orders from the paramount chief to an outlying chief were given via the latter's friend at court. The friend at court had no authority over the outlying chief; he was only an intermediary. These links of the various outlying chiefs to the paramount chief did not preclude their having friendships and pacts with one another. When two outlying chiefs dealt directly, they did as equals.

In a manner entirely consistent, the outlying chiefs did not become commanders in the army of the paramount chief—he had army commanders already. Rather, the entire army of a subordinate outlying chief was added to the right wing, say, of the small local army of the paramount chief, while the army of another outlying chief was added to the main body. In addition, then, to the link through the friend at court, the paramount chief appointed his close clansmen as liaison officials with these attached armies and their chiefs and commanders. The army, in other words, was kept on a strictly territorial basis, yet the whole could be welded into a single fighting unit, based on a cadre of the capital village.

Even in a system as consistent as the Ashanti, however, there were exceptions. Many of the paramount chief's councilors, who were also lineage heads, had villages placed directly under their authority. These villages—most of which grew up from hunting camps in the forests after the division was a functioning entity—had a headman, but not a chief. Most of such villages seem to have been granted to elders as rewards for outstanding services. Others seem to have been villages that originally owed allegiance to the paramount chief, in one of his other offices, which he gave away in order to reduce the confusion that often arose when he was both chief and paramount chief.

There is one step needed to complete the pyramidal picture of the Ashanti state: the king himself, and the organization within his territorial division, and the ways the paramount chieftaincies were organized to form the nation. First of all, in the division that came to be the national capital, Kumasi, the method of organization was even more militarized than in the other divisions: the system of lineage heads had been subordinated to, though by no means replaced by, a system of military companies or batallions. The leaders of these companies usually were appointed by the king, though many of them became hereditary, frequently but not always in the uterine line. Aside from this fact, however, the workings of Kumasi division were much like those of any other division: the outlying paramount chiefs tended to be attached to the king through one of his councilors—an official in the smaller territorial army of the king.

The Ashanti state was thus visualized by the Ashanti themselves in terms of military organization. Actually, the ties between the paramount chiefs and their subordinate chiefs, or between the king and the paramount chiefs, were loose ones. Ashanti history contains many instances in which this or that chief broke off his relationship and revolted against a particular king, though none apparently revolted against the idea of Ashanti kingship. This is a very important point: revolution against a form of government is of a different nature from, and much rarer than, mere revolt against a specific administration or specific man. There are kingships in East Africa in which revolt against a particular king is a constitutionalized aspect of preserving the kingship itself. Revolution to overthrow a constitution appears to have been very rare in Africa until recently; revolt against particular office holders on the other hand seems to have been usual.

Every paramount chief among the Ashanti also had to recognize the tribunal of the king as a superior court—any person could have his case transferred there by committing the tribal taboo of swearing a certain oath, which for religious reasons could be dealt with only by the king. Every paramount chief took an oath of allegiance to the king at the time that he assumed his position, and renewed it every year at the national ceremony known in English as the "Yam Custom." The king also took an oath to govern in accordance with the custom of the realm, and to take the advice of his councilors on matters affecting them all. Aside from military situations, the king's governing functions were slight: the so-called ancestral cults of which he was chief priest and practitioner were national cults. But except in the fields of war and religion, and for the fact that his court was the highest in the land, most of the government was in the hands of the paramount chiefs and their subordinates, the village chiefs.

It would appear that the burden of taxation imposed by the national government was light, and that much of the expense of the national administration, consisting mainly of ceremonies and wars, was borne by the capital division. The king did, however, have special attendants who carried on an extensive trade in his name and for his profit, which provided the major source of the national revenue.

In summary, government officials in the traditional Ashanti system were military commanders. They were also priests. One of the basic obligations of the king or chief was to provide the religious needs of his subjects. The authority structure was, however, very weak, and was easily broken. The greatest change that the English administration made was to give strength to the bonds that united the villages together into divisions and the divisions together into the confederacy.

STATELESS POLITICAL ORGANIZATIONS

One of the best examples of the nonstate societies whose political system is based on nonkinship groups is to be found in the traditional system of the Hopi of northern Arizona. Their political organization was made up of a balance achieved among ritual and religious groups; each man, when he became an adult, joined one of these groups, and the government was achieved, without a hierarchy of officers, through a balance of the ritual groups in an annual cycle of festivals.

The political organization based on the extended family can be found in any society composed of bands or hordes—most of these groups are in fact hunters and gatherers. The Bushmen of the Kalahari Desert and the Australian aborigines are classic examples. Among North American Indians, the Comanche and the Basin Shoshone are good examples.

The political organization based solely on the unilineal descent group is typical of parts of Melanesia and of Africa. The example to be given briefly here is of the Tiv of central Nigeria. Tiv are organized into a system of lineages based on the principle of segmental opposition. Each lineage, at every level, is associated with a territory. Therefore, the lineage system supplies a mode of organizing the view of geography. Each lineage is descended, through males, from a single male ancestor; each also has its territory. That territory is beside the territory of the lineage descended from the brother of the founder of the first. The two, taken together, make up a larger lineage descended from the father of the two brothers. Their combined territories form the territory of the inclusive lineage, and so forth.

In such a situation, how are war and fighting controlled? The main device is one based on a simple rule of self-interest: if two people are fighting, the third joins the one to whom he is most closely related. If both are equally distantly related, the third man does not join in, but rather he stops the fight. Thus, if lineage A fights with lineage B, no member of lineages C or D will join in—they will do their best to stop the fight (see Figure 9). Besides this, there is a series of blood pacts between alternate lineages—those that do not bound one another on the ground. Such pacts make it a mystical and religious sin to draw blood from a person of the other lineage; hence they cannot fight each other—neither can they marry each other.

In the same situation, disputes are settled within the lineage by the lineage elders. Disputes between lineages are settled either by fighting *or* by meetings and activities, which verge on what Westerners think of as diplomacy. If I have a dispute with a member of that lineage over there—if, say, he owes me a goat, I go take a goat from him or one of his kinsmen and bring it home. I immediately tell my lineage what I have done. If I can convince them that he did in fact owe me the goat, and that I have performed my side of the bargain, they will stick by me, and we will use our force to defy the others to take the goat back. If, however, I fail to convince them of the rightness of my deed, then they will make me give the goat back in order to save themselves a fight. In cases of divorce, elders of whole lineages meet with one another to work out a *modus vivendi* and the rights involved in the matter. Courts were established by the British and spread throughout Tivland. But they were not indigenous. For a court, properly so-called, must have personnel with authority granted to them. Tiv grant political authority to no one. Every dispute is settled and every war is fought on the basis of a power system, not an authority system. It is order of a sort—ordered anarchy. It enables one to predict what will happen. But it is not really government, and it is certainly not a state.

We can summarize the points made here by noting that there are two sorts of power systems: those that have a single center of power, and those that have multiple centers of power. States are one example of the first sort—there is a single power system, which, for all that it may have an institutionally pluralistic appearance, can be both analyzed and manipulated as a single hierachy of power. Everything that is part of a multicentric power system we have a tendency to see in analogy to "international relations."

Multicentric power systems are, in one sense, the political nemesis of our age. Much of the thought (international law is the most obvious exception) that goes into international relations is an attempt to reduce multicentric political systems to unicentric ones. The League of Nations and the United Nations have been such attempts. The former collapsed; the latter is faced with acute problems, although some of its achievements in "nonpolitical" fields have taken advantage of its multicentric nature.

There are polities in the world that display multicentric power systems throughout. The Tiv-type lineage system based on segmental opposition is an example of such a polity. Its weaknesses are evident: lack of a single legal authority makes peaceful settlement of disputes cumbersome. Its strengths are also evident: institutionalized accommodation of two or more interlinking authorities is its essence. Modern political thinkers may discover in the next few decades that there are stabilizers in non-national, multicentric authority systems which can solve some of the problems that seem to baffle the nationalistic unicentric authority systems of the twentieth century.

17

Law, crime, and warfare

THE LAST CHAPTER showed us that the typically political task is to control power in a bounded social group with territorial dimensions. Such control is always and necessarily carried out in accordance with a set of norms, more or less overtly recognized. We noted that traditionally two sets of activities have been regarded as representative of political life: law and warfare. Such a statement cannot, however, be left unchallenged. The distinction between law and warfare is a simplistic one. As is the case with many other such faulty distinctions we have examined in the course of this book, it is made on the basis of at least two defining criteria.

"Law" is peaceful decision making in a unicentric power system. "War" is violent decision in a multicentric power system.

TABLE 13

UNICENTRIC AND MULTICENTRIC POWER SYSTEMS

	NON VIOLENT	VIOLENT
UNICENTRIC	"Law"	"Police" action against crime
MULTICENTRIC	Diplomacy	Warfare

The modern world has learned to control the unicentric system, in which the major problems are succession to power and maintenance within bearable bounds of deviation from norms. The "state" performs these functions internally and often performs them well. That same "state" as a unit in a multicentric system is faced with a dilemna—its unicentric internal structure leaves it unprepared to share what it follows the old philosophers in calling "sovereignty" with another similar unit in a multicentric system.

We shall here take up four political problems: first law and crime, which are the problems of a unicentric system; then diplomacy and warfare, the problems in a multicentric system.

LAW

Law is one of the best-studied subdisciplines of anthropology; the literature is small but of high quality. It is nevertheless true that studies in legal anthropology have not always managed to free themselves from the strictures imposed by the categories of jurisprudence. The difficulty can be summed up if we note that jurisprudence tends to begin its investigations from the standpoint of "the law" and to proceed from there to questions about the nature of law, the sources of law, or the qualities of the rule of law. Anthropology, by its nature, must comprehend a dimension that is spared the jurists. Jurists, being for the most part lawyers, can take the lawyer's version of the folk image—no matter how specialized, and no matter for the moment how many generations of first-rate thinkers have contributed to making it up, it is a folk image—and build their analyses firmly on that ground. Anthropologists must, in addition, understand and make overt the folk image of the actors in foreign cultures. The language and concepts of jurisprudence being created for comparative scientific and philosophical purposes are usually inadequate to the job of ethnographic description, even as they are essential to the ultimate task of comparison.

As in all other branches of his subject, the anthropologist must begin with social acts and their cultural interpretation.

To discuss law and legal institutions it is convenient to point out a characteristic of all institutions—a characteristic we have so far said little about, but which we shall examine in detail in this chapter. We have seen that institutions are characterized by a social organization, a purpose, by material and ideal culture. There is one more item: an institution in action is marked by a number of characteristic social acts. Sometimes those social acts are extremely diffuse and complex. Sometimes—as is the case with legal institutions—they are extremely simple and form a recognizable series. Although the forms of legal institutions vary widely from one society to the next, what they do is always simple and straightforward. There is, in fact, a series of three typical actions that mark a situation as legal.

First of all, there is a social act that is a breach of norm. Somebody breaks the law, or goes against custom. Norm here means, obviously, what people ought to do. A norm—be it law, custom, ethical precept, morals, manners, or whatever—is not a social act. It is a guide to social action. Acts can be either in accord with or not in accord with norms. Breaches of the norm are always social acts.

The second characteristic act in a legal situation follows breach of norm. When some norms are broken by what we call "deviant" social acts, nothing happens. But there are, in every society, other actions breaking other norms, that—once they are committed—set off a sort of chain reaction: they lead to the sort of social acts that can be called "counteractions." In our own society, these counteractions are the concerted activities of policemen, of courts, of lawyers, of other agencies of law enforcement and people concerned with the law. The counteraction is, in other words, those acts designed to counter the original breach of the norm.

Finally, there is a third set of activities that follows on the counteraction. We can call it "correction." Correction is a good word to express the meaning here because it contains an ambiguity composed of two meanings: these two meanings each represents a type of final action in the event sequences of legal institutions. Correction, in the first instance, means to make somebody perform the original action in accordance with the norm. Thus, for example, we have a man who does something that is counter to the norm. His action makes another whole set of institutions swing into action, as a result of which the original man is made to perform the original action again, this time in accordance with the norm. Usually such a procedure is then followed by the fiction that he did it correctly all along, and the original breach is forgotten, or at least forgiven. The other meaning of the word correction comes into play in those examples in which a man performs an act that cannot be undone. Say he killed somebody. "Correction" in this sense, then, means that an act is performed that by retaliation "corrects" the initial breach. In the modern Western example, the retaliatory or "corrective" act may be imprisonment or even execution. Thus, correction means either a return to the *status quo ante* or else the establishment of a new *status quo* from which normal action can again proceed.

The "event sequence" of legal institutions can be represented in a simple diagram (see Figure 13). If a social act that breaches a norm leads

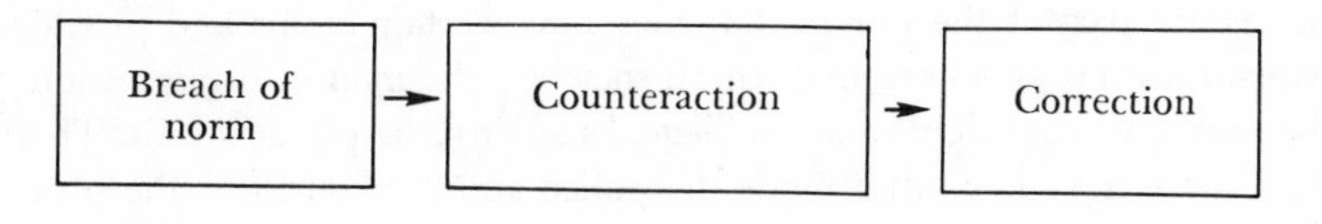

FIGURE 13 Event Sequence in Legal Action

to effective counteraction by a social group of the sort that has been defined as "political," and if the counteraction is followed by some sort of "correction" allowing the processes of society to continue more or less intact, the situation can be said to be a "legal" situation.

Western civilization and the classical cultures on which it has risen examine their legal institutions from a peculiar point of view. Their folk image for viewing legal situations centers on a notion called "the law." The heart of the concept "law" is to be found in the norm that is breached; it has a substantive, empirical element that may well be unique to each given society.

The very word "law" is an extremely difficult one to define. Even a brief analysis of it demands that we separate the way "law" is used by the physical scientist from the way it is used by the moralist, the lawyer's use from the jurisprudent's use, the popular use from the social scientist's use. We must shuck off these various meanings in order to get to the portion legal anthropology has chosen for comparative study. First of all, scientific laws are obviously different from social laws in that they have no ethical element in them. They are merely brief statements of scientific observation and formulation. The law of gravity is a law not because two bodies ought to attract each other in accordance with definite quantifiable principles, but because they in fact do so. Divine law is an even more ambiguous term. It may sometimes be used as a synonym for scientific law, but is also used in the exact opposite meaning—a purely "ought" idea, or statement of the ideal toward which behavior should strive even if it is unattainable. Therefore, "Thou shalt not steal" or "Thou shalt not commit adultery" are divine laws; there may be—and in fact usually are—accompanying social laws wielding more mundane sanctions than the reputed wrath of God. But they are guides and maxims for behavior. They are certainly not *derived* from statistical averages of what people do, even when they in fact reflect it.

"Law" is further complicated from the social scientist's point of view because it is used by two sets of specialists in ways that they consider more or less the same, but that the social scientists can see as quite different. In the parlance of both lawyers and jurists, "the law" is a body of norms that must be obeyed, but is is also the machinery that is set up to "protect" these norms. Thus, the entire police system is "the law" in English; and courts are part of the law in that they have certain rights and privileges which must not be interceded. In all societies, the man in transgression of the norms also has rights and privileges as against the political unit. Therefore, there is a "law" that binds the police and the court, for the protection of the lawbreaker, so to speak. In our society, these limitations on the power of police and court are summed up in what we call the "procedural law" of our society, based on such axioms as "A man is innocent until proved guilty," "Every citizen has recourse to due process of law [which means the courts]," and all the rest of them. Long ago, in the early nineteenth century, John Austin subdivided the law into "substantive law" for the norms originally broken, and "adjectival law" for the norms of the counteracting and correcting institutions.

Lawyers are, furthermore, interested in what people *ought* to do—as that *ought* is defined by statute, precedent, common law, and custom—and with what will happen if they do not. The jurisprudent, on the other hand, must keep his activities strictly separate from those of the lawyer. He is, because of his concentration on comparing several legal systems, interested in what people in fact do; and he compares not only what they do with what they say they ought to do, but he also compares the norms themselves, the degree to which they are maintained or breached, and the methods for coping with breaches from one society to another. Thus, for the lawyer, the datum is that the law says you must fulfill contracts legally entered into, and that in such and such an instance somebody did or did not do so. For the jurisprudent, on the other hand, the datum is that there is a law of contract that does or does not coincide with the other laws in the system, and just as important, that there are basic ideas *behind* this law—what Hoebel (1954) has called the "postulates" for law.

In other words, our lawyers, courts, and police organize our rules or laws for behavior. They are interested in maintaining those laws. Our legislatures, and indeed our courts, *make* laws for purposes of guiding behavior. On the other hand, the jurisprudent studies law not for purposes of behavior, but for purposes of analysis and comparison of one society with another. Lawyers are instruments of their own society, and so are legislators. They help to build the culture of their own society, and they protect and maintain it. A jurisprudent is, on the other hand, something of a social scientist. Insofar as he is a social scientist, he does not build his culture directly, but rather seeks to transcend it and to understand it either philosophically or by comparing it with other cultures or both, thereby changing it (if he is any good) indirectly.

The study of legal anthropology is complicated by the fact that lawyers and jurisprudents use the same words, and by the fact that they are often the same people. In American English, words like "law," "court," "fine," "sentence" have quite a precise meaning. It is lawyers and judges who give them that meaning. When the comparative jurist uses those terms, however, the words have less precise meanings. Sentences, as we know them, are unknown in many African societies. Fines, as we know them, are missing in much of the world. Yet, on a broader level, disputes are disposed of, people are told to do such and such as reparation or correction, and wealth is impounded in retribution for a breach of norm.

Anthropologists must, therefore, study law as jurisprudents do, not as lawyers do. We are interested in what people *do,* and the way they see their actions; we are also interested in what they say they *ought* to do, and how well they think they actually manage to do what they ought to do. Our material is being analyzed for science, not for action. Our problems are scientific problems in the theory of social control, not action problems dealing with specific cases or categories of cases.

There is one further dimension. Anthropologists must, by studying the cases of trouble and dispute that fall within the rubric of comparative jurisprudence and legal anthropology, also elicit from the strained situation the statement of the norm, the values lying behind the stated norm, and ultimately the propositions about the nature of society, the world, and God which are the unstated postulates of any set of laws. Legal anthropology is concerned with the kind of rules people have, how they organize these rules into cultural systems, and the kind of social acts that are performed to maintain or change the rules. It must also go far beyond that point and ask how it is that the rules or laws reflect the most basic values, often so basic that they cannot be uttered by the people who hold them. These basic "postulates" behind the laws can be compared with axioms. In Euclidian geometry, for example, it is an axiom that no two lines parallel with a given line can pass through the same point. Such is, if you will, a scientific way of defining parallel. In much the same way, in Eskimo culture it is a postulate that "Spirit beings and all animals, by virtue of possessing souls, have emotional intelligence similar to that of man" (Hoebel, 1954, p. 69). It is a folk way of defining certain moral precepts. If such a definition of "spirit" is maintained, then certain results follow by more or less logical steps of reasoning. Such a definition of spirit is axiomatic to all Eskimo law; it is the task of the anthropologist, by studying cases of trouble, to discover the axioms a society assumes.

The results attained by legal anthropology, therefore, tend to fall into two categories. On the one hand are the studies of the legal procedures of foreign cultures; to make such studies it is advisable to focus on the "counteraction" and delineate and compare institutions of counteraction from one society to the next. On the other hand are the studies of the basic axioms or postulates lying behind the laws; such studies focus on "values" and ultimately they must accord with studies of religion, cosmography, and morals in the same societies.

To review the position we have adopted: legal anthropology studies the social counteractions to breaches of norm, including the events that precede and follow counteraction; it also studies the basic values that lie at the base of the norms.

Examples of legal institutions are most easily approached by a comparison of institutions of counteraction. Police systems and courts offer one mode for institutionalizing counteraction. Another is to be found in the town meeting or "moot" that assembles to settle disputes or lay down policy. Still another is to be found in those instances in which the principals to a dispute agree to reduce the range of that dispute to the rules of a game or a gladiatorial contest; another version of this sort of counteraction is to be found in the ordeal. A simpler but still effective form is to be found in the institutions of self-help that are exhibited by many cultures of the world. We shall choose examples ranging from the institutionally simple to the institutionally complex, noting that throughout the ultimate aim of counteraction is to reach a state of correction so that social life can continue its accustomed course, as little perturbed as possible.

ESKIMO LAW

One of the institutionally simplest of all societies is that of the Eskimo. Yet, Eskimo law can be seen to be fairly precise in its outlines, and to utilize specific and limited counteractions to achieve its ends. The most common is the counteraction of self-help. Self-help is found to some degree in most societies, although its nature changes with the degree to which special police systems are found. Eskimo society has no police system, and hence self-help looms large in its legal process. Among the Eskimo, when a man breaks the law and in so doing violates your rights, you must help yourself in redressing them.

Right is on your side, but there is no strength or power save your own that you can invoke to claim your rights. You may be able morally to claim the assistance of your kinsmen or your neighbors, but there is no special group such as our own police on whom you can call.

Take the case of Qijuk (Hoebel, 1954, p. 85). Qijuk's wife died. Being without a wife, in Eskimo society, is an extremely serious situation, because the division of labor between men and women is very precise, and it takes two people to run a household. Thereupon Qijuk looked about for another wife, and decided on a woman who was married to Kinger, in a neighboring settlement. So Qijuk had his brothers go with him to get the woman. When he arrived, Kinger was out hunting, so Qijuk moved in and said, "I am now your husband".

Although the Eskimo are liberal with their women, they have definite rights in them, and Qijuk had overriden Kinger's rights. He had breached the recognized law or custom. When Kinger came home, Qijuk told him to be off. Right was on Kinger's side. Everyone admitted that. However, there was no official to do anything about it. So Kinger did the only thing he could do: he killed Qijuk. His friends then came to his aid and killed one of Qijuk's brothers; the other brother escaped.

In this particular case, that ended the matter. The wronged man, through self-help, had created a state of retribution or correction. He had his wife back and the lawbreaker was punished. There was, as it were, restitution and penalty. Self-help of this sort is a legal mechanism, but nevertheless exhibits some dangers and is often precarious. Hoebel goes on to point out that although the brother who escaped was often told he should take vengeance on Kinger, he never felt he was strong enough to be successful.

Self-help in this sense may be looked upon by some members of society as a jural mechanism, although others may look upon it as a fresh breach of norm. Eskimo are willing to admit that, as a general thing, thou shalt not kill—even though, as a specific thing, you must kill to redress a wrong. This case did not lead to a feud, but it might have. Feud occurs when the principle of self-help gets out of hand. In self-help, if I injure you, you kill me. However, my brother is likely to say that the two injuries are not equivalent, and hence he has to take revenge, so he kills you by shooting you in the back. Then your brother says that you killed me in open combat, but my brother killed you by a sneaking low trick, so things are still not evened up, and your brother then kills my brother. This can go on indefinitely, and the feud thus ceases to be a jural mechanism of self-help. You get a new and different series of events (see Figure 14). Here is no jural mechanism, because the group or series of social acts that results in correction is never reached. Thus, though feud or threat of feud is a type of counteraction found very widespread throughout the world, it is usually found to be a faulty jural mechanism, because the almost universally desired state of peace and rectitude is very difficult to arrive at by means of it.

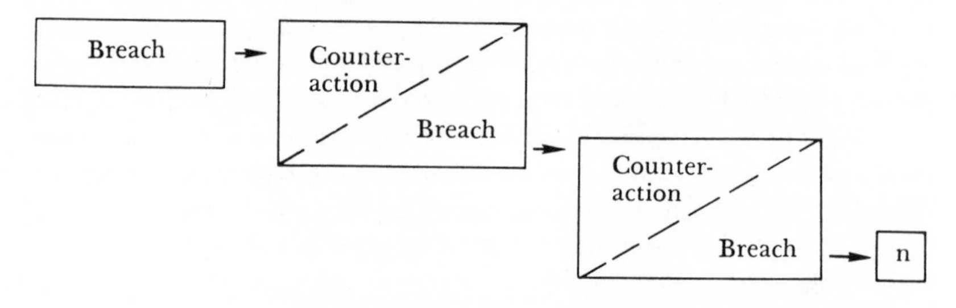

FIGURE 14 Event Sequences in Feud

What are some of the other things an Eskimo can do when somebody infringes his rights? Hoebel (1954) gives some examples of the singing contests for which Eskimo are so well known. If somebody steals my wife, I may not kill him, but merely make up a nasty song about him that makes him ridiculous in the eyes of the neighborhood. He then makes up a nasty song about me so that I will look ridiculous. Among the Eskimo, this sort of contest becomes highly formalized, and it may be accompanied by games vaguely like athletic contests, in which the point is to win by making the other person incapable of further contest. Thus, to generalize, we may say that once a breach of norm has occurred, it is a fairly common way to bring into play athletic contests or games, which reduces the field of counteraction to a definite set of rules that the community will back. If one delves into the history of European law, he will find what is called "ordeal by combat," which is no more than just this sort of reduction of an activity from the overall sphere of real life to the make-believe sphere of a game, in which everyone either does or should take the outcome of the game as the symbolic outcome of the real-life situation.

There is one other sort of concerted counteraction an Eskimo community may take: it may decide that a wrongdoer must be thrown out of the local community—either by exile or, more definitively, by execution. This state is brought about by one of two means. Either the injured party goes about and asks permission from the individual members of the community to kill the outcast, or else the informal leader of the community—either the greatest hunter or the diviner (the *angakok*) initiates the action, gets the permission from the entire community, and then proceeds to tell the closest kinsmen of the condemned man that they must carry out the execution, thus making sure that no feud will develop. Here, in an informal, unorganized way, is a situation that we may liken to a court. There is no officially recognized body of men enacting certain roles; nevertheless, here is organized community action. Let us call such a group a "moot" and save the word "court" for organized bodies responsible to officials in a statelike social organization. The word "moot" is an ancient Anglo-Saxon word for a group of men of the community in a sort of town meeting. It leans on community consensus. A court is a specialized and duly constituted body, appointed by the state.

TROBRIAND LAW

The law of the Trobriand Islands (Malinowski, 1926; Hoebel, 1954, Chapter 8) provides further examples of the various types of counteraction. Most torts and some crimes are counteracted by self-help. A sorcerer caught in the act of performing sorcery can be summarily killed in counteraction. There is always the possibility, however, that the victim of self-help counteraction will be considered by his kinsmen to have been unjustly killed, and hence a feud will be started. There are, within Trobriand society, recognized means by which feuds can be brought to an end—and here we find a development that is not found among Eskimos: Trobrianders pay, and in some circumstances accept, bloodwealth. We are not, unfortunately, told very much about how the bloodwealth is paid. Who brings the kinsmen of the killer and those of his victim together? How is the feud actually closed? These questions are not answered. The important point, however, is this: the counteraction of self-help is recognized, but there are also methods known to control it. Among the Eskimo, self-help is likely to get out of hand. Among the Trobrianders, if it threatens to get out of hand, the community can, one way or another, enforce an ending to the incipient feud.

Indeed, Americans and Europeans recognize self-help, but have rather stringent means for coping with it if it gets out of hand.

Next, there is resort to contest. Breaches of norm can be turned into contests in which quantities of yams are displayed and ritually given to one's enemy, who must either give an equivalent return or else win the contest (and hence the dispute) by topping it. If he fails to make an equivalent return, he automatically loses the contest. In either case, the whole thing is likely to lead to wholesale brawling and fighting, or even to war between the two communities.

The Eskimo community had no real political organization, and certainly no state based on hierarchal ranking. The Trobriand Island group, however, forms a series of small states, and—just as all Melanesians—Trobrianders are among the most rank conscious people in the world. Therefore, they do not resort to town meetings or opinion polls to settle disputes, because of the fact that to do so would be to override the authority of the paramount chief. However, the paramount chieftaincies are not institutionalized in such a way that they can appoint or act as a functioning court. Professor Hoebel, quite rightly, stigmatizes the Trobrianders as having a very poorly developed system of law, even when they have the wherewithal to make a good one. They have, he finds, little talent for law, even as compared with the Eskimo. What the Trobriand Islands show us, then, is a society with a sort of state—for the chiefs and paramount chiefs do form a hierarchy and they are definitely territorially limited. The tiny village states do indeed form the warring units. However, the element of rank has introduced a new problem in how to achieve the settlement of disputes, and the Trobrianders have not been successful in finding a way to get around it. The state, *per se,* does not assure law and order, for it may be based primarily on religious ideas and notions of rank. It is only an organization that *may create* devices by means of which law and order can be achieved. Sometimes it does the job efficiently and sometimes it does not. As Professor Hoebel reads Malinowski, the Trobriand Islands are full of unresolved disputes and the Trobriand state cannot, in this regard, be considered very efficient. It has not solved its own problems of law and order to its own satisfaction.

THE EXAMPLES OF AFRICAN LAW

The last two examples are to be taken from Africa, where some of the most highly developed systems of law in the non-Western world are to be found. We shall take one set of examples from the Tiv, who have a relatively primitive legal system, for Africa, and then note briefly the court system of the Lozi, who have a highly developed and formalized legal system.

The Tiv, just as other people, often utilize self-help. The most stark example that came to my attention was that in which Gu dealt with a thief (Bohannan, 1957, p. 121). In this case, a man named Kuvishar, who was the distant kinsman of the wife of one of Gu's half brothers, had come for a visit. During the night he slipped into one of the huts of the compound and made off with some cloth and a few pence in cash. As he was sneaking out of the compound, he was detected. Gu himself chased Kuvishar almost four miles, caught him, tied him up, and brought him back to the compound. He left him tied to a tree and spent the day teasing him, and encouraging all passers-by to look at him and to join in the general abuse. Gu's half brother, the husband of the kinswoman of Kuvishar, finally persuaded Gu to release the culprit. Gu kept most of the personal property and clothing that belonged to Kuvishar, as well as that which he had stolen, and chased him on his way.

Such is the common Tiv way of dealing with thieves who are caught in the act of stealing, with some other petty criminals, and with adulterers. Disputes of a noncriminal nature are, however, sometimes reduced to contest. One of the most vivid contests occurred when a dispute arose between Torgindi and Mtswen (Bohannan, 1957, pp 142-144). Mtswen's ward had been married to a son of Torgindi, and when the marriage proved to be unsuccessful there was some difficulty about getting the bridewealth refunded. Thereupon, Torgindi hired a songwriter and brewed beer; he gave a party at which the songwriter taught his songs—scurrilous attacks on the behavior of Mtswen—to the guests. They were sung loud, long, and lustily into the night. Everyone in the countryside could hear, including Mtswen. Mtswen did the only thing that an honorable man could do under the circumstances—he too hired a songwriter and began to brew beer and give parties in direct competition to those of Torgindi. This situation continued for more than three weeks with parties every night. Both Torgindi and Mtswen were spending all their money and subsistence. The consensus of the local people was that the dispute would undoubtedly have led to an outbreak of fighting had it not been that the government chief and his appointed judges stepped in and brought the matter to a close by adjudging the case between the two men at the same time that they judged the quality of the songs and entertainment. It is noteworthy that the man who won the prize for entertainment lost the case. Here the officials who properly formed a court acted as a restraining influence on the institution which Tiv know as "drumming the scandal."

Tiv not only resort to self-help and to the contest, but they also settle many of their disputes by means of a moot. The moot, as we have seen, is not a court—it is not made up of officials, but rather is a consensus of the community. Among Tiv it is a gathering, similar to a town meeting, of one's neighbors and peers. Moots are common in Tivland and are attended by all those elders who are able to break away from other duties. Some communities have as many as two or three moots a week; others, especially those with stronger informal leadership, have relatively fewer.

I one day walked into the compound of Ornyiman, just as a moot was about to begin. It seems that Ornyiman, a vastly conceited, rich, and successful man of about forty-five, who had seventeen wives, had seen a young girl whom he thought would do very nicely for an eighteenth wife. He dispatched his eldest son, a lad of twenty, with £8 cash in his pocket for bridewealth, to get the girl and bring her back. When the young man arrived, the girl in question had already married; but he settled down, courted another, and let the second girl believe he was marrying her for himself. After several weeks a marriage took place between Ornyiman's son and the girl; the marriage was consummated. When Ornyiman's son returned to the compound, Ornyiman refused to accept the fact that the son, previously unmarried, had married himself a wife instead of returning with the eighteenth wife for the father. Ornyiman claimed that this girl should be rightfully his own wife. The son denied having consummated the "marriage," although the girl insisted that he did so. Elders of the community were brought in and a settlement was achieved—it might almost be said that a settlement was rammed through by Ornyiman, much the strongest personality of the group. Most of the elders thought that Ornyiman should give this girl to his son as wife, thereby settling the matter to the satisfaction of all save Ornyiman. Ornyiman, however, was adamant; eventually he carried the day. The elders who had come to the moot signaled their concurrence in the outcome by carrying out the rituals that ceremonially separted the young man from the girl and allowed her to become Ornyiman's wife.

There were no further institutions of counteraction to be found among the Tiv until effective occupation by the British in the early twentieth century. The British established courts. That is to say, they appointed a hierarchy of officials who had the specific task of hearing disputes and creating an institution in which settlement could be achieved. The personnel of the courts was made up of the government-appointed chief of an area, the three or four representatives of other lineages within the greater lineage forming the political unit, and a more or less literate clerk who took rough notes and kept the books for receipt and dispersal of court fees and fines. These courts were supposed to meet once a month, but actually did so every six weeks to two months. There were about fifty of these courts in Tivland, called "Grade D native courts" by the British administration. The Grade D courts actually drained most of the disputes that had formerly been settled by self-help, by games, and many of those that would have been settled by moots. However, since the courts could not deal with situations of withchcraft (it was then criminal in Nigeria to bring a charge of witchcraft unless "proof" could be adduced), and since it was considered highly immoral to bring close kinsmen to court, the moots continued to flourish for some purposes.

There were indigenous courts in some parts of the African continent, however. Some of the most highly developed (and best described) were those of the Bantu peoples of southern and central Africa. There the bench is made up of a panel of chiefs that reaches as many as twenty, or even more, and represents all the sectors of the community, however that community may be organized. The dispute is heard by this large group of judges. The litigants present their cases, the witnesses their evidence. The judges, meanwhile, have been seated in a row, with the senior judge, who is usually also the chief, in the middle. The next senior is at his right, the next at his left. And so it goes, by alternate sides, until the most junior men are at each end of the row.

When the evidence in a case is all in, the most junior judge pronounces a sentence. His sentence is followed by that of his immediate senior at the other end, who takes into consideration everything that has been said by the first judge, and again, by the immediately next senior, and so it goes up the line. The litigants are given moral lectures: the rights and wrongs not only of the parties to the dispute, but of everyone else who had anything to do with the matter, are spelled out in detail. Finally, what that particular judge regards as a suitable solution is stated. The last judge is the chief, who sits in the middle. He has before him, when he gives his judgment, the will of the community, expressed in detail by the community's representatives. The final judgment, given by the chief on the basis of evidence and the judgment of his associates, stands. The only thing left to be accomplished is to obtain the concurrence of the principals to the dispute. That concurrence is almost always forthcoming when they, too, have heard all of the judgments. The fullest description of a court of this sort is that given of the Lozi by Gluckman (1954), in which there is extended description and analysis of the court, and several scores of cases reported fully.

We are now in a position to re-examine the diagram of the sequence of legal events. We can see that counteractions are of many types, some of which we have explored. We can also see that the initial act demands two conditions: a norm and an act that breaches it. We can see also that there are several types of correction, the two most common being restitution and retribution (or penalty).

TABLE 14 METHODS OF INSTITUTIONALIZING LEGAL ACTION

BREACH OF NORM →	COUNTERACTION →	CORRECTION
Norms and axioms behind norms	Types of counteraction:	Restitution
	Self-help	Retribution (penalty)
	Contest or ordeal	Fines (including bloodwealth)
	Moot or town meeting	Prisons
	Court	Excommunication

Every society has a set of ideals in accordance with which it trains its people to act. Every society also recognizes that people can never live up to the norms in all situations, and that sometimes the norms are of such stringent moral main that nobody can live up to them. Therefore, in addition to the norms themselves, every society presents us with certain allowable deviations from the norms. The approved deviations are a sort of "gray area" between the ideal and the punishable. Some societies have a very narrow gray area--they demand rigid compliance with high ideals. Other societies have relatively more leeway—they do not demand such rigid compliance, and the ideals themselves may be less uncompromising. A comparative study of the demands that different cultures put on the necessity for living up to the ideals would be of great interest.

It is also noteworthy that societies differ vastly in the sort of punishment they mete out to wrongdoers. So far as I am aware, there is no modern cross-cultural study of punishment. It is becoming obvious that, although legal anthropology has made a good beginning, there are vast unexplored areas in this universal of human behavior.

CRIME

Perhaps no single topic so cries out for cross-cultural comparison as does the whole problem of crime. As is the case in all breaches of norm, there must be two conditions present in order for a crime to exist: there must be an action, and there must be some sort of mechanism for socially defining that act as wrong and for correcting it once it has been committed.

There are two main areas that the comparative study of crime must deal with. First of all, we must compare the acts different cultures brand as crime. It is undoubtedly true that there are some acts which are, at least in some circumstances, universally declared to be wrong, against the law, and criminal in that they excite counteraction and correction. There has been little cross-cultural study of the universality of such acts, however; there has been even less study of the interpretation that might be provided for them in the cultures concerned. It is an interesting fact that if Americans are asked to make lists of the ten most serious crimes, only about a quarter of them—but the proportion increases as age of the sample rises—remember to include the crimes against the state, treason and sedition. The crimes Americans consider most heinous are crimes against the body; most lists of serious crime begin with murder. They proceed from there to various forms of assault, rape, armed robbery, and only later come to crimes against property. Americans claim that all peoples find killing wrong. Such a statement is true in some senses, but it should be added that there are certain areas in even their own culture in which killing is not considered wrong. When the agent of homicide is the "state" and when the homicide occurs after what is called "due process of law"—that is to say, when the killing is an execution—we do not deny that it is legitimate and "correct" for society to carry it out. There are, of course, groups of people within our society who have strong moral convictions that homicide by the state is morally and religiously wrong, and believe that capital punishment as a form of correction should be abandoned; these people want to change the legitimacy of execution. Yet, until they are successful, the fact is that our society does carry out legal executions; so do most others. Within the multicentric institution of warfare, further, killing another human being is by definition not culpable. There may be other practices, several of them religious as is the case with head hunting and human sacrifice, in which homicide is not culpable.

It is undoubtedly true that all of the societies of the world have greater or smaller reaches in which homicide is not a culpable crime—that is to say, in which the act of killing another person is not followed by a counteraction. In short, although the taking of human life may be a universal prohibition, nevertheless in most of the societies of the world there are circumstances in which the prohibition can be—or even must be—set aside.

The other range of comparative problems involves a discussion of the type of social situation to which a significant proportion of members of the society react by committing crimes. Again, it is probably most vividly explained if we take the act of homicide. Homicide occurs with greater or lesser frequency in all societies. That is to say, so far as we know there are some situations in all societies to which at least some of the members react by the commission of homicide. However, the circumstances in which homicide is committed vary extensively from one society to another. In a study carried out in seven African tribes, and comparisons made of them with European and American samples, it was discovered that Africa, containing primary kinship-oriented societies, exhibits a low incidence of homicide, but that nevertheless a very large proportion involves killing kinsmen (Bohannan, 1960). Such a conclusion might have been foretold because people can commit homicide—homicide might be called the definitive social relationship—only in those situations in which they most commonly find themselves. It is unlikely that Americans, who give so relatively little of their time to kinship groups, and among whom retreat from all kinship groups save that based on marriage is so easy, would commit major homicide within any kinship groups save the nuclear family. Yet in the African sample of seven tribes, one of the most striking discoveries was that even when the vast majority of victims were kinsmen of their killers, only two relationships of victim to killer were found in all seven of the samples: all the tribes had instances in which the victims were wives and at least one in which the victim was a full brother. Some tribes killed their father's brothers with regularity, others not at all; some tribes killed mothers with startling frequency, others rarely or never.

The point is that every society exhibits different cultural situations of tension. It is in situations of tension, in which people cannot gain the ends they (and usually the other subscribers to their cultural values) have come to desire, that crimes are committed. If the juvenile and adult criminals in the Western world were able to reach the point of prosperity, status, and satisfaction that is deemed a suitable goal for human endeavor, and reach it by noncriminal means, most would not employ criminal means. The ends that most criminals have in view are ends that the society cherishes. It is the means of reaching these ends that society condemns. There are, of course, criminals in our society, and probably in all others, who commit crimes precisely because their goal is to commit a crime. They want to flout the mores and the laws of their society for one or another psychic reason. Again, a comparative study is badly needed. We would like to know just which crimes, committed in just what ways, are characteristic of different societies and to take the rates and instances so discovered for comparison against what is known of the social structure and the cultural values of the cultures concerned.

One other factor should be noted. Americans and other predominantly Judeo-Christian nations have a tendency to believe that crime is something that not only should be, but ultimately can be, wiped out. Social scientists must nevertheless remind them that although it is the duty of every good citizen of every culture to live so as to reduce the rates, it is also true that were crime totally to disappear, the Kingdom of Heaven would have been achieved, and there would be not merely crimelessness, but also lawlessness. In order for crime to be nonexistent, law must be nonexistent. The moral values and related laws of the community, were it possible for everyone to live up to them, would either be so low and depredatory as to make social life a misery, or would become the "average behavior" upheld by new ideal norms.

We all know that ideal norms, by their very nature, are signposts to conduct. As conduct grows better—that is, as we come closer to living up to our ideal norms—then morals and ideal norms become more precise and more demanding. As conduct grows worse—that is, as we get further from living up to ideal norms—either the "crime rate" rises or else the margin of permissible deviation widens. We say that the crime rate in America has risen—indeed it has. We must also realize that in the process those acts considered crimes have created a situation much more restrictive on behavior. We demand more of our people today than we did at the end of the nineteenth century. Such is undoubtedly of good and real benefit to the culture and the people concerned, in the folk evaluation. From the standpoint of the social analyst, however, it must be seen as a shift in the position of the ideal norm and of the permissive margin, as well as a mere rise in the crime rate.

Probably there is no situation in which the values and the moral and ideal standards of a community are so vividly expressed as they are in the counteractions to criminal activities. In such cases the norm that is desired and the limits of allowed deviation are constantly reiterated within the institutions of counteraction and correction. We know just what the morality of a community may be only when that morality is specifically overstepped. It is necessary for us to achieve a clear statement of demanded behavior and of the sanctions that are brought into play when that demanded behavior is not forthcoming. We all know, and we sometimes bewail, the fact that law follows instead of precedes an outbreak of outrageous acts. The case of the perjured television "experts" of 1959 is a case in point. These people were, in one sense (whatever their moral position), not at variance with the law—they did not disobey the existing law until they perjured themselves before grand juries. There was no law covering their admittedly immoral conduct until *after* they had committed the acts and roused the nation to a pitch which assured that in the future such acts would be illegal. The outrage that the American public felt over being "cheated" by people they considered of high intelligence (never to be confused with moral excellence) resulted in a set of laws which now make it a criminal offense to perform the very acts that they performed: receiving advance information about questions on television quiz shows. A new era had entered American life—the era of television. The law had to be reconsidered and reconstructed so that the morality of American life could be applied to it and, in some instances, legal sanctions also applied. The courts and the legislators stepped in and established new applications of the basic, underlying postulates of the American sense of "fair play." Precisely the same exercise had been carried out when basketball became a widely admired sport—the laws had to be worked out on the basis of acts that, not then illegal, nevertheless outraged the "feelings" of the people. Intellectual games entered the same arena as athletic games—in both cases the American people, in applying their morality to them, had first to tell themselves that their moral standards were going to the dogs.

Obviously, morality constantly changes, and the degree of deviation constantly changes. Both morality and deviation change more or less in accord with the rest of the culture. What is criminal changes constantly. Yet we know perfectly well that crime is not only universal, but that it is necessary to the growth and indeed even the maintenance of ordered society. It is equally necessary that large segments of the population of every society devote a certain part of their time to keeping crime within bounds of the permissible and even to reducing the "crime rate." It is only so that the morality—the basic postulates about the nature of divinity, human society, and the "good life"—is maintained, let alone extended into the new and changing areas of life.

The study of crime is most difficult to divorce from the profferment of programs to reduce crime. Criminology is one of the areas in which the social scientists have been least successful. The reason is that the general populace, and indeed the criminologists and even the anthropologists themselves, think that the social scientists ought to be able to tell them how to reduce the incidence of crime, when as a matter of fact such is probably impossible—certainly until a better theoretical basis for criminal activities is established. That basis comes in learning the psychological and cultural reasoning that leads people to perform acts which are breaches of the norms their cultures establish and strive to maintain.

It may be that norms are impossible to maintain, if on some occasions they are *not* broken. It would seem that certain norms demand certain crime rates, even to gain lip service. It would seem that the free-enterprise system (or any other) cannot exist without a certain amount of "white-collar crime." It may be that sexual morality cannot be maintained at all without a certain proportion of adultery.

The anthropological study of crime will ultimately lead us in the direction of learning about the situations in which people commit breaches of norms. The anthropological study of law will lead us to a fuller understanding of the way in which breaches of norms are handled by society, and to fuller statements of the values and clusters of values that are the postulates of the laws. The point to be studied is the various devices societies use in order to correct the breaches in the norms. We will then be able to study more fully the feedback of such counteractions and corrections onto the norms themselves, and ultimately the moral history of the societies of the world can be spread out before us, studied, and evaluated in its own terms.

DIPLOMACY AND WARFARE

We have been discussing the ways in which a unicentric power system can be organized to carry out its law and to maintain its norms by keeping violence within bounds. We have now come to another and more difficult problem, which is the ways and means that are open to multicentric systems for keeping the use of violence within control and using it for its own purposes rather than letting it go uncontrolled. It is also possible to see at this point that the multicentric system is analogous in some ways to the social relationship, whereas the unicentric system is analogous in some ways to the personaliy. The state (to take its simplest form) is, in its internal organization, a unicentric system and although it is made up of a complex of relationships, social groups, and subcultures, it is possible through custom, writing, and many other devices to create common understandings to which almost all of the citizens of the state can subscribe—multicentrism can be, in short, reduced to a two-party system that argues about details and tactics rather than about ultimate goals and grand strategy.

The state as a unit in a multicentric system must face an additional problem: not only must it work out its own cultural interpretation of situations, norms, and acts. It must also cope with another, more or less equivalent "state," which has quite different cultural interpretations of those same situations, norms, and acts. The stateless societies we examined in the last chapter are examples of multicentric systems reduced to a small, neighborhood scale. The lineage system based on the principle of segmental opposition is one way in which the units in multicentric systems can control their own activities. There are, however, many other sorts of multicentric systems, and as nineteenth-century European history proves, kinship behavior and alliances will not settle international problems above a certain level of size and beyond a narrow range of sort.

The problem in a multicentric power system is always one of communication—just as the problem in a social relationship is always one of communication between the persons playing the roles that define that relationship. Indeed, the problem can be reduced to one of translation. The first task—the task of diplomacy—is to translate one cultural idiom into another, at the same time that the case for one's own cultural values is put so strongly as to win the day. Diplomacy can, obviously, break down in two situations: if the failure of translation leads neither to common understanding nor to what has been called a "working misunderstanding," and if the success of translation makes it apparent that the goals of the two power systems are incompatible. As is the case in simple social relationships, such incompatibility can be countered in two ways: avoidance and the use of force.

One of the necessary elements in a multicentric system is for the units involved to create sufficient complementary expectations that they can begin to know when they are discussing the same thing, so that they can have common (or at least symbiotic) ends in view, and so they can know that they are indeed not communicating. This is probably the greatest single problem faced by the modern West, but it is faced by most other societies as well. On the personal level, the earliest "cures" for faulty social relationships began in the psychic sphere, with psychoanalysis. Only later in its development did psychoanalysis begin to spread out and do something about the social situation that created and perpetuated the psychic problems. Similarly, in the sphere of international relations the first steps have been taken in terms of the state and not in terms of the international relationship itself. Again, the point is a simple one and is now being reinforced at a new level: when relationships are involved, rather than integrations of unitary elements (which of course may themselves be seen from another angle in terms of relationships), the key lies in the two centers of appreciation or awareness of the situation. These two centers of awareness must be able to communicate with each other. They must be able to *know* whether or not their thought and their goals and aims do in fact coincide or whether they are at variance. Only when such is known is it possible to build a structure that enables everybody to get more or less what he wants, or at least to know what he is fighting about.

Diplomacy has taken a tremendous ribbing over the last few centuries; it has been characterized as "the art of saying nothing" or "heaping lie upon lie under the camouflage of charm." In some cases, undoubtedly, there are diplomats who are experts at telling lies under a charming exterior. But to stigmatize the entire activity in such a way is to misunderstand it. To understand it, the notion "lies" must be examined. It is difficult to say what a lie is, even within a single culture. There are, of course, fairly clear-cut cases—when children tell fibs about cookie jars, it is possible to say with some degree of assurance that a "lie" has in fact been told. But the moment greater sophistication enters in, the ambiguity inherent in words and social situations is such that "lies" must be examined by more complex, culturally defined criteria. If the culturally defined criteria of lies in the centers of a multicentric system are sufficiently similar, only then is it possible to agree on what lies are. Only if there is some degree of accordance in the use of language, in aims, in goals, and in means is it possible to make any kind of sensible definition about truth and about lies.

Diplomats, therefore, have the problem that they often "talk past one another." Although they talk, there is little common ground for communication—there are few common understandings. Personally, many diplomats know that such is the case; personally, they are sometimes able to discuss many factors with their "opposite numbers" in the multicentric system and to reach a degree of common understanding (which is not the same thing as agreement). Their achievement however tends to be vastly diluted by the time it is fed back into the official culture, not to mention the popular culture, of the states that make up each unit in the multicentric system. The understanding, if it demands any great degree of self-awareness, is almost impossible to communicate back. Therefore, many of the "lies" of the diplomat obviously come out in the *interpretation* of the diplomat's activities—particularly the diplomat from the other side. Therefore, even if communication is achieved by diplomats, feedback into the unicentric national state is often not achieved.

Diplomacy is therefore a thankless job. Even when the cultures of the two centers are very close together or even all but identical, diplomacy is a thankless task because it gets involved with the egocentric, ethnocentric in-group desires and cupidities of each of the centers, as a unicentric group. Indeed, they may understand each other only too well.

Now, where diplomacy fails, either warfare or isolation must take over. In the case of isolation, the units in the multicentric system cease to interact, and hence the system ceases to exist. In the case of warfare, there is a range of common understandings presented by the nature of the war and the nature of the violence. Warfare is, obviously, one of the most simplistic forms of social relationships; its common understandings are few but definite. In most situations of warfare, however, there is need for communication between the warring parties in addition to mere violence. Kinsmen of both sides are common "go betweens" or peacemakers in warfare. In modern warfare, neutral nations are vital links in the chain—if Switzerland did not exist, she would have to be invented.

Ultimately, the war or even the isolation, must cease—in spite of the fact that warfare may provide normative relationships between two societies over a long period of time, even though it may be universally disapproved as such.

It is now possible to see that there are three sets of activities that form a series and are as characteristic of a multicentric system as is the similar set of three activities characteristic of a unicentric system. First of all, there is a breach. However, in the case of the multicentric system, the breach is not so much one of norm as it is one of relationships. The norms may well be differently conceived on the two sides. It may be that neither group breaches its own norm, but that each may breach the norm of the other. It is the communication and agreement that break down. The breakdown in communication may be either purposeful or nonpurposeful. It may be that the breakdown in communication cannot be avoided because the people do not know that they are not communicating. It may equally well be, however, that the breakdown in communication is a purposeful one—people decide to stop talking and this is the time to start fighting or merely go away.

The second act in this series of three acts characteristic of relationships in multicentric power systems, can be called the counteraction. There are two types of counteraction in multicentric systems: one is in the isolation that we have already discovered; the second is in warfare.

Warfare, as we have seen, is an intense type of social relationship—it is also a limited type. It is the only means of maintaining a multicentric system in the absence of communication and minimal agreement. It is itself a sort of agreement. In many societies of the world, the rules of warfare are so pronounced as to make the warfare seem a game. We can indeed see that warfare is, like a game or a gladiatorial contest, a means of reducing the field so that the outcome within a limited range of activity can be applied to a greater or even a total range of activity.

The return of the activity to a wider scope—the setting of the result of the game back into total social focus—can be seen as the prototype of the third set of activities: the re-establishment of relationships after warfare can be carried out by creation of peace treaties or similar types of agreement. The re-establishment can be made on the old basis, or it can be made on a new basis. One or the other of the two parties to the multicentric relationship may be more dominant, or dominate differently, in the common understandings of the resultant system.

Modern twentieth-century warfare is, if not unique, at least rare in the sense that it involves the total society and an absolute minimum of rules commonly understood by both sides—the game element is minimal in "total war." The ultimate goals of the two parties tend to be diametrically opposed, but their immediate goals to be precisely the same—destruction of the other. The combination of these two facets—the total involvement of society and the breakdown of communication and common understanding—has given modern warfare the characteristics that we recognize.

TABLE 15 EVENT SEQUENCES IN MULTICENTRIC SYSTEMS

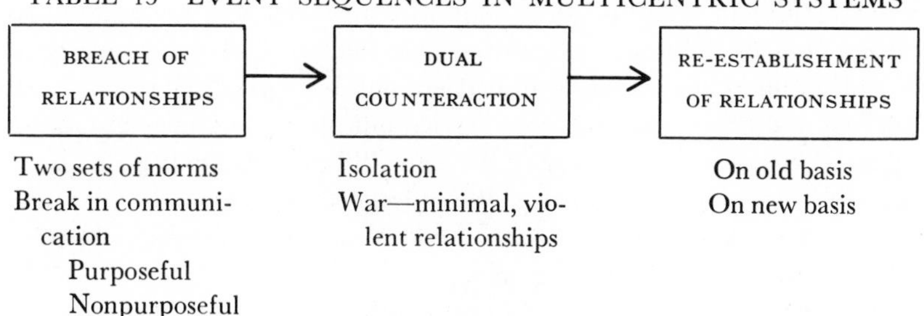

The necessary requirement in understanding warfare is to note that war is a type of relationship leading to a given mode of the multicentric system of political organization—the mode based on violence and minimal communication. There are many types of war, as there are many types of counteracting institutions within the unicentric systems. There are some places in which the war is decided by warriors in contest, and the major parts of the societies are not concerned. There are wars fought by whole communities—mobs in violence. There are wars fought by specialist bodies, called armies. Most North American Indian societies were typified by the first kind of fighting: the exploits of warriors were considered a dominant value in the culture; fighting usually involved only a few people, and consisted in rather loosely organized raids in which young men were given a chance to shine. They then came home, counted coup, and were rewarded with the best women of the tribe. The Comanche are the archetype of such a system of warfare (Hoebel and Wallace, 1952). The raids were sometimes pretty deadly, but often they were not, in their inception, much more than mere aggrandizement of the warriors. The fact that they occurred set the tone and the idiom of the political relationships between tribes—yet their purpose was never to aim at a "just peace" under "our control."

Much "primitive" warfare is of this type. In New Guinea, for example, the main point of much fighting is acquisition of heads, which are needed in religious and prestige ceremonies. In fact, some tribes live in a constant state of enmity with their neighbors and take each other's heads as a regular thing. It may be unwise to call this sort of situation warfare; it is merely a violent social relationship with what seems to us and probably to them an antisocial sort of expression. War is, on the other hand, a contest having as its aim a peace in which the balance of power is shifted. Chronic raiding in New Guinea or among North American Indians is not warfare in this sense—the relationship of enmity is the permanent one and is the end to be maintained.

"True warfare," if we may call it such, is a somewhat different business. It has as its end peaceful settlement with new political conditions, not continuation of fighting. And obviously, when we find it, we are going to find societies in which it is carried out by specialist bodies called "armies" and others in which it is carried out by whole bodies of citizens. In fact, there is here something of the same difference as that between the moot and the court. It is, in fact, the difference between a lynching mob and an army. A lynching mob is a mode of a community; an army is a specialist organization within a state.

The army, as a specialist organization, has been found in many parts of the world. The Maori army has been studied intensively by Vayda (1960) ; the Zulu army was famous in the nineteenth century, and many books on the subject have been written, for all that the definitive analysis is yet to be made. We saw in the last chapter the way in which the army became the skeleton of the Ashanti state.

Comparative warfare is not well studied—a jarringly inconsistent state of affairs in an age in which war is of major concern. Like so many other social activities, the matter has been left to technicians and to moralists. Indeed, the whole multicentric power system is not well studied—the very problem has long lain camouflaged under nineteenth-century ideas about the "balance of power." Our need to know was never so intense.

CONTRACT AND INTERNATIONAL RELATIONS

Contract is, as we have seen, an agreement between persons who were not previously in relationship (or whose previous relationship is irrelevant to the contract). Because the terms of the social relationship determined by contract are usually minimal—that is, they cover a small area of life as compared to relationships based on kinship or community or even rank—extensive contract demands, for its enforcement, some sort of external agency of the sort that we call political. Only in the presence of a firm, stable, and powerful political agency can a law of contract be highly developed. In fact, contract and stability of the state reinforce one another.

Contract is, in short, a type of multicentric social system; ultimate enforcement of its agreements falls on an agency outside the multicentric system. International relationships exhibit a precise analogy—they are relationships in a multicentric social system. The fact that there is usually not an ultimate unitary force does not make the social system the less multicentric; it merely limits the modes of expression of the relationships. One of the unsolved political problems in the world—and it is also a legal problem—is how to achieve the institutionalization of force within a multicentric system without creating an agency of authority. Champions of international governments and international civil services often say that it cannot be done. But the fact it has not yet been done—at least on the level of the nation state—may be only to say that the world awaits political genius.

The image of the unknown

part 5

18

A short history of European thought about magic, religion, and science

THERE IS PROBABLY no single subject with which anthropology concerns itself today on which the literature is larger than that on tribal religion. It is also the only anthropological subject on which there have been more than two or three monumentally original minds at work. In the field of primitive law, there is Sir Henry Maine, and a lot of lesser men. When one thinks of kinship and family, there are Morgan, Rivers, and Kroeber, and a lot of lesser men. When one thinks of primitive economics, one recalls Karl Bücher, and a lot of lesser men. But when we come to cover the subject of tribal religion, half a dozen great names spring to mind—men of the highest intellectual order: Sir Edward Tylor, Sir James Frazer, William Robertson Smith, Emile Durkheim, Lucien Lévy-Bruhl, Max Weber. These men have had lasting effects not merely in the social sciences, but in theology, in philosophy, and in the humanities. Therefore the entire subject of comparative religion, and especially of tribal religion, deals with something bigger and more complex than anything we have so far tackled.

There have been several modern attempts to straighten out the contributions of these thinkers. One of the most successful has been that of Evans-Pritchard (1933a; 1933b). Obscurely published, it is nevertheless the clearest and most economical statement of the contributions of the great scholars; this chapter will lean heavily on his insights. The basic problem Evans-Pritchard and the other writers who have attempted the same task have had to face squarely is that the men who made the greatest contributions to our earlier thought about tribal religions were not themselves ethnographers—they did not know tribal peoples at firsthand. They therefore worked, in most cases, with questionable data, without always being able to question it thoroughly enough. Moreover, their modes of arranging the data into shapes that allowed of comparison gave rise to categories which the nonspecialists who followed them insisted on understanding as data instead of as theory. Perhaps the best-known example is to be found in the term "animism." Tylor, as we shall see, coined this term to explain a series of activities and overt ideas that he found in the data presented by travelers and missionaries. The word has, almost from the first, been misunderstood by students of comparative religion who have insisted that "animism" is "a religion" in the sense that Buddhism, Islam, or Christianity are religions. "Animism" is in fact an analytical system for organizing the data of some tribal religions—it is not a folk or operational system for organizing ritual activities and their underlying "beliefs," such as Christianity is.

The result has been that the "facts" of tribal religion lie hidden in a vast morass of misunderstood theorizing that has been mistaken for fact. Therefore, if we are to comprehend the facts of tribal religion, if we are to take sensible and rational attitudes about the problems of religion and magic, and if we are to understand witchcraft rather than merely decline to believe in it (which takes no thought at all), it is necessary that the facts be separated from the theories—and such a procedure can be done only if the history of European thought on the subject is first bared so that the facts can be relieved of the stringency of interpretations that have themselves become almost superstitions.

EDWARD BURNETT TYLOR

The first great thinker in this field was Sir Edward Burnett Tylor, an English Quaker who held the first recognized university position in anthropology in the English-speaking world. His are the only studies from the period that have lasted.

Tylor published in 1871 a book called *Primitive Culture*. It is (with Morgan's work) the first great treatise on anthropology in English, and it is the first great work in any language on the subject that was then called "primitive religion and primitive thought." It deserves to be read, and it has recently been reprinted. The ideas in it are still vital to an understanding of tribal religion and magic, but unfortunately many of the people who read it do not divorce the ideas from the nineteenth-century idiom in which they are imbedded. Writers on comparative religion, especially, tend to assume that *all* of Tylor is still current. Tylor's information was for the most part of a very low order. It is the more amazing that he got so much out of it.

Tylor was typical of the nineteenth century in that he approached the problem of religion and magic from what Evans-Pritchard has called an intellectualist standpoint. He and others of his own and succeeding generations tried to answer the problems of primitive religion by examining not ideas, but individuals. With what Goode has termed "the thought mould of evolution" (1951, p. 20) fixed tightly upon them, students in the late nineteenth century sought the *origin* of religion. Darwin had made origins popular; and origins, evolution, the genetic method of explanation were all in the air and seldom adequately distinguished. Some of these students of religion sought origins in the phenomena of nature: storms, sun, sea. Others sought them in dreams; still others in the puns and ambiguities of language. As Goode has pointed out, "what is significant is that they all tried to find the origins of religion in individual experiences" (1951, p. 20).

Since the men of the nineteenth century looked within themselves for their own religious experience and knowledge, they considered it obvious that the way to discover anything about the religion of the people they called "savages" was to look within *them*. Today we realize that looking coolly within oneself is difficult enough, and that looking within someone else is probably impossible. Looking within a person from a culture exotic enough that he can be called "savage" is monumentally impossible. But these nineteenth-century men had the brashness that often comes with superficial success, and "look within savages" they certainly did.

Yet, when they "looked within savages" they saw dark reflections of themselves. Since they considered themselves to be rational men, it never occurred to them that they were imputing a very specific type of rationality to the subjects of their study. Their error was compounded because they sought origins. Therefore, they recast the ideas they found within what they considered to be a rational framework and stated the whole in a developmental sequence that was read as historical in the same sense that Darwin's *Descent of Man* could be read as an educated reconstruction of "history."

Then, sensibly enough if these premises are accepted, these students considered that they ought to be able to outline the logic—even though they recognized it to be faulty—and state the premises from which "primitive man" had arrived at his conclusions. Tylor's *Primitive Culture* stands head and shoulders above all others as the most nearly successful attempt at something ultimately impossible. Magicians, he claimed, classified things together because of their likenesses. This procedure, he also noted, was precisely that followed by modern science. However, Tylor said, the magician makes a mistake the scientist does not make: he postulates a causal connection between the things he has classified together. The favorite example of Tylor as well as others was the superstition of modern Greek peasants that gold will cure jaundice. The Greek peasant classified jaundice with gold because of their common color, and made the "mistake" of assuming that this shared attribute enabled them to react on each other.

Tylor's point, as interpreted by Evans-Pritchard, is that "the savage" fails to understand the notion of analogy: he mistakes a connection of analogy for a relationship of causality. Thus, because Tylor saw the logical error of such a procedure, he termed magic a "pernicious delusion."

Yet Tylor did see—and this we must remember and must grant him—

that magic contains a logical scheme of thought. But it is a logic of association rather than one of cause and effect. It is subjective rather than objective: qualities that are perceived similarly are assumed to have an objective similarity, or even a more intimate relationship. The error—whether it is made by "the savage" or by the man attempting to explain the savage—is seeing the analogy as cause-and-effect relationship.

Although the term had not yet been invented, we can see that Tylor charged magical thought with being a subject-object confusion. The difference between magic and science was that between a "false association" of phenomena in which the link is subjective or symbolic and an association in which the link is objective and demonstrably causal.

In the same way as Tylor distinguished magic from science—that is, by leaving the subject matter in doubt and by emphasizing the mode of perception—he also attempted to make a theoretical distinction between magic and religion: religion he reduced to his justly famous minimal definition: "the belief in Spiritual Beings." The rest of the supernatural he left to magic. Tylor thus considered together what he and his successors have all regarded as the three basic ways of looking at the world: that of science, that of magic, and that of religion.

It is interesting that Tylor wanted and kept his definitions elastic. He seems to have seen no point in rigidly distinguishing magic from religion, or either from science. He was himself a very pious man, and saw clearly that religion and science were different ways of looking at the world, that both were valid if the grounds on which they were used were valid. He did his best to distinguish them by behavioral rather than material and external criteria. But he had the whole weight of nineteenth-century "objectivity" against him that mistook such treatment for "subjectivity." He saw that there was no objective dividing line between magic and religion, or between either and science. To argue whether a given practice or statement is magic or religion is the ultimate in futility. In spite of that fact, his successors spent the next sixty years or so trying to do just that without having to refute Tylor, which was very difficult. Tylor's categories were analytical, *not* objective. Understandably, the successors had their troubles.

Tylor is today best known for his masterly definition of culture and for his "minimal definition of religion." Religion, he said, is a belief in Spiritual Beings. From this definition, he developed his main theory, which he called the theory of animism.

Animism, to put it into its simplest terms, is the attribution of soul or spirit comparable to the soul or spirit of man, to nonhuman animals, to plants, and even to things and abstract concepts. Tylor arrived at his theory of animism through wide reading and collecting of ethnographic facts, but also as a logician with an intellectualist bias. Then, succumbing to the nineteenth-century *Zeitgeist,* he sought origins and development. The result was he was led to claim that man's ideas about soul came into being by an attempt to account rationally for the phenomena of death, sleep, disease, trance, and dreams.

Thus Tylor assumed primitive man as logician and philosopher, arriving at his ideas by syllogism, but arriving at false conclusions because he started with false premises. Tylor's was a brilliant analysis, and anthropologists have since found many peoples who actually do, when questioned, *defend* their ideas in this way. They have also found "animism." But many other peoples who claim similar beliefs do *not* defend them in such a way and are not animists. We must carefully differentiate origins in the historical sense from the basic images and rationalizations by means of which people try to make their beliefs sensible to men who do not share them.

Tylor realized that if his theory was true, there must be some explanation for the fact that the "savages" who employed this sort of fallacious reasoning never saw its falseness. Why, his questioning ran, do they believe in magic when it is so manifestly false to the scientific observer? Tylor was the first to ask this question, and his answers were such that they have not since been greatly improved on. He gave five basic reasons why magic, which we on scientific grounds know to be false, does not appear so to the people who practice it:

1. Magic is associated with common-sense behavior that achieves what magic itself does not achieve.
2. Nature often achieves what magic is performed to achieve, therefore the *non sequitur* is not immediately apparent.
3. Failure is attributed to error in the prescriptions or prohibitions that accompany the rite—such matters as broken taboos and mischanted spells.
4. The magic rite may be counteracted by hostile forces; therefore if it does not work, the failure may be chalked up to the machinations of other magicians.
5. What seems to some people a failure may seem to others a partial success. One success outweighs many failures in the interpretation of the evidence: one success in six is inadequate for science, but may be sufficient to prove a magical point.

Thus Tylor contributed two great ideas to the theory of magic: first of all, the ideology and the logical quality of magic, based though it may be on false premises; and, second, an analysis of the causes that prevented magic's exposure as fraud. He may have phrased these ideas in terms of pseudohistorical development, but such a statement does not matter: magic probably did not develop in that way, but it is often practiced and communicated in that way. These two ideas of Tylor are still current precisely because they are capable of being scientifically tested. One can determine with fieldwork the logical processes involved in magical ideas and the ways in which magicians defend their failures.

Evans-Pritchard explained Tylor's notion in this way: "everywhere there is magic and science and religion . . . but in the later stages of development or in the more advanced societies magical and animistic ideas play a lesser part in the thought and behavior of men than in the earlier stages of development or in the more primitive societies" (1933a).

Evans-Pritchard also put Tylor's ideas into diagrammatic form; we have reproduced his diagram in Figure 15.

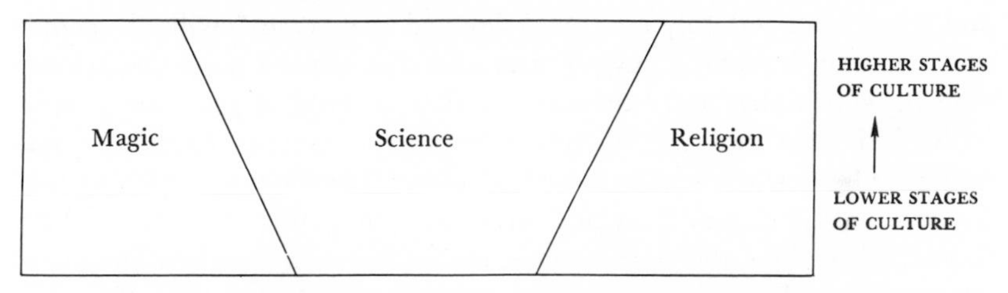

FIGURE 15 Tylor's Conceptualization of Magic, Science and Religion

J. G. FRAZER

Tylor's successor in English anthropology was Sir James Frazer, a Scotsman who wrote his own five-foot shelf, which included *The Golden Bough, Folklore in the Old Testament,* and many others. Frazer came on the heels of such men as MacLennan, Robertson-Smith and others, and was what has been called the last flower of the second Scottish Enlightenment (which had reached its climax in early editions of the *Encyclopaedia Britannica*).

Sir James, who eventually became a professor at Cambridge, was blessed with a wife who had a very able business head. She, convinced that Sir James's work was for posterity, refused his friends admittance to his study and took charge of his relations with publishers. The Frazers were a formidable team.

Sir James Frazer was an active writer from 1885 until about 1935. Reading his work, and hearing the tales of those who knew him, one gets the impression that he wrote 1750 words every day of his life and never looked at any one of them again. It is a fact that he wrote standing at his lectern, pulled up in front of the fire, between a heavy tea and time to dress for dinner. There is a calculated, regulated, scones-and-jam quality about Frazer's writing even when it is at its most exciting.

Frazer was a much less careful scholar but a much greater showman than was Tylor (whose wife was a great helpmeet but scarcely an impresario). He both popularized Tylor's theories and added some of his own. In doing so he fell into some of the more obvious traps that Tylor had successfully avoided. Sir James's hypertrophied *belles lettres* (*The Golden Bough* runs to twelve volumes) have had a tremendous influence on historians and on comparative theologians and classicists: more than any other anthropologist who ever lived.

Tylor had shown that under the ideology of magic was a false association of ideas: that analogies were seen as causal relationships. Frazer took up this idea and gave it a name. He called it the "law of sympathy." Now, Tylor had not called it a "law" at all—but Frazer did. And whereas Tylor had said that "savages" reasoned by analogy instead of by cause and effect (and certainly had never implied that some "civilized" people might not do the same thing), Frazer said that savages perceived sympathies between things and expressed the idea in terms of the "law of sympathy." He was then able to show that there were two kinds of "sympathy." There was sympathy based on observable similarity, such as that between gold and jaundice; and there was sympathy based on contact. Frazer called these the two subtypes of the law of sympathy. Therefore, he created a scheme in the form of a genealogy (1922, p. 12). (See Figure 16.)

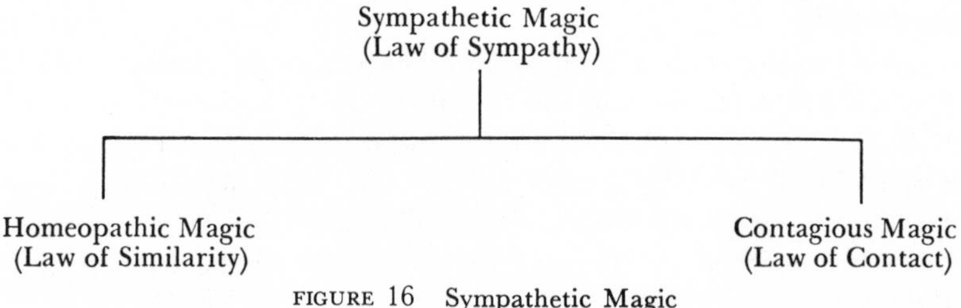

FIGURE 16 Sympathetic Magic

Now, having given a "scientific" classification (in what he considered the sense of Linnaeus' botanical classification), Sir James proceeded to tell us how these laws were "applied" by people: how they look in action. As he put it himself: "Though these laws are certainly not formulated in so many words nor even conceived in the abstract by the savage, they are nevertheless implicitly believed by him to regulate the course of nature quite independently of human will" (1922, p. 11).

This passage displays that Sir James has taken considerable liberty with the thought both of Tylor and of the "savages." He has, in fact, taken the regularities in data that he himself (aided by a deep understanding of and influence from Tylor) had perceived, and claimed that "implicitly" (which means "in Sir James's opinion") the savage "believed" in them (which means the savage did or said something that the travelers and missionaries, whom Sir James used as sources, communicated in this way).

The idea of "belief" is extremely difficult to explain cross culturally. Obviously, it is risky to say that anyone says or does one thing and "believes in" something else. The "belief" is usually a restatement by the analyst, with a confusion of data and analysis at stake.

The point Sir James was making is, however, valid if it is made in another way. When he states that the savage "thinks when he acts in a certain way [that] certain consequences will inevitably follow in virtue of one or another of these laws," he is wrong. As Evans-Pritchard succinctly reminds us, the "savage" acts as he has been taught to act. In a few cases he may explain his behavior to the foreign inquirer by statements that can be translated to one of Sir James's laws. Usually, however, he does not do even that. The law of sympathy is sensible theory—it indeed explains much. It is not, in itself, a part of "savage thought." Ideas, as expressed culture, may be—indeed, must be—studied independently of the thought processes if this particular subject-object confusion is to be avoided.

Sir James is on firm ground with another point, however: the practical aspects of magic rather than the theoretical. Magic, he points out, is a "pseudo-art" as well as a "pseudo-science." Magic as art involves action. There are, Frazer noted, two types of magical action: that designed to bring about certain ends and that designed to avoid certain ends. The first he called "sorcery" and the second he called "taboo." In his own words:

> Positive magic or sorcery says "Do this in order that so and so may happen." Negative magic or taboo says "Do not do this lest so and so should happen." The aim of positive magic or sorcery is to produce a desired event; the aim of negative magic or taboo is to avoid an undesirable one. But both consequences, desirable and the undesirable, are supposed to be brought about in accordance with the laws of similarity and contact [1919, p. 22].

Frazer's collation of sorcery and taboo into the two types of magical behavior has been widely followed. Folk explanations of both that confirm his insight are plentiful. Frazer's own analogy to science and medicine, however, stood in his way. One of the most famous passages from *The Golden Bough* runs:

> Magic is a spurious system of natural law as well as a fallacious guide of conduct; it is a false science as well as an abortive art. Regarded as a system of natural law, that is, as statement of the rules which determine the sequences of events throughout the world, it may be called Theoretical Magic; regarded as a set of precepts which human beings observe in order to compass their ends, it may be called Practical Magic. At the same time it is to be born in mind that the primitive magician knows only magic on its practical side; he never analyzes the mental processes on which his practice is based, never reflects on the abstract principle involved in his actions.

> With him, as with the vast majority of men, logic is implicit, not explicit; he reasons just as he digests his food in complete ignorance of the intellectual and physiological processes which are essential to the one operation or the other. In short, to him magic is always an art, never a science; the very idea of science is lacking in his undeveloped mind. It is for the philosophic student to trace the train of thought which underlies the magician's practice; to draw out the few simple threads of which the tangled skein is composed; to disengage the abstract principles from their concrete applications; in short, to discern the spurious science behind the bastard art [1922, pp. 11-12].

Sir James, in that oft-quoted passage, fails to take only the last step. He saw clearly that the "bastard art" is a folk image, and that the "spurious science" is an analytical restatement of it. What he failed to state sufficiently clearly is the next step: his own rules and devices—his own theory—for recognizing and analyzing the spuriousness. He failed to bisect with sufficient clarity the savage from the anthropologist. Because he did not realize the significance of this step, he went on to assume that magic is merely bad science, based on false premises and perhaps reasoned out through faulty logic. He said that, like science, it embodies the concept of the world run by "laws"—magical laws instead of natural laws, but nevertheless run by laws. There is, in magic, no necessary idea of the supervention of a spiritual or personal agency. If you perform such and such acts and do them right, and there is no countermagic afoot, then it follows that your ritual will be effective. Magic, in such a view, is part of the "natural law." It differs from science only in the validity of its premises and the provability of its results.

Religion, Frazer continued, must be separated from *both* magic and science, because it involves a different principle. According to Frazer, religion is "a propitiation or conciliation of powers superior to man which are believed to direct and control the course of nature and of human life" (1922, p. 50). As in his view of magic, he finds two elements in religion: one of belief and one of behavior. They are "a belief in powers higher than man and an attempt to propitiate or please them" (1922, p. 51).

The implications are now all before us. Science and magic take an impersonal view of the universe. Religion personifies it in the form of deity or spirit of some sort. In science, natural law is to be accommodated; in magic, natural law is to be manipulated. In religion, natural law is the rule of sentient spirits who can change it or manipulate it for the good of their favorites. We have, thus, two conflicting views of the universe: magic and science on the one hand, and religion on the other.

It is this very dualism that Tylor avoided. Tylor was much more firmly pinned to reality than Frazer, and he saw that in everyday life about him, such a scheme did not work. Frazer, locked in his study, never looked about him. Tylor, it will be remembered, said that magic, science, and religion, as he defined them, were all present everywhere, though science tended to cut off some of the territory of both religion and magic in a more sophisticated culture. Frazer, on the other hand, built hypothetical historical stages. In one of the neatest pieces of sophistry ever penned—and he has been widely read and treated as an authority on a subject in which there can be no authorities because there are no facts—Frazer claimed that magic was the oldest form of thought, that it was succeeded by religion, and that in his own and Darwin's time religion was being succeeded by science.

The way in which he did this is revealing. Magic, he said, is logically more primitive than either religion or science, because it is simpler; that is, the recognition of similarity or contiguity in things or in ideas "is not so complex as the conception of personal agents." In short, the personal agent, says Frazer, is a *tertius quid* that explains the similarity which is noted. Merely noting it is simpler than "explaining" it. Frazer cited the poor Australian aborigines as proof: he said that they were the simplest people known (a questionable statement), therefore their ideas were the oldest and nearest to original thought (first error), and that the Australians were magicians and had almost no religion at all (second error).

Now, as a matter of fact, the Australians are anything but simple, and their ideas are as old as anybody else's—or as young. However, this point did not occur to Frazer. The Australians were, to Frazer, by definition the simplest people (probably because of all "savages" they are the ones Sir James would have found it most difficult to join) because they lived by a "stone age culture." They were also magicians by definition. Frazer then buttressed his "proof" with a statement that religion varies widely in different parts of the world, whereas magic is much the same everywhere you find it. That statement can be made with a certain validity even today, but it does not follow from it, as Sir James thought, that magic therefore was "older" and hence more fundamental than religion.

Having thus to his own satisfaction established the "fact" that magic was older than religion, Frazer asked himself what people of his age considered the next sensible question: What "mental" change occurred in the shift from an exclusive belief in magic to a belief in religion? His conjectural answer was that intelligent people began to rise above the limitations of magic and to see that it did not in fact work. Rather than leave themselves in a chaotic world of unpredictable caprice, they postulated "beings, like themselves, who directed the course of nature" and turned their attentions to placating these beings.

We in this age want to go on and ask what happened to the switchover from religion to science that Frazer postulated. It is interesting that Frazer, writing just after the turn of the century, felt no need to mention it: it was, the implications seem to be, well known by his readers. This oversight is one of the most puzzling to be found in Frazer's work.

Professor Evans-Pritchard has set Frazer's theory into a diagram of magic, religion, and science (Figure 17) to be compared with that which he created to summarize the theories of Tylor (see Figure 15).

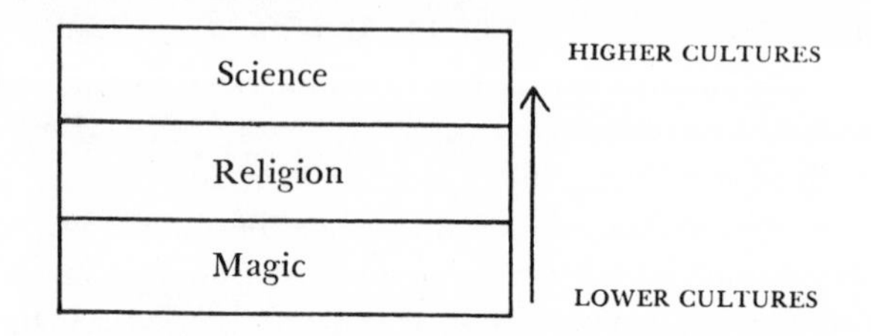

FIGURE 17. Frazer's View of Magic, Science, and Religion

Evans-Pritchard's criticism of Frazer is succinct and revealing:

> The apparent futility of Frazer's analogy between science and magic is due to the fact that he sees both as modes of thinking and not as learnt modes of technical behavior with concomitant speech forms. If he had compared a magical rite in its entirety with a scientific performance in its entirety instead of comparing what he supposes to go on in the brain of a magician with what he supposes to go on in the brain of a scientist he would have seen the essential difference between science and magic. This difference is most strikingly shown in the experimental standpoint on the two modes of behavior. Science experiments and is open to experience and ready to make adjustments in its notions of reality whereas magic is relatively non-experimental and the magician is impervious to experience, as science understands the terms, since he employs no methods for testing or control [1933a].

He clinches his point by noting that Frazer was also wrong in comparing the science of one society with the magic of another: better he compare the empirical behavior with the magical behavior within a single society, or the magical behavior in two.

EMILE DURKHEIM AND LUCIEN LEVY-BRUHL

The main difficulty in all of the early work in the matter of religious and magical ideas is that the early scientists confused ideas with the actual vicissitudes of thinking. We are still interested in ideas, as they are spoken or acted out. Investigation of the processes of thinking has long since been taken over by special branches of science. Ideas, as expressed, can be treated scientifically, as if they were things. Thought, on the other hand, is a biochemical activity that we are scarcely on the brink of understanding. It is the achievement of Emile Durkheim that he took out the "mind" or "thought" of the "savage" and left us with a usable means of dealing with the ideas. There was, however, one other great hurdle that had to be got over before his theories could be understood: the imaginings of another famous Frenchman, Lucien Lévy-Bruhl. Lévy-Bruhl's work became widely known in the English-speaking world before Durkheim's, at least in part because it fitted in with the assumptions of Tylor and Frazer about "primitive man as philosopher." His best-known book is *How Natives Think* (1926).

Lévy-Bruhl, like Durkheim, was his own worst enemy. He insisted on hiding his ideas under a bushel of dross and verbiage. Again I have leaned heavily on the critical analyses of Evans-Pritchard (1933b), in large part because they are almost the only critiques available that both denounce the nonsense to be found in Lévy-Bruhl and extract the usable ideas and the wisdom. I must admit that Lévy-Bruhl makes more sense to Evans-Pritchard than he does to me, and I believe that many of the ideas attributed by him to Lévy-Bruhl are in fact his own. But since his reading gives Lévy-Bruhl the greatest possible advantage of every doubt, it is the one I prefer.

In spite of the fact that Lévy-Bruhl still studied the thoughts of individuals, he did it for a different purpose than did Frazer, for he brought in the determinism of culture in a more sophisticated way. Lévy-Bruhl acknowledged that "the mental content of the individual is derived from, and explained by, the collective representations [read "culture"] of his society" and insisted that "these collective representations are functions of institutions" of the society. He was thus well on the way to studying ideas rather than "thought."

Lévy-Bruhl's best-known work is a series of comparisons between "us" (Westerners) and "them" (primitive peoples). The results are foregone, but he expressed them colorfully. Westerners, in the comparison, appeared logical and scientific; if we are religious, we say that mystical influences can affect the working order of the universe. The primitive peoples, on the other hand, appeared to focus on the mystical rather than the logical. After making this observation many times and documenting it with hundreds of examples, Lévy-Bruhl confused the entire issue by equating the mystical turn of mind with "prelogical" thought.

The term "prelogical" is undoubtedly one of the worst word choices a term-mongering social scientist ever made.

What Lévy-Bruhl meant by prelogical was prescientific, and his theories would have been much better treated had he said so. Scientific and logical seem to have meant much the same to him, and he defined "logical" and "prelogical" quite carefully. But the power of the word being what it is, prelogical meant to most readers and critics—even that minority who read the definitions carefully—the same as if he had said unlogical or illogical. It could, so read, be denied quite rightly on all sides—and Lévy-Bruhl was damned by everyone who read him this way: which included most English-speaking anthropologists until about 1940, when they began to read Lévy-Bruhl himself instead of what people had written about him.

Prelogical does not mean incoherent. It merely means that some ideas do not accord with the rules of logic as philosophers have determined them; especially do they contain inherent contradictions. Evans-Pritchard has pointed out that no place did Lévy-Bruhl indicate he considered the savage intellectually inferior.

The really tremendous step forward that Lévy-Bruhl made was that he was talking about the content of thought, which he clearly separated from the psycho-physical processes of thought as Tylor and Frazer had not. He dealt with the ideas held by the bulk of the members of a society—what he called the "collective representations" and what most mid-twentieth-century American anthropologists would subsume under "values." They are collective because they are ways of viewing institutions so that behavior can be meshed.

Now, obviously, if "prelogical" ideas are socially determined in this way, so must "scientific" ideas be socially determined. It thus becomes possible to ask whether in fact the ideas held in "primitive societies" (whatever that may be made to mean) are in fact mystically oriented whereas ideas of "civilized societies" are scientifically oriented. Such a question is answerable only if by "scientific" we mean subject to a given type of validation and "proof." Most of the ideas of any society are not subject to this sort of "proof"—in anything except science itself, modern Westerners are not more scientific than are "primitives."

The word "mystical," as it is used by Lévy-Bruhl, refers to the undifferentiated natural-cum-supernatural world. He seems to have been the first to point out that the distinction between natural and supernatural is not made in most cultures. The lack of distinction he regarded as "mystical." What Lévy-Bruhl is saying, therefore, is only that the "savage" sees in an event what his culture teaches him to see, and that he structures his perceptions as his culture has taught him to structure them. He thus actually *sees* the common understandings of the culture as if they were *in* the events or objects. So do we all. Evans-Pritchard has summed up the vast contribution of Lévy-Bruhl in this matter:

> In emphasizing that attention is largely determined by collective representations and that it is they which control selective interests, Levy-Bruhl has stressed a sociological fact of the greatest importance. . . . Our interests in phenomena are not the same as savage interests in them because our collective representations differ widely from theirs [1933b].

The main difficulty with Lévy-Bruhl's approach, as Evans-Pritchard points out, is that he, like Frazer, compared the scientific thought of our world with the magical and religious thought of primitive societies, whereas he should have compared, in addition, both from the same society. He would have seen, had he done so, that the scientific and nonscientific are two sorts of rationality, that they are both present to one degree or another in all societies, and that science is not the only way of perceiving what passes in one society or another for truth.

The notion that "collective representation" or "common understanding" is the proper subject matter of the study of exotic religious and magical activity was not new to Lévy-Bruhl. In fact, we have treated Lévy-Bruhl out of strict chronological order precisely because he so plainly illustrates the difficulty inherent in treating the human individual as the source of religious ideas and action. The concept of the human individual has, as a matter of fact, blinded more philosophers and more social scientists than has any other single concept: even the "free will" of which it is a mode. Psychology and psychological anthropology have progressed only since they have got rid of the individual and studied personality or some such analytical entity. Sociology began really to be able to synthesize the various elements in its position only when it could subsume the individual in the concept of the actor. And social and cultural anthropolgy can only rise as far as it is possible to turn the individual into ideas, symbols, reactions, and concepts that supersede individuals. The fact that our data necessarily involves behaving individuals, and that the perceiving instrument of both folk images and scientific images is an individual mind, often terribly alone, must not be allowed to blind us to this point.

The concept of "collective representation" was developed by Durkheim, although the term is older and the source of many of the most important aspects of the concept is to be found in German philosophy. The idea, or understanding (*représentation* in French; *Vorstellung* in German), communicated among many individuals is the only "fact" in this field, which (more than any other) presents the dreadful difficulty of distinguishing fact from interpretation.

One way the anthropologist can get at the ideas is to examine the ritual performed in the society under study, then learn to communicate with the people who perform it about what they think they are doing, and why. He must learn, from priests and suppliants and sacrificers, what purposes their ritual is meant to achieve and what the motivation for achieving those purposes may be. The rite—which is a deed—is central to the idea, which is a mode of explaining the deed.

This method of working has a long and honorable history in anthropology, and it is astounding that it was applied so late to the study of religious and magical ideas, and that it had to be from classicists such as Jane Harrison and sociologists such as Emile Durkheim that it was ultimately learned.

Durkheim's book, *The Elementary Forms of the Religious Life* (1912), sets out, chapter by chapter, a careful refutation of the individualist, introspective views of Tylor and Frazer. But—as often happens in academic debate—Durkheim went too far in the other direction. He was what the French call a rationalist—that is, religiously he was an unbeliever. He can be read by religious persons as an agnostic who has established society as God. Be that as it may, his scientific method was unexceptionable: he pointed to the rites and then to the folk explanations of the rites.

The Australians who provided his primary example are characterized by a religion that has, for several anthropological generations, been called by the North American Indian term "totemism." A "totem" is a species of animal or even plant, which, in the simplest terms, is conceived to be in some sort of a social-like relationship with the members of a kinship group. Thus, in those Australian groups marked by moieties and phratries —that is, the clans are grouped into two main divisions, each of which has again two or more main divisions (each a grouping of "clans")—the natural as well as the social world is divided into four sorts. The four phratries or groups of clans are each at one of the focal points of the social universe, and all of the animals and plants of the universe are also divided into four sorts and assigned to the same categories as one or other of the four phratries. Thus, in one phratry, you will get, say, a group of clans, the kangaroo, the emu, several types of grasses and trees, as well as some vegetable food and rainstorms. In another phratry, the wallaby and the witchety-grub, another selection of plants, with perhaps emphasis on food plants, will appear. The human members of one of these categories are held to be related in some way or another to the animal and plant members, and that relationship is often expressed in a kinship idiom—we have already seen that a system of kinship nomenclature is a good system for classifying other phenomena. This idiom is often spoken of as one of descent: man is descended from the main animal in the phratry; or else the men and animals have common descent from spirits, for spirits may also be divided into these four groups. That is the elementary idea of Australian totemism, and it is found in something like the same form among some American Indians.

The ritual involved in such a belief system is that in a hard environment such as in much of Australia, in the situation of a simple and largely ineffectual material culture, game is scarce, and hence food is often scarce. Therefore, each phratry, indeed each clan, has rituals to perform at certain times of the year every year, which are said to insure the breeding and multiplication of the plant and animal species within their category of the universe, thus bringing prosperity to all. The several clans in each of the several phratries cover all the main elements of nature assigned to the same category as that phratry, and the four phratries cover the whole of the natural and supernatural—the mystical—world.

There is often a food avoidance either permanently or temporarily imposed upon members of the clans not to eat those natural species that are associated with the clan. If they do so, a cleansing ceremony is necessary in order to avoid disaster of some sort. This food avoidance is relaxed in time of famine and may, in fact, be only what the ethnographers describe as the Australians' insisting that if they eat the species related to them, they must do so in a solemn mood, with respect.

Durkheim, taking this information and studying it in great detail, both from the standpoint of the composition of the rites in different acts, and in the ideas expressed about and during the rites, came to a startling conclusion. The Australians, he thought, were not merely worshiping their food. They were not merely worshiping nature. The real purpose of their cosmography was to put the social structure, nature, food, and all the rest into a single mystical system. Not only did man create God-the-personal-force in his own image (as Voltaire had already claimed), he created God-the-cosmography in the image of his society.

Now, expressed in somewhat more general and less poetic terms, we have met this idea before: in Sir James Frazer. Frazer held that religion and magic bolster the political organization of society. A king, he said, was equated with priest and sometimes with deity so that political control was made the easier. Moreover, the king and priest became the focal point of ritual, both religious and political (when they can be separated), in order to allow personalization and hence "worship" of the polity.

At this level, there is no contradiction between Frazer and Durkheim. Both are proving that the social, political, and kinship organizations of a society are reflected in its religion. This is more than merely to say that all of the institutions of a society must be tolerant of one another. It is rather to say that religious ideas and political ideas may be the same ideas and not differentiated. In such societies, the ideas have not been separated. Precisely because they are an undifferentiated unity, this condition must *not* be described as the interrelationship between politics and religion.

Durkheim went so far as to say that all religions are restatements on a mystical plane of the social organization, both family and kinship organization. A more sensible way to make this statement is to say that religion, insofar as it is to be effective either for the individual or for the social group, must be of a piece with the society. You cannot have an ancestral cult in the United States because the political and economic milieu contradict it.

This identity of the religious and the political is also to be found in an identity of the religious and economic postulates of a culture. The best studies along this line have not been done in "primitive" societies at all, but treat historical eras of Western and other civilizations. Among the most masterful of these studies are those of Max Weber.

MAX WEBER

People are brought up in a religion, which is a restatement, in a special mode, of the major ethical postulates and cosmographical viewpoints of a culture. Indeed, if law or drama are life writ small for purposes of control and comprehension, then religion is life writ large for purposes of control and comprehension. The whole of the cosmos and of society is, through religion, brought within the range of comprehension of the people who live by a culture, whatever that range may be and whatever idiom is the one used to express the "truth" as it is comprehended.

Religion is, thus, distilled in action as ritual; ritual is explained in "scripture" or its substitute; scripture must be constantly reinterpreted in order to be kept in phase with the changes constantly occurring in society. The ritual, the narrative or poetic images given to the social ideas that inspire it, and the totality of institutions within the society—all these things are in delicate balance, each responding to changes in the other.

Weber studied the ritual of the great religions and—more importantly for him—the theology that explained them to the practitioners. He then examined his data, including the folk interpretations—the values—in connection with all the other data from the society. He found that religion (just as the drama, and just as law) restated the basic postulates of a culture in new, vivid terms and re-emphasized them in ritual and hence re-emphasized their corollaries in the rest of the culture.

We have finally emerged from terminological darkness to a situation in which the anthropological categories of "primitive religion"—animism, animatism, fetishism, totemism, and all the rest—can be cast aside. Anthropologists have at last discovered a means to translate the religious ideas of people without the "curtain" of *isms* that has so often hidden them in the past. That method is simple: first one must concentrate on the deed (ritual) in order to understand the explanation of the deed in the terms given it by the practitioner (creed); one must set ritual and creed into their larger cultural context. Finally, one must compare rituals and creeds among societies—both in their substantive statements and in their symbolic reflections of the rest of culture.

19

Tribal religions

IF IN THE PAST anthropologists have woven curtains between themselves and any understanding in depth of religious phenomena in exotic societies, it is now up to anthropologists of the future to correct these misrepresentations. Such correction can come only if we know the reasons for the original corruption. It would seem that there are two fundamental causes for the misunderstanding. One lies in the fact that Westerners adhere to religions that have become supranational in the sense that they are supple enough and abstract enough to be applicable to a wide range of social and cultural situations; such a religion also exhibits a theology which takes as its specific and overt task (among many others) the correlation of deity and society. Westerners have, as a result, investigated exotic religions in terms of the type of abstractions they have learned at home—abstractions vital to their own religions, which some of the finest minds of the Western world have labored to create, but abstractions that nevertheless are worse than superfluous in dealing with less universalistic religions.

The other reason the curtain exists probably arises from the isolation of the early anthropological writers on religion from the peoples who practiced the religions they analyzed. There have been, since Frazer and Durkheim, a good number of fine studies of exotic religions. Yet, the differences between what can be called ethnographic theory and what must be called ethnological theory have not as yet been bridged to make possible a wide-range comparison among these fine studies. When an ethnographer gets close enough to a people and familiar enough with their ideas to translate them adequately into English, he finds that those words that are traditional in broad-scale comparative studies are almost wholly inadequate to convey the subtleties and complexities of meaning in the folk image he is reporting. The ethnographer must, thereupon, create specific, low-level "theory" in order to explain his ethnographic data. These low-level theories are not sufficiently generalized, or even generalizable, to form an adequate basis for comparison; rather, the comparison must come from the creation of more generalized theory on the basis of the necessary distinctions that have emerged in the ethnograhpic fact and theory. It is precisely this step that has not been taken.

Distinctions between natural and supernatural, among magic, science, and religion, or between sacred and profane—all beg the ethnographic questions. At best, all are *a priori* matrices in terms of which data can be viewed only with a greater or lesser discomfiture. At worst, they are totally effective blinders. It is true that there are adequate theories of sacrifice, and even of "the holy." But there is as yet no adequate framework for summing up national or tribal religions, comparing them with one another, and generalizing about their cultural and social settings.

UNIVERSAL RELIGIONS AND TRIBAL RELIGIONS

The first of these two problems—that of understanding an exotic national or tribal religion in the already hard-pressed language of a culture given to universal religions—must be tackled first. In a tribal religion participation in rites is limited to a rather specific social group; subscription to and efficacy of the rites and beliefs is limited to the membership of such groups. The religion is, thus, a method of characterizing the group: of creating and recreating that group at the same time that it is ritually "prospered" (to use an Africanism).

A universal religion, on the other hand, is one primarily independent of any specific social group or type of group, and hence, at least to some limited extent, it is independent of specific mores: indeed, it chooses to regard itself as the arbiter of mores. Such a change is reflected in a different basic conceptualization of the universe. The social universe is no longer primary. There is no longer merely "our group" and "outsiders." To that dichotomy is conjoined another: the distinction between the natural world and the supernatural world. The problem of the right way and the wrong way is superseded by the problem of good and evil.

Similarly, it is unlikely that a tribal religion contains any concept "religion." There are, rather, only the ritual and theological conceptualizations of political and domestic organization and of the unknown forces that shape economies and destinies.

Universalistic religions have emerged only in a few places in the world. The rest are national or tribal religions. The error of most students of comparative religion is that they unconsciously—or even consciously—create, on the analytical and intellectual level, the universalism that the religion lacks on the folk level. In short, they create a pseudo-Scripture modeled on those that characterize the universalistic religions they know, thereby sharply misrepresenting the nature of the tribal religion.

MYTH AND RITUAL

Universalization of religion leads to a new mythology. But there are two sorts of universal-myth making. Take the example of Christianity. Although most of the ideas that form the heartland of Christianity existed before Christ, Christianity as a religion obviously did not. Even though the Dead Sea Scrolls tell us of Christianlike groups before Christ, Christianity was nevertheless the achievement of Jesus and his followers—and that achievement was to turn a national religion into a universalistic one. So far as most of the Jews were concerned, their action was wrong. Judaism is still a tribal religion, no matter how similar in its ethical and theological principles to Christianity, precisely because it demands—and gets—a specifically social allegiance that (with the possible exception of Mormonism) even the most strict sects of Christianity do not require. The change was accomplished by means of a great deal of suffering and a great deal of myth making. But the changes were real in the sense that they exist in the world and move human creatures and ultimately mold cultures and societies. These myths are living and vital—they spring from human interactions. Like all living myths, they are played out anew, every day, every year.

The other type of universalization involves just as much myth making, but is the work of scholars and has little or no reflection back into the realm of living. And yet, scholars have found it almost impossible to work with such material if they do not create myths. It is well at this point to examine the nature of myth.

It is unfortunate that the word myth has, in English, accreted to itself, somewhere in the course of its historical development, the association of untruth. It has been repeatedly noted, however, that the historical truth or falseness of a myth is beside the point (Watts, 1953; Malinowski, 1926; Cassirer, 1946). The historical value of a myth must be judged by the same set of rigorous criteria as the historical value of a document—who is trying to prove what when he repeats a myth or writes a memoir? It will be found that all myth bears the stamp of truth—but it is a qualified truth, having perhaps nothing to do with history and but little to do with society. Like the Freudian myth—Freud recognized his formulations as myth, and even gave them recognized mythical characters—the success is empirical. The earmark of success of myth is organization and ultimate comprehension of the idea system. It is also possible—and Freud seems to have succeeded here, too—to create scientific theory out of the very stuff of myth. The difference between myth and theory is—discounting the intrinsic story aspect of myth—the difference between the plausible, or at least the reasonably impossible, and the scientifically provable.

Every society, then, has myths about what it does not understand: about, if we may use the medieval term, its mysteries. Yet, the myths are kept nurtured by something more tangible: the recurrent events in which they are played out, with greater or lesser symbolic nicety. Accompanying every set of myths, there is a set of activities. And it is these activities (or at least some of them) that are most directly available to the anthropologist. They can be observed and, ultimately, they can even be "believed" (whatever we may mean by that complex notion springing as it does from the supranational religions).

Religion is made overt in ritual, whether in any other way or not. A ritual is a repeated act or set of acts—usually but not always ceremonial in nature—by means of which a community (of whatever composition) or, more rarely, an individual, makes manifest its celebration and repetition of the myths explaining the nature of the interrelationship among the cosmographical, divine, and social worlds. Ritual and dogma supply socially safe outlets for emotion and tension.

There are two sets of "facts" open to the anthropologists. One set is to be found in what people do; the other set is to be found in what people say about what they do and why they do it, and the traditions of its efficacy. Such are ritual and myth. There is also usually a more or less rich material culture, much of which is imbued with the meanings assigned by the tradition to the myth and ritual. Myth and ritual may of themselves call up the entire range of cultural awareness, which, when it is perceived by the individual, may be called the religious attitude. And, finally, there is the "community" that we have been discussing: the social organization that maintains and is maintained by religious practice or ritual, myth, and icon.

We are, with this background, in a position to investigate the anthropology of religion with somewhat the same tool kit that we have already used in investigating legal anthropology. Just as the law and its effectiveness in the folk system is unaffected by analysis of an anthropological sort, so religion and its effectiveness in the folk system is unaffected by an analytical treatment of it.

The anthropological method is to observe the ritual; to discuss with whatever members of societies may be aware of it (and that itself is an important fact) the myth and the philosophy that lie behind and explain the ritual; to describe and learn the appreciation of the icons; and, ultimately, to analyze the social system that maintains the whole and the attitudes considered seemly in relation to it. Its second step is to create from this material, as it is known from many societies, a more generalized statement of the place and function of religion in carrying out the world's work.

We have already seen that religion is life writ large for explanation and for the achievement of personal tranquility, just as law is life writ small for social control and for the achievement of personal safety. It follows, then, there are two directions that the anthropology of religions can take—and they are directions that are analogous to those legal studies can take. One of these roads leads toward the creation of a generalized event system that allows the explanation and direct comparison of ritual, myth, icon, and congregation, just as we have sought to create at least the beginning of a statement of comparative law. The other road leads toward the unstated and even unconscious assumptions—the values—to be found in the culture, and its goal is to elucidate the postulates on which behavior and belief are based.

Here we shall examine only two examples, but they will make the point adequately: that life contains an element of ritual, backed by a mythical character that explains man's fate, by an iconography that somehow sums up his most cherished hopes, and by a sort of philosophy that constantly renews that hope. The first is a religion reported by Reo Fortune for the people of Peri, a small village in the Admiralty Islands off New Guinea, belonging to the larger group of people known as the Manus. That description will be followed by a brief generalized description of African religion.

MANUS RELIGION

Manus religion (Fortune, 1935) embodies several familiar ideas. The dead do not merely disappear, but are turned into ghosts or shades and some interaction with the living is still possible. Manus recognize a soul or vital essence in the living. They have the notion that the control of this vital essence is to a large extent, and in the course of nature, in the hands of the ghosts, and out of control of the living. Therefore, it is rationally necessary to postulate, if chaos or caprice are to be avoided, that the vital essence, the soul, can in some situations—for the Manus, it is a condition of trance—approach the ghosts. There is another idea—vital to Manus religion as to many others, but not so nearly universal—that diviners have control over spirits, which allows them, even without trance, to interpret ghostly intention.

Ghosts continue to live in their own houses, to be the same kind of "people," and to follow the same interests as they followed when they were alive. But there is one significant difference: as ghosts they can know the deepest secrets of living people. When they were alive, they had always been interested, and insisted that their fellows follow the correct Manus moral way; they had, by and large, followed it themselves. But it is only as ghosts that it is vouchsafed them to know the secret and innermost thoughts of the living, to recognize that source of guilt in all minds: the intransigent resentment of the unselfishness implied by following the correct moral way.

The vital essence of human beings is called *mwelolo* by the Manus, and if a ghost wants to harm a mortal, he merely takes the *mwelolo* away. Such a loss of *mwelolo* makes a person ill; if the loss is extensive or permanent, the person dies. A ghost should—note that ghosts have rules, too, and that they resemble social rules, and the ghosts are also sometimes resentful while still maintaining and following the rules—take this soul stuff away from one of his kinsmen only if that man has been lax in his kinship obligations or has committed some sort of secret sin. Once reparation has been made for the lapse or the sin, the ghost should return the vital essence to the body of its owner. But in order that the secret sin or laxity be made reparable, it must first be discovered by mortals. One cannot make secret expiation, for to do so is to leave the sufferer unrequited. Obviously, such a belief demands that an oracular mode of communication between ghosts and living be created. The belief follows that ghosts are kind to their mortal kin, merely making them ill instead of killing them; when the reason for disapproval is removed, the vital essence is returned, and a cure effected. Ghosts can, however, kill their nonkinsmen outright, merely out of malice. Obviously, then, the way for mortals to get security against illness and death is to avoid secret sin, to bind the ghosts of one's kinsmen to oneself, and to expiate any sin or laxity that one discovers in oneself, and see to it that others do the same.

As in every such religion, however, there is a "way out" that allows for a certain degree of variation from the strenuous ideals that are imposed. The "way out" for the Manus is the idea that, whatever they may do against it, illness and death are sometimes attributable to black magic —to the living evil rather than the ghosts. Such beliefs are most often called upon to explain illnesses in unweaned children and women's illnesses accompanying childbirth.

As usual, however, the boundary between the black magic and the illness resulting from laxity or secret malice is difficult for the Manus to define. Every adult Manus male has his own Sir Ghost, who is a deceased close kinsman, usually the father or elder brother. The relationship between a man and his Sir Ghost is seen in analogy to a kinship relationship among the living—indeed, it is a continuation on a new plane of such a relationship. Thus, both a man and his Sir Ghost are bound by duties and obligations, and they have a right to certain more or less reciprocal benefits.

We have here one of the favorite analogies people use in bringing their religions to human expression: the analogy in which the relationships between a mortal and an immortal are said to be of basically the same quality as the relationships between two or several mortals. Such an analogy, for all that it is widespread, is not universal—the analogy to imponderable and nonhuman forces of the sort that Westerners see imminent in electricity or atomic energy also find their adherents. To the Manus, however, religion is seen as a basic extension of the human relationship to include the nonhuman world.

Thus the "relationship" of a man to some particular deceased kinsman is enshrined in a set of activities on the part of the living person which are obligations; the consideration that he receives is of a nature that Westerners would consider in some degree divine. The ghost that is said to have entered into such a compact is called the Sir Ghost of that man; the living member of the compact is his ward. Sir Ghost—a translation of the Manus term—is such to one man alone. To everyone else he is merely a ghost, and potentially evil and dangerous.

The terms of the compact between ward and Sir Ghost include several activities on the part of the living member. (1) The ward must make the funeral rites over the mortal remains of the individual who is to become his Sir Ghost; since the exact identity of one's Sir Ghost is not known in advance, one must participate in the funeral rites of all one's kinsmen. The Manus say that such rites serve the purpose of placing the Sir Ghost in the debt of the living ward. Dr. Fortune says specifically that Manus do not admit the great degree of self-solicitude provided for the living by the rituals, but claim it is all done in solicitude for the dead who are the eventual Sir Ghosts of the members of the living community. (2) The ward is obliged to preserve the skull of his Sir Ghost; he puts it in a carved bowl within his house and makes devotional offerings to the skull. (3) The ward has to protect the skull because it is his Sir Ghost, especially because it may be merely a ghost to other people and may annoy them so that they may wish to harm it. The skull gives to mortals an *icon* in terms of which they can honor, dishonor, harm or even extinguish the ghost. The living ward can at any time threaten the Sir Ghost that he will break the compact if the Sir Ghost does not live up to his part in it.

It is part of the compact that Sir Ghost never visits vicarious spite or malice on his ward. This vicarious spite is thought to occur merely because he is a ghost, and resents the translation into the nonmaterial sphere. If he is angry about this, he vents his anger on other people. It is the job of the Sir Ghost to keep his own ward safe from just such vicarious dealings at the hands of other ghosts. A Sir Ghost may fail, however, and it is ultimately in this way that death is visited upon the ward. The Sir Ghost thus is always proved to have done an inadequate job of his part of the contract—if he had done better, death could never have resulted. The former ward, now dead, becomes the Sir Ghost of one of his survivors—specifically, his heir—and the original Sir Ghost's skull is thrown out, usually into the sea. Such discarded Sir Ghosts first become ghosts that hang around the edges of the community, then ghosts of the Middle Seas; ultimately they turn into sea slugs. The imagery is a vivid reminder of the processes of obscuring memory.

Causing illness may be regarded as the righteous prerogative of the Sir Ghost who is head of a house, demanding moral excellence from the members of the household. Upon proper expiation, the Sir Ghost desists and the disease goes away. However, a great deal more of illness, particularly serious illness, is laid to the breach in the defense of the Sir Ghost so that other ghosts can create the damage. Any kind of offense against the moral code is a human fault and reaction against it by the Sir Ghost is to be expected. It can therefore be expiated. However, some types of misfortune occur in situations in which no human fault is discoverable, or even surmised. In such cases, the blame is placed on the general malice of ghosts, turned incarnate by death and hence deprived of the many delights of mortality. Human weakness is never asked to carry the entire burden of misfortune a community suffers. The malice of jealous spirits, or even the greater wisdom of God in the total pattern, affords at least some relief. In the Manus case, such jealous ghosts may penetrate the defense of a man's Sir Ghost and attack him or his close kinsmen, which means that there is comparatively little the mortals can do about it. Such is another "way out" of a system of explanation that, if carried to its rational extreme, would prove unbearable.

As has so often been found in Africa, there is a tendency for Manus within the household to say that illness is ghost-caused or the result of malice and a concomitant tendency for other people outside of the household to say that the death resulted from sin and the retaliation of the Sir Ghost.

The Sir Ghost may not take the vital essence of the sinner himself, but rather that of somebody else in the household. Therefore, it is not always possible to know who in the household committed the sin simply because somebody falls ill. One member of a household may have to confess a sin in order to save another.

Any man can talk to his Sir Ghost all he likes, but in order to be sure of the communications he receives back, he must use a diviner or medium. The diviner must have the permission of his own Sir Ghost in order to become a diviner, and must then be initiated by an already initiated diviner. As Dr. Fortune assures us: "The oracle himself or herself is by no means a fraud. It is only necessary to believe that after one is consecrated whatever . . . comes into one's mind when one sets out to divine or to conduct a seance, is suggestion from the ghosts" (1935, p. 33).

The oracles can come to three decisions in the case of serious illness: sin and Sir Ghostly correction, ghostly malice, or a combination of the two. The latter alternative is the most common. As Fortune points out, gross malarial fever is so common that the Manus cannot possibly account for it by new sins; old sins have to be raked up over and over again, and complications arising from them must be newly invented and churned about. Ultimately, only malice from ghosts who are jealous of the potentialities of human beings in good health can be blamed for the undermining of that health. In short, ghosts overcome Sir Ghost and all overcome men.

The greatest number of offenses that Sir Ghosts punish are sexual offenses. Others are failure to pay debts on time and tardiness about funeral feasts for the dead. Sir Ghost punishes disobedience to the head of the household on the part of kinsmen or economic dependents. He may punish his ward for not keeping the house in good repair, or for being greedy and concentrating too much wealth for show purposes—but, conversely, for not utilizing wealth properly for show purposes (diverting a pig from economic exchange merely to eat it is a sin), and for not making the best possible showing in wealth displays. In fact, Fortune found that the moral code supported by Sir Ghost is very well kept; the oracles are sometimes hard put to it to find a sin with which to explain a misfortune.

The Sir Ghost may not only cause illness; he may also spoil the fishing to which the main economic subsistence is geared. A Sir Ghost may, in fact, take the essence *(molua)* from the fishing gear in much the same way that he may take the vital essence *(mwelolo)* from a person. Sir Ghosts are also said to be able to control the movement of fish. Hence the basic economic activities are thought to be in the hands of the Sir Ghosts, and ultimately, via the compacts between wards and Sir Ghosts, in the hands of the human wards.

Manus religion is best fitted to deal with emergencies and disasters. It has only minimal component of prevention, so to speak. Although there are rituals that, it is said, should be performed at the various stages of an individual's life when he passes from one status to another—the well-known *rites de passage*—they are seldom performed except in cases where disaster has struck and the diviners reveal that anger of the ghosts, or of the Sir Ghost of the ill man or his household head, lies behind the difficulty.

Dr. Fortune has adduced the moral postulates underlying the religion and ritual of the Manus, and has set them forth in the form of sixteen commandments reminiscent, on the one hand, of those handed to Moses, and, on the other, of Hoebel's postulates underlying Eskimo law. These commandments are, of course, axioms that lie behind the moral behavior of the Manus. The postulates themselves need not be repeated here (they are to be found in Fortune, 1935, pp. 345 ff.); what is important is that "Manus religion exemplifies on the lowest level of the ancestral cult, the thoroughgoing coalescence of religion and morality that has been characteristic also of the Christian religion" (Fortune, 1935, p. 37).

MORE ABOUT AFRICAN TRIBAL RELIGIONS

Much has been written, particularly concerning the tribal religions of Africa, about the lack of association between morality and tribal religion. It is true that most tribal religions—including that of Manus—do not set out ten principles in the imperative mode to govern the major areas of social life. But the claim that tribal religious are "amoral" would seem to be a sign either that the ethnographer did not understand the deeper significance of the ritual and myth to the people he studied, or else that the ethnographer was by the exigencies of his own nature, and through confusion of association with cause, required to deny the religious basis of morality.

The basic moral tenet of African religion—indeed, it is the basic tenet of many Near Eastern religions, at least three of which have become supranational—is the tenet that unselfishness is the primary virtue, and that human selfishness lies at the root of the world's ills. The tremendous variation in African religion makes this idea difficult to generalize in any terms save those of a coordinating myth. Yet, such a myth has value and can be used to explain the basis of African tribal religions if it is clearly stated and firmly understood that the myth, in this form, cannot be discovered empirically in any African society, although most of the myths that can be collected might be recognized as variants of it. African religion is complex in its ritual and in many places it is complex in its theology. But the basic postulates that lie behind it—postulates that can be stated as a narrative myth—are simple and eternal.

In the beginning, the myth might run, God made the heavens and the earth, and all that is in them. He created man, or alternatively the beings whose descendants became human. He gave to man—or caused to be given to man—the knowledge that is necessary to keep the firmament running smoothly and in good repair. Then God retired. God, in African religion, has often been called an "otiose" God, which means literally that He is at rest, or idle; such a concept would seem to be somewhat wide of the mark. God, in many (not quite all) African religions, may be distant, and the route between man and God may be long and maneuvered only by special spiritual or divine messengers. But God remains the creative force in the universe—and He can be reached. The statement is often encountered in

African ethnographies that prayers are not addressed to God, but rather to some minor deities. Such statements should be examined closely for the folk images that explain the activities they are meant to describe; under such scrutiny these assertions often turn out to be false.

Throughout much of Africa, the maintenance of the firmamental forces is done through the agencies of ancestors, of spirit, or of totemlike wraithes or some other intermediary. As we shall see in the next chapter, the forces of evil (represented also by spirits or, in many cases, by human beings of ill will generally called "witches" by those who report on them in English) try to disrupt the world or to pervert it to their own selfish ends. They do so by using the very techniques that God gave to lesser spirits and man specifically to maintain the world in good running order.

African religion tends, therefore, to have two fundamental event sequences. One is a sequence of ritual that follows the seasons and has definite associations with the economic life of the people, and in many cases with the political life as well; there is usually an accompanying sequence of ritual that follows the life cycle of maturing human beings. The second event system centers in a sequence of ritual that is triggered off when misfortune appears in the community, either in the form of illness and death or of drought or epidemic. The two event sequences may be closely interlinked, because the appearance of misfortune may be attributed to failure to carry out properly the ritual for keeping the forces of the firmament in good working condition.

The ritual centers around prayer and offerings and around sacrifice. And although prayer is of importance in African religion, it is in sacrifice that the whole can be most vividly portrayed, for sacrifice lies at the heart of African religion.

A SUMMARY

In summary, it can be said that there is a widespread tendency in human society—indeed, it may be a psychic necessity—for events of vital importance in the personal or social lives of the members of society to be marked on two levels: to be carried out in the mundane manner and then, further, to be celebrated in a religious manner. The emotional difficulties engendered in the first can often be unraveled in the second. Moreover, in most parts of the world (but not quite universally) the vital steps in the life cycle are noted and underscored by ritual.

Birth and death are marked by christenings and funerals; marriage is celebrated in almost all societies (but not quite all) by a ceremony or a whole series of ceremonies in which the new status of the individuals is underscored, and in which the new situation in the community is broadcast. Other personal life crises, such as initiation or retirement, may be marked by specific ritual.

A nonrecurring danger point in the life of the individual may also be buttressed by ritual. Such, for example, are the curing and healing ceremonies found in so many parts of the world. Illness obviously puts the individual into jeopardy, and it is precisely in situations of social and personal jeopardy that religion comes fully into play.

It is also evident that crises in social life as well as in personal life may be marked by religious ritual. The annual agricultural or herding calendar may be the subject of an equally binding religious calendar. Such is true among Christians just as it is true among Admiralty Islanders. All the other major social activities may also be given a religious dimension: oaths in courts are of a religious nature, and so are ordeals. War is often—in fact, one can say usually—marked by ritual that is intended to ease the pressures and assure success in a questionable undertaking. Family life is often the center for religious activity, either in the form of an ancestral cult or merely in the form of common worship.

It would seem, then, that religion and ritual serve as a mode of underwriting and making overt certain aspects of daily life of all sorts. Religion is a means by which the fundamental value system or idea system of the society can be given cultural form to which symbolic value can attach, at the same time that the event system, which lies behind important economic, political, and familial activities, can be made more precise and secure.

Through the study of religious ritual and of whatever theology a society has developed, whether it be a complex one such as that of Dahomey or a simple one such as that found in Manus, the anthropologist can expose the postulates that form the foundation of the entire culture. As in legal anthropology, the discovery of the postulates is an exercise beyond ethnography, but dependent on good ethnography. The postulates of a legal system and those of a religion are probably in almost all cases the same. As a Tiv judge once told a criminal: "Divine rectitude will punish you for this breach; but it may be a little slow in coming and meanwhile the court shall punish you."

Ogden and Richards have claimed that language is "duplicate, a shadow-soul, of the whole structure of reality" (1946, p. 31). So is religion.

We are not reducing religion to "mere" epiphenomena of society; but whatever else it is, religion is also an accompaniment and a mode of underlining—of duplicating on another plane—the whole of society and culture. It is this part of religious phenomena that is available to and of interest to the social scientist. Theological truth, whatever that may be, is not in any wise affected by sociological truth, unless it be to drive deeper the level of theological analysis and understanding.

The anthropology of religion has suffered a different sort of ailment from most other branches: in many fields, too few students are interested enough to get sufficient background. In religious anthropology, too many students are too self-interested to get sufficient background. Few students of legal anthropology or of economic anthropology are looking for a way of life or an answer to personal problems. Yet, all but a few students of religious anthropology seem to be carrying on such a search. Indeed, the anthropology of religions is the most difficult of all branches of the subject. Not only does it require a most rigorous discipline to do well: in field research, it is the religion of a people that the fieldworker learns last, and usually after greatest probing. Even when he has been shown the ritual early in his field research, it is only when he knows the culture the ritual reflects and can understand the theology as it is explained to him, that he can comprehend any except the superficialities of what is being shown and told him. Undoubtedly, religion supplies the anthropological area in which the possibilities of misunderstanding are maximal: both misunderstanding of the subjects and misunderstanding of the self. In analysis of religion, the necessity to rid oneself of simplifying ideas, always difficult, is the harder because it is to these very simplifying ideas that so much emotionalism adheres, either in the form of commitment or in the form of disillusion. For life, either commitment to a creed or disillusion with it may provide a driving force to be valued differently by different peoples. Anthropology, just as any science, also demands commitment and excitement. But the commitment must be to scientific analysis itself, rather than to any specific way of life. Therefore, anthropology also demands recollection in tranquility; the degree to which that tranquility can be achieved is directly related to self-knowledge.

20

Witchcraft

THERE IS TO BE FOUND, in many parts of the world, a sort of belief that battens on religion but that is in fact a *non sequitur*—it is often used to link religion and the malice that gnarls so many human relationships. The spirits or the forces of the universe may, it is believed in many places, be captured by selfish and evil people and used to their own uncharitable and antisocial ends. The devil is to be found all around us; witches may be everywhere; witches may, indeed, do the bidding of the Prince of Darkness.

Witchcraft beliefs have been effectively absent from Western society for some two centuries, and therefore Westerners tend to know comparatively little about witchcraft. We read histories of the Inquisition and the Reformation and cannot quite grasp how some of the finest minds of the late medieval and early modern world could be so obtuse, so foolish, and so cruel. Obviously, when we think thus, we are having trouble getting at the reasoning and the social milieu in which these ideas took root and persisted.

DEVELOPMENT OF EUROPEAN IDEAS ABOUT WITCHCRAFT

The so-called Dark Ages, before the twelfth cenutry, were not much bothered by witchcraft.[1] The ideas of witchcraft current in the classical world—and some of them were hair-raising, even by medieval standards—seem to have had little effect on the Early Middle Ages. The Church, during the tenth century, stated unequivocally that witchcraft was a false belief. Here is a quotation from an authentic church text of the tenth century:

> Some wicked women, reverting to Satan and seduced by the illusions and phantasms of demons, believe and profess that they ride at night with Diana on certain beasts with an innumerable multitude of women, passing

[1] The discussion presented here of medieval European witchcraft derives mainly from an account by Trevor Davies (1947).

> over immense distances, obeying her commands as their mistress, and evoked by her on certain nights. . . . Innumerable multitudes, deceived by this false opinion, believe all this to be true, and thus relapse into pagan error. Therefore priests everywhere should preach that they know this to be false, and that such phantasms are sent by the Evil Spirit, who deludes them in dreams. Who is there who is not led out of himself in dreams, seeing much in sleeping that he never saw in waking? . . . It is to be taught that he who believes such things has lost his faith, and that he who has not the true faith is not of God, but of the Devil.

You cannot get much more skeptical about witchcraft than that. And although the ideas and beliefs were obviously present, they were present in much the same way as they were among ourselves: we have a lore of witches, though it is not a very deep or impressive one, and we do not, any of us, worry much about witches or being bewitched. "Bewitched" is merely a word found in perfume ads. Beliefs, however, are present—at least, ideas that some of us might, given the right social milieu, instill with belief.

Early medieval skepticism about witchcraft was strengthened by the fact that people in those times had what they considered extremely good protection against evil spirits of all sorts. No devil or evil spirit could harm a Christian. The sign of the cross, or judicious use of holy water, was proof against witches and even against the devil himself; talismans against witches were sometimes found, just as talismans against witches are found in many peasantlike subcultures (the Pennsylvania Dutch provide a sophisticated example) where the belief is not very powerful. Most important, the law codes of the Early Middle Ages contain no mention of witchcraft.

However, about the time of the Crusades, the religious milieu of Europe began to change markedly. The situation is usually described by historians as a weakening of religious belief and action, accompanied by the growth of heresies of all sorts. The eccelesiastical sceptics who denied that witches were possible had their position weakened. At the same time, the traditional protection against evil of all sorts—holy water and the power of an Ave Maria—were taken less seriously. There were a number of famous school men who began to set forth, in a new and organized way, those ideas of witchcraft held by the populace in a somewhat similar manner to that in which we hold ours: they began to clothe them in logic and philosophy, backed by scholarship and the weight of the academia of the time. It is as if Margaret Murray were taken up by the Republicans and made part of their platform. The Church, in its form of the Inquisition, changed its attitude, in part to accommodate the changing social and cultural times, and in part to direct and even to slow the change. It sheltered some of the best brains in Europe, who were making a case for the truth of and pointing out the danger of the peasant beliefs that had been current all along.

The idiom—as is the idiom of most witchcraft—was religious. Therefore, the devil and his witches had to be accounted for. The mode of doing so was fairly simple: God created the world and all that was in it, including evil. He assigned the administration of evil to the devil. Witches were, *ipso facto,* a department under the devil because they were evil. They were thus brought within the range of the interests of the clergy, which we can see today were leading up to the Inquisition. Suspected witches began to be tried on charges not of witchcraft, but of heresy and devil worship. Amazingly enough, the confessions began to pile up. By no means were all confessions of witchcraft wrung by torture from those accused. Confessions and trials led to further spread of belief, and the tremendous weight of the clergy added still more to the credibility of the ideas. As more confessions were gathered, and records kept, the amount of documentary evidence to support belief in witchcraft became overwhelming. And at the end of the fifteenth century, belief in witchcraft became so prevalent and so dangerous that the pope himself issued a bull on the subject and (as we would say today) created an ecclesiastical commission to write an exhaustive report on the subject. It is a pseudosociological study (if one can use the term for an era in which the "society" had not been discovered, let alone studied) on the theory and practice of witchcraft. Here is an extract of the Bull of Pope Innocent VIII from December of 1484, which shows how far the position of the Church had been reversed:

> Many persons of both sexes, unmindful of their own salvation and straying from the Catholic Faith, have abandoned themselves to devil, incubi and succubi, and by their incantations, spells, conjurations and other accursed charms and crafts, enormities and horrid offenses have slain unborn infants and the unborn offspring of cattle, have blasted the produce of the earth . . . nay, men and women, beasts of burden . . . vineyards . . . wheat and other cereals; these witches furthermore afflict and torment men and women . . . with terrible and piteous pains . . . over and above this they blasphemously renounce the Faith which is theirs by the Sacrament of Baptism, and at the instigation of the Enemy of Mankind do not shrink from committing and perpetrating the foulest abominations and filthiest excesses . . . [quoted in Davies, 1947, p. 5].

Coming as it does from the head of the Church, we can see that the belief in witchcraft was pronounced normal.

Shortly afterwards, apparently about three years after the papal bull, there was published more or less simultaneously in Köln and in Rome, a book called *Malleus Maleficarum,* or "Hammer of the Witches." This book was translated into English only in 1928 by the Reverend Montague Summers, a Church of England clergyman who led an interesting life in pulpit, publisher's office, police station, and coven. In any case, the *Malleus* is excellently translated. And a most horrible book it is—one of the few really terrifying books. It is a legal tract that proves conclusively, by the most formidable logic and the most meticulous scholarship into sources ancient and contemporaneous, with full play given to the classical scholars and to the commentators, that witches, incubi, and succubi exist, that they work out their compacts with the devil, and that they attack mankind in order that the devil might gain more souls. Passages of Scriptures are cited; for example, "Thou shalt not suffer a witch to live," which is from Exodus, but the point is made even more fully in Deuteronomy.

The thesis of the book is this: devils, being spiritual, cannot do their own dirty work. They therefore must get physical bodies in which to do it. They acquire the bodies either by entering them—that is, the phenomenon of possession—or by signing pacts with human beings to do as they are bid in return for mundane considerations. Here is the last paragraph of the first chapter of the *Malleus:*

> This then is our proposition: devils by their art do bring about evil effects through witchcraft, yet it is true that without the assistance of some agent they cannot take any form, either substantial or accidental, and we do not maintain that they can inflict damage without the assistance of some agent, but with such an agent diseases and any other human passions or ailments, can be brought about, and these are real and true. How these agents or how the employment of such means can be rendered effective in cooperation with devils will be made clear in the following chapters [Summers, 1928, p. 11].

The book provides what one latter-day commentator has called "a complete guide, theoretical as well as practical, for the discovery, examination, torture, trial and execution of witches" (Davies, 1947, p. 6).

The book was republished at least a dozen times in the century following its publication; it was used as a sort of handbook by both Catholic and Protestant clergymen. Suspects charged with witchcraft could be tried in either the secular or the ecclesiastical courts, and the movement grew apace because of the fact that it was fortified by a "logic," no matter how spurious, that created the situation it sought to eradicate: the more witches who were tried, found guilty, and executed, the more witches the community spawned. Moreover, convicted witches were often executed in public, which added still more to the intensity of the mania and the awareness of the populace. It has been estimated that tens or even hundreds of thousands of people died at the stake as a result of these witchcraft accusations and trials. Indeed, the proportion of the population so to have died has been estimated to be about the same as the proportion of the population to have died in the political frenzies of our own time.

Although the Protestant Revolution occured in part as a reaction against the Inquisition, the Protestants nevertheless did not stop witchhunting In fact, in many areas, they even added to its impetus. Luther, as is well known, was a believer in witches. Calvin was almost a zealot in the matter. Geneva, Calvin's native city, became the very center for witchhunting and its clergy and elders became authorities. They gave advice to other cities on how to go about this pursuit successfully.

At this time, Geneva—like most other cities—was the center of many epidemics of disease and pestilence. The cause, in the absence of what we today would call scientific knowledge, was assigned to witches working at the instigation and in the pay of the devil, and to the medicines or "unguents" they were said to have prepared. In a well-attested case, which occurred on the twenty-second of January, 1545, one Bernard Dallinges was arrested. He confessed to having joined with other people in a plot to put ointment on the foot of a man who had been hanged for witchcraft, and then "by Satan's malice" to smear this unguent on the doors of the citizenry of Geneva for the precise and overt purpose of spreading the plague. The people who were implicated by Dallinges were immediately arrested, brought to Geneva, and put to the torture. The "leader" in this case, one Lentille, endured two twists of the rope without confessing; he was then put to the strapado and died from loss of blood. His body was dragged through the city streets to the Plainpalais and burnt. (Davies, 1947, pp. 5-6).

This event put the city authorities on their guard, and as a result quite a large number of men and women were apprehended at spreading the plague, consequent to making a pact with the devil. They were accordingly tortured and burned. Calvin, during this time, is known to have appeared before the Council of the city of Geneva with the request that the prisoners' death agonies not be "excessively prolonged." He was successful in having an order given to the executioner to be diligent and see that death was quick.

In fact, Calvin himself acted as witness against witches, and held a firm belief in witchcraft. In light of the letter that he wrote on the twenty-seventh of March, 1545, the point can scarcely be gainsaid:

> Here God is trying us sorely. A conspiracy of men and women has been discovered, who for the space of three years have spread the plague through

> the city, by what sorceries I know not. Fifteen women have already been burnt. Some of the men have been punished even more severely. Some have committed suicide in prison. Twenty-five are still in custody. Notwithstanding the conspirators do not cease to smear the locks of doors with their ointments. Behold the perils that beset us. Hitherto God has preserved our household uninjured, however frequently it has been assailed [quoted in Davies, 1947 p. 7].

Shortly after that letter was written, the drive against witches was intensified: all people of bad reputation were rounded up. Many confessed under torture; others were walled up, burned, decapitated.

The judges of these trials heard, and apparently believed, evidence stating that people accused of witchcraft had committed such unlikely acts as to "kiss, in token of homage, the posterior of a black dog named Margaret, who was the devil in disguise," in order to be provided with the power to make or otherwise acquire the unguents to be used for spreading the plague.

Geneva, in gaining her reputation in successful dealings against witches, of course also got a reputation as the home of witches; it was even suggested that witches of other communities had emigrated from there. In addition to this outburst of witch mania, there were others, fairly well documented, in 1568, and 1615. These beliefs were prevalent in Geneva—in Scotland and in New England—in the eighteenth century.

There are several reasons that stand behind the Calvinist fear of witches. Some were doctrinal. Calvin and his followers were convinced not merely of the reality, but also of the inevitability of sin. The *Institutio* claimed the fall to be in accordance with man's nature, showing absolute depravity:

> All of us, descending from an impure seed, come into the world tainted with the contagion of sin. Nay, before we behold the light of the sun we are in God's sight defiled and polluted . . . even infants bringing their condemnation with them from their mother's womb, suffer not from another's but from their own defect. . . . Their whole nature is, as it were, a seed-bed of sin and therefore cannot but be odious and abominable to God [quoted in Davies, 1947, p. 10].

Thus, in Calvinism natural man was of the same sort as the devil.

Second, Calvinists were fundamentalists: they went directly to Scripture for their tenets, and they interpreted Scripture with a sureness and unequivocality that has seldom been matched. If the clergy was not infallible, the written word was. Obviously, as one scholar has noted, "the Bible literally interpreted text by text without regard to historical background or historical criticism of its documents seemed quite decisive on the subject of witchcraft in general, and on many of the current accusations in particular. The command 'Thou shalt not suffer a witch to live' seemed . . . to settle the matter once for all"[2] (Davies, 1947, p. 10).

The political soil in which Calvinism could flourish also was congenial to witchcraft beliefs. The state at that time was dominated by the votes of the church members. The inherent democracy, like democracy everywhere, meant that social institutions represent the entire population rather than merely the educated segments of the population. Hence, witchcraft was kept alive even after the intelligentsia had ceased to respond to its fundamental ideas.

Finally, too, Calvinism was a heritage of all the dualistic heresies—the Manicheans, Paulicians, Cathari and Albigenses—who claimed that all matter was evil, all pleasure save love of God was a sin. All of these heresies had an elaborate system of demonology that could be seen without difficulty in terms of witchcraft. The last known burning for witchcraft in Scotland was 1722; the belief in witches lasted even more decades.[3]

ELEMENTS OF BELIEF IN WITCHCRAFT

This short survey of European witchcraft allows us to make some few generalizations that can be compared with those derivable from some other systems of witchcraft. There are, in fact, several necessary elements for any belief system of witchcraft. First of all, such a system, to make sense, must have a theory about the force or power in the cosmos. In the Judeo-Christian scheme, all the power had to come from God. However, for God to be both all powerful and good, He had to delegate the capacity for evil. Hence we have the devil. The devil, then, was the source of evil power, and the proposition had to exist (if witchcraft was going to be admitted) that there existed some sort of a pseudorelationship between the evildoers and the devil. The lore on this point is tremendous: usually, however, the relationship was established by some sort of rite, most often of a purposely disgusting nature.

The second important point about witchcraft is that it must be said to be carried out in some way or another; ritual is one of the most commonly postulated ways for doing it. The ritual may be an obvious one: the "good ritual," so to speak, may be performed backwards, as in the well-

[2] Further underwriting of witchcraft ideas is to be found in Deuteronomy VIII, 10-17; I Samuel XVIIII; Job I, 7-12; and many other passages.

[3] Just to insure that no modern Western religion comes off too lightly, it should be noted that Menassah ben Israel wrote a very effective and influential tract on witchcraft.

known black mass. It may be almost any method for negating symbolically the main religious values of the society. There is another common method, however: that is, the magical use of substances variously called unguents, medicines, potions, or poisons. Sometimes, however, witchcraft is considered to be a psychic act, pure and simple; this psychic act may be thought to be accompanied by a physical act, as in the case of the evil eye: some sort of substance is formed by the glance of some people, which gets into the bodies of the victims and causes all sorts of troubles. The evil eye may, however, be merely a metaphor in some cases; there is said to be no substance, but only a ruinous quality in the glance—a sort of psychic deathray.

It has been traditional for some years now for anthropologists to draw a distinction between witchcraft and sorcery among these various techniques of bewitchment. The basis is a simple one: Does anything actually take place or not? In the case of witchcraft, any act that takes place is only a psychic act. It is obvious, then, that witchcraft is a system of thought for interpreting misfortune by assigning (by tradition) psychic acts of human beings as the cause of misfortune. Sorcery, on the other hand, is performed. It is a system of magic for bringing about the destruction of another person. Leaving the causal effectiveness of sorcery to one side, we can say that sorcery is an act, carried out with attendant ritual. Such acts are certainly carried out in many societies.

This distinction between witchcraft and sorcery is different from the one sometimes made in traditional thinking, which says that witches are women and sorcerers are men (sometimes the latter are called wizards). It is true that in our own recent experience—that is, up to 250 years ago—most witches were women. But there were witches in Europe throughout the time of the Inquisition and the later Prostestant continuations of it; there were male witches in Salem and the other American Calvinist colonies. Witches are, in our lore, predominantly female, however. This is a peculiarity of our society, and of some others; there are other societies in which witches are predominantly male.

In Chistian belief, the power the "witch" wields has been acquired from a greater source of power: ultimately, via Satan, from God. The witch was supposed to be a knowing agent—the most common sort. This power, and its association with a greater power, is often accompanied by a special ability in divination—the Witch of Endor herself was not a witch Geneva would have recognized, but was merely a woman who became possessed of a spirit and foretold the future—in short, she was a seeress or an oracle. However, oracular capacities assume, in the Christian cosmography, the same set of assumptions as witchcraft—foreknowledge is the work of the devil.

Third, another extremely important point: witches become important socially only in time of misfortune or crisis. In the Geneva case, the misfortune was plague in the city. The theory of germs was unknown; plague obviously spread. What was the agent of its spread? The answer was at hand: the evil power in the world. Who had it? Satan. By definition. But Satan was a spirit and therefore could not transport a medium of sickness from one place to another; hence, he had to utilize living creatures for that purpose. He usually chose human beings because he could cause them to transport the sickness and could gain a soul into the bargain. The reasoning, in time of plague, then, went like this: plague is caused by magical ointments of Satan spread by witches. There is a plague in the city. Therefore, there are witches in the city.

Now note that we have here a logical system. It even goes into neat syllogistic form.

> Major premise: Illness is spread by witches.
> Minor premise: Illness is spreading.
> Conclusion: Witches are present.

The weakness, obviously, to twentieth-century Americans, is in the major premise. But the validity of that major premise was never questioned in the folk system concerned. Indeed, we shall find a syllogism with an unproved and probably erroneous major premise of this sort to lie behind all systems of witchcraft.

There are, then, three basic points that have been isolated for consideration: (1) A belief in witchcraft requires some doctrine of evil power that can reside in human beings, but that is connected with a greater power (the major premise). (2) There must be a situation of misfortune (the minor premise). (3) There must be some supposed method for activating this power, whether it be by ritual, by a supposed psychic willing, or by some totally external means (allowing the conclusion to be reached).

The syllogism, indeed, gives us our major points for examining other instances of witchcraft. It would seem that there must be misfortune either in the social world or in the personal world of some "victim." There must be a belief that evil can reside in human beings (even as it is derived from perversion of a greater power), and that the evil power can be activated by ritual, a supposed psychic act, or some other means. There must, moreover, be a recognized mode of reaction—indeed, a quasi-legal "counteraction." When witches are "proved" to be present there must be a countervailing act: that is, there is an action that can follow upon the syllogistic conclusion.

In short, then, witchcraft is a body of beliefs for explaining misfortune in terms of evil power thought to reside in human beings and to influence their action. It is, moreover, a system of action that is believed to be at least to some extent effective in taming and vanquishing that power. Witchcraft operates in a milieu of social tension, and it is a set of ideas that both explains the misfortune and justifies the action taken against it.

Indeed, "witchcraft" is the set of ideas lying behind the institutions of *counter*witchcraft—curing, reparation of the social fabric, and attempts to ease tensions within social groups. That it is not *always* effective does not make it any different from any other sort of curing practice or religious observance.

COUNTERACTION OF WITCHCRAFT

It can now be seen plainly that what is present to be studied is the counterwitchcraft activities and the idea systems— the "witchcraft" beliefs —that accompany them. It is just as necessary, however, to look at the social situations that are attacked by counterwitchcraft and to consider whether or not the attacks are effective; obviously, the idea system that lies behind is not "true" in any logical, provable sense. That does not mean, however, that some activities of counterwitchcraft may not be socially and personally effective. The analyst is, in short, in a position to study the situation from two angles: first, the social use to which the witchcraft and counterwitchcraft institutions are put; and secondly, and much less importantly, the rationality of the system of beliefs. Judgment is to be made, by social scientists, only on the first problem. It may be that these institutions do not perform the tasks they are expected to perform. Only if that is the case are we entitled to judgment about the second problem.

Such an idea—that misfortune can be caused by the psychic states and secretly malicious acts of others—is found in almost all parts of the world. Obviously, it is so: social tensions and neurotic reactions to them are omnipresent. One of the simplest modes of institutionalizing them is to find a scapegoat and "get rid of the cause" of the misfortune. The regularity with which witchcraft appears and the similarity of its logical and belief structure everywhere is one of the astounding facts of ethnography. "Human beings can cause misfortune to others" is the axiom underlying it. Such an idea scarcely needs explanation—rather, one might almost say that overcoming this view is a major achievement for any culture, and the very absence of the idea should be examined: how, in the absence of witchcraft, does the society achieve the balance, the equilibrium, and the "mental health" that it requires? Before we can answer such a question, however, two more examples of witchcraft should be studied: one from native North America, the other from Africa.

THE NAVAHO AND WITCHCRAFT

The cultures of American Indians are ordinarily not thought to be hotbeds of witchcraft—we see Indians in a stereotype of the Plains Indian who goes out in search of a vision and personal power. And yet, this concept of power, even among the Plains Indians, has many attributes of witchcraft; outside the Plains, witchcraft of an easily identifiable variety emerges. The best studies on American Indian witchcraft have been done on the Navaho of Arizona and New Mexico, (Kluckhohn, 1944) and on the Owens Valley Paiute, an Indian group who live in southeastern Oregon (B. Whiting, 1950) and who formed a part of the Basin Shoshonean peoples—and who had one of the materially most primitive food-collecting cultures in the world at the time they first came into contact with whites.

Navaho say that there are several methods of bewitching, and they give each a name. Kluckhohn has translated each of these forms with an English word, noting that the translation is not always perfectly congruent with its usual English meaning: (1) witchery, (2) sorcery, (3) wizardry, and (4) frenzy witchcraft.

WITCHERY

The technique of "the witchery way" is a part of the Navaho emergence legend. The medicine, usually called a "poison" when Navaho discuss these matters in English, is said to contain the flesh of human corpses—one of the major elements in the well-known fear of the dead exhibited by Navaho. The two preferred parts are the head bones and skin whorls, such as those found on fingerprints. The "poison" is said to look like pollen, and to be thrown into houses or hogans, or else administered as inhalations to sleeping victims or to members of large crowds. Soon afterwards, illness is said to ensue. The usual ceremonial treatments for illness are considered not to be of any avail—actually, of course, when the ceremonial treatments are of no avail, a reason must be found and the reason is found in witchcraft—again, the "reasoning backward" that is characteristic of witchcraft beliefs.

Among Navaho, more men are witches than women; almost all female witches are old. Witchcraft is associated with the dead, and also with incest.

Navaho say that witchery is most often learned from a close kinsman or spouse, although other kinsmen and some spouses may not know that a person is a witch. As is true in many other parts of the world, it is sometimes necessary to give as a victim in one's initiation, a close kinsmen. Witches may become such in order to get vengeance on someone they dislike, Navaho say. They also hold that witchdoctors sometimes perform witchcraft in order that they may get the fees that come from performing cures. Navaho often track witches over long distances at night; sometimes the "witch" turns out to be an animal (which may be associated with enemies by means of totem beliefs), but at other times he turns out to be a human being. The exact signs followed in tracking are hard to elicit from them.

Witches are said to meet at night in a sort of coven, where they initiate new members, practice cannibalism, or kill victims at a distance. There is said to be a hierarchy of offices with a headman, workers, and a division of labor.

Most of these ideas are, of course, found both in European and in African witchcraft. The social group of witches is called a "coven" in English, and they are said to have ridden to their special black rituals or "sabbaths" on broomsticks or else disguised as animals. The supposed social organization of the witches is patterned on more familiar organizations.

SORCERY

Another sort of activity is that which the Navaho called by the word Kluckhohn translated as "sorcery." "Sorcery" was regarded by most of his Navaho informants as a branch of witchery, and sorcerers participated in the witch's meetings, but they used different techniques in working their ill effects. Navaho sorcery is said to be performed by means of spells, with no face-to-face encounter between the sorcerer and his victim. The former must, however, obtain a sample of hair, fingernails, or body dirt—any item that has been in close association with his victim. This token is buried with human flesh or other "poison" beside a grave or in some other frightening place. The sorcerer is said to recite a spell, after which his victim will die. As in the case of the "black mass," a good spell said backward in sometimes used as the technique, although various other techniques are also said to exist. The spell may be murmured while the sorcerer merely walks around the house of the victim; he may make esoteric spells, uttering them over the opened belly of a horned toad. Sorcerers make images and damage them, much as witches were said to have done in medieval Europe.

WIZARDRY

Just as the others, the third type of nefarious human being among the Navaho is distinguished by his way of working. He is called by a term that has been translated "wizard." The main technique wizards are said to use is the introduction of a foreign substance, such as a stone or a piece of charcoal, into the body of their victim. Bits of bone or teeth from a corpse are said to be favorite materials. English-speaking Navahos sometimes refer to this particular form of witchcraft as "bean shooting" and say that it is of recent origin. The way in which these projectiles are thought to be inserted into the body of a victim remains a mystery, although it is subject to much speculation.

Wizards seem not to participate in the witches' sabbaths, and women are never named as wizards, although when asked directly, Dr. Kluckhohn's informants saw no reason a woman could not act as a wizard. The objects inserted into the victim are removed by sucking—this operation is carried out by doctors.

Now, in this information we can see another constant attribute of witchcraft: the unsureness of just how the dirty work is done. The reason is easily apparent: when nothing is actually done there must be some mystical explanation if the belief is to be maintained. Everyone will profess ultimate ignorance about how these things are done not just because to do otherwise would make one appear to know too much about it, but also because one actually does not know. It is only with patient questioning and long residence in a community that the commonly held ideas on these subjects are forthcoming.

As we have already seen, what exists in the world of Navaho social reality is a set of activities for counteracting misfortune, and an extensive idea system that links human misfortune with human malice.

Institutions of counterwitchcraft may take the form of frenetic legal trials, as they did in our own history. They may take the form of charms or rituals to counteract the evil. Kluckhohn has examined these ideas for the Navaho and found that they say tangible and intangible ceremonial goods are their surest protection against witches. The thing most often mentioned was "good songs and prayers and stories," which witches are afraid of—note the similarity to the medieval Christian tradition, which said that if a true Christian made the sign of the cross, or carried his rosary about with him, he was safe. The most common Navaho specific against witchery is gall medicine, an immediate antidote to corpse poison. The gall of some animals—eagle, bear, mountain lion, skunk, wolf, badger, deer, and sheep—is mixed with ground corn; the mixture may be carried or kept in the hogan. Possession of certain plants, or anointing the body with certain plants, is also good medicine against witchery: often the same plants are said to be used *in* witchcraft.

*Anti*witchcraft is in most, but not all, societies associated with medicine, doctors, and curing. Curing among the Navaho is done by several means. A confession by the witch is effective in itself unless the victim has been destroyed beyond cure—confessions can only stop disease, they cannot undo its ravages. Divination, or community agreement that certain acts are suspicious, may lead to charges against a man, who is thereupon questioned publicly, and possibly tortured until he confesses. Confession usually includes, in the Navaho idea, the absorption by the witch of the forces that have been killing his victim, and hence death is commonly supposed to follow confession within the year. A few confessed witches were allowed to live in exile. Navaho claim that even unconfessed witches will eventually be killed by lightning.

Navaho witchcraft is a reality in the sense that belief in it is a social force: thirty out of thirty-two houses that Dr. Kluckhohn knew well in Ramah had gall medicine. Prayers and chants against witchcraft are performed. Moreover, there is the undisputable fact that people have been killed as witches.

> Accusations of witchcraft are based upon revelations by divination . . . or upon observation of the accused picking up spittle or engaging in other behavior attributed to witches. When is a diagnosis of witchcraft likely in divination? The evidence is unmistakable on this point: when an illness is persistent, stubbornly refusing to yield to usual Navaho treatment; when an illness is in any way mysterious from the Navaho point of view; when the symptoms correspond to those expected in such cases—sudden onset, fainting, emaciation, sharp pain in a localized area and a lump or other evidence of a foreign object there; and when the sick person has quarrelled with some powerful person, especially one previously suspected of witchcraft [Kluckhohn, 1944, p. 31].

Thus, to sum up: the constellation of ideas described as "witchcraft" comes to the fore when a situation of misfortune occurs—it may be sickness and death, or it may be community calamity. In such a situation, the community subscribes to the postulate that misfortune of this sort can be the result of human causation—in fact, it may be that, as the authors of the *Malleus Maleficarum* did, the community ideas state that there is no other way for this misfortune to happen.

In short, a culture may need the concept of the witch to explain cosmography or human biology or social tension, or all three. With the postulate in mind, "This misfortune is caused by a witch," the next step is to discover just who is the witch. This may be done by divination of some sort as among the Navaho and most Africans, or it may be done by extracting confessions from "suspicious" people. The point is that since there is no empirically provable connection, the "authorities" are dependent either on nonempirical means of knowledge or on confessions. Then, having found their "scapegoat"—that is, the human agent who can be blamed for having caused the present situation—the society is capable of carrying out some sort of activity, be it ritual, legal, or whatever, which is assumed to clear up the matter they ascribed to that activity.

The point about witchcraft is that misfortune exists and the counteraction exists. But a *non sequitur* links the two. Scientifically we know that the cause did not produce the effect—and that ideas of witchcraft are false ones. But scientifically we also know that human malice must be counteracted to achieve mental health.

Perhaps a better way to put it is to say that the institutions of counterwitchcraft have idea systems that can be called "witchcraft" or "belief in witchcraft." We have thus taken into account the social reality: society, giving itself the impression that it is doing something, curing something. And with the social values and the norms thus reaffirmed, it may make it easier to live down the misfortune, to cope with it morally. That at least is the opinion of many social scientists and even of some of the sceptics among the primitive peoples.

THE AZANDE AND WITCHCRAFT

The belief in witchcraft can be overpowering, and yet before any sort of rational questioning of the premises, it must be proved false. How can a people live with irrational beliefs and false premises without discovering that they are false? The question was investigated in detail by Evans-Pritchard, who studied witchcraft among the Azande of the southern Sudan.

We are fortunate in having two great ethnographic monographs on witchcraft, both written in the 1930s. Evans-Pritchard's book (1936) has, in fact, made assimilation of Kluckhohn's work and the historical material on the subject possible.

In the very briefest of terms, Azande suspect witchcraft when misfortune strikes. They place the names of possible witches before their various oracles, and the oracles tell them which of the suspects are innocent, and which may be guilty. The guilty persons are then presented with the evidence from the oracular consultation and, almost without exception, claim innocence or lack of knowledge of their deed, ceremonially "withdraw" any malice they might inadevertently have turned on the victim, and thereby open the path for effective medical treatment. When witchcraft is the means of explaining misfortune, and since misfortune ultimately strikes everyone, all "witches" ultimately get their comeuppance. The community may or it may not recognize that the comeuppance would have occurred regardless of whether or not counterwitchcraft is said to lie behind it; different groups in the community may indeed take different views in any specific case.

Yet, people do not see that witchcraft is illusory for precisely the reason that almost all human relationships are inadequately performed, and therefore may lead to feelings of guilt on the part of the actors. The guilt felt about relationships is probably not guilt of carrying out acts that can be construed, in any culture, as witchcraft—it is, rather, a more general inadequacy. And yet, as Reik (1958) has so convincingly shown, guilt communicates itself, and the bystanders assume that it is guilt of the act of which the charge has been made. We are all guilty—few are guilty of witchcraft, but if witchcraft is the learned and accepted mode of interpreting overt guilt, then it may not be possible to see that witchcraft is false.

There can be little doubt, I think, that witchcraft and witchcraft trials clear the air. The question is, of course, whether a community can be satisfied with that mode of clearing the air, and whether or not a *non sequitur* can be made, ultimately, into a positive social force.

Social change

part 6

21

Institutions: their process, history, and evolution

IT REMAINS FOR US to examine one of the most vital of all the problems in social anthropology: social and cultural change. Three different factors must be distinguished—recurrent social process, history, and evolution.

A FUNCTIONALIST MODEL

In order to analyze change, it is first necessary to review the position we have already attained, and to make an overt "model" of the theoretical elements so far considered. This model is one that derives from structural-functional theory, which has been quite correctly criticized as being static in character; but it is wrong, as we shall see, to *oppose* a functionalist to dynamic theory, as has too often been done.

Functional theory in anthropology is based on two interrelated axioms. The first is frankly teleological[1] and states that culture fulfills the physical needs of human beings for expression and for survival, and the symbolic and material needs of societies for persistence.

The second is pseudomathematical and can be written with the symbol $\int$—culture is an organized whole, the parts of which adjust in a regular manner to perturbation in any other part.

The functionalist model that has been used in this book is one developed from Malinowski's concept of the institution (1945). It fulfills the requirements of a model: an elegant analytical framework that can be used to organize data with economy and without serious distortion. The institution, as Malinowski defined it, is characterized by a group of people united for a purpose. They have the organization for carrying out the purpose, and they have the culture, both material and ideal, to assist them.

[1] Teleology in physical sciences is suspect because it is anthropomorphic; this very anthropomorphism is obviously, however, inherent in social phenomena involving human beings.

They have a set of ideas, which Malinowski called the "charter" of the institution, about the way things should be done and the reasons why they should be done.

Social life can, thus, be divided (for purposes of analysis) into institutions each of which is characterized by a social system, a system of material culture, and an idea system; institutions fulfill the needs of human beings and of social groups, and they are functionally interrelated because change in one is likely to precipitate change in some or all of the others. With this model, as it is set forth in Table 16, it has been possible to survey some of the most important aspects of the nature of man as an animal—a sentient and communicating, social and organizing mammal. We have also surveyed the major institutions of his social and cultural life: kinship and family, work and production, politics and war, and finally those institutions that center about the explanation of man's place in the cosmos—religion, witchcraft, and magic. We have seen that language and art are a dimension—indeed, the very fabric—of all these institutions. It is in language and art, as it is in technology and science and in moral and legal precepts, that mankind grasps its own condition, understands it, and communicates about it.

It is also obvious that this model in itself has not proved adequate to all our needs, and that we have found it necessary to add a time dimension, the baby Malinowski threw out with the bath water of "reconstructed history." We have discerned repetitive series of events, which have been called "event systems," in the working of institutions.

Recognition of an event system introduces the element of time into the model of the institution by adding a third axiom to the two functionalist axioms already enunciated. Stated briefly, the axiom reads: Only through repeated series of acts or events can purpose be achieved and various aspects of culture interrelated. That is to say, in order to achieve the desired ends, actors must be able to predict, within certain limits, the range of events that will normally follow other events. Therefore, acts must recur and must follow one another in an order that is substantially known to all. It is thus possible to elicit series of recurring events that carry out purposes and interrelate the various dimensions of human experience.

Mere recognition of an event system does not, however, make a suitable theory of change; for the institution can still be regarded as static and unchanging, even if there is a cyclical and recurrent dynamic. The "event system" has been added to the model in Table 16. The life cycle, the events surrounding marriage, the jural cycle of events—all such event systems can be treated in a nonhistorical way in which a limited view of time is recognized in the system that is nevertheless still fundamentally nondevelopmental.

However, with the introduction of the concept of the event system we are no longer bound to treat institutions *only* in a frame of reference that either omits time or allows only of cyclical time. We can add time which is the very organizing stuff of history.

It is only with the introduction of the concept of the recurrent event system that social change can be understood, for the simple reason that all events do not fit into such cycles that are predictable to actors in the situation. There are, everywhere and no matter how rarely, unpredictable events, which disrupt the institution and its characteristic events. Such disrupting events, by changing the nature of the cycle, lead to new adjustments within all the institutional systems and hence to new repetitive event systems. At one level of generalization, the nonrepetitive events are equivalent to what computer analysts call "random shock." At another, they comprise history.

History is, among other things, a noncyclical lineal arrangement of events, each of which can be seen as an alternative occurrence to some other occurrence, which limits or at least redirects all subsequent events. Some of these historical events come from quite outside the institutional system—in the next chapter we shall examine some of the ways in which the historical events marking the expansion of the West were external to the societies and institutions on which their impact was most strongly felt. Historical events may also, of course, be generated by tensions within an institution, which rearranges itself in such a way that its cyclic event structure is changed: such was the need for expansion in the West.

Evolution is quite another matter: evolution studies not just the event structure and not just the historical events *per se,* but rather the sequences of the event structures that follow on a line of nonrecurrent historical events. The argument among students of social and cultural evolution lies in whether or not such sequences are regular and predictable: early evolutionary theory, which can be typified by Morgan, assumed that there were regularities in evolutionary sequences, and therefore that stages of social and cultural development could be determined. Neoevolutionary theory, which can be typified by Steward, assumes that such regularities are unprovable, and hence that stages of social and cultural development are either misconceptions or are fortuitous.

We now have a model before us in terms of which it is possible to review everything that has gone before in this book, and then to understand, in the rest of this and in the next chapter, the principles of social and cultural change.

A REVIEW

To review again at somewhat greater length: We have found first that every concrete and empirical institution is characterized by—indeed, it is defined by—a social organization. A social organization is a system of differentiated and interlocked roles, relationships, and syndromes that provide guideposts to behavior and motives to compliance. We have, for example, given a purely formal definition of the family and have discussed its extension into different sorts of social groups by multiplying and overlapping roles. The item "social system" heads the first column of Table 16, which represents a diagrammatic summary of the characteristics of institutions. The social system was the major system we studied in the institutions of family and kinship groups. It was not, however, by any means the only system we studied.

We began our kinship studies with an investigation of marriage. Marriage is an act, or a concatenated series of acts, performed on the part of many people. It is an event, perhaps even a series of events as is the case among the Nuer where different rights in the wife are transferred at different times, the whole taking as much as three or four years; indeed, the Swedes of northern Europe legally demand an engagement announcement a definite time prior to the actual wedding, and domestic rights may, with social accord, be in certain instances exercised after the "official engagement" but before the wedding. Marriage is, however, only one of the events characteristic of a family. Births and deaths are other important and universal events in the event system of family institutions. Additional events may also be recognized: coming-of-age parties or initiations, retirement or grandparenthood, and an almost numberless group of events that different societies have picked out and made a structural part of the event sequences of their family institutions. The life cycle is, thus, a series of acts going to make up the activities of kinship groups, especially families.

The cycle may and probably will have ramifications in other institutions—sometimes definitive ones—but the passage through the life cycle is always related to kinship groups in that it represents a characteristic series of events by which they are known. It is the "event system" of the group; it is placed at the heading of the second column of Table 16, as the second summarizing characteristic of institutions.

The household, just as any other identifiable group, has a typical event structure in every society. Among ourselves, for example, a new household comes into existence at marriage, let us say. The young couple usually form a household from the time of their marriage—in certain classes and in certain areas this statement is not true, but it is usually the ideal. The house or apartment is usually too small for the family once there are two or three children. They need nursery space, play space, trees, air—whatever is dictated by the subculture and its mores. In any case, a large proportion of American middle-class family households move into bigger houses, arranged on a different plan, from the original apartment they lived in. Then, as the children grow up, and leave the household, a new arrangement again is called for: the "younger generation" marries or goes to college; the older generation may cling to the house for a while because the children will come home—but only for short periods. The elders often leave the big house and go into an apartment or a smaller house. Finally, the household may be terminated by the death of one of its spouse members, certainly with that of both. Here we have a pattern of events characteristic of the households of a greater or lesser sector of our own society. There are at all times households in all phases of development, at all places in the cycle. This sort of event system can be computed for every household recognized in any society (Fortes, 1949; Goody, 1958). There may, indeed, be several different patterns all operating at the same time in different reaches of the community.

There are two other event cycles in the household in our own society. There is the daily routine of getting up, eating, cleaning, the departure and return of the husband/father, more eating, watching television or whatever. Such a daily event structure—a routine of greater or lesser rigidity—is characteristic of all households everywhere, and of the family groups that form their basis. There is also an annual cycle associated with the seasons and with work and recreation.

There is a further factor to be mentioned—so obvious as almost to escape notice: the household is characterized by a certain material culture. In the ordinary primitive societies—and indeed in our own society—these material things comprise primarily the houses themselves. All known people build some sort of shelters. They may be extremely rudimentary as were the Bushmen windscreens or the leaf-hatched shelters of the tiny hunting tribes of inland Borneo. But there are houses of some sort—and the house is probably the most important material culture item associated with the household. There have been world surveys of house types, in which the buildings of all the known peoples of the world have been examined. (These studies were usually done in German.) The material culture of the household also includes domestic implements and perhaps clothes, treasures—all sorts of things may be associated with the family and its household.

This system of things is of relatively greater importance to archeologists and to economists than it is to ethnologists and social anthropologists.

Or at least, we think today that it is so; yet probably as much as half of all anthropological literature is thing-oriented, and describes things—often without any reference whatever to social systems, events, ideas, or any other aspect of the institutions of which things are characteristic.

Now, we have a social system, an event system, and a system of material culture. What is left? Obviously, the ideas that are characteristic of every institution. Ideas about how things ought to be done, and even more importantly about *why* they should be done. In the family and kinship institutions, there are always definite ideas behind the social system, which give the cues to the people who live there about how they ought to feel about the other members of the family. That is to say, there are ideas of the "proper" behavior of brothers and parents; and even more important, there are given, learnable ideas about what a relationship of brothers ought to consist in. Moreover, there are definite ideas and evaluations about all of the events in the event system, and there may even be a sort of philosophy connecting all these ideas into a sensible whole. There are ideas about the value and quality of the relationship between people and houses ("home" is an American example), or between things and certain people. The family is the subject of a whole set of morals, ethics, legal obligations, and attitudes. So are all kinship institutions. Every society has a family morality and kinship ethic, which to a finer or coarser degree systematize the ideas about kinsmen and give one standards of how to act toward and perhaps even feel about kinsmen. This family philosophy is a series of the larger genre, the "idea system."

The system of material culture and the idea system are summarized as columns 3 and 4 of Table 16. It is also evident that the institutions of family and kinship form, as a large and internally varied category, the first row of the table: we have considered the social system, event system, system of material culture, and idea system of the kinship institutions.

We can then proceed to another major area of institutionalization: that of the control of power. In our discussion of politics, we centered on the social system and on the event system. It would seem that the event structure of political institutions is probably simpler and more overt than is the event structure of other major institutions with which we have been concerned. Two event structures were discussed: that for handling disputes or crimes in a society, and that for analyzing warfare. We saw that we could generalize and say that jural activity consisted of a breach of norm (either law, custom, or whatever), which was followed by a social counteraction that might be of any general type—court and police action, moots, contests, and ordeals. The counteraction is then followed by some sort of a correction—either a carrying out of the norm or an approved substitute for it.

Now, there are obviously many other event structures in the political organizations that could be selected and looked into. For example, how do people achieve or acquire the roles in political institutions? In our own society, this is the subject of "politics" par excellence. We have a complex system of elections—an event system that runs in cycles of two, four, and six years with definite acts repeated at each election, and the whole thing carried out with the purpose of putting the so-called "right man" in office. We even say, sometimes, that we want to keep the courts free of politics—very well; but to say so requires a special use of the word "politics," for the activities of the courts are politics in essence whereas the activities leading to selection of officeholders may be somewhat tangential, even though they take up a disproportionate amount of time both of the members of the political institutions and of the general populace—those whose role, we might say, is voting. All, however, seem to think the time well spent. Certainly, in our elections there is a complex event system that can be examined. Similarly, there are elections or succession fights or some other such device by means of which officeholders are chosen in many societies. Such event sequences are described by political scientists; they certainly form an extremely important part of the event system of the political institutions.

The social system of any political institution is, however, of great importance. The political events may be acted out by kinship groups or by contractual groups or by some other form of social group. We studied briefly some examples of various kinds of social groups that are available for carrying out these acts—the royal family and state religion of the Swazi, the army organization of the Ashanti, and so forth. It is apparent, indeed, that there are several forms a political organization may take: it may be hierarchial as is the case with modern nations, African kingdoms, and Greek city states. It may, on the other hand, be an "acephalous" organization such as the lineage system of the Nuer, the Tiv, or the Bedouin Arabs, which carries out all the political activities, as we have here defined them, without a centralized organization and utilizing instead a form of balance of power called the principle of segmental opposition. Small kinship groups such as extended families may indeed carry out all the political activities in small-scale societies, usually those based on economies of hunting and gathering.

The system of material culture connected with political institutions deals with land and space and with the trappings of majesty, badges of authority, and symbols for focusing patriotism. Because of the symbolic nature of the material things, the range is as broad as life itself.

The idea systems of political institutions are often highly articulate, and indeed almost become reified into things: the word "democracy" and the idea systems it stands for provide a case in point. The idea system may, moreover, take overt form as a legal code or a set of stated and recognized jural precedents. These overt and systematized ideas have behind them and beneath them another set of less highly formalized and perhaps unstated ideas that Hoebel (1954) has called the "postulates" on which the law is based. The postulates might, indeed, be called the given axioms of moral political behavior, and like axioms everywhere they may remain unstated. In the case of our own society, we base our legal activities not merely on written law and stated custom, but on a series of proverblike sayings (many written into the law) that have the force of axioms in our legal reasoning and acting: "A man is innocent until proved guilty," "No man can be forced to testify against himself," and the rest. These proverblike principles, moreover, can be distinguished from deeper, more covert postulates such as those about the inviolability of the human body that Sykes (1958) found in his study of a maximum-security prison.

In short, we can approach any political institution from the standpoint of the social system, the event system, the system of material culture, or the idea system. Hoebel (1954), as we noted, chose to study the idea system behind law and created his analysis of postulates. Here we have chosen to recast some of his material, with other case histories as well, in terms that emphasize the event system.

In discussing economic institutions it is usual to begin with the system of material culture and those items that are seen in analogy to material items (we have already noted that "services" is a concept in terms of which economists can deal with social factors that social anthropologists would deal with in terms of social structure and human relationships). Economics deals with production of things, with distribution of things such as subsistence, treasure, and prestige items. Throughout, *things* are concerned —indeed, the whole study of the economy is sometimes branded as "materialistic" in a pejorative as well as in a literal sense.

There are social organizations behind any sort of allocation or movement of things, and behind their production as well. There are social groups having as one of their purposes production of goods—a good is a thing with a prescribed social value—and other social organizations or groups dealing with distribution. The *kula,* you remember, was best seen as a far-flung organization of trading friends, which passed things along its links of social relationships. It *could* be seen as the necklace structure of Melanesian society, which it is if one looks at it from the thing-oriented view. Obviously, a family or even a political group may be, for specific purposes, a production group; in studying production the family or political aspects may be beside the point.

There is, in fact, a new and special field of sociology that deals primarily with the social systems of economic institutions: because of the fact that it developed in examination of the economic institutions of our own society, it is usually called "industrial sociology." Industrial sociology is, however, fast growing beyond the society that nurtured it and that it first explained: it is becoming comparative, utilizing insights and theories that can be applied cross culturally. Industrial sociologists—and economic anthropologists—can predict many things about the sort of group organization found in a specific work situation, which can be divided into, say, six processes. With an amazingly high ratio of probability, the organization of production groups can be predicted on a knowledge of the production processes. In short, industrial sociologists are finding correlations among the social system, the event system, and the idea system.

The event system in any economic institution tends to center around the technology of producing or distributing the item the institution sets out to produce or distribute. Thus, the event system in a cattle economy will be determined in part by the cattle themselves, and in part by the way in which cattle are handled and valued by the people. A farming technology will create an event cycle consisting of tasks running from farm selection and preparation to planting, weeding, harvesting, and storing. Another sort of event system is the various acts encountered in a trading institution. The *kula* has a relatively complex event structure—complex even by modern market standards.

The idea system of economic institutions is another matter: and it is a matter that is very little explored. Aside from the science of economics itself, the ideas surrounding economic institutions have, in the past, most often been explored in terms of the Western concept of "property." However, property is another one of those simplifying ideas such as "money" and "time." Property is a conceptual way in the folk system for linking the system of material culture with the social system. Property ideas assume a set of social relations; they also assume a set of things. "Property" is only one of the possible relationships of people to things. The relationship of people to things is universal; in that sense and that sense alone is "property" universal.

Finally, when we came to the institutions of religion, magic, science, and witchcraft, the emphasis was placed on the idea system, precisely because it is here that the data are richest. We, in our society, tend to think of magic, science, and religion all as having an intellectual dimension. We even confuse them with "ways of thinking." In probably no area of cultural endeavor are the idea systems as overt in almost all societies as are those which deal with religion and magic. In the Western world there have been centuries, indeed millenia, of writers and thinkers dealing with the problems of cosmology and theology. The idea system of a religion or a set of magical practices is itself an explanation in myth, story, or history of all the rest of the systems contained within that institution, and indeed perhaps many in the other institutions as well.

And yet, religious and magical institutions are raised on a foundation of social groups. Congregations are social groups with memberships, organization, hierarchical structure, and the like. These congregations participate in a series of social acts that are basically repetitive. These acts and the various secular activities leading up to them are ritual and ceremonial. Some of these activities in the event system of the religious institution are performed on a weekly basis, others on a daily basis, and still others on an annual basis. The repetitive and cyclical character of the activities in a religious institution is very often given specific value: the very repetition may give positive benefit and comfort, more perhaps than in any other institution.

When the anthropologist approaches the study of religion in the field, it is the event system and the system of material culture that are immediately observable. He must, in short, start with the ritual he can see performed. Only later can he learn the social system behind it and the idea systems that give it meaning.

The systems of material culture involved in religious and magical institutions is well known for revealed and modern religions: it even has a name–iconography. There is a large literature, written for the main part around the turn of the century, on what is called the "migration of symbols" or holy objects; the point was to see how they spread, trace their voyaging around the globe, and then check into the ideas that became associated with them. Today, we could see these studies as concerned with the differential rate of travel of the material and the idea systems of the institution, and hence as a primary problem in social change.

When it comes to science, with its theoretical idea system, we can also study the social organization of universities, foundations, and laboratories; we can study the ritual of experimentation, and the material system of scientific paraphernalia ranging from Bunsen burners and blast furnaces to mazes and couches. And yet, primary interest in religious, magical, and scientific institutions is always in the idea system.

A warning should be repeated: we have been discussing a model for reviewing and comparing the institutions of societies. The student should not assume that the empirical division of a whole society into institutions will correspond exactly with the model, but only that the different categories in the model will be found somewhere in the empirical situation; that is to say, the family may be the only organization present and must be listed as the social structure in every box under "social system" in the model.

Taking this oversimplified model, which is summarized in Table 16, we must note that the investigations in this book have focused on the rows of the diagram: kinship, polity, economy, religion, and science; the rows have been chosen on the basis of function—of necessary preconditions for the existence of society (Levy, 1952). The student may, by changing or refining his concepts of function, change the criteria used for the rows. Such is the strength, not the weakness, of the model.

It would have been equally possible—but it would have been another book—to deal with columns instead of rows. We can study the social systems, event systems, material systems, and idea systems of all the various institutions of any given society. There are in fact some disciplines or subjects that do precisely this. Archeology, in the nature of its subject matter, is limited to the systems of material culture: to things and their distribution in space. Archeologists can never dig up ideas unless there had been a literature in the society whose remains they are excavating. They can only infer an idea system; an event system and a social system can only partially be seen in the material remains. Often any inferences are shaky, as archeologists admit.

In the early days of anthropology—and in the consideration of these problems, the early days extended into the middle twenties—most anthropological studies dwelt on the spatial distribution of material "culture traits" and their diffusion. Those traits that were nonmaterial, such as the themes of myths or a type of marriage or a term for mother's brother, were treated with the same set of theoretical tools and hence were quasimaterial (just as the idea of "services" is quasimaterial to the economist, who by this means can get both personal relationships and nonmaterial "products" such as electricity or good will into his theoretical model) Distribution studies made some simple assumptions: that culture traits, once invented, spread outwards in ripple fashion, and that therefore if the distribution of a trait is known, the process can be reversed intellectually and a sort of "history" can be reconstructed. Even when these scientists were studying living peoples they tended to study mainly the material system, to treat social organization as merely another culture trait, to break ideas up into "themes" and trace them back. When they paid any attention to event systems at all, such systems were made up on more or less "logical" grounds, not based on the observations that would, in many instances, have corrected the error—that is, the event sequence *could* have been got into the data instead of being implied in the analysis.

The development of anthropology since the late 1920s can be seen as an increasingly precise focus on the social system and the idea system. The event system remained unplumbed in any "scientific" sense, until neo-evolutionism emerged in the late 1940s. To sum up, American anthropology developed in analogy to archeology and for decades took its subject matter primarily from the system of material culture, branching into the other systems only in terms of analogy or if it was vital to explain a point in that material system.

Another example of a discipline that deals primarily with one of the vertical columns—though of course it may, after its fashion, utilize all—is sociology. One of the primary tasks of sociology is to make sense out of the vertical column headed social system in Table 16.

In somewhat the same way, the idea systems are the province of philosophers (without, of course, belonging solely to them—none of those columns or rows belongs solely to any discipline). Philosophies include systems of family morality, and political ethics, ideas about justice and honesty. They reach their peak in epistemology, which investigates how we know what we know. Philosophy, in short, sets out to organize the guiding ideas behind the major institutions of any culture, usually following the humanist tradition of moral commitment to one or the other of these ideas, no matter how critical the examination may be.

RECURRENCE AND CHANGE OF EVENT SYSTEMS

Imperfect perception of the event system has, up to the present day, lurked behind several of the bitterest—and least enlightening—schisms in anthropology: the false opposition of history to functionalism, the confusion of evolutionary theory with reconstructed history, and the strife between neoevolutionism and the followers of Franz Boas who have (for the good reason that they have done almost everything) been called almost everything. Here we want to point out again that the axioms lying behind classical functionalism also necessarily lie behind evolutionary theory, and that history not merely connects the two, but is a logical necessity to both schemes. Indeed, the clarification of the nature of the event system and the overt statement of the third axiom make the point obvious.

Recurrent events can be investigated and recorded. So can rare events or nonrecurrent events. It is also investigable that in the process of recurrence, certain strains may be created within the institution, which ultimately must either be corrected (by recurring events with an atypical pattern of recurrence) and the strain so eased, or which lead to nonrecurrent events that make recapturing the older event system impossible, and hence lead to change in all aspects of the institution. The first of these two modes of correction does not lead to change, but merely to what can be called a gyroscopic event, often unrecognized, in the event structure. The second is the very essence of change.

Some event sequences work smoothly and would seem to proceed over and over again, without noticeable tension or with only self-resolving tension. Yet, there are other event systems which seem to contain elements that so wobble the system as to make exact repetition extremely difficult—events which, even when performed in accordance with the basic ideas and postulates of the accompanying idea systems, throw the institution out of kilter. Such systems would seem to contain the seeds of their own destruction.

Yet a second event sequence, often called into action by the tension created in the first, is found to be widespread; interestingly enough, these gyroscopic event structures that maintain the operation of the other event structures within the institution are often disapproved by the actors. One of the best examples is to be found in American political activity. America is beset every couple of decades with witch hunts on a national scale. Such witch hunts always take a political form; they are universally deplored at the same time that each individual one is well-nigh universally deemed necessary to maintain the most precious of political ideas and organizations. Extremist groups of both the right and the left "get out of hand," make their points, even change minor aspects of the national political organization, and then are brought to heel. Thus, they constantly refortify the middle: the fundamental dynamic of the political process.

Similar activities have been observed elsewhere. Among the Tiv of central Nigeria, a "witch hunt" of similar mien recurs about every ten years. The event system of the political institutions allows power to be thrust into the hands of fewer and fewer individuals. The Tiv political ethic allows authority to no one. Therefore, in order to maintain the political institutions so that authority does not become crystallized in given offices, the Tiv revolt and throw out the leaders to whom the authority is accreting. Only so is it possible for them to maintain their particular type of "democracy." The revolts are generally deplored; but the results are considered necessary and worth the candle. (Bohannan, 1956).

The other alternative is, of course, that the institution will not have such a built-in or even an improvised gyroscope which brings it back to its keel of regular events; it will instead change its nature, especially its event system. If the Tiv did not have their periodic revolts, they would become some sort of centralized system. If the Americans did not regularly produce Huey Longs, Senator McCarthys, and John Birch societies, in all of their many incarnations and reincarnations, or if they were not just as regularly rejected, the American political system would have changed fundamentally.

We can say, then, that the repetition of an event system, over and over, is the dynamic of an institution. It may or may not contain institutionalized correctives. When it does not, or when it suddenly feels an impact from outside, the events characteristic of the insitution may change, and if that is the case, then social and cultural change throughout the society and in all reaches of the culture are to be expected. If the event system, with its repetitive dynamic, becomes wobbly, eventually it will change in such a way that the series of events forming the system are different—and therewith the entire society is different. If the institution is brought into contact with foreign intruders, whose presence disallows a cyclic continuation of the event system, unchanged, the entire society will again be different.

SOCIAL PROCESS, HISTORY, AND EVOLUTION

We are now in a position to make the vital distinction among social process, history, and evolution. Social process (sometimes called "dynamics") is to be found in the repetitive pattern of events, including gyroscopic events. History, on the other hand, is a chronological statement of events that upset the systems—even if that "upset" is no more than an intensification of a trend, or the presence of a particularly virulent corrective movement. To paraphrase Gertude Stein, process (she said "fiction") happens all the time, but history happens all the time from time to time. History is a record of the events that intensify change in the cultural and social process; good history further explains what is changed and why.

What then of evolution? Social evolution deals not in events but in forms and in processes, even though (like culture) these forms and processes are momentarily manifest in the form of events. Each institution has a number of possibilities for change, depending on its social and nonsocial environment and on the weaknesses and strengths inherent in itself. The actuality of change is an historical event that can be seen as a realization of one of these alternative possibilities. The very realization creates a new process—some of the old possibilities for change are no longer possible, whereas new possibilities have been added.

It is not the event *per se,* but the relationship of the former event

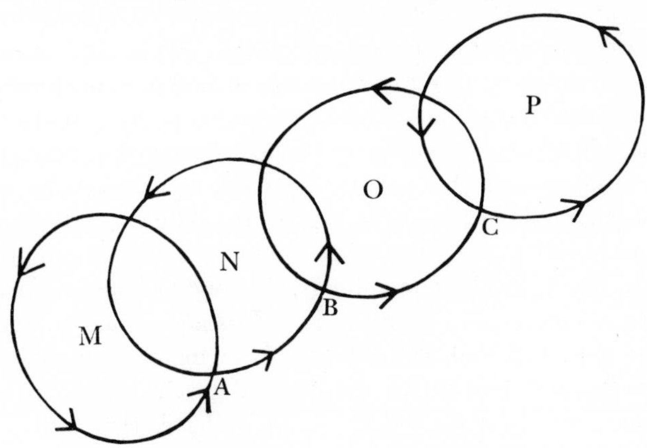

FIGURE 18 Evolution and Social Process

structure to the later event structure which is the stuff of evolution. A diagram may help (see Figure 18).

The event sequence of the institution is marked by an oval, M, made up of many lines, standing for repetitions. Then, at point A on the oval, a break in the accustomed event sequence occurs, whether it result from a "built-in" point of tension or an externally triggered occurrence. The sequence or dynamic of the institution is then thrown out of shape, and the dynamic becomes something of the sort represented by oval N. The event system proceeds on its new round, its process proceeding either rapidly or slowly, its tensions mounting or easing, until at point B another change can be assessed as having occurred, a new oval of event sequences, O, follows to point C, where another change occurs, and event sequence P ensues, and so on to infinity.

In such an explanation, the dynamics or process of institutions is to be studied in each event sequence—an integral part of such a study is the tension generated by the system, leading to greater or lesser change. The history in the situation is an analysis of the actual "choice" of events A, B, and C, showing the way in which individuals and social pressures, the vicissitudes of "historical accidents" and "psychological accidents," actually brought about one of the potential changes rather than others. Evolution, then, is a generalization from the relationships among M, N, O, P. M, as an event sequence in motion, has certain potentials. Historical and psychic accidents of the sort studied by history emerge—one might almost say "strike"—at certain points in the system. The momentum of system M, plus the impact of event (or events) A, create system N. N, as a system, can be seen to have different potentialities than M as a system. The potentialities for change in N may be as great or even greater as those in M, but at least some of the potentialities in M have been lost. A shift has been made—new potentialities have emerged in the new dynamic, waiting for new historical and psychic accidents to trigger their weaknesses and intensify their strengths and thus to produce further evolutionary change.

We have, here, a scheme for looking at institutions and their development and change. Institutions serve ends, and in so doing fulfill the functional requisites of man's continuing biological and social life. Man must reproduce and socialize his young; he must maintain order while he exploits his environment; he must explain the nature of his place in the universe. There are many other things he must have and conditions that must be met (Levy, 1952). These things and conditions are summed up in a concatenation of interlocked institutions. It is the essence of functionalist theory that the social and biological needs of mankind must be met by cultural means and that all of the cultural means which requite such needs form a sort of interlocked unity. As we have seen, both conditions are necessary in functionalist theory.

It need hardly be added that all these theories are of a piece: human needs are satisfied by cultural means; all cultural means are associated with all the other aspects of institutions; all aspects, at different rates and in different degrees, may be diffused; in the diffusion, new tensions arise in the event systems of old institutions, which ultimately lead to change and to social and cultural evolution.

It has, thus, been possible to summarize under this rubric of the institution (with only a modicum of warping that invariably comes with oversimplification) the theories of diffusion, of functionalism, and of cultural and social evolution. Such an analytical system allows us to compare institutions, even though the total theoretical system would not be discoverable in any empirical institution (though most of its manifestations would be). Like all analytical systems or models, it must be seen as the work of the social scientist, and must be distinguished from the type of systemization that is done by the people in a society. The cardinal error in anthropology is making up a systematic explanation for purposes of comparison, and then projecting that explanation into ethnography and hence into the reported consciousness of the people who were studied for information.

INSTITUTIONS AND SOCIETY

There is one more point that must be made: a society or a culture, because it has meaningful organization, is more than just the sum of its institutions. Every society institutionalizes many aspects of its culture and its ideas and social relationships. But there are some that are only very weakly institutionalized. We can all pick out examples of weak institutionalization in our own society. In addition, there are in every society institutions that are not part of the approved and acknowledged social milieu, but that are nevertheless there. Take the institution of criminals that in 1958 held a meeting of its personnel in upper New York State. It would be possible for an analyst, studying that institution, to find something to go in all of the columns, all of the pigeonholes. And yet that institution is *sub rosa* and not acknowledged by the general population as desirable or perhaps even existent. Such can be called "interstitial" institutions because they establish themselves in the interstices of the society and perform functions that are performed in no other way. As we have seen, some such institutions may perform positive functions as well as dysfunctions. Many of our political and economic institutions would be very different were it not for major or minor interstitial institutions. And, ironically enough, some of the aspects of our institutions which we admire most may be those very ones that depend on an interstitial organization to set them up or to keep them going.

The institutions of a society, including the interstitial institutions, can be—indeed they must be—studied as of a piece. Ideas from one institutional area are influenced by ideas from other institutional areas. Such is, perhaps, the main point Max Weber (1930) made in his study of the Protestant ethic. There, Weber's argument ran, the developing capitalistic enterprises utilized the ideas and values, as well as the sentiments, of the breakaway Protestant sects. Given this sort of theology and ethics, he said, the way was open for development of technology, and what he called an "economic ethic," which made capitalism possible. It might well be possible within any virile and developing society to see the institutions change—all sorts of institutions, not just the economic ones—in response to a new and pervasive set of ideas.

Anthropologists, then, in studying culture and society must take into consideration both the unity of institutions, productive though it may be of greater or lesser strain, and the disparity of the sources of change. Event systems may change because of built-in tension. Material cultures may change under the impact of the inventions of creative minds. Idea systems may change because they develop discomforts or contradictions; social systems may change because they are unwieldy or because they do not offer the satisfactions men need.

Yet institutions, and ultimately whole societies and cultures intertwined and overlapping one another, also change by impact from the outside. A Portugese explorer may suddenly stand with his cohorts on a strange coast of Guinea, face to face with Africans. New social relationships have been brought into being, and the struggle for a predictable and comfortable culture to express them must begin. Institutions of trade may turn up new material culture—as when the metal axe was brought to Australia, or the wheel to the Papago Indians (Spicer, 1952)—which changes the entire system of institutions. A steel axe replaces a stone axe and in the process affects the sexual division of labor, all aspects of the institutions of production, and ultimately the rank system and even the religion of the society. And an idea like "Savior" or "evolution" can with the appearance of all innocence enter into an institution and take root, ultimately ripping it apart at the seams.

Social and cultural change is an integral part of social and cultural life. It is, in fact, change that keeps us working by keeping us guessing. Yet social scientists today know quite a bit about change. The only major thing they cannot do is predict just which historical events will occur, leading to just which evolutionary direction. Perhaps they never shall—it may be man's destiny to follow in the race of change, as Achilles followed the tortoise, never quite catching up. It may also be, however, that a couple of geniuses can devise an equation to show that our problem, like the problem of Achilles and the tortoise, is a false one.

TABLE 16 INSTITUTIONS

	SOCIAL SYSTEM	EVENT SYSTEM	MATERIAL SYSTEM	IDEA SYSTEM
Family and Kinship	Families	Life cycle Family cycle	Pertains to the household and not to the family	"Family philosophy"
	Kinship groups			
Political Organization: Law and War	Hierarchal or egalitarian structuring of power roles	The jural sequence	Emblems	Axioms for man's relationship to man in power terms Jural postulates
		The war sequence	Land and space	
Economic Institutions	Production groups Distribution groups	Technology	Subsistence and other material things in space, and how they got there	Idea of property
		Trade or other distribution functions		Science of economics
Religious, Magical, and Scientific Institutions	Congregation, and so on	Ritual	Religious goods and symbols; icons	Explanation in myth, theory, story, history, and so on, of the nature of the world and society
			Scientific paraphernalia	

22

The other side of the frontier

WE NOTED IN THE LAST chapter that institutions may be changed by blows from the outside as well as by accommodation of the tensions created by their own workings. This chapter concerns the impact of the West on the outside world, and, increasingly since the middle of the twentieth century, the counterimpact of that outside world on the West.

Tensions within Western institutions in the last few centuries have been met by expanding geographical boundaries and technology—the two have been constantly intertwined. The resultant frontier has been of constant and fundamental importance to Western society.

But seldom did anyone look at the other side of the frontier, where ancient civilizations and primitive societies were both hit by what were to them blows occasioned by the sheerest historical caprice. These situations, whatever influence they may have had on the conscience of Westerners—and the poignancy and pathos of the lot of "primitive man" as the forgotten man of history have been played upon for all they are worth in many anthropological treatises—provide a superb laboratory for dispassionate study of institutions under stress.

To review some of these changes and problems, two examples serve as an introduction: the story of the impact of the Dutch on a people of the central Celebes called the Toradja, and an account of the reaction of a Plains Indian tribe to American impact.

THE TORADJA

The Toradja are a fortunate people, for a most unusual missionary—a pastor named Kruyt—settled among them. His account (1929) of his own experiences and theirs is extremely valuable because he has no axe to grind: although he wrote in the late 1920's, he is innocent of Freud, of Marx, of Durkheim, and even of Herbert Spencer. His basic bias is that of Protestant Christianity, theologically simple and morally strict. He recounts, in simple language, an experience that he shared with the Toradja, and that he assimilated by means of his Christian belief. His account unwittingly reflects the bleak tone of self-accusation pervading much of the ethnographic material on social change—the white man's burden has become a load of guilt.

Kruyt assures us that before we can understand the influence of Western culture on the Toradja, we must have an idea of their lives before the contact.

Before the arrival of the Dutch the Toradja lived together in communities, the only ties that kept the communities together being those of kinship. The members of such a community built their houses close to each other, thus forming a village consisting of one or more great houses in which a large number of families had their abode.

The head of the community was not exactly elected by the members, but one of the villagers came to assume this responsibility because of local custom that enabled him to give advice on all matters when called upon. People came with their problems and asked for his help. The headman was also a leader in raids. If he was hospitable and unselfish his influence might be very far-reaching. As soon as the headman became too old, his successor emerged precisely as he himself had, and the transfer of authority took place gradually and without difficulty.

The headman was unable to force anybody to carry out an order; the only effective sanction was that of public opinion. The headman therefore always acted in the spirit of that public opinion, and if anyone did not wish to submit to the will of the community, the only thing left for the recalcitrant was to move to another village. But he would be accepted only where he had kinsmen.

In this way, the community maintained discipline among its members by playing on the dependency of one another, since none had any refuge outside the community. The miserly were forced to give away part of their possessions to others in need if the latter asked for it. If they refused, they would find that no assistance was forthcoming when they themselves needed it. The fear of sorcery was the ultimate sanction.

Although every family in the community had its own property, the other members had claims on it in crisis or for purposes of a clan feast. The families who had had most success with their livestock were required to supply the most animals. It was impossible to store goods such as salt —the undeniable demands of neighbors soon depleted the supply.

Among the Toradja, the possession of goods was obviously of little importance. What treasure there was was kept largely in the form of long swatches of white cotton cloth, stored in the rice sheds, and used only for payments of fines or as wrappings for corpses at funerals. There was no general-purpose money, and no need for it.

In 1892 missionaries started work among the Toradja, but attempts to convert them were not signally successful. Kruyt notes that they listened to the sermons purely out of politeness toward the missionaries, who had been kind to them and for whom they therefore were quite willing to do a favor. There were few conversions, for conversion meant isolation from the community not so much of the living as of the dead. They claimed that if the worship of their gods and ancestors were to be discontinued they were doomed to destruction. In Kruyt's words: "The God of the Dutch interfered just as little with the [Toradja] people as the gods of [the Toradja] did with the Dutch" (1929, p. 3).

The same situation applied to the schools. For years no one sent his children to school. A few small schools, with two to eight pupils, were started. But, again, support came only from friendship individual Toradja felt for individual missionaries "whom they did not like to disappoint any longer" (p. 4). These schools, Kruyt believed, had no influence whatever on social life.

In 1905, however, the entire picture changed. The reason was that the Netherlands Indian government changed its policy to a more active pursuit of political mastery and concomitant "repayment" to the Indonesians, with the goods and ideas of modern civilization, for the upset that had been noted and profit that had been reaped. The Protestant ethic had taken a new turn. The result was an effective intervention with internal affairs in all of the islands of the East Indies. The Toradja came under direct Dutch rule. At first there was no resistance—the Toradja believed that the government would act the same as the other rulers to whom they had paid tribute. These rulers had never interfered with village affairs. But when it became known that the new colonial government would require people to work as indentured laborers and to pay tax, resistance began. Resistance was increased when farming methods were changed by fiat. The resistance was, however, quickly broken by soldiers. The Toradja, like so many colonial peoples, resigned themselves to new conditions. The collision with the West was violent, but they made superficial adjustments: they paid head tax, they worked at road building, and they brought their disputes to be settled by the new government.

The change, however, was not an easy one, and the cultural wound did not heal quickly. Probably the greatest difficulties were experienced by the chiefs. The administrative officials took them for men who could successfully give orders to their people. Such actually was not the case. If the chief gave an order that fell outside his ordinary jurisdiction, the people merely ignored it. They did this now to the headmen who were appointed by the officials. If the headmen ordered them to make roads and carry burdens for military patrols, they refused. The headmen were then held responsible for the inhabitants' failure to carry out orders. The headmen were unable to demand obedience, and the misunderstanding was complete.

The chiefs were also held responsible for permitting conditions that, no matter how natural to them, ran counter to the ideas of the Dutch administrative officers. It was impossible for the Toradja to regard slaves and free men in the same light and give them equal treatment. It was equally impossible for them to sentence people who had killed witches and werewolves, which they considered to be in the same category as mad dogs. The headmen found themselves helpless in a strange world. They did not know what they were expected to do; when they "failed" or withdrew, few were found to fill their places.

The Dutch administrative officers also decided that it was incumbent upon them to "develop the country," and one of their devices for so doing was to move the villagers to spots they considered more "accessible," on roads that had been constructed at the instigation of the Dutch themselves. The general move that resulted was all but disastrous for the Toradja. They were a highland people who did not feel at home closed into the valleys. Many of them began to lose interest in life—a life that they no longer controlled, for they had now to follow minute instructions in order to achieve what they had merely known how to achieve in their accustomed habitat. The death rate—as is common in these circumstances—rose precipitously. Uncertainty, disgust, boredom, and apathy weaken the morale of any people.

"For their own good," Kruyt tells us—nowhere does he attach any blame to the Dutch government actions—the people were persuaded to make irrigated rice fields; before the move they had grown rice in dry fields. The order to plant wet rice was obeyed with considerable reluctance, and the fact that the rice crops that were planted on these fields were a failure during the early years was undoubtedly due to lack of interest arising from ignorance of the demands of the new methods.

Although Toradja were willing to pay tax by village units or by families—they had, indeed, paid tribute to earlier masters—the officials demanded that the unit of taxation be the individual. The old community, by this and other means, was torn apart; people were forced to act as individuals. The individual, as the unit of society, was a disturbing notion, because it left one in so vulnerable a position.

The shock to Toradja religion was equally violent. The Dutch stopped head hunting. They did so for two reasons: they did not understand its religious significance, and—even if they had understood—it was repugnant to European sensibilities. The Toradja considered head hunting—or, more specifically, the possession of heads—necessary to insure health and crops.

A temple connected with head hunting had stood in every village, and the village gods lived in the temple, bringing prosperity when appeased with new heads. The old people among the Toradja were convinced that if the ritual were discontinued a heavy death rate and failure of crops would follow. Since (for different reasons, to be sure) heavy death rates and crop failures were to be seen all about, their point was underscored and they believed more firmly than ever in the necessity for head hunting, even as they were denied an opportunity to practice it.

The Toradja originally took the bodies of their dead out of the graves several months after burial, cleaned the bones, and replaced them. For reasons of health and sanitary protection, the authorities banned this practice. The Toradja were allowed to celebrate the Feast of the Dead, which accompanied the cleaning of the bones, but they were not allowed to remove the bodies from the graves. The authorities did not realize that they were banning the essential features—so long as the dead stank, they could not enter Death City; after the bones were cleaned the pure soul was carried to Death City to the accompaniment of the chants of priests; what good were the ceremonies if they were not allowed to clean the bones?

In sum, Kruyt assures us, the contact with the West made the Toradja uncertain of themselves and confused. They understood little or nothing of the objectives and rules of the new government. Again and again they unwittingly did things for which the authorities punished them. Spiritually they became uncertain because the religious rites, which they had performed to invoke strength and success in their conflict with nature, had been banned.

In their uncertainty the people turned to the missionaries, who spoke their language and knew something of their customs. From all sides came the requests for teachers and schools. At first there was not so much a desire for instruction as a desire to be free of uncertainty. The teachers could tell them what to do in order not to come into conflict with the new administration.

Under the tutelage of missionaries, and learning from experience, the Toradja slowly began to emerge from their confusion and depression. The Dutch, at the same time, learned more about the Toradja and even something about the degree of deprivation they had created among them. The authority that had been taken away from the indigenous political officials during the first years was again placed in their hands. Court cases, instead of being heard by foreigners who did not know the custom, were again followed with interest by people who came to discuss matters with their own headman; and the Toradja were tried according to customary law insofar as custom did not conflict with Western "human feeling."

New interests were created—the new wet rice began to be successful. Rice culture developed rapidly, and sale of rice brought economic change and new goods. The rice fields were instrumental in allowing the people to adjust to a fixed abode; the new, stable village began to form the center of a new social world. Economic prosperity followed successful introduction of coconut and coffee trees. At night the houses came to be illuminated by kerosene lamps; sewing machines became abundant and better clothing became common.

Living conditions in what Kruyt calls "the properly equipped houses" were more hygienic; hospitals were built. The people came to attend mission meetings—originally, Kruyt insists, not through any religious desires; but nevertheless they became acquainted with Christian teachings. After a few years, small groups presented themselves for baptism. This movement continued until by 1930 the greater part of the Toradja were Christians.

Kruyt's account is as valuable for the way it tells the story of the Toradja as for the details of the ethnography and history. He insists —like so many of his colleagues—that the missions left people "to their old ways and customs as much as possible." What he means is not that people were not disturbed, but rather that the missionaries tried to explain the new situation in terms of old ideas and patterns. He firmly believes that "all customs which did not actually come into conflict with the principles of Christianity were not interfered with," the very while he gives evidence that ideas which made these "customs" meaningful were undermined and destroyed. The missions did not forbid the dancing of the Toradja—but Kruyt predicted that "the sinful features" often accompanying the dances would disappear as Christianity penetrated more deeply. Marriage in the old community was "a civil affair," and was "left unaltered." The mission exercised "a certain amount of influence on the moral side of the marriage by consecrating it" while insisting that refusal to do so "in cases of immorality" did not affect legality. (Quoted material from Kruyt, 1929, p. 7.)

Important ceremonies to which the people were attached and which could be vested with a Christian mantle were allowed to remain. The harvest festival came to be celebrated as a thanksgiving day. The missionaries considered it important to preserve the pious attitude toward the dead that was shown during the "death feasts," but decided to stamp out the "heathen idea" that the dead would help Toradja in their agricultural labors, and so changed the time of the death feast to harvest and celebrated it as a harvest festival, to be held on Easter Monday. The Toradja piety and the missionaries' doctrine were both, they considered, satisfied.

Many young Toradja, themselves products of the mission schools, began to teach in the mission schools, and fewer "strangers" were required in the land. The form of the community was changed out of recognition, however. Just as the force of public opinion had acted as disciplinarian to the members of the traditional community, the new Christian community expelled members for disobedience. However, the old community had not been merely Christianized, it had been dissolved into a collection of individuals, and the chains of dependence were loosened. The congregation was the new community, and Christian communities are communities of individuals: "The members have to fall in line with the Christian opinion ruling in the community if they do not wish to be ignored" (Kruyt, 1929, p. 9).

The astounding part of Kruyt's report is the lack of irony with which he can write that:

> If we regard the situation in the right light, it can be said that a basis has been laid down both by the Administration and the Mission, for a healthy development of the [Toradja], both socially and spiritually. This basis is to allow the people to remain in their old atmosphere as much as possible and to let them develop in it. In this way it is possible that the development will take place from within and that the people will be saved from an artificial development which only touches the surface [1929, p. 12].

To recapitulate the facts of this account in general terms, we find that the impact of Western civilization on the Toradja reached into every corner of Toradja life. Indigenous political ideas were upset. Dutch misunderstanding of Toradja authority ideas was complete; new authority patterns were imposed, which destroyed the old political system. The geographical disposition of the people was changed without an accompanying ecological change—this sort of movement is probably the surest way to break the institutions of a society and has, indeed, been known to military commanders and princes since the dawn of history for its effectiveness. The methods of production and the crops were altered radically: the startling effect such a change of produce and production has in advanced societies is well known and has been the subject of study for many years. Further, a man's security about immortality was removed by the same stroke that branded his sex life as evil. Religion and morality were linked, and those of the Toradja were declared inadequate. A man's social security—that group of people who must in the reciprocal arrangement of rights and duties back him up, be on his side, take care of him when he is ill and aged—was removed when the social groups that supplied it were no longer allowed to function. He was recognized as an individual in what was to him a new light—he was not now an individual merely in the sense that he was Tom, Dick, or Harry; he was now an individual in the sense that he had no effective kin and no trustworthy kith: he was an individual in a world based on contract. Western civilization changed the Toradja's politics, his local group, his type of work and with it his food; it banned his religion and his morality, undermined his emotional life, and left him without the active protection of the groups in which he had formerly found security.

The latter-day reader must marvel that the good Pastor Kruyt could think—and we cannot for a moment question his sincerity—that now, after all this, the Toradja were free to develop along their own lines.

It remains to underscore Kruyt's leitmotiv: "The Toradja," he tells us repeatedly, "didn't know what to do." Such is the chronic difficulty in all situations of impact of mutually exotic societies: people don't know what to do. Policy, in all colonial countries, changes with the domestic situation in the metropolitan country, and from that point of view it is consistent. But from the point of view of members of the small societies within the colony, governmental policy is a matter of personalities at best, and often seems the result of caprice; being capricious, it offers no possibility of sensible planning or prediction. Only after such a community comes to have educated and informed members can it again begin to build a pattern of prediction, necessary to everyday living. In the early stages of social change, people do not know what to do. They are living a life in which they do not know the rules.

To put the Toradja material into institutional terms allows still another view of it. Before contact with the West, the Toradja had a social structure, divided up into various social organizations each of which was characteristic of an institution. These social organizations fitted into each other and formed a sensible whole. Then, with the appearance of the Dutch, new social relationships were necessarily formed. Two men, a Dutchman and a Toradja who had never before seen one another, stood face to face. The new social relationships had to be accommodated by both, and they had to be fitted into the other relationships. New institutions of government, trade, and missionary Christianity were introduced; and all had social systems. By participating in the social systems of the government, the missions, and the traders, the Toradja had to make allowances and adjustments in the other social systems in which they participated.

Because the social system is one with the event system, the material system, and the idea system, the life of the Toradja began to assume an almost unrecognizable form. With the Dutch and their social organization came new things that superseded the old ones and that, by upsetting the production, created chaos in the economic institutions. With the introduction of taxes, road building, and new methods of cultivation of rice, the entire event system of all Toradja institutions was altered. And what is most important—the idea systems, which had fitted perfectly or at least adequately into the old institutions, now were knocked out of kilter with the new institutions.

It seems to be true that people can assimilate new *things* without much difficulty. Material things carry with them a minimum of assumption in the social and idea spheres. A thing can, within certain obvious practical limitations, mean anything. Mere introduction of a few new pieces of material culture is probably not enough seriously to upset a people—but there is a cumulative effect, even with things: and people cling to old things because they are known and signify old associations, familiar ideas, and comfortable muscular movements. Yet, everyone will accept new things, especially those that make life easier or work more quickly accomplished. They will accept them so long as they do not see in them a threat to fixed and comprehended ideas, accustomed events, and valued relationships.

Any group of people can accommodate new social systems—if they do not depart too radically in required behavior, ideas, and values, from those social systems they already know and in which they already participate. It was the quantity of adjustment and the radical nature of the new social systems that were difficult for the Toradja.

Perhaps the greatest difficulty comes with ideas, particularly those that are covert—ideas, however, that are implicit in institutions, in behavior, in the very language. Ideas people know about and can see objectively are never as difficult to change as those covert concepts made to seem a part of the "natural" world. Among a people who live in a small and nonphilosophical society the fixed nature of metaphysic and lack of inquiry gives a very much more rigid conception of the "natural" than Westerners have. Westerners are used to changing their notions and their customs because they have done it so many times in the course of each of their lives.

Things, social groups, events, ideas—all were changed by the impact of the West. The Toradja world had fallen apart and had to be mended by principles that could be discovered only in the process of mending.

THE "ANTLERS"

The "Antlers" are an American Indian tribe described in any early study of Margaret Mead (1932). She had used this pseudonym for the Omaha Indians in order to protect her informants and to assure that possibly libelous or just uncomfortable information be divorced from the people it concerned, and charges of unfairness not be made. Since much time has passed between the writing of her monograph and the writing of this chapter, and since several other writers have published the true identity of the Antlers, and since there has been no study of the Omaha in the interim, their true identity can in all conscience be noted here.

It is possible to select from Dr. Mead's data three institutions in the society of this Mississippi Valley tribe, and to show the progressive disparity of those institutions from the ideas that activate them. We shall examine some of the economic, political, and religious institutions of that tribe, and check them against the idea the Indians held of what they should have been. The "anthropological present" is 1932 when Mead's study was made.

The Antlers live on a reservation in Nebraska, which corresponds very closely with their original habitat. There was no adjustment to a strange locality such as some Indian tribes had to make in their move before an advancing frontier. However, a broad change in the economic base of the tribal society was necessary. The Antlers had not only hunted buffalo, but had also planted maize and maintained permanent villages.

Disturbance of Antlers economic life began with infiltration by French trappers, many of whom took Indian wives and lived much like Indians. At the time of the initial contact, the Antlers lived a three-seasonal life: in villages of earth lodges during spring and autumn, in small camp groups of tipis during the winter, and in buffalo camps during the summer. The villages of earth lodges did not correspond to any aspect of the social organization, but houses of relatives were often close together; a lodge was usually occupied by two or more families. With the demand for furs, this economic cycle began to break down. However, the breakdown and the reduction of the social horizons of both sexes, brought about by technological changes, was offset by a drive to get more furs.

This period of contact with fur traders continued until the influx of white settlers and the establishment of agency administration. At that time, more serious adjustments had to be made: the buffalo had disappeared, and trapping areas were vastly curtailed. Loss of power by their chiefs and intrusive agents of Christianity led to government schemes for the improvement of the Indians.

The reservation was surveyed and 160 acres of land were given to every adult. The government began erecting frame houses and purchasing agricultural tools for the Indians. People abandoned earth lodges, tipis, hunting, trapping, and fishing. They settled down in the last quarter of the nineteenth century to an existence with a superficial resemblance to that of rural Americans. But the settlement patterns of the Indians were completely changed—dwellings had been built on isolated farms, sometimes as much as ten minutes' walk from each other. For people accustomed to living in village communities, this isolation was a very great hardship.

At this time, the Antlers made serious attempts at farming. Some dairy farming was done; new vegetables were introduced by the missions. Women who went to mission schools were taught to use sewing machines, make bread, preserve fruits and vegetables; they also retained most of their old techniques of food preparation and preservation. There was, at this period (about 1880), enough land for everyone and it had not been fenced; prosperity seemed assured. Antlers took well to the quick-shooting, hard-drinking type of Middle Western life in the days of Abilene and Dodge City.

Problems soon began to appear, however, in the adjustment of the two sexes to the newest situations. Antlers had, all of them, made a fairly good adjustment to the conditions brought about by trapping. However, in the new settled conditions, women fared better than the men. As we have seen, the former lost none of their old techniques, and acquired new ones. The same could be said of their social position—it had changed relatively little, and they had lost little or no status.

With men, however, the situation was different: all of their old techniques were abandoned. They were encouraged to farm, but there was no basis in their old culture on which to graft farming as an ideology —there was no prestige attached to agriculture. The prestige men acquired under the old conditions was involved with gift giving and feasts, but the materials for these activities came from a hunting and raiding life, and were no longer available.

Thus the prestige system was never brought into the settled way of life, and a successful transfer to a new prestige system was never made. In the old system, a man became a man—in every sense of the word—by participating in war, counting coup, and hunting. Trapping, when it was added, changed the situation very little. Wars may have grown fewer and degenerated into individual fights; the buffalo disappeared, but the notion of being a good hunter easily assimilated the notion of being a good trapper. But what about farming? Farming was women's work. Moreover, hunting and trapping techniques did not enable man to cope with lame plow horses and leaking barns or broken harnesses, and at this early stage no one taught the Antlers how to do so. The women were systematically taught domestic science in the Indian schools, as well as the three R's. The men learned a little manual training, but actually they were not properly equipped with technological knowledge. The result was that in their own eyes they were being made to do women's work, and then found that they could not do it. Far from being men, they were not even successful women. When an entire community of men is left in such a position, they will go a long way to prove their virility. A great deal of the carousing, fighting, and shooting can be traced to this search of masculinity. Men had to be men, if not on the preferred level, at least on some level.

Most of the Indians soon gave up much pretense of farming. The number of white settlers increased, and a system of Indian landowners came into being. Indians leased their land to white farmers, usually keeping the house for their own use, and lived on the rent money. Through this means, their income was usually as great as it would have been from their own mediocre efforts at farming. Most Indians gave up the struggle to be farmers. Their wives' gardens produced the basic food; rent money purchased clothes, meat, and kerosene. There was no incentive to improve the standard of living, which was already completely alien. A period of lethargy set in.

The Antlers had made a second adjustment, of sorts, to white culture. The first had been changing their economy from a substantive economy based on hunting, to a money economy based on trapping, with concomitant changes in the way of life. They had encompassed it ably. Then, no sooner had they got themselves well adjusted than a second change ensued. They, who were hunters turned trappers, were now asked to turn farmers. Their second adaptation to white culture was not as adequate as the first. But, they made it—they had become landlords instead of farmers, and that in itself comprised an adaptation. They had made even this adjustment without sacrificing their tribal individuality, without giving up their language; they achieved it by the surrender of half of their institutions, their political autonomy and existence as a self-governing community, and by absorbing a fair number of traits of white material culture. But they had made for themselves a sort of existence, although it was only the shadow of the rich complexity of their former lives.

But the pattern of adjustment to European and American culture is more complex than merely adjusting to a single and stable new situation: one must adjust to adjusting. White American culture is in constant and rapid flux, and white Americans are used to constant and rapid change. Indian culture, although it changed, was not in such turmoil—at least it was not so in the minds of the Indians.

New changes were in the offing. No sooner was one adjustment set into habitual and predictable patterns than new changes occurred and still another set of adjustments was demanded. The tide of settlement rushed on; the end of the period of governmental trust meant that the Indians were getting their lands in fee simple. Again, a new set of adjustments had to be made. Antlers had not become farmers; as landlords and government wards they had an even less realistic idea of money than they had had in the trapping days. With each new set of changes, they became less well equipped to meet the new conditions. Now individual land ownership—and the possibility of sale—created new problems. In the traditional culture, there had been no inheritance of property other than ceremonial property and privilege: personal property was destroyed at the death of its owner. The association of land with private property or inheritance was an alien idea. Even at the time the study was done, the Indians had two sets of economic ideas and vacillated between one and the other when faced with economic expenditure.

Many Indians, when they got fee patents to their land, sold it. They spent the money, then became pensioners on their relatives. Between 1920 and 1930 the number of dependents increased vastly, as the amount of land to provide income for them decreased. Leasing became almost total, and family incomes continued to get smaller. At the same time, goods such as automobiles and clothes became more desirable. The "giveaway" and other economic institutions of conspicuous distribution disappeared. Before 1920, the old pattern could still be followed—bureaus, bedsteads, clocks, lamps, all were given away with a lavish hand, being luxuries and not necessities. After 1920, the giveaway disappeared: poverty had settled over the reservation.

There was still in 1932, however, the compulsion to provide freely for anyone who entered one's house, especially for one's kinsmen. Economic obligations to kinsmen were very difficult to avoid for fear of public ridicule. When Dr. Mead's study was made there was the beginning of a movement to call sponging relatives "servants" and at least make some use of their labor. It is seldom in tribal society that obligatory hospitality works hardships. The society will be found to have arrived at a situation in which reasonable limits of mutual aid are seldom transcended. When the social and economic institutions are disturbed, however, and when opportunities for earning or acquiring wealth are open to some members of the community but not to others, this customary behavior may become a definite barrier to social and economic adjustment.

There were other difficulties involved in giving the Indians farmland and requiring that they treat it with a Western property concept: no attempt was made to deal with the problem of inheritance. So far as the whites were concerned, the laws of the state were assumed to be in operation. The Indians did not, of course, know what they were, and had no precedents of their own to handle inheritance of this sort of property. Fractionalization began very soon. Sometimes fifteen or twenty heirs shared an estate, each receiving that portion of the original allotment. If a widow remarried, her shares went to her husband and children.

The original allotments soon came to be subdivided in a manner utterly incompatible with farming on the Nebraska plains. Eventually, the only sensible alternative was to sell land; each heir then took his share of the market price. Even government officials, many of whom disapproved of Indians' selling land, came to approve of "heirship" land sales because of the difficulty of leasing land with multiple owners. White men made the law of the state work by means of wills and of rules excluding collaterals and stepchildren; Indians would not willingly make such exclusions.

Alienation of land was steady and devastating: twenty-five years of landlordism and lack of interest in farming did little to prepare the Antlers for handling unrestricted rights in their lands. The government made granting of fee patents individual instead of doing it all at once, but this practice merely postponed the foreseen calamity. Fee-patent land was taxable; it could be deeded and sold at the will of the Antler owner, who got his money directly. Under the guidance of land sharks, Indians developed expensive tastes—their neighbors, the Oil Indians, added further incentive. Money from land sales—sometimes as much as $10,000—was spent by the individual, not dispersed into the kinship group. When the money was gone, big cars and fine clothes were sold and the seller came back to the reservation. All the other Indians felt that they, too, wanted to get a share of the windfall. Land sales increased.

Antlers applied their Western-derived notions of economic individualism to money derived from land sales; but in other respects the kinship hospitality rules of the traditional culture still held. Small sums—rent, crop sales, and the like—were fair game for relatives. Any Antler who failed to provide for a kinsman, no matter how distant, was accused of having "gone white," even when his means were inadequate to provide for his own family. But large sums, such as those derived from land sales, never became subject to pressure from kinsmen.

In the political sphere, disjunction between basic ideas and the rest of the institutions was just as great. Traditional political organization had been based on rank and wealth. By distributing his wealth cleverly, a man acquired merit and might ultimately become a minor chief, although many of the offices were heritable in families or in the descent groups into which the tribe was divided. Above the minor chiefs was a council of seven, whose function was to maintain order, keep the peace, and preserve decorum within the tribe. The Antlers had a well-organized tribal government. There was also a number of sacerdotal groups, which served to bulwark the formal unity; a group of tribal fetishes relating to the hunt and to war served to integrate the feeling of unity.

The twentieth-century Antler community was in sharp contrast. Every Antler is a U.S. citizen subject to a federal and state law, with full claims to citizenship. But he is also a ward of the federal government, which places him in a peculiar legal and moral position. He gets free medical aid and free boarding-school education. Much of his property is held in trust by the government. Nominal citizen though he may be, except for the right to vote and formerly to serve in the armed forces, his position is that of a child. An Indian's political status lacks the realities of obligation, participation, strong local feeling. The chief political fact in the Antler's mind is that he is an Indian. Being an Indian is centered in a sense of home, of kinship, of security, of familiar phrasing of experience; but it has no referent to a political status.

There was, at the time Dr. Mead carried out her study, an elected tribal council of some twenty members, but its political capacities were largely fictitious. The council legislated about (but could not sell) tribally owned lands; they planned the annual camp ceremony. Many of the Antlers stayed aloof from this sort of political organization.

Thus, in the political field, indigenous institutions disappeared completely. New ones were created by the Indian agencies, but neither the old ideas nor the new ones had succeded, at the time the study was made, in activating these new institutions. An institution that has no activating idea system cannot survive except by artificial means.

Examination of the religious institutions of the Antlers shows an even greater disparity between ideas and institutions. The aboriginal religion was in the hands of an hereditary priesthood who manipulated fetishes that were intimately related to the economic and political life of the tribe, including their hunting and warfare. With settlement, both hunting and warfare disappeared. The rituals were conspicuous and the missionaries attacked them early and with great success. Fetishes belonging to individuals, called medicine bundles, were more tenacious.

Of less general scope, but more vigor and influence, were the shamanistic societies to cure disease. Membership in these societies was obtained by payment, but was also connected with obtaining visions.

At the time of Dr. Mead's study, the priesthoods had vanished completely; no tribal cult existed at all. Most of the shamanistic societies had disappeared, and those still in existence no longer functioned. The personal fetishes could still be found. Young people, knowing nothing of the old religion or the ritual, and often not even cognizant of the name of the fetish or the society to which it belonged, were often still mortally afraid of it. Many Antlers welcomed the acquisition of these sacred objects by museums, for they thought museums could cope with the power in them better than they themselves could after the loss of their old men. Youngsters did not question their old religion, but they neither knew anything about it nor followed it. They did not doubt that their ancestors found visions, but they did not themselves go in search of them. The old religion died through the elimination of its social system and want of a predictable event system, not through the weakness of its spirits or ideas; it decayed through the progressive outmoding of its institutions, but without any diminution of the faith and fear of the younger generations. The most highly institutionalized and integrated aspects of religious life disappeared first—priesthoods and tribal fetishes, followed by the societies. The least integrated—those nearest to individual values and ideas—are still present: fear of the dead and personal fetishes.

Christianity was introduced in the middle of the nineteenth century. The first missionaries were hard-working Presbyterians who learned the language. The tribe was "converted" to the point that in 1890 all professed Presbyterianism. But the assimilation of Indian concepts to Christian concepts helped obscure the points of misunderstanding between missionaries and Indians, and communication between them was difficult because each side thought it knew the meanings of the ideas. Church attendance at the mission was very small. No emotional value was attached to allegiance to the church, no sense of the imminence of the supernatural, no compulsion toward any form of behavior based on the Christian ethic. Meanwhile, old religious forms had vanished. The Antlers were ripe for new religious stimulation, and they found it in the Peyote cult, which was introduced from another tribe.

Peyote, the "medicine road," was open to all, though to become a full-fledged member was expensive. The principal rule was against drinking. Priesthoods in the Peyote society were becoming hereditary, and when Dr. Mead did her work they cost between $100 and $300. Peyote religion took the form of a prestige-giving society involved in spending. In days when the tribe was prosperous from land sales, and the cult was new, there were many meetings and much time and energy were devoted to them. By the time of Dr. Mead's study, however, Peyote had begun to pale in importance and interest. As people grew more impoverished, they attempted to keep the meetings quiet and private, inviting only small groups of kinsmen. The function of the cult as a curing institution, however, became more important. In cases of illness, one's whole kin group might strain every resource to put on at least one meeting.

Thus, a new cult, which incorporated many of the ideas both of the traditional religion and of Christianity, was found in the Peyote cult; but it contained many new ideas of its own. It was a new institution that arose in a situation in which old institutions had broken down. The new one, however, had not been given sufficient content, and even religious ideas had been forgotten or badly warped.

It is time for a new study of the "Antlers." The years since Dr. Mead's study have undoubtedly changed them. It must be noted, however, that American Indian studies, on which so much American anthropology was based, have deteriorated in the twentieth century; the able scholars in the field cannot begin to encompass the vastness of the subject.

Since the middle 1950s, studies in social and cultural change have necessarily taken a new tack. The reason is obvious: as the new institutions have been more and more successful—and they have been so in much of the world—they have become expanding institutions in growing and expanding societies. The two sides of the frontier are being reversed: as non-Westerners expand, Westerners are now on the other side of the frontier.

In the middle years of our century it has become obvious that new types of leaders and of people have emerged in many parts of the world. The whole of the international scene became filled, not with just Westerners and their counterparts from the Communist and Oriental worlds, but rather with people from the many new nations, especially in Africa but not limited to Africa. These people, coming from countries and from areas formerly disregarded because they were "backward," emerged onto the scene and actually upset the balance of world power. Morover, the ancient civilizations and the formerly "primitive" societies, now becoming educated in a Western sense and forming nation-states also in that sense, have joined hands to form the "neutralist" bloc. Hundreds of links are being forged between the older, exotic civilizations and the formerly "primitive" peoples, who have now come to be the most active and most effective of international lobbyists.

Western impact led, simply enough, to a search for a new culture in which social relationships between Westerners and non-Westerners was possible, and in which disrupted institutions could be refurbished. Because of the generally acknowledged technological superiority of the West (even if it is sometimes declared by non-Westerners to be beside the point of a culture or even inimical to decent social life), and because of the power relationships that were created in colonial and imperial structures, Western culture contributed much to the new creation—much, but not all, for it was usually the idea systems of Western institutions that were either repudiated or misunderstood. The result, then, can be seen as basic institutional imbalance in the new structure. And such imbalance, as we have seen, leads to further change.

THE DETRIBALIZED SHALL INHERIT THE EARTH

It was only in the 1930s that anthropology began to look seriously at the peoples of the formerly primitive world who were undergoing a tremendous transference of culture, and who in many cases were unable to cope in total comfort with the new situations in which they found themselves. Whereas many anthropologists, as we have seen, turned to examining the ways in which culture changed, ignoring by and large the impact such change had on people, there was at the same time a tendency throughout the world to look at the problems of the human individual living in a changing society. A stereotype arose of the deprived man who in his deprivation merely turned inward to his memories of an older culture, or backward to despair. Such a man, it was said, was detribalized—he had been robbed of his own values and his own culture but he had been given nothing to take its place. Detribalization was the only fate that could be seen in store for the American Indians and for the Bantu peoples of southern Africa. Detribalization was looked upon as a necessary concomitant of progress, terribly to be worried over, but demanding the entire reorganization of society to cure, making every cure "impractical."

The word "detribalization" came into common anthropological currency in the early 1930s, but it has about it the tang of officialese. The word does not appear in any of the standard dictionaries and must be taken at its face value. Detribalization means "removing from tribes" or "untribing." A tribe is a social or political group; the etymology of the word goes back to the Latin and means a group, sort, or kind. A detribalized person is, then, someone who is removed from his kind or from his sort, divorced from his political and social groups. We can establish an Elizabethan ambiguity and say that he has been un-kind-ed.

Detribalized persons are deviant persons, but with a difference. There are in all societies deviant persons of one sort or another; all societies have a way of taking care of misfits. But, when there are two or more accepted cultural media in a single space, the methods for dealing with deviant persons become indistinct. Deviant persons may escape from the sanctions of either culture merely because the other is present. This is a primary difference between detribalization and ordinary social mobility.

Detribalized persons, being deviant, face problems and make choices other than those for which their culture has prepared them. Yet there is no difference in kind between the adjustment that leads to detribalization and that which is required of us all every day. When the West expanded and formed new social relationships with formerly unknown or very little known peoples, and when these relations were structured into new sorts of social groups, a new cultural medium had to be sought for these new relationships. People had to communicate, and to act with some degree of reciprocal expectations. This sort of thing happens to all Westerners every day. Throughout their lives all people must learn new ways in response to new social situations and to new culture.

Rather, the difference is a matter of degree. Most Westerners have never had completely to reorient their lives, but only to make minor changes. Even the difficult adjustment that so many displaced persons made in the decades following World War II is quantitatively insignificant when compared to that required of the many peoples of Africa and Oceania, the Indians of North and South America.

The personal problem of adjustment that detribalization creates may be aggravated by the fact that extensive culture learning may come at a time of life when a person is not prepared for it. Among all peoples a child, as he grows up, must change his outlook and the quality of the social relationships from which he gets satisfaction. From having only a single important relationship—that with his mother—he learns to become a member of several small groups: his family, his peer groups and play groups, and a little later his school groups. Then, at about the time of puberty, he must undergo another change of social perspective: he must look out to a wider social life than merely the small groups in which he has grown up. Anthropologists have known since pioneer studies such as Margaret Mead's of New Guinea (1930) and Samoa (1928) that these changes of perspective need not be traumatic or sudden. But they nevertheless must be made.

Few Westerners are called upon to go through still another extensive social and cultural reorganization after they become full adults. It is precisely this demand that is made of "detribalized" persons. Such people are having to make themselves into new sorts of people; not merely are they adding to or changing their knowledge, as we all are, but they are changing the categories and values by means of which they see the entire world.

Each small process that goes to make up the entire new experience may be merely a matter of learning new facts and new acts and attitudes, such as happens to us all every day; but when enough of these small processes occur simultaneously, suddenly one's social center of gravity is shifted; the entire course of life is redirected.

Detribalized persons, of this sort, came to be regarded as almost synonymous with the anomic social condition created by rapid or forced cultural change. The magnitude of misery could be seen readily. However, the ultimately more impressive adjustment of the people who succeeded in encompassing the problems of detribalization was not at first apparent, precisely because those who were successful were "ordinary people." The number of people who were successful in reorienting their lives has grown until, in the 1960s, it became necessary completely to readjust our thinking about the processes of detribalization and of the impact of the West on the formerly primitive world. Indeed, it is these very people who are beginning to make a mighty impact on the West.

People who successfully reorient their lives after the detribalization experience have had to find a new personal equilibrium. They have had to find a new tribe—a new "tribe" is indeed to be found among those very detribalized persons. And it is an expanding society with a progressive culture. Its stage is the entire world. Far from being merely "detribalized," such people have become "multicultural," and people who are multicultural come into a new inheritance: the leadership of nationalistic movements and of new states, as in Africa and Asia, and the less blatantly heralded but no less important independent countries of Oceania; new cultural and political awareness as is to be found among Navaho and a few other American Indian tribes.

It is true that these men must learn to live with an internal division. They have what Han Su-Yin (1952) has called "split, two-layered souls." From her experience at being both and simultaneously European and Chinese, she writes: "Underneath are deep emotions, taboos and compulsions, repulsions and loves unexplained and dark. Above, a glut of words . . . ideas intellectually acknowledged and emotionally impotent".

Such is the nature of the successful answer to the impact situation and to detribalization. People learn, at whatever cost and with whatever personal problems, to be bicultural. Even more difficult, they learn—as Han Su-Yin herself so clearly illustrates—to translate quickly and surely between their two cultures. The difficulties are immense, but the rewards are correspondingly large: the modern world demands multicultural individuals.

The question of demand for certain types of human being must not be confused with the mere capacity for acquiring Western culture. Learning new culture is only one of the phases of personal readjustment to an impact situation. The impact situation also changes the demographic balance. The question of the personality types demanded by different demographic situations has been explored by David Riesman in his popular book, *The Lonely Crowd* (1950). Riesman's hypothesis is that there is a connection between different types of human character and certain demographic factors found in different societies: "It would be very surprising if variations in the basic conditions of reproduction, livelihood and survival chances, that is, in the supply of and demand for human beings failed to influence character" (p. 9).

Riesman has postulated that in a society having both a high birth rate and a high death rate, people are taken up with existence, oriented toward the quest for food and for replacing themselves. They seldom seek beyond the technological traditions in which they grew up. However, given another state of technical development and medicine, quite another situation is to be found: when the death rate is lowered, but the birth rate remains high, there is a sudden increase in population that alters the supply of human beings. Technological advance (which has, in Riesman's hypothesis, a symbiotic relationship with the new demographic situation) alters the demand for human beings. Such societies grow rapidly, and there is a demand for persons who can change and improve conditions to accommodate the new members. One type of successful person, by no means always approved by his contemporaries or even by posterity, is the one who breaks his old bonds of thought and action. Riesman claims that such a man must, to emerge successfully, have a much more highly developed and more rigid code of behavior than is necessary for the man in the stable society. Right and wrong no longer follow from tradition, but must be made into moral codes that can be applied to new and different situations as they arise. A man must, to be successful in this newly developing world, carry his own code of behavior within him and learn at the same time to be pliable in its application. Such a man is "inner-directed."

Riesman's own investigations are concerned with the shift to still a third demographic position: when both death and birth rates are low. There is an accompanying shift, he says, in the type of human being demanded: a shift he has characterized as from "inner-directed" to "other-directed" persons. It seems from our vantage now that both the demographic and character changes that Riesman studied were themselves illusory.

For us the interesting part of Riesman's book is that which deals with the change from traditional direction to inner-direction. In examining Africa or Oceania, and the sort of people they are producing, we can see that it is an oversimplification merely to blame the difficulties on the impact of the West. Such is, indeed, a grossly ethnocentric and even smug view of the matter. A more thoroughgoing and impartial statement would be that Asian and African peoples, at the same time that they are trying to get along with the West—and also the East—and cope with continuing impact, are having to accommodate themselves to the divergent demands of an expanding society and a developing technology. Oceanians, whose societies underwent terrible epidemics and depopulation, are now once again living in societies whose populations are increasing; their problems are just as complex as those of Africans. These emergent people have problems beyond merely adjusting to the West. They are making the adjustment on Western demands and their own desires, but more important, they are today after the tools the West can give them in order to live in their new, expanding societies. They do not want Western things and ideas for their own sakes—their being Western may be the least desirable thing about them. They are seeking the technology that will enable them to encompass an order of some sort within their expanding societies at the same time that it enables them to take their places in the front ranks of it. The impact situation is not one merely of "acculturation," but is accompanied by a necessary change of character type in response to changed demographic as well as cultural conditions.

Response to the impact situation has led to the development of exceptional human beings: people with an extraordinarily wide range of cultural capability. It is a remarkable achievement that an African can one day participate with full commitment in a ritual, the next day step into a helicopter and go campaigning for votes, the next day board a plane to London or Paris and hold a successful conference there with representatives from many countries and cultures, and the next day fly to New York to manipulate international tensions in an appearance at the United Nations. All with the ease and assurance that come with knowledge.

The Problem of the Western World

Face to face with more and more of these amazing people from what might almost be outer space, Westerners have reacted in a conservative —almost a "facesaving"—sort of way. Many of them still think in terms, or at least in the words, of the nineteenth century.

It has become apparent that, to paraphrase the words of an American statesman, the world cannot continue to exist half developed and half underdeveloped. The developed world sees before it a responsibility, even if it be for the purpose of maintaining its own position, to aid the aspiring nations that have sprung up. And yet this aid is often given in what appears to be colonial terms. Americans, in particular, have for so long considered their culture totally superior merely because it is technologically irresistible, that even in the situation of the modern world they have great difficulty in overcoming the idea that they are "experts" in civilization, and that theirs is a role of providing tutelage to the world. The result has been that even when they know that they must help, and indeed want to help, they have proved themselves incapable of giving aid in such a manner as to make it acceptable. The irony is that a "new nation"—and America, two hundred years later, still guards that stereotype of herself —conceived in liberty and dedicated to the proposition that all men are created equal, thinks that it is still the last word; believes that it knows what it means to be "equal" in all situations—and mistakenly reads its own ideals to mean that equality depends upon everyone's being birds of the same feather. Americans have been rejected and will be rejected so long as they go out into the world merely as teachers. They must go to learn. There are ideas abroad in the world that Westerners *must* learn if their society is to continue to exist and if the part of their culture they most value is to be maintained. The counterimpact may be greater than we think.

It all comes, in the long run, to a necessity for more and more Americans to learn to look into themselves and into the basic assumptions of their culture. Socioanalysis is probably as difficult as psychoanalysis. The difficulty is multiplied when we realize that, as in some cases of psychic adjustment, we are dealing with types of social adjustment to which we have grown emotionally attached, and for which we have a high cathectic regard. We want to stand by our idiosyncratic social adjustments no matter what effect those particular adjustments may have in the greater social, cultural, or psychic unit.

Just as biological sciences have learned not to apply human motivations to nonhuman beasts or to cells merely because all are mammals or all are animals, so the social sciences of the Western world must develop the firm knowledge that there are many modes of being a human being. The great necessity is to separate knowledge from commitment and evaluation. It is not necessary to give up commitment—indeed, life falls apart if there is no commitment to a fairly narrow range of values and goals. But it is necessary for a few scientists, as scientists, temporarily to suspend commitment to the values they live by in order that they can see them clearly. Only so is it possible to learn to distinguish the totally human from some mere specific manifestation of humanity. Only so can ethnocentrism give way to social science.

Anthropology in its major application has been and will always be a device through which it is possible for men to examine themselves by examining others, and to explain their own societies and cultures on a par with those of other people so that ultimately the modes of cultural, social humanity can be understood as natural phenomena. Anthropology must turn inward, onto Westerners, at the same time that it works with the peoples of other cultures not in order to change them the more effectively or the less painfully, but in order to make them see themselves as we must learn to see ourselves—without *amour-propre and* without commitment to outmoded or ridiculous values, or, worse, to anomic institutionalizations in which ends and means are at loggerheads.

References Cited

ADAM, LEONHARD

1948 " 'Virilocal' and 'Uxorilocal'." *Man,* 48: (73).

AKIGA (B. AKIGA SAI)

1939 *Akiga's Story.* Trans. by Rupert East. London: Oxford University Press, for International African Institute.

ARDREY, ROBERT

1961 *African Genesis.* New York: Atheneum.

BARBER, BERNARD

1957 *Social Stratification.* New York: Harcourt, Brace & World, Inc.

BARNES, J. A.

1949 "Measures of Divorce Frequency in Simple Societies." *Journal of the Royal Anthropological Institute,* 79: 37-62.

BEATTIE, J. H. M.

1951 *Checks on the Abuse of Political Power.* Unpublished B. Litt. Thesis, Oxford University.

BENEDICT, RUTH

1940 *Race: Science and Politics.* New York: Modern Age, Inc.

BENOIT-SMULLYAN, EMILE

1944 "Status Types and Status Interrelations." *American Sociological Review,* 9: 151-161.

BERNARD, JESSIE

1956 *Remarriage.* New York: Holt, Rinehart and Winston, Inc.

BLOCH, MARC

1952 *Apologie pour l'Histoire ou Métier d'Historien.* Paris: Librairie Armand Colin.

BLUMENBACH, JOHANN FRIEDERICH

1775 *On the Natural Variety of Mankind.* Edition cited in *The Anthropological Treatises of J. H. Blumenbach.* Trans. by T. Bendysche. London: Longmans, Roberts and Green, 1865.

BOHANNAN, PAUL

1954 *Tiv Farm and Settlement.* London: Her Majesty's Stationery Office.

1957 *Justice and Judgment among the Tiv.* London: Oxford University Press, for International African Institute.

1958 "Extra-Processual Events in Tiv Political Institutions." *American Anthropologist.* 60: (1): 1-12.

1960 *African Homicide and Suicide.* Princeton: Princeton University Press.

BOHANNAN, PAUL AND GEORGE DALTON, EDS.

1962 *Markets in Africa.* Evanston: Northwestern University Press.

BOULDING, KENNETH

1956 *The Image.* Ann Arbor: University of Michigan Press.

BULFINCH, THOMAS
n. d. *Mythology*. New York: Modern Library, Inc.

CASSIRER, ERNST
1944 *An Essay on Man*. New Haven: Yale University Press.
1946 *The Myth of the State*. New Haven: Yale University Press.

CODERE, HELEN
1950 *Fighting with Property*. New York: Augustin. Monographs of the American Ethnological Society, No. 18.

COLSON, ELIZABETH
1948 "Rain-Shrines of the Plateau Tonga of Northern Rhodesia." *Africa*. XVIII.
1951 "The Plateau Tonga of Northern Rhodesia." In *Seven Tribes of British Central Africa* (Max Gluckman and Elizabeth Colson, editors) . Manchester: Manchester University Press.
1951 "Residence and Village Stability among the Plateau Tonga." *Rhodes-Livingstone Journal*, (12).
1954 "Ancestral Spirits and Social Structure among the Plateau Tonga." Leiden: *International Archives of Ethnography*, XLVII: (1) .
1958 *Marriage and the Family among the Plateau Tonga*. Manchester: Manchester University Press.

DARWIN, CHARLES
1859 *On the Origin of Species*. London: J. Murray.

DAVIES, R. TREVOR
1947 *Four Centuries of Witch-Beliefs*. London: Methuen.

DAVIS, KINGSLEY
1949 *Human Society*. New York: Macmillan.

DIXON, ROLAND B.
1923 *The Racial History of Man*. New York: Scribner.

DRY, D. P. L.
1950 *The Family Organization of the Hausa of Northern Nigeria*. B.Sc. Thesis, Oxford University.

DUBOIS, CORA
1936 "The Wealth Concept as an Integrative Factor in Tolowa-Tututni Culture." In *Essays in Anthropology* presented to A. L. Kroeber (R. H. Lowie, editor). Berkeley: University of California Press.

DURKHEIM, ÉMILE
1912 *Les formes élémentaires de la vie religieuse*. Paris: Alcan.

EGGAN, FRED
1950 *Social Organization of the Western Pueblos*. Chicago: University of Chicago Press.

EINZIG, PAUL
1949 *Primitive Money in its Ethnological, Historical and Economic Aspects*. London: Eyre & Spottiswoode.

EMBREE, JOHN F.
1939 *Suye Mura.* Chicago: University of Chicago Press.

EVANS-PRITCHARD, E. E.
1933 "The Intellectualist (English) Interpretation of Magic." Cairo: *Bulletin of the Faculty of Arts,* 1: part 2.
1933 "Lévy-Bruhl's Theory of Primitive Mentality." Cairo: *Bulletin of the Faculty of Arts,* 2: part 1.
1937 *Witchcraft, Oracles and Magic among the Azande.* Oxford: Clarendon Press.
1940 *The Nuer.* Oxford: Clarendon Press.
1945 "Some Aspects of Marriage and the Family among the Nuer." Livingstone: *Rhodes-Livingstone Papers,* (11).

FISCHER, JOHN L.
1958 "The Classification of Residence in Censuses." *American Anthropologist,* 60: 508-517.

FORDE, DARYLL
1939 "Kinship in Umor—Double Unilateral Organization in a Semi-Bantu Society." *American Anthropologist,* 41: (4): 523-553.

FORTES, MEYER
1945 *The Dynamics of Clanship among the Tallensi.* London: Oxford University Press, for International African Institute.

FORTES, M., AND E. E. EVANS-PRITCHARD
1940 *African Political Systems.* London: Oxford University Press, for International African Institute.

FORTES, M., R. W. STEEL AND P. ADY
1947 "Ashanti Survey, 1945-46: An Experiment in Social Research." *Geographical Journal,* 60.

FORTUNE, R. F.
1935 *Manus Religion. An Ethnological Study of the Manus Natives of the Admiralty Islands.* Philadelphia: The American Philosophical Society.

FRAZER, J. G.
1922 *The Golden Bough* (abridged ed.) London: Macmillan.

GILBERT, WILLIAM HARLEN
1944 *Peoples of India.* Washington: Smithsonian Institution.

GLUCKMAN, MAX
1954 *The Judicial Process among the Barotse.* Manchester: Manchester University Press.

GOODE, WM. J.
1951 *Religion among the Primitives.* New York: Free Press.
1956 *After Divorce.* New York: Free Press.

GOODENOUGH, WARD
1955 "A Problem in Malayo-Polynesian Social Organization." *American Anthropologist,* 57: 71-83.

1956 "Residence Rules." *Southwestern Journal of Anthropology,* 12: (1) : 22-37.

1961 "Kindred and Hamlet in Lakalai." *Ethnology,* 1: (1) : 5-12.

GOODY, JACK, ED.

1958 *The Development Cycle in Domestic Groups.* Cambridge: Cambridge University Press.

HAN SU-YIN

1952 *A Many-Splendored Thing.* London: J. Cape.

HARRISON, JANE

1903 *Prolegomena to the Study of Greek Religion.* Cambridge: Cambridge University Press.

HATT, PAUL K.

1950 "Stratification in the Mass Society." *American Sociological Review,* 15: 216-222.

1950 "Occupation and Social Stratification." *American Journal of Sociology,* 55: 533-543.

HERSKOVITS, M. J.

1937 "The Ashanti Ntoro: A Reexamination." *Journal of the Royal Anthropological Institute,* 62: 287-296.

HJELMSLEV, L.

1953 *Prolegomena to a Theory of Language.* Baltimore: Waverly Press. University of Indiana Publications in Anthropology and Linguistics, No. 7.

HOCART, A. M.

1950 *Caste, a Comparative Study.* London: Methuen.

HOCKETT, CHARLES F.

1954 "Chinese vs. English: an Exploration of the Whorfian Hypothesis." In *Language in Culture* (H. Hoijer, editor). American Anthropological Association Memoir No. 79.

HOEBEL, E. A.

1949 *Man in the Primitive World, an Introduction to Anthropology.* New York: McGraw-Hill.

1954 *The Law of Primitive Man.* Cambridge: Harvard University Press.

HOEBEL, E. A., AND E. WALLACE

1952 *The Comanches: Lords of the South Plains.* Norman: University of Oklahoma Press.

HOLLINGSHEAD, AUGUST

1949 *Elmtown's Youth, the Impact of Social Classes on Adolescents.* New York: Wiley.

HOMANS, G. C., AND D. M. SCHNEIDER

1955 *Marriage, Authority and Final Causes.* New York: Free Press.

HOOTON, EARNEST ALBERT

1932 *Up from the Ape.* New York: Macmillan (2d ed. 1946).

HOWELLS, W. W.
1959 *Mankind in the Making*. New York: Doubleday.

HSU, FRANCIS L. K.
1963 *Clan, Caste, and Club*. Princeton: Van Nostrand.

HULZINGA, J.
1944 *Homo Ludens* (English Edition). New York: Roy, 1950.

HUTTON, J. H.
1946 *Caste in India*. Cambridge: Cambridge University Press.

KALMUS, HANS
1948 *Genetics*. West Drayton: Pelican Books.

KINSEY, ALFRED C., W. B. POMEROY AND C. E. MARTIN
1948 *Sexual Behavior in the Human Male*. Philadelphia: Saunders.

KLUCKHOHN, CLYDE
1944 "Navaho Witchcraft." *Papers of the Peabody Museum*, XXII: (2).
1949 *Mirror for Man*. New York: McGraw-Hill.

KLUCKHOHN, CLYDE AND HENRY A. MURRAY
1949 "Personality Formation: The Determinants." In *Personality in Nature, Society and Culture* (C. Kluckhohn and H. A. Murray, editors). New York: Knopf.

KROEBER, A. L.
1909 "Classificatory Systems of Relationship." *Journal of the Royal Anthropological Institute*, 39: 77-84.

KRUYT, A. C.
1929 "The Influence of Western Civilization on the Inhabitants of Poso." In *The Effect of Western Influence* (B. Schrieke, editor). Batavia: G. Kolff.

KUPER, HILDA
1947 *An African Aristocracy*. London: Oxford University Press, for International African Institute.
1950 "Kinship among the Swazi." In *African Systems of Kinship and Marriage* (A. R. Radcliffe-Brown and Daryll Forde, editors). London: Oxford University Press, for International African Institute.

LAWRENCE, W. E.
1937 "Alternating Generations in Australia." In *Studies in the Science of Society* (G. P. Murdock, editor). New Haven: Yale University Press.

LÉVI-STRAUSS, CLAUDE
1949 *Les Structures Élémentaires de la Parenté*. Paris: Presses Universitaires de France.

LÉVY-BRUHL, LUCIEN
1926 *How Natives Think*. Trans. by Lilian A. Clare, London: G. Allen.

LEVY, MARION J., JR.

1952 *The Structure of Society*. Princeton: Princeton University Press.

1955 "Some Questions about Parsons' Treatment of the Incest Problem." *British Journal of Sociology*, VI: (3) : September 1955, 277-285.

LINTON, RALPH

1936 *The Study of Man*. New York: Appleton.

LIVINGSTON, FRANK B.

1962 "On the Non-Existence of Human Races." *Current Anthropology*, 3: (3) : 279.

LLOYD, P. C.

1953 "Craft Organization in Yoruba Towns." *Africa*, 23.

LOWIE, ROBERT H.

1920 "Relationship Terms." 14th Edition of *Encyclopaedia Britannica*.

1936 *Primitive Society*. New York: Liveright.

1948 *Social Organization*. New York: Holt, Rinehart and Winston, Inc.

MALINOWSKI, B.

1922 *Argonauts of the Western Pacific*. London: Routledge.

1926 *Myth in Primitive Psychology*. New York: Norton.

1926 *Crime and Custom in Savage Society*. London: Routledge.

1929 *The Sexual Life of Savages*. London: Routledge.

1945 *The Dynamics of Culture Change*. New Haven: Yale University Press.

MEAD, MARGARET

1928 *Coming of Age in Samoa*. New York: Morrow.

1930 *Growing up in New Guinea; a Comparative Study of Primitive Education*. New York: Morrow.

1930 "Melanesian Middlemen." Natural History, XXX: (2) : 115-130.

1932 *The Changing Culture of an Indian Tribe*. New York: Columbia University Press.

1935 *Sex and Temperament*. New York: Morrow.

MITCHELL, J. C.

1951 "The Yao of Southern Nyasaland." In *Seven Tribes of British Central Africa* (M. Gluckman and E. Colson, editors). London: Oxford University Press.

MITFORD, NANCY, ED.

1956 *Noblesse Oblige; an Inquiry into the Identifiable Characteristics of the English Aristocracy*. London: H. Hamilton.

MONTAGUE, ASHLEY

1942 *Man's Most Dangerous Myth* (3d. ed.). New York: Harper and Row, 1952.

MONTESQUIEU, CHARLES LOUIS DE SECONDAT, BARON DE LA BRÉDE ET DE
1750 *The Spirit of the Laws*. London: Printed for J. Nourse & P. Vaillant in the Strand.

MOORE, WILBERT E.
1951 *Industrialization and Labor*. Ithaca: Cornell University Press.

MORGAN, L. H.
1871 *Systems of Consanguinity and Affinity of the Human Family*. Washington: Smithsonian Contributions to Knowledge, Vol. 17.

MORRIS, R. T. AND R. J. MURPHY
1959 "The Situs Dimension in Occupational Structure." *American Sociological Review*, 24: 231-239.

MULLER, H. J.
1962 "Human Evolution by Voluntary Choice of Germ Plasm." *Science*, 134: (3480), Sept. 8, 1961, 643-649.

MURDOCK, G. P.
1949 *Social Structure*. New York: Macmillan.
1950 "Family-Stability in Non-European Cultures." *Annals of the American Academy of Political and Social Science*, CCLXXII: Nov. 1950, pp. 195-201.
1959 *Africa: Its Peoples and Their Culture History*. New York: McGraw-Hill.

NADEL, S. F.
1954 *Nupe Religion*. London: Routledge.

NEEDHAM, RODNEY
1962 *Structure and Sentiment*. Chicago: University of Chicago Press.

NIDA, EUGENE
1952 *God's Word in Man's Language*. New York: Harper & Row.

OGDEN, C. K. AND I. A. RICHARDS
1946 *The Meaning of Meaning* (8th ed.). London: Routledge.

OLIVER, DOUGLAS
1955 *A Solomon Island Society*. Cambridge: Harvard University Press.

OPLER, MORRIS E.
1941 *An Apache Life-Way*. Chicago: University of Chicago Press.

OTTENBERG, SIMON AND PHOEBE
1960 *Cultures and Societies of Africa*. New York: Random House.

PARSONS, TALCOTT
1951 *The Social System*. New York: Free Press.
1954 "The Incest Taboo in Relation to Social Structure and the Socialization of the Child." *British Journal of Sociology*, V: (2): 101-117.
1959 "The Social Structure of the Family." In *The Family, Its Function and Destiny* (Ruth Nanda Anshen, editor), 2d. ed. New York: Harper & Row.

POLANYI, KARL
1944 *The Great Transformation.* New York: Holt, Rinehart and Winston, Inc.
1947 "Our Obsolete Market Mentality." *Commentary,* 13: 109-117.

POLANYI, KARL, CONRAD M. ARENSBERG AND HARRY W. PEARSON, EDS.
1957 *Trade and Market in the Early Empires.* New York: Free Press and Falcon's Wing Press.

RADCLIFFE-BROWN, A. R.
1950 "Introduction." In *African Systems of Kinship and Marriage* (A. R. Radcliffe-Brown and D. Forde, editors). London: Oxford University Press, for International African Institute.

RATTRAY, R. S.
1923 *Ashanti.* Oxford: Clarendon Press.

REIK, THEODOR
1958 *Myth and Guilt.* London: Hutchinson.

RIESMAN, DAVID
1950 *The Lonely Crowd.* New Haven: Yale University Press.

RIVERS, W. H. R.
1924 *Social Organization.* New York: Knopf.

ROYAL ANTHROPOLOGICAL INSTITUTE
1951 *Notes and Queries on Anthropology* (6th ed.). London: Routledge.

SCHAPERA, I.
1941 *Married Life in an African Tribe.* New York: Sheridan House.

SCHAPIRO, MEYER
1953 "Style." In *Anthropology Today* (A. L. Koeber, editor). Chicago: University of Chicago Press.

SCHÜRTZ, HEINRICH
1902 *Altersklassen und Männerbunde.* Berlin: G. Reimer.

SMITH, M. G.
1954 "Introduction" to M. F. Smith, in *Baba of Karo.* London: Faber.

SMITH, WILLIAM CARLSON
1953 *The Step Child.* Chicago: University of Chicago Press.

SOROKIN, PITIRIM A.
1953 "What is Social Class?" In *Class, Status and Power* (R. Bendix & S. M. Lipset, editors). New York: Free Press.

SPENCER, HERBERT
1892 *Principles of Sociology.* New York: Appleton.

SPICER, EDWARD H.
1952 *Human Problems in Technological Change, A Casebook.* New York: Russell Sage Foundation.

SPIER, LESLIE

1925 "The Distribution of Kinship Systems in North America." *University of Washington Publications in Anthropology*. 1: (2).

SPITZ, RENE A.

1949 "The Role of Ecological Factors in Emotional Development in Infancy." *Child Development*, 20: 145-155.

STEINER, FRANZ BAERMANN

1950 *A Comparative Study of the Forms of Slavery*. Unpublished. D. Phil. Thesis, Oxford University.

STREHLOW, CARL

1908 "Die Totemistischen Vorstellungen der Aranda. Die Aranda- und Loritja-Stamme u. Loritja in Zentral-Australien." Frankfurt am Main: J. Boet & Co., 1907-20. *Veröffentlichungen aus dem Städtischen Volker—Museum*, Frankfurt am Main, Vol. 1.

SULLIVAN, ANN MANSFIELD

1904 Letter in *The Story of My Life* (Helen Keller, Author). New York: Doubleday.

SUMMERS, MONTAGUE (Translator)

1928 *Malleus Maleficarum*. (Edition used: London: Pushkin Press, 1948).

SUTHERLAND, EDWIN H. AND DONALD R. CRESSEY

1960 *Principles of Criminology* (6th ed.). Philadelphia: Lippincott.

SYKES, GRESHAM M.

1958 *The Society of Captives*. Princeton: Princeton University Press.

TEGNAEUS, HARRY

1952 *Blood-Brothers; an Ethno-Sociological Study of the Institutions of Blood-Brotherhood, with Special Reference to Africa*. Stockholm: Statens Ethnografiska Museum, Publication No. 10.

THOMSON, DONALD F.

1949 *Economic Structure and the Ceremonial Exchange Cycle in Arnhem Land*. Melbourne: Macmillan.

THURNWALD, RICHARD

1916 *Banaro Society*. Memoirs of the American Anthropological Association, Vol. 3: (4): 251-391.

TITIEV, MISCHA

1943 "The Influence of Common Residence on the Unilateral Classification of Kindred." *American Anthropologist*, 45: 511-530.

1944 *Old Oraibi*. Papers of the Peabody Museum, 22, (1).

TYLOR, E. B.
1871 *Primitive Culture.* London: Murray.

VAYDA, A. P.
1960 *Maori Warfare.* Wellington, N. Z.: The Polynesian Society, Maori Monographs No. 2.

VEBLEN, THORSTEIN
1899 *The Theory of the Leisure Class.* New York: Macmillan.

WALLACE, A. F. C.
1961 *Culture and Personality.* New York: Random House.

WARNER, W. LLOYD AND PAUL S. LUNT
1941 *The Social Life of a Modern Community.* New Haven: Yale University Press.

WATTS, ALAN W.
1953 *Myth and Ritual in Christianity.* London: Thames and Hudson.

WEBER, MAX
1930 *The Protestant Ethic and the Spirit of Capitalism.* London: G. Allen & Unwin. Translated by Talcott Parsons.
1958 *The Religion of India; the Sociology of Hinduism and Buddhism.* Trans. by H. H. Gerth and Don Martindale. New York: Free Press.

WEIDENREICH, FRANZ
1946 *Apes, Giants and Man.* Chicago: University of Chicago Press.

WHITE, LESLIE
1948 "Man's Control over Civilization: An Anthropocentric Illusion." *Scientific Monthly,* 66: 235-247. (Reprinted in *Readings in Anthropology,* M. H. Fried, editor).

WHITING, B.
1950 *Paiute Sorcery.* New York: Viking Fund Publications in Anthropology, No. 150.

WHORF, BENJAMIN L.
1956 *Language, Thought and Reality.* New York: Wiley.

WILSON, MONICA
1951 *Good Company.* London: Oxford University Press, for International African Institute.

Index